MIRRORS OF VIOLENCE

Communities, Riots and Survivors in South Asia

MIRRORS OF VIOLENCE

Communities, Riots and Survivors in South Asia

edited by
VEENA DAS

DELHI
OXFORD UNIVERSITY PRESS
BOMBAY CALCUTTA MADRAS

Oxford University Press, Walton Street, Oxford OX2 6DP

Oxford New York
Athens Auckland Bangkok Bombay
Calcutta Cape Town Dar es Salaam Delhi
Florence Hong Kong Istanbul Karachi
Kuala Lumpur Madras Madrid Melbourne
Mexico City Nairobi Paris Singapore
Taipei Tokyo Toronto

and associates in

Berlin Ibadan

ISBN 0 19 563221 4

Printed at Ram Printograph (India), New Delhi 110020
and published by Manzar Khan, Oxford University Press
YMCA Library Building, Jai Singh Road, New Delhi 110001

Contents

Preface

This book has grown out of papers presented in a conference on ethnic violence in South Asia which was held in Kathmandu in February 1987 and sponsored by the International Centre for Ethnic Studies (ICES). It was a privilege to work with Neelan Tiruchelvan and Radhika Coomaraswamy of the ICES in bringing this project to fruition. Their quiet courage in the face of the apocalyptic conditions prevailing in Sri Lanka was an inspiration to all the participants.·

The reader will find different styles of work reflected in this volume. There are scholarly essays written by historians or other social scientists, researched in libraries and duly documented in the true spirit of academic research. There are also papers by activists who have documented particular riots in all their specificities, even as they themselves were engaged in the herculean tasks of organizing relief, filing petitions in courts, and arranging for the security of victims. I believe it is the dialogue that developed between these different kinds of concerns that helped to define the problem of violence in the South Asian context.

Some participants who did not contribute papers acted as discussants. Their comments were a great help in the subsequent revisions of these papers. I should like especially to thank Asghar Ali Engineer, D. L. Sheth, Bashir Ahmad, Neelan Tiruchelvan and Radhika Coomaraswamy for their thoughtful criticisms. In editing this volume and writing the overview I have been helped by many people. I must particularly thank Jeevan Thyagaraja and Mukulika Bannerji for help in editorial work.

I have not been able to cultivate the kind of serenity with which one is advised to approach the study of violence. In reading and working on these essays I was often overcome by a terrible anxiety. In such phases it was the affection of my children Saumya, Jishnu and Sanmay, and of my students in the Delhi School of Economics, that sustained me.

I want to thank the research and reference staff of the Robert Frost Library in Amherst, the Widener Library in Harvard, and the Ratan Tata Library in Delhi for their help in tracing books and journals. Savita Aggarwal typed some of the papers, while the final typescript was prepared at the Institute for Studies in Industrial Development. I am grateful to all of them for their efficient handling of the manuscript. I warmly thank the editorial staff of Oxford University Press for their courteous and efficient handling of various editorial details, and the anonymous referee for carefully considered suggestions. Thanks are, finally, due to Sanmay for help in making the index.

The participants in the conference on ethnic violence who discussed the prospects of a new South Asia till the early hours of the morning for four days hoped to create alternative visions of peace in the region. Together, they would like to dedicate this book to all those who are working to establish human rights in South Asia.

Notes on Contributors

ASHISH BANERJEE is a Fellow of the Nehru Memorial Museum and Library. He has published several articles on Indian politics and co-authored, with Nirmal Mukarji, *Democracy, Federalism and the Future of India's Unity*.

SUNIL BASTIAN is a Fellow of the International Centre for Ethnic Studies, Colombo. He has participated in the research projects of the Centre and contributed to several research reports on political economy and problems of ethnicity in Sri Lanka.

UPENDRA BAXI is Professor of Law and Vice-Chancellor, University of Delhi. His publications include *The Indian Supreme Court and Politics* (Lucknow, 1980), *The Crises of the Indian Legal System* (Delhi, 1982), *Courage, Craft and Contention: The Indian Supreme Court in the Mid Eighties* (Bombay, 1985), and *Liberty and Corruption: The Antulay Case and Beyond* (Lucknow, 1989).

DIPESH CHAKRABARTY is Lecturer in History and Anthropology at the University of Melbourne. He is the author of *Rethinking Working-Class History: Bengal 1890–1940* (Delhi, 1989).

VEENA DAS is Professor of Sociology at the University of Delhi. She is the author of *Structure and Cognition: Aspects of Hindu Caste and Ritual* (Delhi, 1977), and editor of *The Word and the World: Fantasy, Symbol, and Record* (Delhi, 1986).

AKMAL HUSSAIN is an economist who has written extensively on the political economy of Pakistan.

SUDHIR KAKAR is Senior Fellow at the Centre for the Study of Developing Societies, Delhi. He teaches annually at the University of Chicago. His books include *The Inner World: A Psycho-analytical Study of Childhood and Society in India* (Delhi, 1978), *Tales of Love, Sex, and Danger* (with J. Ross; Delhi, 1986), *Shamans, Mystics and*

Doctors (Delhi, 1986), and *Intimate Relations: Exploring Indian Sexuality* (Delhi 1989).

VALLI KANAPATHIPILLAI is currently working for her doctorate at the Institute of Social Studies, The Hague. She was previously with the International Centre for Ethnic Studies, Colombo, where she participated in several research programmes on ethnicity and society.

ASHIS NANDY is Senior Fellow at the Centre for the Study of Developing Societies, Delhi. His publications include *At the Edge of Psychology* (Delhi, 1981), *The Intimate Enemy: Loss and Recovery of Self under Colonialism* (Delhi, 1983), and *The Tao of Cricket* (Delhi, 1989).

MICHAEL ROBERTS is Professor of History at the University of Adelaide. He has contributed several articles on the social history of Sri Lanka and is editor of *Collective Identities, Nationalisms and Protest in Modern Sri Lanka* (Colombo, 1972). His next book, *People in Between*, is due soon.

FARIDA SHAHEED works for Sharkat Gah, Women's Resource Centre, Lahore. She was previously Senior Research Fellow at the Centre for South Asian Studies, Punjab University. She has co-authored *Invisible Workers: Piecework Labour Amongst Women in Lahore* (Government of Punjab, 1983), and *Women of Pakistan* (Lahore, 1987).

AMRIT SRINIVASAN is Senior Lecturer in Sociology at Hindu College, Delhi University. She has published several articles on gender and society, kinship, and the study of texts.

Chapter One

Introduction: Communities, Riots, Survivors—The South Asian Experience

VEENA DAS

The decade of the eighties has been a period of intense uncertainties in South Asian societies.[1] The goals of rational organization of life, the scientific management of society, modernization and development, to which great energies had been devoted in the sixties and early seventies, now seem like signposts to cities that are abandoned and empty. There is an exhaustion of utopian energies which does not simply reflect a passing mood of cultural pessimism but relates to fundamental changes in modern society and polity. This entire region has seen an escalation of violence; industrial accidents such as Bhopal have made us question our created environment; and the energies with which smaller groups are claiming their rights to cultural survival against the state have brought the concept of the state as a neutral umpire in the management of differences to its limits. Even legal and administrative measures for the implementation of social welfare policies are not seen as a passive medium but as the means through which reified and alienating power flows into the smallest capillary branches of society. In a word, these societies are engaged in an intense interrogation of themselves.

The contributors to this volume have taken up the themes of

[1] I am grateful to Deepak Mehta, Ranendra Das, Shahid Amin, Gyanendra Pandey and Michael Roberts for comments and suggestions. Hans Joas shared his thoughts on these issues with generosity. I am very grateful to Upendra Baxi for patiently showing me the hazards of using the normal language of the social sciences when considering these issues. An earlier version of this paper was given as the Fourth Puneethavathy Tiruchelvan Lecture in Colombo in September 1988.

ethnic, caste and communal violence when these crystallize in urban riots, as well as forms of writing about these, as the objects of their investigation. In the process of this analysis they have been inevitably led to an interrogation of the categories of the social sciences, as also to a re-examination of the relationship that societies have to institutions—whether these be located in their own past or in recent colonial history. Obviously, such institutions, regardless of the degree of 'otherness' that they present, cannot be simply expelled; they can, however, be re-appropriated on the basis of a new relationship established through the process of relocating them in new practices. The essays presented here do not represent a consensus on these issues; nor do they strive for a consensus. Instead it is hoped that social science scholarship in these countries will discover its own voice in this process of mutual engagement: and more importantly, we may learn to treat each other as the addressees of our discourse.

The essays herein can be divided into three parts. The first set places the moment of violence encountered in riots in the context of a general discussion of societal and individual processes, with the assumption that the riot constitutes a moment in the system—it directs attention to the nature of religion, polity or the individual unconscious. The second set of essays takes for its object certain instances of violence in South Asian history and society, such as the violence against Tamils in Colombo in 1983, against the Sikhs in Delhi in 1984, the anti-reservation movement in Gujarat in 1985, and the Pathan-Muhajir riots in Karachi in 1986. In these essays the concern is with understanding the particular instance in its concreteness and specificity, so that general arguments about communal or ethnic violence can be given body and form. An examination of earlier riots in the nineteenth century pertaining to Buddhist-Christian conflicts in Sri Lanka and Hindu-Muslim conflict in India gives us an opportunity to look at this problem in some historical depth. In the last section the experiences of survivors are described, as also the processes through which they reformulate their worlds.

State, Communities and Collective Violence

The existing sociological and historical studies of social action present us with three distinct points of view. The first is that collective action can be analysed by the same categories as conventional behaviour. The genealogical connections of this theory can be traced to the theories of social action that have their origin in Weberian sociology. According to the second view, collective action constitutes a distinct break in normal social life. With its roots firmly located in Durkheimian sociology, such a view of collective behaviour emphasizes the collective effervescence, the break in everyday life, the intensity of exchange and the Dionysian punctuation in an increasingly Promethean world, that moments of collective action provide. In the third view, which has its roots in Marxian interpretations of society and history, collective action often expressed in the behaviour of crowds is best understood if we focus upon the sense of injustice which crowds try to redress through their actions.[2] We shall see how these diverse views are reflected in the essays in this volume.

The most comprehensive expression of the view that the theory of social action as developed by Weber and Parsons is competent to deal with collective behaviour is found in Smelser (1962). Lamenting the tendency in sociological analysis of treating collective episodes as if they were the work of mysterious forces, Smelser states that although the nature of interaction is different in small group behaviour and collective behaviour, the latter may be analysed by the same categories as conventional behaviour. In his definition of collective behaviour Smelser includes not only what he calls the hostile outburst, but also protest movements, including both norm-oriented movements and value-oriented movements. Although the goals of these movements are quite distinct, the social processes underlying them, he argues, are similar. What, then, are these social processes?

For Smelser, collective behaviour is a compressed way of attacking problems created by strain. Normal social action, according to him, moves along a map or a flow chart, with definable components. However, under situations of protest the established ways or actions fail. In the face of such unstructured situations, different kinds of collective behaviour, ranging from hostile outburst to normative protest movements, arise as reactions to stress. Solutions are sought to be produced to situations that short-circuit the normal socia█████████████world is sought to be

---

[2] See Moore (1978), Tilly (1█████████████71) and Rudé (1959, 1964).

re-ordered on the basis of non-institutionalized action and social mobilization. In the specific cases of the hostile outburst under which he carefully considers the literature on race riots, Smelser believes that the responsibility for the stress is placed upon well-defined groups or categories of people, rather than upon impersonal forces. Such groups are sought to be expunged or punished by the use of violence. Thus the moment of violence presupposes the development of generalized beliefs that are hostile to the targets that are later attacked. Despite the many important insights on the phenomenon of riots contained in Smelser's work, I find his model somewhat mechanical in its application. It also relies rather heavily upon the distinction between instrumental and expressive action that I shall have occasion to question later.[3]

In the literature on communal riots in India, the historian Bipan Chandra (1984) has made an argument somewhat similar in its component to that of Smelser. He argues that communal riots occur because there is a development of communal ideology in society. The components of this communal ideology are difficult to define clearly. However, Bipan Chandra makes the point that popular religion, being syncretic in nature, should be distinguished from communal ideology. The latter, in contrast to the former, he argues, is exclusive in its orientation as it is based upon hatred of other religions. The development of communal ideology reflects for Bipan Chandra the state of affairs when religion moves out of the bounds of the private and enters the realm of the public. It becomes the basis for the organization of political and economic interests along religious lines. This definition is close to that proposed by Mohanty (1987), who states that

As an ideology, communalism refers to the belief that people belonging to one religion also share common socio-economic, political and cultural interests. As a social phenomenon, it refers to an exclusive assertion justified in the name of a group—in this context, a religious group. . . . We emphasize the aspect of exclusiveness as a characteristic of communalism which ordinarily sees an antagonistic relation between groups. (p. 58)

Although both Bipan Chandra and Mohanty see communalism in terms of a disease in the body politic, there is a difference in the

---

[3] For a critique of the distinction between instrumental and expressive action in the study of violence, see Das (1987).

space where this is located. The former sees it as a disease of civil society, whereas for the latter it reflects a process of alienation from the authoritarian practices of the modern Indian state. Neither addresses the question of the alchemy by which communal ideology, as they describe it, becomes transformed into violent conflict.

In a sense these views, which are widely shared between writers of very different persuasions, reflect the conventional wisdom on Indian society in particular, and on South Asian societies in general. In this view South Asian societies are threatened by the lack of cultural homogeneity and the absence of institutionalized mechanisms for the regulation of differences. Hence a strong state is necessary to ensure order in society and to proclaim a new order based upon rational and scientific principles of management.

The theory of the state underlying these conceptions derives its significant concepts from what Schmitt (1985) called 'secularized theological concepts'. For Schmitt modern politics was merely the secularized version of a theology in which the sovereign was seen as a profane divinity with all the omnipotent attributes of its alleged sacred predecessor. As he put it, 'Like god, the political sovereign is not bound by normative constraints of any kind, but is rather their prior ground.' From the perspective of this strongly centred notion of power that informs much of the sociological and historical writing on communalism, there is an appropriation of legitimacy, especially in the public domain, by ideologies that propound the importance of the state.

Nandy's paper in this volume sees communal and ethnic riots in the countries of this region in an entirely different light. Rather than view these as pathologies located in the nature of civil society, he places the increase in violence as being due to the nature of the state in these societies. Nandy, too, makes a distinction between religion as faith and religion as ideology, corresponding to the distinction between syncretic popular religion and communal ideology. As faith, religion is located in the domain of everyday life and shares in the heterogeneity of everyday life in which it is the 'whole man' who is involved (cf. Heller, 1984). Nandy does not deny the possibility of conflict in traditional societies, even when these were marked by syncretism, but his argument is that conflict was contained and managed in the context of principles that were concrete, and which had evolved in the process of the living together of different communities. He points to the specificity of the riot as an urban phenomenon, and also argues that the nature of organization, the new technologies, and the involvement of agencies of the state in sustaining these conflicts point to the fact that riots cannot be seen as if they were a disease of civil society which are to be corrected by the enlightened state.

Bastian and Hussain's essays provide other kinds of evidence—from Sri Lanka and Pakistan, respectively—that economic policies of the state may play a crucial role in the development of ethnic conflicts. This is especially interesting because Bastian is able to show how an ethnic majority may capture state power in a democratic society; whereas for Hussain it is the failure of welfare policies that makes individuals look towards their communities for protection and support. How such legitimate functions of the community are transmuted into a violent protest that encompasses the state, as well as other communities that are defined as the 'enemy'—is a question of great interest and is beginning to be documented in the new historiography.

It is also important to ask whether or not our understanding of 'community' needs to be deepened. For instance, in Bastian's analysis, the Sinhalese are treated as a single community. Yet, in terms of their capacity to capture state power, the differences in class to which Bastian alludes are surely important. The question is how these differences come to be muted in order for the 'Sinhala–Buddhist–Chauvinist' ethos to arise in Sri Lankan society. Conversely, as Hussain and Shaheed's papers show, there is no agreement in Pakistan as to what constitutes the 'correct' interpretation of Islam. Here I feel that a theory of interests is not sufficient and must be complemented by a theory of political passions.[4]

These arguments lead us to question whether even in democratic regimes in the region we can assume that there is an identity between the rulers and the ruled, the governed and the governing, the subjects of state power and its objects. As Habermas (1986) has forcefully argued, if we assume such identities we may be led into a

---

[4] I do not view passions as instincts, but rather as having the revelatory possibility of confirming one's place in the world through engagement with the 'other'. This formulation of passions may be found in Unger (1984). See also Das (1988).

position of 'authoritarian legalism'. Thus, communal ideology may reflect hatred of other groups, but in Nandy's reckoning it may also be an expression of a group's attempt to create a legitimate space for itself in the public domain—especially in view of the homogenizing pressures of the modern state.

At this stage we must ask whether the syncretism of popular religion prevented the development of conflicts. Bayly (1985) has argued in an influential essay that, despite the syncretism of popular religion, periods of economic and political uncertainty led to conflict and violence. However, his conclusion that the nature of riots observed in the late-eighteenth and early-nineteenth centuries was the same as those observed in later periods is questionable. The contribution by Pandey in this volume is especially important from this point of view. Through a close analysis of the early texts produced by British administrators, he shows how a narrative of communal riots came to be 'fixed' within this discourse. Social categories were bestowed with 'natural' characteristics, so that engagement in collective action of any kind that were seen as threatening law and order became an index of the biological charac-teristics of groups engaged in such actions. What is fascinating in Pandey's account is that we can see how a particular language is evolved by the state so that 'riots' may be seen as evidence of mob fury, of the 'centuries old' hostilities of Hindus and Muslims, rather than as evidence of the erosion of the moral order of the cities brought under colonial control. What gives power to this narrative is not only that it becomes the narrative of the state, but also that it is presumed to belong to the order of mimesis and thus to have a referential truth. Thus, false images and deceptive signs are circu-lated in the body politic, providing the historian of these events with a readymade way of looking at such events. In fact, Pandey is able to show how even contemporary accounts become vulnerable to this description.

The power of the colonial narrative may be witnessed in many contemporary accounts of communal riots wherein the authors, consciously or unconsciously, occupy the language of the state. I shall take only two examples to demonstrate this point. My first example is from Shah's (1984) analysis of the 1969 communal riots of Ahmedabad. He states:

Hindu and Muslim communities have deep rooted prejudices against each other and tension between the two has been persisting in one form or another for several centuries. The extent of tension, however, varies from time to time. Often it is at low ebb and members of both the communities interact in socio-economic or political spheres.... But occasionally tension reaches a high pitch, turning into mad fury. (p. 175)

This preamble provided by Shah has that timeless quality to which Pandey draws attention in his delineation of the colonial narrative. Instead of the careful investigation of the particular conditions that lay behind the emergence of communal conflict, such as the nature of immigrant communities in industrial cities, the state's intrusion into sacred spaces, and the enactment of offensive legislation, Shah only sees 'mob fury' and 'tension persisting for several centuries', and these provide his backdrop for the 1969 events.[5]

Even more insidious is the kind of conclusion that Gopal Krishna (1985) draws from his investigation of riots. Basing himself upon the statistical compilation put together by the ministry of home affairs, Government of India, Krishna concludes that communal incidents are not only steadily increasing but also that they are the direct results of the diversity of Indian society. According to home ministry sources, the incidents of communal riots between 1964 and 1970 averages out at 1025 per year. It does not occur to Krishna to ask whether the police characterization of an incident as a 'riot' needs to be examined and deconstructed by the social scientist. He sees in these 'riots' the fact that more power has devolved to communities on account of the democratic process in India, and that this can 'aggravate communal conflict and ultimately disrupt the state'. There is not even the hint of a suggestion that the state might itself be party to these riots, for, as he says, 'There is no evidence of a pre-planned conspiracy behind any of the riots that

---

[5] For an analysis of riots that emphasize the historical specificity of the moment, see Joshi (1985) and Chakravarty in this volume. Joshi, however, seems to make the assumption that popular religious attitudes formed in the village are not only carried over into the urban setting but also explain the communal conflict that emerged in the industrial city of Kanpur. She also notes, however, that widespread resentment of the new legislations to control plague, as also the intrusion of the colonial state into sacred spaces, were important causes of unrest. It is a pity that such resistance is labelled 'superstition' in her work. For an alternative view of resistance to the plague legislation, see Arnold (1987).

have been carefully investigated by various inquiry commissions.'
Not only is he incorrect when concluding that all inquiry commissions have exonerated the state, his essay also offers evidence of the manner in which the social scientist can become an apologist of the state. He unhesitatingly accepts a view of the state that would enable it to establish greater control over the life of society and to exclude alternatives. Thus, he quotes J. C. Furnival in arguing that the 'heterogeneity of plural society has but few creative possibilities', thus providing an ideology for the worship of homogeneity as the only basis of a civilized society.[6]

The Form of the Riot

One of the important questions addressed in these essays is about the form of the riot. What is the web of signifiers through which such ideologies as communalism and ethnicity are organized and communicated? Have these symbols remained constant through history, or, if they have changed, what does this change signify? There are three kinds of symbolic structures that are analysed in these papers directly or in terms of implicit categories. These are: the organization of symbolic space, the temporal structure of riots (different kinds of riots relating to ritual or political calendars in different ways), and, finally, the repertoire of symbolic actions that is called upon in the case of ethnic or communal conflict. Not only is such a repertoire available to the crowd, the mob, or the procession, it is available to the state in its management of collective behaviour. The papers in this volume suggest that although conflict along lines of religion or ethnicity may be traced back to the eighteenth century, there has been an important change in the repertoire used in episodes of collective violence. Further, the changes in symbolic forms are not changes in some kind of passive medium which convey the same content; rather, these changes are of such significance that we may not be justified in talking of content as if it lies in or under form. The form pervades

---

[6] The literature on the creative possibilities of pluralism abounds but is not noticed by these social scientists. For a philosophical statement about pluralism, see Deleuze (1983), and for an analysis of pluralism in contemporary Indian culture see Borden (1988).

the content and is better thought of *via* the Saussarian image of the wave—rather than as a vehicle which, so to speak, contains the content.[7]

The Sacred Space

The question of form has been raised in a very direct manner in the work of Michael Roberts who, in a closely argued essay, shows how British attitudes to noise as well as their notions of governmentality led to the formulation of the Police Ordinance of 1865 in Sri Lanka, regulating the use of music and drumming by Sinhalese Buddhists in front of mosques and churches. This led to a struggle on the part of the Sinhalese Buddhists to protect their sacred spaces from governmental claims. The interesting point that Roberts makes is that although the British self-image was that of mediators between different religious groups that were seen as locked in conflicts, it was the Police Ordinance which led to a new space being created for this conflict. As Roberts says, 'my argument in this essay implies that drumming–cum–music was generally tolerated by Sinhalese of all faiths till the British and the missionaries taught them to regard it as a "disturbance" and a mark of disrespect.' Thus it was the interest of the colonial government in the regulation of time and space, including sacred space, that invested these issues with special significance, creating new forms of conflict for which the British could then appear as neutral mediators. The argument I made earlier about the state in South Asia being an important party in communal or ethnic conflicts rather than a neutral referee of these has an important historical dimension clearly shown by this essay.

One may argue that control over sacred spaces such as pilgrimage centres or temples, mosques and churches, had always been important in the self-definition of a religious community. However, the fact that these spaces have been of political interest to rulers of

[7] In Saussure's words, 'Visualize the air in contact with a sheet of paper; if the atmospheric pressure changes, the surface of the water will be broken up into a series of divisions, waves; the waves resemble the union or coupling of thought with phonic "substance".' Saussure (1974), p. 12. In Indian historical writings, it is the pioneering work of Guha (1983) that establishes ways of analysing form.

earlier periods should not obscure the fact that new forms of governmentality led to new ways of regulating the access of a community over its sacred spaces. Roberts makes the significant comment that time was sought to be regulated by the British in accordance with notions of industrial discipline. Thus, the division of day and night was seen as corresponding to the rhythms of work and leisure. These notions of time were in direct opposition to Sinhalese Buddhist ideas about the characteristics of night—a period which could be devoted to healing rites, or rites of passage; or on appropriate calendrical days for noisy celebrations. Yet the British notions were assumed to be universal and were thus imposed (to the extent possible) by law. The introduction of this legal and bureaucratic rationality masked the fact that an alien power was trying to legitimize its position as a neutral protector of universal rights according to 'the rule of law'. The use of police ordinances, curfews and litigation were then to become part of the repertoire of management of future communal and ethnic conflicts.

The control of sacred spaces and their protection continues to be an important symbol around which communal conflicts tend to be organized. However, it is not only sacred space but also ordinary space which has important symbolic elements. Each riot leaves its own signature, and one way to decipher this is to pay attention to the spaces involved. We see in several studies of communal riots that authors speak of 'spaces of traditional configurations' *versus* new areas in which violence may have spread. For example, the violence against the Sikhs in 1984 in Delhi or against the Tamils in 1983 was a traumatic experience for the entire Sikh and Tamil communities because the violence penetrated into spaces that had been considered relatively immune. In contrast, the Hindu–Muslim riot in 1987 in Delhi remained confined to the walled city, a traditional area in which riots have occurred with some regularity.[8] These were ignored by the wider populace of the city, which went about its tasks in the spirit of 'business as usual'. It seems that we have to consider the role that repetition plays here. Certain patterns of violence become routinized if they follow expected paths in

[8] For an analysis of riots in the walled city, see the People's Union for Democratic Rights (PUDR) Report of June 1987.

terms of their spatial and temporal location, and are somehow felt to be less traumatic than new patterns of violence. A rise of novelty is signalled when violence spreads into areas which are not those of traditional conflagrations. Thus, I would consider that the violence against the Sikhs in the aftermath of the assassination of Indira Gandhi was saying something 'new' about Hindu-Sikh relations, as against the Hindu-Muslim riots of the walled city. The latter were interpreted as part of the same pattern because the spaces in which they occurred were well recognized—confined and localized, and thus bounded even in the consciousness of people. Similarly, the spread of violence against upper-class Tamils in Colombo, who in previous riots had been protected by their class positions, signalled a new phase in this cycle of violence and was interpreted as such by many Tamils who decided to migrate from Sri Lanka.

The structure of modern cities in South Asia has special significance for the understanding of collective violence. It is true that urbanization is not a modern phenomenon in these societies. Yet the modern city is quite different in character from the traditional city. The modern city has a large number of new migrants who live on the margins of the city, whose integration into the economy and polity is of a special kind. Generally, such migrants constitute the floating populations which become potential recruiting ground for the underworld activities of smuggling, drug-peddling and hired assassination. For example, Farida Shaheed shows the involvement of refugee Pathans in the smuggling of drugs and illegal weapons in Karachi through the institution of slum lords. The inhabitants of these slums and 'unauthorized colonies' also become a human resource for conducting the underlife of political parties. These are the people employed as strike-breakers; they make up crowds to demonstrate to the world the 'popularity' of a particular leader; and they form instruments for the management of political opponents. It is not surprising then that in the organization of riots they should play a pivotal role in the perpetration of violence. Baxi, in his contribution to this volume, refers to their role when the leaders of the anti-reservation movement in Gujarat complained that their movements had been 'hijacked' by anti-social elements.[9]

[9] I am not arguing for a causal sequence of immigration—relative depriva-

In two cases—of Pathan-Muhajir riots in Karachi and the violence against Sikhs in Delhi—it has been shown that the character of the slums had special significance for the understanding of violence. A disproportionate number of victims among the Sikhs came from the slum areas in Delhi, as did the perpetrators of this violence. In the case of the Karachi riots, the development of slum lords—who controlled strategic spaces in the city for the storing of drugs and illegal weapons (important because of the incorporation of Karachi into a global political economy)—led to violence between Pathans and Muhajirs. It seems that the kinds of political networks that have developed in our modern cities—wherein the unorganized labour sector provides personnel for smuggling drugs, weapons, and the crowds and processions for various political parties—is also responsible for providing the personnel that can be mobilized into a hostile crowd.

One of the intriguing features of the riots examined here, which also came up in discussions during the conference where these papers were presented, is the differentiated character of the violence when we view its spatial distribution. For example, while it is true that the violence against the Sikhs took a very heavy toll in the slum areas on the outskirts of Delhi, not all such localities were equally affected. In the case of Sultanpuri, from where the survivors described in my paper in this volume came, the brutal killings took place in three blocks of the locality. Other streets which also had an equally heavy concentration of Sikhs were not so severely affected; some escaped the wrath of the crowds completely. Similarly, in the violence against the Scheduled Castes described by Baxi in this volume, the spatial spread of violence followed a pattern which is difficult to understand in terms of a general theory

---

tion—floating aggression; nor am I suggesting that we can assume the participation of slum populations in underworld economic and political activities on a priori grounds. In a city like Delhi, however, resettlement colonies have come into being as a result of political decisions, and people who own houses in these colonies are dependent to a large extent on political overlords. People often pointed out to me that the route of social mobility in resettlement colonies lay through such nefarious activities. From the point of view of those who occupy the central spaces in Delhi, the peripheries are feared as slums. For the dwellers in these colonies, it is the city which is a landscape of fear. See also Obeysekere (1984).

of communal or caste ideology. It is possible that we have to bring a bifocal perspective on collective violence. Thus, while the kind of violence encountered by the Sikhs, the Tamils, the Muhajirs, etc., may be narrated as part of a national or regional history, it may also be simultaneously understood within a different sequence of events that have local relevance. In the case of Sultanpuri, for instance, described in my paper, the block A/4 was especially targeted since it had been locked in an ongoing feud with the adjoining block of Chamars, who were the main perpetrators of violence during the riots. The penetration of local issues by regional or national events appears again in the case of one of the Tamil families described by Valli Kanapathipillai. She shows how the Sinhala-Tamil conflict translated itself in the case of one of the families she studied into landlord-tenant conflict, leading to prolonged harassment of the Tamil family by the Sinhala landlord. Smelser noted in his analysis of race riots that when a hostile outburst begins, it becomes a sign that a 'fissure has opened in the social order and that the situation is now structurally conducive for the expression of hostility'. Thus, all kinds of latent hostilities are drawn towards the avenues that open up. While it is certainly true that all kinds of hostilities become conjoined together in the case of collective violence, I should like to turn Smelser's argument on its head. It is not that once a riot starts other hostilities become conjoined to the master symbol of the major hostility; it is rather that, in order for diffused hostilities to translate themselves into violent conflict, a contiguity has to be established between specific, concrete, and local issues on the one hand, and a master symbol on the other, in terms of which the conflict is viewed in the public consciousness. This may be control over a sacred space, or avenging the death of a leader. This may help us to see the connections between the everyday life of the people engaged in such violence and the extra-ordinary events around which narratives of violence are woven.

The Temporal Structure of Riots

The form of the riot is seen not only in the organization of space but also in its temporal structure. Time in this context, however, cannot be understood purely as an external dimension, as duration, but also as constitutive of the phenomenon itself. As Bourdieu (1977) has stated in a different context, there are certain social practices which are defined by the fact that their temporal structure, direction and rhythm are *constitutive* of their meaning. Let us consider this statement in the context of two questions regarding time. The first question relates to the event structure of the riot and the narrative sequence within which it is placed. The second examines the relation between the unfolding sequence of violence and the objectified calendars, either ritual or political, of the society.

The task of fixing the 'origin' of riots is not an easy one, for the precise sequence of events within which it is to be placed remains one of the most contested sites in the interpretation of violence. In a careful consideration of violence against Tamils in July 1983 in Colombo, Tambiah (1986) makes the point that the official story of a riot is always challenged by alternative interpretations. For example, the most proximate cause of the Sinhala violence against the Tamils was the ambushing of an army truck by 'Liberation Tigers' and the killing and mutilation of thirteen soldiers. The official story supported even by the holder of the high office of President was that those who had served with the officers as well as the relatives had gone berserk with grief and attacked Tamils. Thus, it was the brutality of the Tamil guerrillas which was said to have provoked a retaliation on such a massive scale by the Sinhalese. Many Tamils, on the other hand, traced the genealogy of the conflict differently. They argued that ever since the passing of the Prevention of Terrorism Act of 1979, Tamil youths had been arrested and tortured; this in turn was traced by the militant Sinhalese to the necessity of protecting ordinary citizens from the acts of terror conducted by the Tamil guerrillas, who in turn could point to the systematic discrimination against Tamils—the story can go on and on. The point is not that 'scientific histories' of such riots cannot be written but that these alternative interpretations constitute the *meaning* of the violence for people located in different social positions. Similar contested versions were also produced for the violence against Sikhs. For example, many Hindus felt that the violence against the Sikhs expressed an anger that had been building up against acts of terrorism against Hindus in the Punjab. The fact that more Sikhs than Hindus have been killed in terrorist violence in Punjab does not figure in their narrative. For others, this was of crucial significance. Thus, the meaning attached to violence is differently construed in the popular consciousness of different sections of society.

The temporal sequence in which a riot is placed, then, results from the exercise of imagination in the sense in which Hume used the word when he insisted that the capacity to contract two instants into a single sequence is not a reflection, properly speaking, but rather that it forms a synthesis of time. He implied that it is in the context of a living present that certain moments of a past are retained, while others are actively forgotten. Similarly, it is in the context of a living present that the future is constituted by an anticipation of the other events that are likely to follow. The papers on the experience of survivors are especially concerned with this range of issues. I would like to emphasize that the narrative constructions of a 'living present' by the perpetrators of violence would be of equal importance for the understanding of the nature of collective violence today.

The unfolding of future events, however, may follow different kinds of patterns. The simplest is that in which we have a simple repetition connecting two events such that the occurrence of event A leads to an anticipation of event B. Farida Shaheed gives an example of Shia-Sunni riots that follow this pattern every year with monotonous regularity. The two sects come in conflict at the time of Moharram. In such a case, the violence is a signifier of an ongoing conflict and since the martyrdom of Hussain crystallizes this conflict, the occasion of Moharram becomes an appropriate time for the expression of this conflict. It may also be noted that a marked and sacred event structured around the symbol of martyrdom perhaps results in a heightened awareness among members of the community who experience the intense force described by Durkheim for piacular rituals (Durkheim 1915). This does not mean that scapegoating and conflict would inevitably result on such occasions but rather that its occurrence can be anticipated on the basis of a construction of the past.

Conflicting temporalities in different religions may also lead to conflict. Roberts gives examples of the tensions generated when a Buddhist festival, for example, falls during Easter week and the route of the Buddhist procession with its use of music and drumming has to be negotiated so that it can avoid the churches en route. This feature of conflicting temporalities as a source of conflict, has been noted, for instance, by Zerubaval (1981) in the case of Jewish and Christian calendars.[10]

At one level, we have told the story of Shia-Sunni conflict on the occasion of Moharram as if it repeated an ageless pattern. Yet, the imputed repetition here is a function of the crystallization of representation. We have only to compare Farida Shaheed's brief and unproblematic description with an account of the management of conflict at Moharram in January 1911, contained in the report of the police commissioner of Bombay. In the report which was submitted to the secretary of the government's judicial department, Bombay, following disturbances in Bombay during Moharram in which police had to resort to firing, the commissioner explained the nature of the conflict. What is interesting to observe is that the major source of conflict seems to have been located in traditional rivalries among the different *mohallas* in which different caste groups of Shias and Sunnis lived. The rivalries related foremost to precedence and to challenges by new caste groups to the established hierarchies of caste among the Muslims as these were displayed during Moharram.[11]

What is equally important is to note what happens when such rivalries are treated as law and order problems. In this case, the police were anxious not only to fix routes of processions so that the possibilities of clashes were minimized, but also to ensure that the traditional *tabuts* were taken out, for, as the commissioner put it, 'the non-appearance of a *tabut* could lead to great disturbance'.

It is worth quoting those parts of the report that relate to the management of this conflict in some detail.

On the ninth night (tenth January) we exerted all our influence to keep the various *mohallas* in a good temper. Mr Vincent went with his most trusted C.I.D. officers to the E division *mohallas*, spoke with the crowd listened to their *waaz* or nightly discourse, subscribed to their funds and finally left them apparently happy and determined to carry out their *tabuts* properly. Meanwhile Mr Gadner and I visited the B division *mohallas*, talked with the *tabutwallas* and endeavoured to allay the tensions obviously

[10] A similar conflict is noted when Moharram and Holi fall close to each other. See Ghosh (1971), p. 26.

[11] For a description of this conflict and its implications for understanding power and influence in the *mohallas*, see Masselos (1975–6) and Ghosh (1971).

spreading through the Muslim quarters. At the four chief *mohallas* we visited, we were received in friendly style; but I was made to understand secretly that none of them would lift their *tabuts* unless Rangari *mohalla* gave the lead and that the Konkani *mohallas* were absolutely obdurate and hostile.[12]

Thus Moharram, which is a marked time, since it is the time of reversals, now receives a second mark from the perspective of the law and order machinery as a time of potential disturbance. In the 1911 report we find that the pattern of signification corresponds to what Castoriadis (1975) calls a magma of significations, in the sense that these have not crystallized into a clear pattern. Also, the important markers for the police are the caste backgrounds of the *mohallas* (e.g. the Juhallas are described as easy to incite) and they try to create 'normalcy' as a sign of their own efficiency.

To complete the story of this particular conflict, despite all the efforts described above, there was trouble when the Rangari *mohalla* *tabut* was joined by a hostile crowd that shouted, whistled and hurled obscenities. Finally the processionists and the police were stoned. 'The torch-bearers of the Rangari *mohalla* put down their lights and fled.... The *tabut* was within an ace of being abandoned when the police seized the bearers and forced them to carry on.'[13] Obviously, the hostility of the crowd included the policemen who were heavily stoned and who, in turn, had to resort to police firing in which several onlookers died.

The Governor-in-Council's resolution which exonerated the police commissioner for the deaths also stated that the 'Mohamedan' community could do much to assist the cause of law and order by explaining to the people that the *tabut* procession and *tolis* were in no way necessary to the celebration of Moharram. In 1914, when the conflicts seem to have been satisfactorily managed, the commissioner of police reported that he was greatly aided by leading men of Sunni *jamats* who had tried to persuade people that money should be spent on orderly religious discourses, illumination and charity rather than on 'irrelevant' and 'turbulent' processions.

From the perspective of the administrator responsible for law and order, it is the *quality* of time brought into being during such

---

[12] See Edwardes (n.d.), quoted in Ghosh (1971), p. 31.
[13] See Ghosh (1971), p. 34.

'orgiastic' expressions of popular religiosity that becomes problematic, for such expressions traditionally conveyed hostility and
protest against those in authority. The long-time resolution of
the problem was sought in changing the quality of time. Perhaps
the repetitious monotony with which conflict occurs on Moharram
(although the character of the conflict has altered) is a reminder of
its double mark and consequent over-determination. In other
words, within the religious calendar, festivals that express the
carnival principle and which reverse the normal body orientation
to that of the grotesque (Bakhtin 1969), there is the potential of
interrogating and mocking the normal social arrangements of
power and hierarchy. In addition, these occasions become marked
through the law and order discourse as potentially dangerous
occasions. Thus they can simultaneously express contempt for
the higher echelons of their own society defined by status, and also
defy the representatives of the state.

When we consider the other conflicts described in this book, it
seems that the pattern and meaning of the violence is in the process
of being shaped. An effort to crystallize the magma of these significations is reflected in the effort to graft the various points of
transition of a conflict to the already existing objectified calendars,
both ritual and political, of the society. Thus the conflict over
reservations described by Baxi, for instance, develops along significant political events which serve as markers of time—such as
ministerial announcements, release of judicial committee reports,
regional examination schedules, etc. This points to the clearly
political character of the conflict.

In contrast, the violence against Sikhs left both communities
uncertain as to whether the conflict was over religion or politics.
One indication of this uncertainty was that significant religious
festivals such as Holi, Diwali or the birthday of Guru Nanak Dev
were viewed with apprehension of fresh or retaliatory violence, but
so were occasions of national importance such as Republic Day or
Independence Day. The effort to use the objectified calendars of
society to make statements in a conflict marked by an antagonistic
reciprocity signifies the attempt to introduce order. However,
that the order is in the making rather than representationally
complete is evident in the oscillation between the political and
religious calendars. This oscillation also shows that the conflict is

seen as simultaneously involving two communities as well as the community *versus* the state. Reciprocally, the state's interest in regulating community practices is shown in the way in which transitions and boundaries of the ritual calendar become marked as occasions on which law and order problems are anticipated and dealt with.

We are now in a position to see how the imaginative institution of a narrative sequence to give form to acts of violence may be related to the extant objective calendars of a society. The form is sought to be given by two different, though not unrelated, rhetorical devices. The first is the use of metonymy and mimesis; the second is the use of metaphor and resemblance.

Consider the following two sequences of events. The relatives and the associates of the soldiers in Sri Lanka, who had been killed in an ambush, went into a frenzy of grief at the expectation of seeing their dead and mutilated bodies in the central cemetery. Violence against Tamils followed, in which the bodies of the dead mimetically displayed the wounds, literal and metaphoric, to the whole society. In making other innocent Tamils repeat the fate of the dead soldiers, processes of mimesis and metonymy were being used which linked the killing of soldiers to the killing of innocent Tamils.

The case of the assassination of Mrs Gandhi is even clearer. After her assassination by her Sikh guards, rumours were rife that the Sikh community had celebrated her death by distributing sweets and lighting candles as 'if they were celebrating Diwali'. The structure of these rumours provided a metaphoric linkage between death and celebration on Diwali, and thus legitimized the 'punishment' of members of the community. Like the innocent Tamils, the Sikhs were made to metonymically imitate the fate of the assassinated prime minister. These rhetorical devices are by no means, *causes*, and should not be so confused. What they point to is the manner in which events are linked in temporal sequences through metaphor and metonymy, giving form to fluid significations.

The Cultural Repertoire

In his study of popular protest in France, Tilly (1986) introduced the notion of the limited repertoire of a society for collective action.

'Any population', he said, 'has a limited repertoire of a social action' (p. 390). By this statement Tilly did not wish to imply that the actions of a crowd are predetermined as in a script, but rather, to use his apt analogy, that they provide the crowd with a kind of musical score which gives pattern to its activities and also provides notions of limit. As he says: 'far from the image we sometimes have of mindless crowds, people tend to act within known limits, to innovate at the margins of existing forms, and to miss many opportunities available to them. . .' (p. 390) In the case of France, Tilly says that there have been different kinds of collective actions in different periods of time. In the seventeenth century the typical form of collective action was the assembly to seek redress; in the eighteenth it was the *charivari* that was used to shame people in power for transgression of norms; the nineteenth century developed the strike as its mode of collective action, while the demonstration is typical of the twentieth century. Tilly also suggests that the repertoire of collective action in France remains constant from mid-seventeenth to mid-nineteenth century, and then changes its form. In the mid-seventeenth to the mid-nineteenth century, collective protest, whether over food or tax, was parochial in scope. It addressed local action or local representatives and it relied upon local patronage. From the mid-nineteenth century onwards, the scope of political action becomes national, as shown by the modes of co-operation among localities. Also, the action becomes autonomous, freed of local patronage.

An examination of conflicts described in this volume would show not only that there has been an expansion of scope from local to national levels as far as communal, ethnic, or sectarian conflict is concerned, but also that some of these conflicts have international dimensions. In contrast to earlier conflicts which were local in scope, now it seems that local issues are transformed and have become national or international in their scope.

Changes in communication and modes of organization clearly play an important role in this expansion. However, what is crucial is also that the definition of community has widened considerably. As regards the management of conflict in 1911, it was the different *mohallas* that were locked in battles over local rivalries relating to questions of precedence. The same issues would now have regional or even national implications, so that Shia–Sunni conflicts in one city, for instance, can become a major issue in the emergence of conflict in other cities.

Tilly's argument about the type of collective action that is particular to a period is important. It should, however, be noted that in the unfolding of a conflict, various kinds of collective action can be used. Both Farida Shaheed and Akmal Hussain show how a demonstration organized to protest against the city transport may be transformed into a violent conflict between two ethnic groups; conversely, when a community has been exposed to brutal violence by members of another community—as were the Sikhs in Delhi or the Tamils in Colombo—it may retaliate not by innovating on the margins of existing forms (by organizing a riot for instance), but by using new forms of collective action (such as organizing demonstrations or boycotts). The movement between different forms is one way in which contemporary violent conflicts between different religious or ethnic groups may be distinguished from similar violence in earlier times.

If the community has a repertoire for the organization of collective action, then so does the state for the management of these collective actions. One may argue that the development of the police force and the army for the management of internal conflict and the suppression of protest is an important arena in which the power of the state expresses itself. Traditionally, social science literature had made a distinction between violence and legitimate force, the latter referring to the monopoly enjoyed by the state in the exercise of force. Thus, for instance, the French president Giscard d'Estaing appointed a committee to study violence, crime and delinquency which expressed its deep disquiet at the fact that life itself seemed to be becoming more violent in France.[14] Yet, in its deliberations it did not take into account the violence of war, political terrorism and violent sport. The concentration was upon individual violence, especially crime. The limited nature of this approach may be seen in the fact that the experience of most societies shows that considerable violence is perpetrated by the agencies of the state, such as the police or the army, in such processes as 'riot management'.[15] In his study of collective contention in

[14] See Payerfille *et al.* (1977).

[15] For an insightful analysis of violence in the hands of the state, see Baxi (1988).

France, mentioned earlier, Tilly found that the bulk of the killings over the ages had been done by professional soldiers and the police against protesters, rather than by those engaged in popular protest.

The manner in which the armed forces and the police have been engaged in South Asia in the management of internal conflicts leads one to seriously question the notion of *legitimate* force. Although there is a well developed repertoire that the state has at its disposal for the management of collective episodes of violence, including the use of curfews, the deployment of limited force, preventive arrests, etc.—the manner in which these measures are used by the police can be shown to be partisan.[16]

In all the cases described in this volume, the timing of the declaration of curfew, for instance, was such that crowds could inflict considerable damage before they were brought under control. Saroja, one of the protagonists in Kanapathipillai's account, said: 'We waited, hoping that curfew would be declared but nothing happened.' In the case of the carnage following Mrs Gandhi's assassination, several Citizen's Commissions noted that the police were simply not available to protect ordinary citizens. This failure of the police during such periods of crisis is not new and was noted earlier by such authors as Sorel (1950). However, the meaning of this delay and its consequences may vary considerably from case to case. In the case discussed by Sorel there seems to have been some hesitation in the use of force against the striking workers:

One of the things which appears to have most astonished workers during the last few years has been the timidity of the forces of law and order in the presence of a riot; magistrates who have a right to demand the services of soldiers dare not use this process to the utmost, and officers allow themselves to be abused and struck with patience hitherto unknown to them.[17]

This reluctance to use force may be an expression of solidarity with those against whom the police or the army is being asked to use force. Baxi, in his paper, warns quite explicitly that the tendency of the state to settle differences by the use of force may ultimately

---

[16] Rajgopal (1987) shows that the police are reluctant to register riot cases. In the Bhiwandi riots of 1984, out of 611 cases only 185 were sent up to the courts, and of these only 4 secured convictions.

[17] Sorel (1950), p. 82.

lead to a situation in which the state may lose its legitimacy. He further warns that the policemen are part of society and cannot remain unaffected by the nature of public discussion in society. He recommends, therefore, that differences should be sought to be settled much more by mutual discussion and debate than by the use of force.

In cases of ethnic or communal conflict, the sympathy of the police is often with the members of the majority community. This is partly a result of recruitment policies. In Sri Lanka, for example, Tambiah (1986) has noted that 'for nearly thirty years there has been no recruitment of Tamils into the armed forces, and very little into police forces'.[18] In India, between 1954 and 1960, out of a total number of people killed in riots (according to official calculations) 86 per cent were Muslims, and this proportion shows a steady increase.[19] Studies of particular riots, such as the Hindu–Muslim riots in Delhi and Meerut in 1987, show that more people were killed in police violence than in communal clashes.[20] Secondly, the number of Muslims killed in police violence was larger than Hindus. In certain cases, as in Meerut, the Provincial Armed Constabulary seems to have unleashed unprecedented brutalities upon innocent Muslims in the guise of controlling riots. Thus, official principles of riot control set out in manuals do not take into account the fact that the so-called 'legitimate force' applied by the state transmutes itself into brutal terror when the agencies of the state are used to control the expressions of discontent, especially since the perpetrators of such violence tend to go unpunished.

It would, however, be a simplification to assume that police brutalities are limited to minorities in every case. The case of the violent conflict that developed in the anti-reservation movement in Gujarat points to the complexity of the issues. Baxi, I think, goes to the heart of the matter when he states that in a democratic society repeated repression of dissent by the use of force may threaten the very fabric of that society. Policemen, he says, are also members of society. If they are repeatedly compelled by governments in

---

[18] Tambiah (1986), p. 15. In Sri Lanka, of a national police force of 25,000, only 600 (2.4 per cent) are Tamil. See *The Island*, 18 August 1987.

[19] See Ghosh (1971), p. 52.

[20] See Engineer (1988), for a detailed documentation.

power to push decisions arrived at without discussion and debate on a resistant population, then they can themselves become alienated from the state. The use of the army to discipline the police force which we are repeatedly witnessing in our societies points to the 'illegitimacy' of legal force.

The repertoire of the state to deal with collective violence consists not only of the legal measures available, such as declaration of curfew and preventive arrests, but also the brutal terror which the agencies of the state use to break up collective action. Even in the case of individual crime and violence, the police often use muted violence, as Perkin (1986) has argued recently. In the case of collective violence, we can see the transmutation of such mute violence into publicly applied terror.

Crowds and the Unconscious

Although the different ethnic, communal, or caste conflicts described in this book are located in specific socio-historic contexts, there are certain symbols that recur in all of these. First of all, the symbolism of death seems to be an important organizing image around which volatile emotions are released.

In the riots in Colombo, the mutilated bodies of the soldiers were expected to be displayed in the public cemetery and the initial violence was said to be the work of close associates who had become unhinged with grief. In the Delhi violence against the Sikhs, the public display of the slain body of Mrs Gandhi was a central symbol around which themes of vengeance were articulated. Although all the studies of these riots point to the organized nature of the violence, we cannot ignore the evidence that powerful symbolic images were evoked and that crowds were perpetrating violence in states of heightened emotion. Sudhir Kakar asks whether one's experience in crowds leads to a lowering of normal defenses, so that 'the crowds assault on the sense of individuality, its invitation to transcend one's individual boundaries and its offer of a freedom from personal doubts and anxieties is well-nigh irresistible.' Kakar goes on to argue that 'the need and search for self-transcending experience, to lose one's self in the group, suspend judgement and reality testing, is, I believe, the primary motivational factor in both religious assembly and violent mob, even though the stated purpose is spiritual uplift in one and mayhem and murder in the other.'

The image of crowds as emotional, capricious, temperamental and flighty has dominated the literature of mass psychology.[21] The characteristics had led Le Bon (1952) to declare that 'Crowds are everywhere distinguished by feminine characteristics.' As Muscovici puts it, 'There was no need for Le Bon to invent the idea that there are strong links between the eternally feminine and the eternally collective. The crowds of the French revolution were largely made up of women, and the women who harangued them haunted the nightmares of the leaders of the mobs for years to come.'[22]

Similarly, studies of Nazi crowds have also suggested that the same process of feminization was at work. In all these cases, however, we see that corresponding to the image of the feminine crowd is the image of the hyper-masculinity of the leader. Muscovici (1985) suggests that the crowd comes to be spoken of as a woman simply to mask the exchange of homosexual images between the 'active' leader and the 'passive' crowd. There seems to be a strong element of analogical reasoning in these arguments, as well as a slippage from analogy to concept. The image of Nazi crowds posits the corresponding image of the strong leader. But what about crowds that are formed not around the image of a strong, masculine leader, but around the images of a dead leader, or a raped woman, or a child killed by a demonic other? In these cases it seems that it is the masculinity of the crowd which is being challenged and which is sought to be recovered through punitive murder and pillage. Farida Shaheed gives the instance of the Pathan-Muhajir riots in which one of the motifs in the mobilization of the Pathans was that they could lose the rights to their own women if they did not avenge the insults to which they felt they had been subjected by the Muhajirs. Similarly, I describe how Sikh men were made to feel that they had lost their masculinity by the violent actions of crowds. In fact one of the dominant images repeated by these crowds was that of vengeance, since the 'Sikhs had killed the mother of us Hindus'. The fact that in this case it was the people lowest in the caste and class hierarchies who responded to the idea that they were the pro-

[21] Cf. Muscovici (1985).
[22] Ibid., p. 110.

tectors of 'Hindus', as well as of the 'nation', points to the fact that the masculine/feminine dichotomy cannot be applied to crowds in the simple fashion that Le Bon formulated. Where punitive violence emerges as the major theme around which crowds are mobilized, the whole question of masculinity and femininity is renegotiated through crowd actions.

Almost in direct opposition to the view that crowds are moved to action by deeply buried unconscious urges is the view of crowds as agents of rational action. The best known account of such crowds is by Thompson (1971), who argues in his study of food riots that the English crowds in the eighteenth century reformulated traditional rights in a new moral economy of the poor: 'The food riot in the eighteenth century was a highly complex form of direct popular action, disciplined and with clear objectives.'[23] This view of the rational crowd, whose actions are contained within a moral economy, seems in many respects directly opposed to the kinds of crowds described in this volume. Perhaps we should pay attention to Tilly's suggestion that 'collective action', 'contention' and 'collective violence' should be distinguished. In the case of collective action and contention, he argues that violence constitutes only a *moment* in the system; it does not give value to the system.

Useful as this suggestion is, and though great is our own need to be able to distinguish between protesting peasants looting food and avenging crowds killing innocent people, we come to the painful realization that such crowds are also disciplined, that they have clear objectives, and they are often fighting for the restoration of a moral order defined by the rules of feud, or of sacrifice, as I have suggested elsewhere.[24]

How are these opposite images of crowds—one stating that they are ruled by reason, the other that they are ruled by passions; one documenting the organized nature of mob violence, the other showing the capricious nature of crowds—to be reconciled within a single framework? Tilly suggests that violence is not a coherent phenomenon after all.

Without pretending to give any authoritative answer to these

---

[23] Thompson (1971), p. 78. This view of the rational crowd has been used by Lynch (1981) in describing Jatau violence in Agra in 1978. However, the ethnography in this paper is thin, based largely on newspaper accounts.

[24] See Das and Nandy (1986).

questions, it seems that we need to build our empirical knowledge on several issues relating to crowds before we may be in a position to attempt answers. These are:

1. It must be recognized that crowds are not built out of passive pools of people. Hence networks of people and relationships that already exist have to be mobilized in the creation of crowds. Such networks need to be studied and documented, regardless of the distinctions between collective action, contention, and collective violence.

2. There is no contradiction between the fact that, on the one hand, mob violence may be highly organized and crowds provided with such instruments as voter's lists or combustible powders, and on the other that crowds draw upon repositories of unconscious images. This is no more contradictory than the fact that the use of torture is institutionalized in modern police practice and yet that the torturer must draw from his own unconscious fantasies to enter into such intimacy with the body of the victim through violence. Hence, just as we study the organization and networks through which crowds are recruited, so must we document the organizing images, including rumours, that crowds use to define themselves and their victims.

3. All this is not to suggest that in moral terms all crowds are the same. However, we need to understand more clearly the non-violent crowds who, following Gandhian techniques, are willing to allow their own bodies to be violated, and, conversely, violent crowds who must inflict pain and injury upon surrogate victims in order to be avenged. Although Kakar would argue that there is no difference between the two in terms of the unconscious processes involved—it seems to me that the manner in which participants in the former experience transcendence is different from the latter—who cannot integrate the theatrical transformation experienced in the crowd into their continuous, narrative, selves. If such a view is to be tested, the world views of participants and crowds must be studied not only at the moment of collective action or collective violence but also after such a moment has passed.

One of the greatest lacunae in our understanding of collective action, including collective violence, is the lack of an organized body of empirical knowledge on these issues, as compared to what is available on the composition of crowds in the French revolution, for instance. The essays in this volume cast only a sideways glance at issues which need to be brought to the centre of our attention.

The Experience of the Survivors

If the world view of the perpetrators of violence does not find adequate description in this volume, an attempt has been made to describe the reformulation of the self and the world by the survivors of the riots. A survivor was defined by Lifton (1968) as someone who has been touched by annihilating violence and death. Disasters in South Asia in the eighties, to which reference was made in the first few pages of this essay, have led to the emergence of voluntary-activist workers who have tried to provide immediate relief and long-term rehabilitation to the victims/survivors of these disasters. They have also tried to document the plight of such victims and to secure justice for them. Their work has challenged the natural as well as the social scientists to view their own disciplines critically.

In Lifton's work on the survivors of Hiroshima, the survivor appears as a unitary person. In reformulating his world and re-establishing the narrative continuity of the self, he does not seem to be bound by the structures of his society. Powerful as Lifton's descriptions of the survivors of Hiroshima are, he does not seem to give a central place to the manner in which one's social class or gender shapes one's experience of survival. The conclusions which emerge from the third section of this volume point to a different direction. They show that there is a sliding relation between social structure and the experience of survival. There are at least three identifiable domains in which this relation is shaped. First, the social class of the survivors has a decisive impact on the manner in which violence is experienced and the world reformulated. Second, one's position within the family and kinship structure is related to the type of violence encountered, not only during the catastrophic moments of the riot but also in the course of subsequent events. Finally, the division of labour in the roles played by men and women in the work of mourning during normal deaths stretches into the field of political deaths and makes women the special interlocutors between the worlds of kinship and politics.

In the two detailed studies of survivors presented in this volume, we encounter immediately the question of social class. The slum dwellers of Delhi who are the subjects of my paper lived in an environment steeped in violence and crime, whereas for the middle or upper class Tamils, described in Kanapathipillai's paper, the ethnic riots were the first direct experience of violence. For the Tamils, the violence was the work of hoodlums and thugs, but for the Sikhs living in the slum area of Sultanpuri it was the work of neighbours with whom the leaders of their own community were locked in a long and bitter feud. Consequently, we find that riots broke open whatever solidarity the kin-neighbourhoods of the Siglikar Sikhs normally displayed. It was common to see bitter fights in the Sikh *mohallas* as accusations about betrayals were hurled across among the survivors. Those who had lost their husbands or sons were suspicious that others within the community had betrayed them. These conflicts were further intensified because of the bureaucratic procedures of separating those who could be considered legal heirs, for purposes of giving compensation, from other kinsmen or kinswomen.

The pattern of re-victimization was the most cruel for young widows within the community. Recipients of Rs 10,000 from the government as compensation, they were often beaten and abused by male conjugal kinsmen who felt *they* should have been the compensated heirs of dead sons or brothers. This pattern of intimidation continued till the caste panchayat deliberated on the issue and finally pronounced that the money received in compensation was to be equally shared between a widow and the dead man's father or brother.

Intimidation from within the community was not the only hazard that survivors had to face. They also faced serious threats to their lives from the men they had identified as murderers to various civil rights organizations. Women were threatened with rape and abduction. Threats of kidnapping and killing of children were dealt out in order to silence many survivors. In addition, powerful politicians and police officers who had played a major role in the killings during the mob attacks were not arrested, despite having been identified by the survivors; and they flaunted their freedom for all to see. Thus, a major difference in the experience of these lower-class Sikhs in comparison with members of the upper or middle classes was that they were literally assaulted by a continuous violence from every possible direction. This unrelenting assault and the threat of annihilation bestowed a heroic dimension to the task of surviving. The very bureaucratization of relief constituted a powerful pattern of re-victimization. It is true that in the Tamil case the bureaucracy was also involved in providing help to the Tamil victims. But whereas for the middle-class person (who has encountered the bureaucracy in other contexts of his life) the filling of forms, the presenting of oneself in court or in the office of a relief commissioner, holds no insuperable terror, for the slum dweller it constitutes a traumatic experience. Ravirajan (1988) has given a sensitive description of this process in writing about Bhopal victims who had to undergo further agonies waiting in long queues in hospitals in order to receive appropriate forms that would certify them as MIC victims, the wounds on their bodies not being sufficient evidence. I have shown that help received in a manner that inferiorized the receiver, even though greedily accepted, was classed as counterfeit.

Whereas there are various institutional and symbolic processes through which re-victimization takes place, it would be a mistake to see the survivor as a passive being, completely controlled and moulded by these processes. Kanapathipillai's contribution is especially valuable here because she shows how the family as a unit reconstructs its reality. The role of the outsider in helping the family in periods of crisis has been well documented in the researches of Reiss (1981). Kanapathipillai develops one of the suggestions contained in this work, that this 'outsider' may well be an aspect of the self that has earlier been an outsider in the family. We see the central role played by women in the Tamil families during the process of reformulating their world. Similarly, women survivors in the Sikh community came to play an important role as they learnt to operate the bureaucratic and judicial systems for procuring help and justice. The role of women in periods of crisis sheds a new light on their ability to transform social reality not only in the interiority of their lives but also in the public realm.

Writing and Violence

In the last section, I stated that the traditional arrangement of roles in mourning, according to which it is the women who lament the dead, places them in a special position to be the interlocutors between the domains of kinship and politics. In the case of the survivors among the Sikhs described here, women were under tremendous pressure to terminate mourning. They, however, stubbornly held on to the pollution of mourning, and although traditional laments were not sung or spoken they found new languages for giving expression to their grief and the utter injustice of their situation. It is important to realize that repeated attempts were made to censor their speech. This was done not only by wily politicians but also by well-meaning scholars who feared that if the plight of the victims came to be known it would lead to a backlash by the Sikhs. Thus, both a utilitarian morality fearful of consequences and an utterly corrupt political regime tried to control the survivors for their own purpose.[25] In a certain sense we have the motif of an Antigone, a Sorel myth, insisting upon her right to *mourn* in defiance of superior male authority.

The two essays on survivors together constitute an important critique of a theory postulated by Bloch (1982), that women's role in mourning is indicative of their low status. It is, however, strange that whereas Bloch points out how women are made to take the pollution of death and the responsibility for negated male solidarities upon themselves, he does not consider it necessary to look at their laments as meaningful speech. The arguments in our papers point to the way in which a transition is made from the realm of kinship to that of politics by women's access to a privileged form of speech which, however, if it is to speak, must be treated as meaningful.

In her essay in this volume, Amrit Srinivasan examines the epistemic space occupied by the survivor in the task of history writing. As she points out, the testimony of the survivor demonstrates the fundamental social fact that the artificial disorder at times of crises can only be understood as a function of the artificial order of normal times. Her essay not only gives us an insight into how the survivor constructs his world and learns to see the self in the eyes of the other, but also how the microcosm of violent space

---

[25] One is reminded of Derrida's observation: 'If light is the element of violence, one must combat light with certain other light in order to avoid the worst violence, the violence of the night which precedes or suppresses discourse.' Derrida (1978), p. 115.

and time that s/he inhabits is a reflection of the macrocosm of the violent modern state.

The question of writing, however, poses many new problems. What is the form through which violence may be written about when its foundation, as Bataille (1957) said, is that it exceeds limits? A crucial issue here is whether the form evolved in writing about survivor experience is simply used to titillate. Does it tear the facts of violence out of context? Does the author stand in relationship of a voyeur to the narratives of suffering? Most of the work on survivors done in this context would suggest that the distinction between the author and his/her object dissolves in the study of violence. To be the scribe of the human experience of suffering creates a special responsibility towards those who suffer. While there cannot be a single answer to the nature of this responsibility, one cannot simply hide behind the axiological neutrality of Max Weber. We shall have to ask: did we take this responsibility seriously?

In a world threatened by annihilating violence, the testimony of the survivor has special importance. Suffering may transform a person in two directions. It may become a mark of special status, and the survivor may view his own historical mission as a prevention of the repetitions of that suffering. This was the case of the Hiroshima victims who dedicated themselves to peace, as also of the Bhopal victims who, despite grinding poverty, refused to accept the meagre compensation offered by Union Carbide, insisting that responsibility for the disaster must be judicially fixed. Suffering, however, can also lead to the belief that, having suffered, one has acquired a right to impose suffering upon others.[26] It is the special task of the survivors of violence to show us how such suffering may be transformed into redemption.

While it is true that moments of violence create an atmosphere of intense exchange in which boundaries between the self and the other are broken, the nature of signs through which such Dionysian communities are created needs careful consideration. The intense exchange of May 1968 in Paris seems to have been created over words. It broke barriers of all kinds, including those between French professors and their students. When the sign changes from words to human lives over which the euphoria is created, we have

[26] See Das and Nandy (1986).

to recall Durkheim's words that the sacred can be evil and eminently so: then the right of final pronouncement over the nature of this violence must rest with the survivor. It is he, or more often she, who is charged with the responsibility of creating a reflexive understanding of our situation and our times. This is a difficult historical burden that we place on the survivor: but it is a burden that will have to be borne for suffering to become redemptive.

REFERENCES

Arnold, David, 1987: 'Touching the Body: Perspectives on the Indian Plague 1896–1900', in *Subaltern Studies V*, ed. R. Guha. Delhi: Oxford University Press, pp. 55–91.

Bakhtin, M., 1968: *Rabelais and his World*. Cambridge: MIT Press.

Bargar, B. L., 1907: *The Law and the Customs of Riot Duty*. Published by the author.

Bataille, G., 1957: *L'Erotisme*. Paris: Les Editions de Minuits.

Baxi, Upendra, 1988: 'Violence, Dissent and Development'. *Law and Social Change: Indo American Reflections*, ed. R. W. Meager. Delhi: Indian Law Institute, pp. 72–93.

Bayly, C. A., 1985: 'The Prehistory of Colonialism? Religious Conflict in India, 1700–1860'. *Modern Asian Studies*, pp. 177–203.

Bloch, M., 1982: 'Death, Women and Power', in *Death and the Regeneration of Life*, ed. M. Bloch and J. Parry. Cambridge: Cambridge University Press, pp. 211–31.

Borden, C. M., 1988: *Contemporary Indian Tradition*. Delhi: Oxford University Press.

Bourdieu, P., 1977: *Outline of a Theory of Practice*. Cambridge: Cambridge University Press.

Castoriadis, C., 1975: *L'institution imaginaire de la societe*. Paris: Editions de Seuil.

Chandra, Bipan, 1984: *Communalism in Modern India*. Delhi: Vikas.

Das, Veena and Ashis Nandy, 1986: 'Violence, Victimhood and the Language of Silence', in *The Word and the World: Fantasy, Symbol and Record*, ed. Veena Das. Delhi: Sage Publications, pp. 177–95.

Das, Veena, 1987: 'Anthropology of Violence and the Speech of Victims'. London: *Anthropology Today*, pp. 106–9.

———, 1988: 'Cultural Rights and the Definition of Community'. Paper presented to the Melbourne Conference on the Rights of Subordinated People, organized by La Trobe University and the Indian Law Institute.

Deleuze, G., 1983: *Nietzsche and Philosophy*. London: The Athlone Press. Trans. from the French by H. Tomlinson.

Derrida, J., 1978: *Writing and Difference*. Chicago: University of Chicago Press.

Durkheim, Emile, 1976: *The Elementary Forms of the Religious Life*. London: George Allen and Unwin. Translated from the French by J. W. Swain. First published 1915.

Edwardes, S. M., n.d.: *The Bombay City Police*.

Engineer, Asghar Ali, 1988: *Delhi Meerut Riots: Analysis, Compilation and Documentation*. Delhi: Ajanta Publications.

Ghosh, S. K., 1971: *Riots: Prevention and Control*. Calcutta: Eastern Law House.

Guha, Ranajit, 1983: *Elementary Aspects of Peasant Insurgency in Colonial India*. Delhi: Oxford University Press.

Habermas, J., 1986: 'Civil Disobedience: Litmus Test for the Democratic Constitutional State'. *Berkeley Journal of Sociology*, vol. xxxi.

Heller, A., 1984: *Everyday Life*. London: Routledge & Kegan Paul. Translated by George Campbell.

Joshi, Chitra, 1985: 'Bonds of Community, Ties of Religion: Kanpur Textile Workers in the Early Twentieth Century'. *Indian Economic and Social History Review*, vol. 22, no. 3, pp. 251–80.

Krishna, Gopal, 1985: 'Communal Violence in India: A Study of Communal Disturbance in Delhi'. *Economic and Political Weekly*, vol. xx, no. 2, pp. 61–74.

Lacan, J., 1977: 'The Agency of the Letter in the Unconscious or Reason since Freud', in *Ecrits: A Selection*. London: Tavistock Publications. Translated from the French by Alan Sheridan.

Le Bon, G., 1952: *The Crowd*. London: Ernest Benn.

Lifton, R. J., 1968: *Death in Life: Survivors of Hiroshima*. New York: Random House.

Lynch, Owen M., 1981: 'Rioting as rational action: An interpretation of the April 1978 riots in Agra'. *Economic and Political Weekly*, vol. xvi, no. 68, pp. 1951–6.

Masselos, J., 1975–6: 'Power in the Bombay "*Mohalla*", 1904–15: An initial exploration into the world of the Indian Urban Muslim'. *South Asia*, vol. 6, pp. 75–95.

Mohanty, M., 1987: 'Communalism: A democratic rights perspective'. *Lokayan Bulletin*, vol. 5, pp. 55–65.

Moore, B., Jr., 1978: *Injustice: The Social Bases of Obedience and Revolt*. New York: M. E. Sharpe.

Muscovici, S., 1985: *The Age of the Crowd: A Historical Treatise of Mass Psychology*. Cambridge : Cambridge University Press.

Obeyesekere, G., 1984: 'Political Violence and the Future of Democracy in Sri Lanka'. *International Asian Forum. International Quarterly for Asian Studies*, vol. 15, pp. 39–60.

Payerfille, A. *et al.*, 1977: *Reponses à la violence*. 2 volumes. Paris: Presses Pocket.

Perkin, D., 1986: 'Violence and Will', in *The Anthropology of Violence*, ed. David Riches. Oxford: Basil Blackwell.

PUDR, 1987: *Walled City Riots: A Report on the Police and Communal Violence in Delhi*. Delhi. June.

Rajgopal, P. R., 1987: *Communal Violence in India*. Delhi: Centre for Policy Research, published by Uppal Pub. Co.

Ravirajan, S. R., 1988: 'Rehabilitation and Voluntarism in Bhopal'. *Lokayan Bulletin*, vol. 1, pp. 3–30.

Reiss, D., 1981: *The Family's Construction of Reality*. Cambridge: Harvard University Press.

Rudé, G., 1959: *The Crowd in the French Revolution*. Oxford: Clarendon.

———, 1964: *The Crowd in History, 1730–1848*. New York: Wiley.

Saussure, F., 1974: *Course in General Linguistics*. New York: Fontana. Translated from the French by Wade Baskin.

Schmitt, C., 1985: *Political Theology: Four Chapters on the Concept of Sovereignty*. M.I.T. Press. Translated by George Schwas.

Shah, Ghanshyam, 1984: 'The 1969 Communal Riots in Ahmadabad: A Case Study', in *Communal Riots in Post-Independence India*, ed. Asghar Ali Engineer. Delhi: Sangam Books, pp. 175–209.

Smelser, N. J., 1962: *Theory of Collective Behaviour*. New York: Free Press.

Sorel, G., 1950: *Reflections on Violence*. Glencoe: Free Press. Translated by Hulle and Rath.

Tambiah, S. J., 1986: *Sri Lanka: Ethnic Fratricide and the Dismantling of Democracy*. London: T.B. Tauras and Co.

Thompson, E. P., 1971: 'The Moral Economy of the English Crowd in the Eighteenth Century'. *Past and Present*, pp. 76–136.

Tilly, C., 1986: *The Contentious French: Four Centuries of Popular Struggle*. Cambridge: Harvard University Press.

Unger, R. M., 1984: *Passion: An Essay on Personality*. New York: The Free Press.

Visvanathan, S. *et al.*, ed., 1988: Bhopal: An Interim Appraisal. Special Issue of *Lokayan Bulletin*, vol. 6.

Wood, S. A., 1952: *Riot Control*. Harisburg, PA: The Military Service Publishing Co.

Zerubaval, E., 1981: *Hidden Rhythms: Schedules and Calendars in Social Life*. Chicago: University of Chicago Press.

Chapter Two

'Comparative Curfew': Changing Dimensions of Communal Politics in India

ASHISH BANERJEE

I

The communal problem in India, it has been argued, is a modern phenomenon.[1] Through the major part of this century the problem of communalism has signified Hindu-Muslim conflict. Only in recent years have the diffused conflicts between Hindus and Sikhs become crystallized into a communal conflict. Even though occasional instances of rioting between Hindus and Muslims are known to have occurred as early as in the eighteenth century, it is from the late nineteenth century that the problem becomes more endemic. The marginalization of the Muslim ruling class in this period and the rise of a new Hindu national assertiveness are widely accepted as a basic explanation for the emergence of communal conflict between the two communities.

It was, however, the politics of representational government after the 1920s which brought the communal issue to the centre stage. Communal quotas, communal representation, communal electorates and a communally oriented federal system—all these were openly debated between the Muslim League and the Congress. While the Muslim League represented only Muslim opinion (though not the opinion of all Muslims), the Congress claimed to be a secular party even though it housed within itself sections of

[1] See Chandra (1984).

articulate Hindu opinion, just as it harboured groups of various other ideological persuasions.[2]

With the complete breakdown of dialogue between the Muslim League and the Congress, the demand for the separate state of Pakistan was raised.[3] Thus the communalism of the Muslim League translated itself into an alternative nationalism, an alternative to the nationalism of the Congress. The period preceding the formation of Pakistan witnessed some of the most gruesome and violent Hindu–Muslim riots, which, in a sense, hastened the division of India. One era of communal politics thus came to an end, with the antagonism between communalism and nationalism resolving itself by creating the avowedly religion-based state of Pakistan and another secular state, India. During the transfer of power some voices were raised in favour of a separate homeland for Sikhs but the issue was resolved fairly quickly and a potential Hindu–Sikh confrontation was diffused.[4] Muslims constituted roughly one-fourth of the population of undivided India. After the partition they were reduced to less than one-sixth of the Indian population. The Muslim League leadership and the bulk of the wealthy and influential Muslims went across to Pakistan. Those who remained were either committed to Indian nationalism and secularism—and were consequently prepared to adjust to the changed circumstances—or were too poor and weak to be embroiled in any kind of politics at all. The Congress under Nehru distanced itself from avowedly Hindu organizations, and the new Constitution provided for freedom of religion as well as for the protection of all minorities.[5]

The post-partition period, except for the immediate aftermath, was marked by the absence of major communal riots. The two-nation theory (i.e. Hindus and Muslims as constituting two nations)

[2] The Hindu Mahasabha, for instance, was a part of the Congress, and so was the Congress Socialist Party.

[3] The experience in UP between 1937 and 1939 was crucial. The Muslim League felt let down by the Congress after the 1937 elections. See Naidu (1980), pp. 60–1, and Gopal (1976), pp. 224–8.

[4] See Kapur (1987), p. 204.

[5] There were differences within the Congress over the role of the RSS. Patel is said to have had no objection to its inclusion, whereas Nehru was vehemently opposed to this. See Kothari (1982), p. 156n.

had worked itself out. Indian Muslims began to settle down to their new status as a considerably reduced minority. For most of them the logical choice of political party was the Congress, though getting Muslim candidates to contest on behalf of the Congress continued to be a problem.[6] A fairly large section of Muslim intellectuals were also either members of the Communist party or in broad sympathy with the left.

Even though the historical juncture was full of possibilities for the Indian nation as a whole, the experience of partition and its bitter memories remained in the minds of Muslims and Hindus. As widely noted by contemporary observers, a formidable Hindu political opinion continued to hold the Muslims responsible for the partition—even those who had stayed back in India. Muslims were, in their turn, baffled and insecure under the new circumstances, and to the reality that parts of their own families were now to be citizens of another country. Besides, for many, the economic support structures which they had taken for granted had collapsed. That is why even after the initial exodus was over a steady trickle of late decision-makers continued to leave for Pakistan. Muslim fears were further compounded by the fact that Hindu political opinion continued to be aggravated on account of the forced migration of Hindus from Pakistan.[7]

The primary task before the Indian leadership was therefore to contain Hindu communal aggression and channelize it into nation-building activity. At this stage Muslim sectarianism or communalism was not perceived by it as a significant challenge. Nehru's appeal to the Hindus to be tolerant and liberal must be understood in this perspective. Besides, he also tried to shift the plane of discourse towards the need to inculcate a scientific temper and the spirit of rationalism, which he considered were the essence of secularism and modernism. It is necessary to emphasize this point because Nehru is sometimes said to have followed a policy of appeasement towards minorities. Ever since his strong advocacy

[6] See Naidu (1980), p. 39.

[7] Nehru wrote to chief ministers on 3 May 1948, warning them against a 'recrudescence' of the RSS. He reminded them that the Congress had undertaken not to recognize or encourage communal organizations with political ends. See Rajagopal (1986), p. 119.

for the reform of Hindu Personal Law, and its successful implementation, sections of Hindu opinion have held that he should have been as thoroughgoing with the reform of Muslim Personal Law. The erstwhile Jana Sangh held, for instance, that Nehru was unwilling to reform Muslim Law because Muslims served as vote-banks for the Congress.

It is not the case, however, that the Congress was at this stage desperately in need of Muslim votes for electoral purposes. If at all, the Muslim vote was necessary to establish secular legitimacy.[8] Nehru believed that Hindus, who constituted eighty-five per cent of the Indian population, had to show the way to reform. Some Indian intellectuals, however, argue that Nehru need not have been 'soft' on the Muslims, and that if he had taken a firm and equitable position at that stage Indian Muslims would have been very clear about the conditions of citizenship in this country. This would have put to rest controversies which still plague the Indian nation. In any case, under the circumstances, Muslims gradually evolved three central symbols of their identity as Indian Muslims—Muslim Personal Law, a proper status for Urdu, and the Aligarh Muslim University. Nehru, we might argue, started the struggle to realize the secular principle in India, but made compromises which he perceived as politically judicious. He certainly could not establish unshakeable roots for secularism during his life-time.

The communal peace that obtained between 1950 and 1960 can then be explained in the following terms. Firstly, in the aftermath of the partition, Hindu communal forces were kept in check by the national leadership, even as the partition had left Indian Muslims weak and leaderless qua Muslims. Secondly, an accommodation was worked out between the remnant Muslim elite and the Congress to the extent that certain symbols of Muslim culture would be protected. Besides, constitutional guarantees were given to all minority religious groups. Finally, there was an adherence by the Congress leadership to the principle of secularism, but with the understanding that secularism would be realized through a gradual process.

[8] Though opposition politicians such as Ram Manohar Lohia, and even Ambedkar, accused the Congress of using caste and communal factors to win elections, even at this stage.

II

In 1961 a fairly serious riot broke out in Jabalpur which left over fifty persons dead and many injured.[9] This marked a new phase of Hindu–Muslim communal rioting. It has been observed that from 1964 onwards there was an upward trend in riots until about 1971.[10] When discussing communal riots, which are essentially irrational outbursts of brutality, it is difficult to provide specific explanations for their occurrence. It is fairly obvious, though, that the foremost prerequisite for a riot is the persistence of communal perceptions. These are generated by communal ideologies and political myths. Concrete political and economic issues are also usually involved in inter-community competition, but communal ideologies are primarily responsible for the felt need to destroy and perpetually subjugate the rival community in order to win in the competition.

It has also been suggested that the absence of a strong central authority in India coincides with the rise of communal violence.[11] While there is a great deal of truth in this suggestion if taken at face value, it may seem to imply that a strong law and order regime is sufficient to contain communalism and communal riots. The significance of proper policing and adequate vigilance for the prevention and control of riots cannot be minimized. However, the other significance of a strong authority in India is in its ability to affect stable intra-elite alliances. Needless to say, such alliances are easier to sustain under a stable regime, when sufficient room is available to manipulate inter-communal adjustment.

Thus, the upswing of riots between 1964 and 1970 is largely attributable to the passing away of Nehru and the crisis of stable leadership which followed. Seen from a more limited perspective the sudden eruption of riots may appear to be purely accidental, or as a series of coincidences. The following paragraph is interesting:

In 1964 serious riots broke out in various parts of East India like Calcutta, Jamshedpur, Rourkela and Ranchi in what appeared to be a chain reaction. Tension erupted in Kashmir earlier over the theft of a holy relic of the Prophet from the Hazratbal mosque. The relic, preserved under strict

[9] Mayer (1983).
[10] See Saxena (1984), p. 53.
[11] Saxena (1984), p. 53.

security conditions, was found missing on 27 December 1963 and this caused an immediate reaction among the people in Kashmir. Their anger was mainly directed against the carelessness of the government and had no trace of communal colour. Although the relic was discovered within a week, the incident led to serious riots in Khulna (Bangladesh), which caused panic among the Hindu population. They began migrating to India, carrying with them harrowing and sometimes exaggerated tales of their woes. As a reaction atrocities were committed against Muslims in the above mentioned places in India. According to Shri S. K. Ghosh, who was then Additional Inspector General of Police in Orissa, two thousand people, mostly Muslims, were killed in Rourkela alone in riots which lasted for about 15 days.[12]

The fourth general elections of 1967 proved to be a major turning point in Indian politics. Due to a variety of reasons the Congress could not form a government in eight states of the Indian Union and the 'Congress System' came under eclipse for the first time. Among the groups disenchanted with the Congress were large sections of the Muslims. These felt that the Congress had not been able to protect their interests, and that it had taken their vote for granted in the previous elections. It is not certain what the specific grievances were. The recurrence of riots in the period immediately preceding must have been one of the reasons. The Indo-Pakistan war of 1965 also had adverse consequences upon Hindu–Muslim relations. It is noteworthy in this context that Indo-Pakistan conflicts have had a general tendency to worsen Hindu–Muslim relations as they invariably exacerbate Hindu patriotism, which turns into mistrust towards Muslims.[13] This is naturally resented by the Muslim community as a whole. But another reason for the failure of the Congress to retain the Muslim vote in 1967 was its inability to manage elite-level adjustments on account of unsettled conditions within the Congress. Thus rival political parties could wean away a sizeable Muslim vote.

It is also interesting to note, however, that it was around the late 1960s that many Muslim families had begun to do somewhat better economically than in the previous decade and a half. Muslim

[12] Ibid., p. 53.
[13] It is, for instance, alleged that Muslims work as Pakistani agents, harbour spies, give signals to Pakistani aircraft during blackouts, etc.

political articulation in this period was also a reflection of this relative economic stability among sections of the Muslims. It is equally important, though, that the condition of the economy as a whole was extremely poor. A major devaluation had occurred and economic prospects for the country looked disturbing. This had led to a general disenchantment with the Congress, especially among the middle classes. Besides, most of the SVD governments (coalitions) which came to power in the wake of the 1967 elections were weak and wavering, and consequently not in control of the law and order situation.

Thus, the changing as well as unsettled political and economic conditions in India allowed the process of communal polarization to grow. Some of the worst communal riots occurred in the years 1968 and 1969, in which according to Home Ministry Reports there were 865 incidents of communal disturbances.[14] In Bihar, where between March 1967 and December 1971 there had been nine governments (with the shortest lasting four days and the longest ten months), there were 197 communal disturbances in these two years. In Gujarat there were 217 incidents and 111 in Uttar Pradesh. The all-India figure for 1970 and 1971 was 842. In the subsequent years upto 1977 the figures were nearer half the figures for the years 1968–71. There was another upswing from 1979–80 onwards.

During the 1971 general elections most Muslims returned to the Congress fold. The main reason for this seems to have been the insecurity caused by the riots of the preceding period. But soon after, there was considerable discomfiture among large sections of Muslims over India's role in the Bangladesh War. It has been noted, though, that the longer-term effect of the emergence of Bangladesh was that it put the remaining credibility of the two-nation theory to rest. This reconciled Indian Muslims to a more settled Indian identity. The oil-boom of the 1970s provided new avenues of employment in the Middle East to many Muslim crafts-men and skilled labour.[15] This brought a renewed confidence and economic stability in many Muslim homes.

Muslims broke with the Congress again during the Emergency

[14] Saxena (1984), p. 54.
[15] Ahmad (1984), p. 125.

over the issue of forced family planning drives and over other incidents, so that in the 1977 elections the Muslim vote was more decisively split than ever before. Curiously, in December 1976, the son of the then Prime Minister and perhaps the most important political figure of the day held a joint rally with the RSS in Delhi.

In the foregoing I have attempted to provide a brief history of the episodes which shaped communal politics upto the 1970s. I have primarily dealt with relations between Muslims and the Congress. It is all the more necessary to understand the politics of the Hindus. The secular character of the Congress has often been somewhat overrated. Even though as compared to the Hindu Mahasabha and Jan Sangh the followers of the Congress—which was a larger party—consisted of a larger number of secular Hindus, they had to be continuously exhorted by the national leadership to remain on the secular path. But the Congress was also the sole ruling party for a long time, so that communal interests often sought to work through the Congress as well. Because of its overwhelming Hindu membership, the Congress, especially at the local levels, found it difficult to reach out to the average and poor Muslim. Consequently it reached for the Muslim vote either through its social influence or through its religious leadership. In this sense the Congress could rarely engage the Muslims in its day-to-day organizational and party activities and therefore, organizationally, the Congress continued to be dominated by Hindu factions.[16] It needs to be emphasized, however, that before the 1980s the Congress was never overtly a proponent of the ideology of Hindu nationalism. Through the fifties and sixties political Hinduism was mainly the preserve of upper-caste Hindus.

Also, the Hindu political phenomenon was primarily north Indian. Its strongest base was in the Hindi-speaking areas, the main platform being the promotion of Hindi and Hinduism. This is not to overlook the strong presence of the RSS in states such as Maharashtra and Gujarat. But in some ways the political rhythm of the Hindu phenomenon in north India was different from that in the other parts. We might venture to say that though the sentiment for Hindu nationalism was to be found in almost all parts of

[16] This statement does not hold entirely for towns where Muslims constitute a very large minority, say 25 per cent or above.

India, this sentiment did not have national political cohesiveness. The disaggregation of the Hindu political phenomenon can be explained by many other political factors such as the North–South divide and so on, but there can be little doubt that it was the best (negative) guarantee for Indian secularism.

Just as the Muslims had broken away from the Congress in the 1967 elections, going by the improved performance of the Jan Sangh a sizeable number of Hindus too seem to have moved away. However, India's performance in the Bangladesh war enabled the Congress to recapture the Hindu imagination. Overtly Hindu organizations suffered a temporary eclipse after the 1972 elections. Soon, however, they found a major issue in the inflow of petro-dollars, which were allegedly financing Muslim communalists. The role of petro-dollars became ubiquitous. If a mosque were renovated, or new properties acquired by a Muslim, it would be attributed to petro-dollars. Not that such money was non-existent, but the hue and cry seemed far out of proportion. However, enough mileage was extracted by Hindu communalists. A campaign to construct more temples was started, so that every crossing in some of the towns of north India had a little temporary temple under a peepul tree, which would ultimately be made permanent. And, after all, who in the state administration could be so bold as to demolish a temple!

The RSS and Vishwa Hindu Parishad (VHP) stepped up the other usual points of propaganda, such as the scrapping of a special consti-tutional position for Jammu and Kashmir; the scrapping of Muslim Personal Law; the point that Muslims bred faster and would over-take the Hindu population in India; that Hindus and Muslims were not only religiously but also culturally antithetical and could never live together; that Muslims ate beef; that Muslims were the source of riots, and so on. Jayaprakash Narain's movement of 1974–5, because of its loose organizational structure, gave them the crucial political opening and a legitimacy that had been unavailable since 1971.

During the Emergency Mrs Gandhi's political axe fell on the RSS. A large number of RSS activists went to jail and since anti-authoritarian sentiments became popular the RSS and the BJP acquired new respectability among the common people. When the Janata party came to power in 1977, the BJP as well as the RSS became part of the ruling coalition. It being the first instance when they became part of a national ruling coalition, some national imperatives seem to have become apparent to them. Their inadequacy as a party with a predominantly north Indian base seems to have prompted the RSS to develop pockets of strength in the southern states, especially Kerala, Karnataka and Andhra Pradesh. This has obviously entailed a change of emphasis from the Hindi-Hindu idea to the primacy of the Hindu idea.

After Mrs Gandhi's return to power in 1980 she made positive attempts to win over this powerful Hindu political factor. Causal connections are difficult to establish, but some of the most gruesome and long-drawn-out riots with the complicity of the police, and the administration in general, occurred between 1980 and 1984. The following are some of the instances: Moradabad (UP) 1980, Allahabad (UP) 1980, Godhra (Gujarat) 1980–1, Ahmedabad (Gujarat) 1982, Biharsharif (Bihar) 1981, Vadodra (Gujarat) 1981–2, Pune and Solapur (Maharashtra) 1982–3, Hyderabad (Andhra Pradesh), 1983, and Bhiwandi-Bombay (Maharashtra) 1984. These were all major riots with many killings and with the destruction of property worth millions of rupees. In this period so much did Mrs Gandhi's credibility with the Hindus go up that she was able to drive a wedge between the BJP and the RSS. The covert link with the RSS was carefully nurtured through a series of actions, speeches and political signals. It can only be assumed that she also used the services of various Hindu religious leaders whom she used to visit frequently during this period.

In 1983 the whole strategy became quite explicit. In a speech on 15 May 1983 at Hardwar she refused to blame the PAC (Provincial Armed Constabulary of UP) for the heinous acts it had committed in Moradabad, Allahabad, Meerut, and so on. She put the blame for communal riots on the Janata party alone. In Bhiwandi too she refused to allocate blame, though the role of the Shiv Sena chief in fomenting violence was well established. She went a step further and said that minorities should learn to adjust in India. In the Jammu elections of 1983 she showed her ability to play the Hindu card and repeated the performance with the help of the RSS in the Delhi elections. Under her leadership a close political relationship was forged between the Congress and the Shiv Sena in Maharashtra. The RSS leader Balasaheb Deoras tilted the entire weight of the RSS in favour of Mrs Gandhi and her party. After her death the RSS openly backed the Congress in the 1984 general elections and this alliance continued into the assembley elections of 1985.

The 1980–4 phase also saw a diversification in the activities of the RSS. Not only was the Vishwa Hindu Parishad strengthened and its activities widened, the VHP was treated as a mass front by the RSS so that those Hindus who hesitated to identify themselves with the RSS could also join in the spreading of the Hindu political message. In regions where the RSS was not looked upon with favour, other front organization were floated, for instance the Hindu Front in Tamil Nadu. Organizations under different banners have also been floated to attract the upwardly mobile backward castes, such as the Marathas, Yadavas, etc., with the knowledge that many of these groups would feel organizationally dominated by the old hard-core upper caste RSS, and be disinclined to work through the RSS. More recently attempts have also been made to woo sections of the scheduled castes, mainly by pitting them against the poorer sections of the minorities. Maharashtra has seen a proliferation of these front organizations, for instance the Patit Pawan Sangathana. Shiv Senas have also been founded in Punjab, Delhi and other parts of north India.

Political Hinduism of the variety cited above is also predominantly against the government's policy of reservations (positive discrimination), whether it be in favour of scheduled castes and tribes or for any other group. It espouses the cause of a modernized national meritocracy. It is consequently opposed to the constitutional recognition of linguistic, religious and other groups as minorities, and to constitutional safeguards in their favour. However, the conversion of a group of scheduled caste Hindus to Islam in Meenakshipuram (in Tamil Nadu) in January 1981 sent shock waves through the communalized Hindu mind. Shankaracharyas and other religious leaders protested against it; political leaders warned against the increasing power of petro-dollars and Hindu *sammelans* were organized to face this new threat from 'Islamic fundamentalism'. Counter-conversions were also arranged in Rajasthan and other places in north India within a short space of time.

Whatever may have happened to the poor scheduled caste converts of Meenakshipuram, it gave political Hinduism a popular tool to attack Muslims, Christian missionaries, and indeed all minorities alike. The VHP and other front organizations painted a diabolical picture of 'Hinduism under seige', and launched a sort of self-respect movement among Hindus which was symbolized in the form of stickers saying 'I am not ashamed to be a Hindu'. This campaign, which was sustained effectively, though at a low political key, took deep roots among the middle- and lower-middle-class Hindus. Whatever the numerical size of this class, it includes the average intellectual, the civil servant, the professional, clerical personnel and large sections of skilled labour. The communal phenomenon, which was by and large confined to the middle-sized towns earlier, spread to small as well as large cities.

Since Hindus perceive all other religions as being more organized than Hinduism, positive attempts were made to get Hindus organized. Thus processions and large-scale festivals came into being, and middle-class participation in the public demonstration of Hinduism increased in this period.

III

In the 1980s the most important political factor responsible for the communalization of India has been the Punjab problem. It will not be possible here to go into the background of the Akali agitation in Punjab. I shall mention only three factors which seem the most significant. Firstly, that in 1978 the Akalis (a Sikh party) revised an old resolution of 1973 formulated at Anandpur Sahib in Punjab, to press for some long-standing demands which were not essentially communal in nature. Secondly, the Congress party in Punjab, which since the mid-sixties represented a coalition of Hindus and Sikh with the Hindus as the dominant section, was deeply factionalized, and constantly needed to dig into the Akali support base which, naturally, was Sikh. And thirdly, though there had been intense economic competition between the Sikhs and the Hindus, and though considerable undercurrents of cultural tension existed since the 1950s, there had been no open communal hostility between the two communities. It was with the purpose of out-doing the Akalis at being the protector of Sikh interests that the erstwhile chief minister of Punjab, Giani Zail Singh, with the encouragement of Mrs Gandhi and her younger son Sanjay Gandhi, promoted a little known Sikh priest called Sant Bhindranwale to challenge the Akali leadership. Through Bhindranwale the capture of the Shiromani Gurdwara Prabandhak Committee (SGPC) was attempted. Even though that attempt failed, Bhindranwale emerged as a fundamentalist factor in Sikh politics. His militant brinkmanship was ignored by the central government till he began to pose a serious armed challenge to the Indian state. The Akali agitation had, by this time, been usurped by Bhindranwale and his followers, especially as the centre and the Akali leadership could not come to any agreement about the Akali demands. I believe that an agreement was possible but Mrs Gandhi was not inclined to reach one. Not only was she unwilling at that time to concede to any of the states' demands but was actively engaged in toppling governments in Jammu and Kashmir, Andhra Pradesh and Karnataka.

'Operation Bluestar', which was a military action on the Golden Temple to eliminate Sikh militants, took place in June 1984. I, among others, had warned that such an action, even if it were to improve the election prospects of the Congress, would be extremely dangerous as it would fuel the fire of terrorism in Punjab. It has been suggested by many observers that there was no option to Operation Bluestar as things had already gone too far. This is a contentious question and I shall leave the issue here. What happened, in any case, was that the base of Sikh fundamentalism and terrorism did widen. For a fairly long period the followers of Bhindranwale indulged in selective killings not only of politically important people such as Sant Longowal and others, but also of innocent Hindus who were shot in buses, on the streets, and so on. The purpose was to start a communal conflict, but this took a long time to come. Gradually Hindus began to organize in towns where they had a substantial majority. The Hindu Shiva Sena was formed and this exhibited some retaliatory force in places such as Hoshiarpur in Punjab.

However, the most successful act of communalization was the assassination of Mrs Gandhi in November 1984. Her assassination unleashed a massive reprisal against the Sikh population in Delhi. I was witness to the lynching and burning of Sikhs on that day. Sikh gurdwaras in Delhi went up in flames. Shops belonging to

Sikhs were robbed and burnt, their homes looted. Some Congress leaders of Delhi are alleged to have incited riots which took their worst toll in the next two days in poor and working-class localities on the fringes of Delhi. Sikhs reported to First Aid Centres and dispensaries with massive sword injuries, burn wounds and all manner of other serious injuries. This was not so much a Hindu-Sikh riot as an organized attack by Hindus on Sikhs to vent their pent-up anger. To the extent that Sikhs could resist, they did. And that might qualify these incidents to be called riots. Subsequently, however, Hindu-Sikh riots have taken place in Delhi.

In the post-assassination riots, the middle-class Hindu had nearly complete sympathy with the killing and lynching of Sikhs, even though many felt that beatings and arson could have been sufficient to teach the Sikhs a lesson. There was not much sympathy for the view that most of the Sikhs killed or hurt were innocent. Middle- and lower-middle-class youths, under cover of mob anonymity, took active part in the riots. Workers, especially those of the Delhi Transport Corporation, allegedly had a major hand in the riots and the Delhi police are widely believed to have behaved in a most partisan manner.[17] Trade unions affiliated to leftist parties such as the CITU were the only ones to resist rioters, and this has been the case in riots all over India. In Delhi many students and socially committed persons also displayed exemplary courage in trying to prevent rioting and in providing crucially necessary relief about which the Delhi administration was astonishingly lax.[18]

What have come to be called anti-Sikh riots also took place in several other parts of India, but these were quickly brought under control. The entire episode has left the Sikhs outside Punjab feeling extremely insecure and more aware of their communal identity than ever before. Hindus who live in Punjab have felt equally insecure ever since the rise of Sikh terrorism. The forced migration of Hindus from Punjab to Delhi and other places has communalized the atmosphere in an unprecedented manner. Hindu communalism inevitably turns against Muslims, whatever the source of its origin

[17] It seems worth mentioning that a large proportion of the DTC work-force is drawn from the Hindu Jats of Haryana who are traditionally hostile towards Sikhs.

[18] See Sethi (1985), p. 61.

at any given time. A few Hindu-Muslim clashes have also occurred in recent months. And thus, while the Hindus have set up a *trishul*-wielding Hindu Shiv Sena in addition to the already formidable RSS in Delhi, Muslims have also set up an Adam Sena. No other city in India is as much in the grip of continuing communal frenzy as Delhi.

As a result of the threat from Punjab, political Hinduism has almost become synonymous with Indian nationalism. The elections of 1984 and 1985 were implicitly fought from this ideological platform by the Congress. The official media, especially the TV, was blatantly manipulated to plug a chauvinist Hindu line. A separate analysis needs to be made of the ways in which this was done.

Several other methods of political Hinduism need to be taken note of. In 1983 a massive Ekatmata Yagna was organized in which holy waters from all the four corners of India were brought to meet at a point. In 1984 the Ram Janaki Rath was similarly taken out in procession over various parts of north India as a part of the Ram Janma Bhoomi Andolan for the 'liberation' of Lord Rama's birth place from the hands of Muslims. The subsequent court order to unlock the Babari Masjid (the spot claimed by Hindus to have been the birthplace of Lord Rama), which had been sealed by the administration many years earlier on account of a previous dispute, was claimed as a victory by the Hindus. This led to a heightening of tensions between the two communities.

At the same time, a suggestion by the government to introduce a common civil code following an *obiter dicta* in a Supreme Court judgment (in the Shah Bano case) brought out a great deal of Muslim resentment. The government initially seemed to be in favour of a common civil code, then for electoral reasons it prevaricated, and finally capitulated in favour of not disturbing Muslim Personal Law. Debate over the whole issue became communally coloured and secularists were ignored. The issue of an optional Uniform Civil Code has been reopened in recent months, but in the presently communalized atmosphere it is likely to sharpen Muslim apprehensions. I was witness to a recent public meeting (8 January 1987) of Muslims at Lucknow called by the Muslim religious scholar and leader Maulana Abul Hasan Ali Nadvi, on behalf of the Muslim Personal Law Board, to enjoin them to reject the proposal for a Uniform Civil Code in any form. Thousands of

Muslim men and women left the meeting with badges displaying 'We Reject Uniform Civil Code'.

The controversy over personal law resulted in the proposal by the apex Muslim body, the Majlis-i-Mushawarat, that Muslims stay away from the Republic Day celebrations. The call was later withdrawn but it was a powerful communal Muslim protest against what was perceived as the appropriation of Indian nationalism by political Hinduism

IV

From the foregoing it is clear that communalism has acquired political centrestage in India in a manner that it has not since Partition. As suggested earlier in this paper, the single most important factor which gives rise to communal violence is the prevalence of communal ideologies and perceptions. But unscrupulous political manipulation in a no-holds-barred electoral game makes matters worse. And, unless a positive commitment to secularism comes to prevail, democratic politics itself becomes a prisoner of communalism. In fact the very idiom of democratic politics becomes communalized. The variety of politics that has come to obtain in India in recent years has had a catalytic effect on the process of reinforcement of communal ideologies. These in turn are used by communal groups to further parochial ends. And all this goes on under the cover of espousing one kind of secularism or another.

There are, of course, many local-level causes for communal riots as well, and most often these are the ones which are immediately perceptible. However, before we come to a discussion of these local factors, the wider factors must be understood. Firstly, the overall atmosphere in which politics operates is one of immense economic scarcity. There are a large number of young, and not so young, men who are unemployed and frustrated—angry with their own condition and without any perception of the future for themselves. And even for many who have a job, or other forms of petty employment, the threat of losing it is real. Secondly, a great deal of illiteracy prevails. This makes youth vulnerable to political manipulation and scare-mongering. The semi-literate (who predominate among the so-called literates) are worse as regards communalization, for they can be moulded into any kind of fanaticism provided they are fed on the right kind of poisoned literature. In the absence of a hegemonic secular national culture, semi-literacy can be the source of dangerous political tendencies. And, thirdly, there is a great deal of corruption in the economic and administrative spheres. Corruption in the economic sphere gives to the upwardly-mobile elements the opportunity to make a quick buck, whether it is by acquiring another person's property or by destroying a rival's business premises or by manufacturing illicit liquor, etc. These elements often take a communal cover for their operations. Administrative corruption has led to a general fall in the objective standards of administration, manipulation of the administration by communal interests, and above all to the sacrifice of the element of vigilance.

Riots in pre-independence days were caused by local issues such as the 'playing of music before mosques', cow slaughter, the throwing of meat into temples and other such things. Nearer the point of independence incidents such as these became more political and saw mass participation from both communities. The Calcutta riots of 1946 serve as an adequate example. The riots in the immediate aftermath of partition were the fall-out of a forced transfer of populations and mutual recriminations of a political kind. This, as has been noted earlier, was followed by a period of relative calm, with skirmishes over the routes of religious processions, the throwing of colour during Holi, and often over boy-girl affairs. The Jabalpur riots of 1961, for instance, were sparked off by the news of a Hindu girl disappearing with a Muslim boy.

The riots of the late 1960s began to acquire a greater communal ideological character and the beginnings of economic conflict. This was the case in the Ranchi riots of 1967 which started over the issue of making Urdu the second official language in Bihar and ended up with the destruction of Muslim workers' colonies where 150 Muslims were killed—according to official estimates.[19] Riots in Indore (1968), Ahmedabad (1969), Bhiwandi, Mahad and Jalgaon (1970, 1984), for instance, exhibit similar patterns.[20] At any rate

[19] See Naidu (1980).
[20] See Naidu (1980), and Engineer (1984), for detailed documentation on this issue.

during the riots which were sparked off by some form of religious or political confrontation, properties and business premises were destroyed. In the Godhra riots (1965–6) refugee Sindhis and Ghanchi Muslims clashed primarily on account of economic rivalry.

During this phase elements of pre-planning also begin to appear. Houses were marked out in advance. For example, if Muslims happened to live in, or have shops in, Hindu-owned houses, the houses were spared, whereas their own property was destroyed and the men themselves were killed or injured. In the Tellicherry riots (1972), property owned by Muslims was meticulously destroyed but no Muslim killed. The riot started over the issue of some Muslim boys teasing Hindu girls and the Hindus, led by the RSS, sought to teach the Muslims a lesson. Interestingly, it was just the beginning of the period when Muslims had started bringing in some of their earnings from the Middle East, and economic jealousy was, according to some people, the main reason for the disturbances.

Violence by Muslims in this phase was usually retaliatory. But this does not imply that Muslims refrained from taking aggressive postures during the build-up to the riots. The course of events that led up to the Ahmedabad riots, ably chronicled by Shah (1984), included aggressive processions by Muslims in the wake of the Al Aqsa mosque episode and slogans such as, 'Jo Islam se takrayega, chur chur hojayega' (anyone who clashes with Islam will be destroyed). This phase, further, though often indicative of administrative slackness and political prevarication, does not provide evidence of police partisanship or administrative complicity. In the subsequent phase which begins in 1980 (Moradabad, Allahabad, Godhra, etc.) economic issues seem to predominate. Even though tension starts off with some overt religion-related issue such as a pig entering an Idgah during prayers (Moradabad), the economic factors are relatively easy to discern. The rivalry between the up-coming Muslim brassware manufacturers and exporters of Moradabad and the already entrenched Punjabi refugee dealers was the cause of communal tension in Moradabad.

In Biharsharif (1981) the Yadava's had an eye on the substantial urban lands which served as Muslim graveyards and had been attempting to grab them for cattle grazing. The riots were precipitated due to a drunken brawl but the economic origins were clear. In fact, the Biharsharif riots are a typical example of violence between two upwardly mobile groups. Not only have the Yadavas here done well from potato cultivation and preservation, some Muslims too, as in Moradabad, have acquired a share in trade and commerce with their own markets, cinema halls and cold storage. They have also set up schools.[21] Economic rivalry between Dalit and Muslim labourers appears to have laid them open to manipulation by communal elements in Ahmedabad in 1982. The Bhiwandi riots of 1984 were also a result of the economic competition between Hindu and Muslim powerloom owners, but communal violence was, according to Engineer, fanned by the Shiv Sena chief Bal Thackeray who, on 22 April 1984, delivered a virulently anti-Muslim speech that described Muslims as a cancerous growth in India which needed to be operated upon.[22]

Some of the riots in this period were also sparked off by riots elsewhere, though the triggers were local. Thus the Allahabad riot of 1980 was part of a chain reaction which started in Moradabad. However, some of the riots were the consequence of sustained political campaigns by the VHP, RSS and other front organizations after the Meenakshipuram conversions. We may include among these the Meerut, Pune and Solapur riots of 1982. In Meerut, the Muslims, who comprise 49 per cent of the population, do have a reasonably high economic profile, but no crucial economic rivalry with the Hindus seems to have existed. In part the problem in Meerut was political competition in respect of the municipal council elections, in preparation for which the BJP was trying to break into other parties' strongholds. But the most significant feature of the riots of the 1980s has been the partisan role played by the police and the district administration—especially by the police.[23] And even where administrators try to be upright they are pressurized by politicians into taking partisan positions. Two instances with regard to the last point will suffice. Before the Solapur riots the commissioner was disinclined to allow a Shiva Jayanti procession under the prevailing conditions and he refused permission. Subse-

---

[21] See Engineer (1984), p. 241.
[22] See Engineer (1985), p. 210.
[23] See Hasan and Sabherwal (1984), pp. 224–6.

quently he had to yield to political pressure and the processionists did start the riot. Even more significantly, in Ahmedabad (and other places in Gujarat) when the anti-reservation agitation was at its peak and was proving to be a political embarrassment, it was widely alleged that the chief minister ordered the police to give the agitation an anti-Muslim turn.

It is necessary to return to the role of the police because it is blatant police partisanship against minorities and unmitigated brutality that has today undermined the credibility of the Indian state in the eyes of the minorities. To my knowledge the first instances of police terror and looting began before the 1980s. It has been reported that in Varanasi (1977) the PAC indulged in indiscriminately beating, maiming and looting ornaments from the homes of Muslims.[24] In Aligarh (1978) this story was repeated. The beatings were accompanied by abuses and accusations of Muslims being Pakistanis, etc. In Jamshedpur (1979) the Bihar Military Police and RSS are known to have acted in unison in indiscriminate killing and burning. This took a worse turn in Moradabad and Allahabad (1980), and has continued since then. This was, for instance, also the case with the State Reserve Police in the Gujarat riots of 1985 and the PAC in Barabanki (1986).[25]

I have noted that in the earlier phase the pre-planned destruction of property and business premises was indulged in by rival groups, especially Hindu communalists. But in the present phase it is the police which undertakes to destroy private property such as televisions, refrigerators, etc., and in the name of searches walks away with other valuables such as watches, ornaments and cash.

Lower personnel of the State Reserve Constabulary, at least in north India, have usually been communally biased on account of the social class from which they are recruited and the predominant religious group to which they belong. But in recent years this has worsened. This is largely explained by the fact that often senior officials themselves are not secular. This does not imply that all

[24] See Khan and Mittal (1984), pp. 308–9.
[25] This paper was written well before the May 1987 riots in Meerut. Details of Meerut have thus not been discussed here, but the systematic killings by the PAC in Malliana, outside Meerut, are part of the rising trend of police brutality.

officials are communal, but even a few in crucial positions are sufficient to cause enormous damage.

Finally, another new feature is that communal riots now seem
to be affecting rural and peri-urban areas. This was clearly noticed in
Biharsharif (1981). In fact it may be suggested that *rath yatras*
through rural areas are designed to carry the communal message
to the countryside. However, as yet no clearly discernible pattern
has become available and this new phenomenon needs further
investigation. If this does emerge as a pattern, it would pose a major
administrative challenge, given the sparse policing that exists in
rural areas today.

As noted earlier, middle-class Hindus as a whole have succumbed, to a lesser or greater degree, to the process of communalization
which has spread apace over the last few years. The Punjab disturbances have jolted many a secular Hindu out of his Nehruvian
framework. Peer. group and other kinds of pressures have done
the rest. It is, indeed, alarming to note the speed with which this
has happened in these few years. The alienation of the Muslims
can only be gauged from the attitude of the majority community.
In towns such as Allahabad it is critical.

However, the major part of the Muslim wrath has turned against
the PAC and the local police. Muslim youth who live in sensitive
areas say that they have nothing against the Hindus but hate the
PAC. This is, of course, not entirely true, for they also nurse a
strong feeling of being discriminated against by Hindu-owned
establishments. They feel handicapped in terms of jobs and bank
loans, even when the banks are state-owned. While such difficulties
are faced by much of the middle- and lower-middle class, Hindus
have a wider network of extra-official support to fall back upon—a
relative here, a fellow-caste brother there, and so on. Muslims,
since they form a minuscule section of officialdom and occupy
few places among the higher business executives, have fewer
contacts to get by.[26] Besides, Muslim youth are fed upon their
own form of communal propaganda whereby, in many cases, even
the will to try is sapped.

Muslim youth, even when they have not taken to fundamentalism, are subjected to a great deal of revivalist propaganda that filters

[26] See Rajgopal (1986), pp. 64–5.

in through pan-Islamic organizations, and which is'also generated locally. With propaganda, money comes in, sometimes. And even if the money is not considerable, it can be just enough to get by, or to invest in a small business. This is how Muslim communal organizations such as the Jamaat-e-Islami maintain an active presence among Muslim youth.

Lack of employment among Muslim youth often drives them towards illegal and underworld activity. This reinforces antagonism towards the state and is used by communal elements. It is not that this phenomenon is not found amongst Hindu youth, but in proportion to population this factor is more prominent among Muslim youth. It is all the more unfortunate that many among these young men, merely because they have acquired the skills to use minor weapons, have a sense of bravado. And if in riot situations the police is out to 'teach the Muslims a lesson', these youngsters get into a 'we will see these police dogs this time' state of mind. This steps up the scale of violence.

One of the major issues confronting Muslim youth is education. Statistics are available which conclusively establish that the dropout rate among Muslim children is very high.[27] The bulk of the Muslims being poor or lower-middle class, higher education is a luxury, especially in an environment which teaches that education does not necessarily mean employment. Yet the general pressure to be educated does exist, socially if not economically. This creates anxiety and double-mindedness. It is often the case that Muslim parents positively discourage children from going in for higher, or even secondary, education because they fear that these children would not be able to work with their hands once they are educated and will end up as good-for-nothings. Instead, they are encouraged to go in for apprenticeships and/or self employment. Since apprenticeships and jobs of this nature are more readily available with fellow Muslims, there is a reinforcement of minority identity. In many metropolises and middle-sized towns, such as Allahabad, *mohallas* (localities) have evolved which are exclusively Muslim or Hindu. These areas are crowded and ghetto-like. Sharply demarcated communal identities are nurtured here. This is not to suggest that communities live their lives exclusively. There

[27] See Rajgopal (1986), p. 63.

is usually a fair amount of economic interdependence. In Varanasi, for instance, this is very high due to the variety of handicraft industry that exists there. But leisure hours are invariably spent within the community, and social interaction, especially in sensitive areas, tends to be low. In times of communal tension this dips further.

V

The riots that took place in Allahabad towards the end of June 1986 were not remarkable in terms either of the issues involved or in terms of the nature of the riot. The entire riot period lasted for about six to seven days. In this sense too it cannot be said to have been major. It started over a small mosque in a bylane in the crowded city area. The mosque, which is situated at the edge of a Muslim locality, is said to have been built many years ago by a Muslim dancing woman. In recent years it has not been in use. A Hindu petty tradesman who had a shop on the adjoining footpath for nearly ten years wanted to bore a few holes on the outer wall of the mosque in order to construct a makeshift support for an awning. This was objected to by the local Muslims, which led to altercations. This, given the dense population, brought out crowds on both sides.

It must be noted that the Babari Masjid–Ram Janma Bhoomi Andolan was at its height at the time. Besides, Hindu organizations had declared that just as they had 'liberated' the Ram Janma Bhoomi they would also liberate that part of the Vishwanath temple at Varanasi which they alleged had been forcibly converted into a mosque during Mughul rule, and the Krishna Janma Bhoomi in Mathura. Also, about two months before this episode there had been a major police firing on a Muslim gathering in Barabanki, resulting in the death of a large number of Muslims. Muslims in the sensitive localities of Allahabad had been tense, and trouble was expected. But the 'Black Day' called by the Muslims in protest against the reopening of the Babari Masjid and the ensuing flag war (black vs. saffron) had passed off peacefully. The administration seems to have taken it easy after that. So much so that on the day the trouble started neither the senior superintendent of police, no the district magistrate were in town.[28]

Altercations had started in the forenoon, but by the afternoon crowds had gathered on either side of the bylane. No responsible police officer was present, so a few constables tried to disperse the crowds with their sticks. The groups momentarily retreated but kept regrouping. By the time the police really arrived on the scene, brick-batting and bottle-throwing had already started and the trouble had started spreading to other localities. From available reports it appears that the SP (City) reached the scene of disturbance late at night. At this stage there was no option but to impose curfew. Six police districts were brought under curfew that night and another district the next day. It has been reported that some Muslims attacked the *kotwali* (city police headquarters) with a fairly heavy bomb the same night, damaging a portion of the wall. Muslims were resentful as they felt that the police could have intervened earlier and stopped the tradesman from 'destroying' the wall of the mosque. Police reinforcements arrived the next day and swung into action. From available reports it seems that, firstly, except for the opening episode in which Hindus and Muslims clashed, the fighting was between the PAC and the Muslims. Secondly, that some Muslims were prepared for such a situation and were equipped to the best of their ability.

Searches into Muslim localities continued over the next few days and a large number of arrests were made. Especially in the narrow bylanes, Muslims put up resistance with hand-bombs and minor sniper fire. As the curfew was indefinite, and curfew passes were as usual difficult to obtain, it was not possible to assess the exact degree of fighting; but intermittent bomb-blasts could be heard outside the curfew-bound area.[29] The curfew continued for six days without a break, and though the administration claimed to have undertaken relief work, reports indicated that far less than was necessary was being done.

Given the fact that there were no Hindu-Muslim clashes after the first day, the popular impression was that the indefinite curfew

[28] This led many observers, including some in the district administration, to believe that the riots were preplanned.

[29] In any case, curfew passes were often not honoured by the police. They were reported to have been torn up, with the bearers being asked to go back.

was not necessary. In fact it was widely believed that if the police withdrew, things would return to normal on their own. From private sources I also learnt that many among those arrested were innocent youth upon whom fabricated charges had been imposed. The apparent severity with which curfew was imposed gave the impression that the state government was acting more out of panic than on the basis of an objective assessment of the situation. The Barabanki killings had been a matter of deep embarrassment to the state government and it probably did not want to take any chances. Besides, the absence of both the administrative and police chiefs of the district (the DM and SSP) on the day the riots started seemed to have unnerved the administration.

On the seventh day, concerned citizens and political leaders from all parties, barring the ruling party, met in another part of the city to decide upon the future course of action. The meeting decided to offer all help to the administration but noted that adequate relief was not reaching the curfew-bound areas, that hygienic conditions had deteriorated and that innocent persons were being harassed by the police. It also felt that the curfew had become unnecessary. A resolution to this effect was passed. It was also added that unless the curfew was lifted by the next day, citizens would be obliged to break it and march to the kotwali, which fell within the curfew-bound areas. The resolution was delivered to the district magistrate, the commissioner and the SSP sometime around noon.

Curfew was lifted from one of the police districts that afternoon. There were no further disturbances and the following day curfew was lifted completely. Whether the citizens resolution had any impact will probably never be known. Since an important opposition leader (H. N. Bahuguna) was due to visit Allahabad the following day, the administration may have decided to lift the curfew in order that the opposition could not capitalize on the riot. Whatever may have been the circumstances under which the judgement was made, there were no further incidents of violence. Since then many instances of police high-handedness have come to light. I have met young men who were picked up from their homes for no apparent reason. There is an instance of a poor ice-cream vendor whose knees were permanantly damaged by a police beating. There is also the case of two sisters who had saved up for their own weddings by rolling bidis, a most ill-paid job, whose belongings were taken away by the police. Such examples can be listed *ad nauseum*. Concerned citizens have compiled detailed evidence of such police action after a door-to-door survey.

It needs to be recorded, however, that sections among the Muslim community had prepared themselves with arms and ammunition. The Barabanki affair and continuing tensions over the disputed Babari Masjid had probably contributed an extra element to this preparation. There had been flag wars between Muslims and Hindus in many UP towns, including the capital Lucknow, during the protest-day celebrations. Some Muslim youth in Lucknow frankly admitted that they had equipped themselves with arms in that period, even though they normally did not keep any.

In Allahabad, it was reported that some respectable Muslim gentlemen were helping youth behind the scenes. But during the disturbances the head of the district RSS organization was unmoved, probably because in the RSS perception the PAC were in any case doing the job for them. Later, he told me that the RSS had also made armed preparation. Exact casualty figures are not available, but they were not very high. Most often Muslim youths exploded small crackers or hand-bombs in order to distract the police from search operations. The effect of the blasts was to give signals to adjoining Muslim localities that they were still around. It was a sort of confidence-restoring exercise.

Several months after these disturbances, I spoke to a senior police officer, who has a good reputation, to ascertain his point of view. The officer emphasized the necessity of prolonged curfew as in his opinion things could have taken a turn for the worse if curfew were lifted earlier.[30] He said that search operations are invariably messy affairs and very time-consuming. Residents invariably resent searchers and refuse to open their doors; consequently homes have to be broken into. Besides, the police begins to get tired after the first couple of nights and efficiency goes down. Fake phone calls and explosions keep the police perpetually on the run.

He also admitted the partisanship of the police and the communal attitude of the PAC. He also said that often senior officers betrayed

---

[30] He admitted, however, that the absence of the DM and SSP had led to chaos within the administration.

a communal attitude in their behaviour. He attributed the communal attitude of the PAC to their backgrounds and to inadequate education. The PAC, he said, shared all the prejudices which were commonly prevalent in society. He said also that while imposing curfew the police tended to be lenient with the Hindus and inordinately strict with the Muslims. In a good-humoured vein he described this situation as 'comparative curfew', which sums up the attitude of the state quite succinctly, however ironical it may be.

This officer gave another reason for police brutality. According to him PAC battalions are usually stationed at their headquarters, which are often several hundred kilometres from the site of disturbances. When they have to move at short notice they grudge leaving their families and moving on arduous operations. Once they arrive on the scene of action they feel that they must crush the trouble-makers for good. That is why they act out of vengeance and commit excesses. From this it is obvious that their training in discipline as well as professional indoctrination leaves much to be desired.

I asked the officer why the district administration does not take citizens into confidence while handling riot situations. To this he said that very often the very notables whom the administration would pick up as likely model citizens are responsible for abetting communal violence from behind the scenes, even though they could be expected to say the right things in a public forum. Peace committees and the like were therefore of little use in a riot situation. Upon my suggestion that this indicated an enormous gap between the state and the citizens, he said that it is absolutely necessary for the administrator to keep himself aloof from the citizen. Too much familiarity came in the way of taking necessary action at appropriate times.

VI

What should be done to avoid communal conflict? It is sometimes suggested that India should learn to live with communal conflict.[31] Communalism should be seen as another form of ethnic competi-

[31] Naidu (1980), suggests that 'enlightened communal leadership is crucial for the development of the country' (p. 139), but also adds that enlightened secularism is as important for the development of a pluralist state system.

tion, or that communalism should be treated at par with any other kind of ethnic identity assertion.[32] But, given the historical roots of communalism in India and its continuing ability to shape antagonistic identities, it cannot be treated as yet another form of group assertion within the normal political (i.e. democratic) process. It questions India's ability to sustain a larger Indian identity. It distorts the political psyche of the citizen by feeding him on diabolical myths. Hindu communalism, in particular, can generate the power to transform the entire state system under certain conditions by the sheer weight of numbers. And even though in the past it has been comforting to the secular Indian to understand that Hindu communalism tends to be more disaggregated than cohesive, the rapid growth of communication and a range of other factors have contributed to the emergence of a national Hindu political factor which was not the case even at the height of communal conflict at the time of independence.[33] This, taken together with the communalization of the state machinery, can do incalculable damage.

It is not my case, however, that Hindu communalism is qualitatively more dangerous than other communalisms. The persistence of deep communal tendencies among a large section of Indian Muslims, whatever its causes, has kept them alienated from the rest of the citizenry. If the Hindu communalist wishes to see Muslims as second-class Indian citizens, the Muslim communalist ensures that such a status is accepted. How else can the Muslim communalist sustain his role? Reforming the less educated Muslims is not an easy task, for reasons discussed earlier. But in my view this task has not been taken up seriously enough at the social and cultural level by either the progressive sections among Muslims themselves or by others.

Too much has come to be expected out of *politics* in India. This sentence obviously needs elaboration, but what I wish to imply is that, increasingly, politics has been taken to be so versatile a tool of communication that other levels of social action have inadvertently been dispensed with. In India, and perhaps in many other developing countries, there is a poverty of popular culture—

[32] Ahmed (1984), p. 132.
[33] Mukarji and Banerjee (1985), p. 26.

especially modern secular culture, which is at the same time sophisticated enough to absorb or even compete with tradition, and is also able to relate to the problems and aspirations of people.

Communalism among the Sikhs, as previously stated, was earlier a form of sectarianism. With the granting of the Punjabi Suba their religio-ethnic identity was also recognized by the state. That, however, has not necessarily led to any positive gain in terms of integration. I have already granted that Punjab, in recent years was mishandled by Mrs Gandhi, but I would be less than objective if I were not critical of the Akali party for throwing tantrums when out of power—as though inspite of the democratic process only the Akali party is destined to rule Punjab. Sikh communalism today, which has led to Sikh separatism, is therefore not just the creation of Bhindranwale and his men. It must be seen to have deep roots in Sikh sectarianism which has been nurtured by the political process in Punjab.

Communalism in India has a historically determined antagonism with nationalism, which is probably not the case in many other countries, such as Malaysia, which also have a communal problem. This is why the only way in which Indian nationalism can sustain itself is by continuing the struggle to establish the secular principle at all levels of social action. And this need not imply cultural, religious or non-religious 'homogenization'. A religio-cultural identity is not the same as a communal identity. For a long time this distinction was obscured in India because of an intellectually vague distinction between 'Gandhian secularism' and 'Nehruvian secularism'; the former implying tolerance for all religions, and the latter implying the scientific temper, rationalism, and so on.

In India we are just beginning to disentangle these knots and think about the contours of the interface between religion and the state at more concrete levels. Those who are impatient with legal niceties will probably not even have perceived these changes—for instance the provision that electoral campaigns cannot be conducted on the basis of overt religious appeal. The debate on maintenance for divorced Muslim women which arose out of the Shah Bano case is another instance. These are no substitutes for an ideological struggle for secularism, but in the present phase we need to get down to the nitty-gritty of day-to-day problems and move towards a closer definition of the political limits of religion. Once this homework is done, on a quieter keel we are likely to find that many irritants which explode into riots will disappear.

In this context certain aspect of administrative action could also be discussed. Take, for instance, the issue of Muslim graveyards. In most cities these traditional graveyards are not fenced, and since with the expansion of cities these have now become parts of the inner city, the price of these lands has soared. There are attempted encroachments almost everywhere and disputes go on for years. Ways must be found to resolve such disputes speedily. I admit that not all such disputes are amenable to quick resolutions, especially in a country like India where, for many, litigation has become a way of life. But that is why ways must be found, legal and administrative, to bring these disputes to an end before they are politicized.

Serious thought needs to be given to the reorganizating and training of the police. This, I realize has been said often, but it still bears repetition. I am not entirely convinced that by increasing minority recruitment in the police we would come to terms with the problem of police indiscipline. However, a greater presence of minorities, especially in the higher cadres, would be preferable to the present situation. Further, in order to avoid the delay in deployment of the reserve constabulary in riot situations, the north Indian states could think of a system of district reserve police on the lines of some of the southern states. If a district reserve constabulary is created, especially for sensitive towns, special care can be taken to train them for the problems of the particular district or region. This would familiarize them not only with problems but also with the urban terrain where riots occur. Once the district constabulary is pressed into action, further forces, if necessary, can be garnered without undue panic.

The question of urban renewal in the middle-sized and smaller towns needs to be considered. Modern housing, whether state sponsored or through housing societies, can relieve the pressure from the densely populated areas where trouble starts. It is, however, not always easy to move people out of their areas of business and social networks, but in many cities the process has started. Modern localities are also likely to be more mixed than at present.

But there is no real substitute for sustained social action. Usually, concerned citizens and politicians tend to get activated only after riots have occurred. While the secular political parties have a major role to play on account of their organization, social action cannot be left to them alone. In any case very little grassroots activity is done by most of the political parties on a day-to-day basis. In fact, communal organizations do much more grassroots activity than the more enlightened. It has been observed that the Hindu and Muslim communities are further apart today than they were at the time of independence. This, in many ways, is true. But that is mainly because not enough attention is given by citizens with secular commitments towards generating countervailing currents to the communal current.

A large number of well-meaning citizens are willing to bridge the social gap and actively engage in secular social reconstruction. But they shy away from direct party activity. They are often not concerned with the whole gamut of questions that a political party is. Therefore, under the present conditions of heightened communal conflict, it is both necessary and possible to set up informal and open platforms which would allow people from all communities and walks of life to interact. Exchange of information and the airing of grievances goes a long way towards promoting better understanding, not only of the communal problem but of a host of related social issues.

REFERENCES

Ahmed, I., ed., 1983: *Modernization and Social Change among Muslims in India*. Delhi: Manohar.

———, 1984: 'Tamil Nadu Conversions, Conversion Threats, and the Anti-Reservation Campaign: Some Hypotheses and Perspectives on the Communal Problem', in A. A. Engineer, ed., *Communal Riots in Post-Independence India*. New Delhi: Sangam Books, pp. 118–130.

Banu, Z., 1984: 'Two Sides of a Coin: A Comparative Study of Riots at Godhra and Udaipur', in *Communal Riots in Post-Independence India*, ed. A. A. Engineer. Delhi: Sangam Books.

Chandra, B., 1984: *Communalism in Modern India*. Delhi: Vikas Publications, pp. 228–38.

Engineer, A. A., ed., 1984a: *Communal Riots in Post-Independence India*. New Delhi: Sangam Books.

———, 1984b: 'Case Studies of Five Major Riots from Biharsharif to

Pune', in *Communal Riots in Post-Independence India*, ed. A. A. Engineer. New Delhi: Sangam Books, pp. 238–71.

———, 1985: 'Bombay Bhiwandi Riots: A National Perspective' in A. A. Engineer and M. Shakir, ed., *Communalism in India*. Delhi: Ajanta, pp. 205–14.

Gopal, S. 1976: *Jawaharlal Nehru: A Biography*, vol. I. Bombay: Oxford University Press.

Hasan, M. and Saberwal, S., 1984: 'Moradabad Riots 1980: Causes and Meanings', in *Communal Riots in Post-Independence India*, ed. A. A. Engineer. Delhi: Sangam Books, pp. 209–28.

Kapur, Rajiv A., 1987: *Sikh Separatism: The Politics of Faith*. Delhi: Vikas Publishing House.

Khan, R. and Mittal, S., 1984: 'The Hindu–Muslim Riot in Varanasi and the Role of the Police', in *Communal Riots in Post-Independence India*, ed. A. A. Engineer. Delhi: Sangam Books, pp. 305–13.

Kothari, P. B., 1982: *Politics in India*. Delhi: Orient Longman.

Mayer, P. B., 1983: 'Tombs and Dark Houses: Ideology, Intellectuals and Proletarians in the Study of Contemporary Indian Islam', in I. Ahmed, ed., *Modernization and Social Change among Muslims in India*. Delhi: Manohar.

Mukarji, N. and Banerjee, A., 1984: 'Is Indian Unity Under Threat?', *Indian Express*, May, pp. 26–29.

———, 1985: 'New Nationalism', *Seminar*, September.

Naidu, R., 1980: *The Communal Edge of Plural Societies*. Delhi: Vikas Publications.

Rajgopal, P. R., 1986: *Communalism and Communal Violence*. Delhi: Centre for Policy Research.

Saxena, N. C., 1984: 'Nature and Origin of Communal Riots in India', in *Communal Riots in Post-Independence India*, ed. A. A. Engineer. Delhi: Sangam Books, pp. 51–68.

Sethi, H., 1985: 'The Citizens Response: A Glimmer of Possibilities?', *Lokayan Bulletin*, vol. 3, 1 January, pp. 59–73.

Shah, G., 1984: 'The 1969 Communal Riots in Ahmedabad: A Case Study', in *Communal Riots in Post-Independence India*, ed. A. A. Engineer. Delhi: Sangam Books, pp. 175–209.

Chapter Three

The Politics of Secularism and the Recovery of Religious Tolerance

ASHIS NANDY

I. *Faith, Ideology and the Self*

A significant aspect of post-colonial structures of knowledge in the third world is a peculiar form of imperialism of categories. Under such imperialism a conceptual domain is sometimes hege-monized so effectively by a concept produced and honed in the West that the original domain vanishes from our awareness. Intellect and intelligence become IQ, the oral cultures become the cultures of the primitive or the preliterate, the oppressed become the proletariat, social change becomes development. After a while, people begin to forget that IQ is only a crude measure of intelligence and some day someone else may think up another kind of index to assess the same thing; that social change did not begin with development, nor will it stop once the idea of development dies a natural or unnatural death.

In the following pages, I seek to provide a political preface to the recovery of a well-known domain of public concern in South Asia, ethnic and, especially, religious tolerance, from the hegemonic language of secularism popularized by the westernized intellectuals and middle classes exposed to the globally dominant language of the nation-state in this part of the world. This language, whatever may have been its positive contributions to humane governance and religious tolerance earlier, has increasingly become a cover for the complicity of the modern intellectuals and the modernizing middle classes of South Asia in the new forms of religious violence. These are the forms in which the state, the media and the ideologies of national security, development and modernity propagated by the modern intelligentsia and the middle classes play crucial roles.

To provide the political preface I have promised, I shall have to first describe four trends which have become clearly visible in South Asia during this century, particularly after the Second World War.

The first and most important of these trends is that each religion in South Asia, perhaps all over the southern world, has split into two: faith and ideology. Both are inappropriate terms, but I give them, in this paper, specific private meanings to serve my purpose. By faith I mean religion as a way of life, a tradition which is definitionally non-monolithic and operationally plural. I say 'definitionally' because unless a religion is geographically and culturally confined to a small area, it has as a way of life, in effect, to turn into a confederation of a number of ways of life which are linked by a common faith that has some theological space for the heterogeneity which everyday life introduces. Witness the differences between Iranian and Indonesian Islams, two cultures which can be said to be divided by the same faith. The two forms of Islam are interlocking, not isomorphic, in relation to each other.

By ideology I mean religion as a sub-national, national or cross-national identifier of populations contesting for or protecting non-religious, usually political or socio-economic, interests. Such religions-as-ideologies usually get identified with one or more texts which, rather than the ways of life of the believers, then become the final identifiers of the pure forms of the religions. The texts help anchor the ideologies in something seemingly concrete and delimited, and in effect provide a set of manageable operational definitions.

The modern state always prefers to deal with religious ideologies rather than with faiths. It is wary of both forms of religion but it finds the ways of life more inchoate and, hence, unmanageable, even though it is faith rather than ideology which has traditionally shown more pliability and catholicity. It is religion-as-faith which prompted 200,000 Indians to declare themselves as Mohammedan Hindus in Gujarat in the census of 1911; and it was the catholicity of faith which prompted Mole-Salam Girasia Rajputs to traditionally have two names for every member of the community, one Hindu and one Muslim.[1] It is religion-as-ideology, on the other hand,

[1] See Lokhandawala (1985), p. 98.

which prompted a significant proportion of Punjabi-speaking Hindus to declare Hindi as their mother tongue, thus bringing the politics of language to bear upon the differences between Sikhism and Hinduism and sowing the seeds for the creation of a new minority. Likewise it is religion-as-ideology which has provided a potent tool to the Jamaat-e-Islami to disown the traditional, plural forms of Islam in the Indian subcontinent and to create a disjunction between official religion and everyday life.

Second, during the last two centuries or so there has grown a tendency to view the older faiths of the region through the eyes of evangelical Anglican Christianity and its various offshoots—such as the masculine Christianity associated with nineteenth-century missionaries like Joshua Marshman and William Carey, or its mirror image in the orthodox modernism propagated by the likes of Frederich Engels and Thomas Huxley. Because this particular Eurocentric way of looking at faiths gradually came to be associated with the dominant culture of the colonial states in the region, it subsumes under it a set of clear polarities; centre *vs.* periphery, true faith *vs.* its distortions, civil *vs.* primordial, and great traditions *vs.* local cultures or little traditions.

It is a part of the same story that in each of the dyads, the second category is set up to lose. It is also a part of the same story that, once the colonial concept of the state was internalized by the societies of this region through the nationalist ideology—in turn heavily influenced by the western theories and practice of statecraft—the nascent nation-states of the region took upon themselves the same civilizing mission that the colonial states had once taken upon themselves *vis-a-vis* the ancient faiths of the subcontinent.[2]

Third, the idea of secularism, an import from nineteenth-century Europe into South Asia, has acquired immense potency in the middle-class cultures and 'state sectors' of South Asia, thanks to its connection with and response to religion-as-ideology. Secularism has little to say about cultures. It is definitionally ethnophobic and frequently ethnocidal, unless of course cultures and those living by cultures are willing to show total subservience to the modern nation-state and become ornaments or adjuncts to modern living. The orthodox secularists have no clue to the way a religion can link

[2] On nationalism as an internalized Western category the most detailed work is Chatterjee (1986).

up different faiths or ways of life according to its own configurative principles.

To such secularists, religion is an ideology in opposition to the ideology of modern statecraft and, therefore, needs to be contained. They feel even more uncomfortable with religion-as-faith—which claims to have its own principles of tolerance and intolerance—for such a claim denies the state and the middle-class ideologues of the state the right to be the ultimate reservoir of sanity and the ultimate arbiter among different religions and communities. This denial is particularly galling to those who see the clash between two faiths merely as a clash of socio-economic interests, not as a simultaneous clash between conflicting interests and a philosophical encounter between two metaphysics. The westernized middle classes and literati of South Asia love to see all such encounters as reflections of socio-economic forces and, thus, as liabilities and as sources of ethnic violence.

Fourth, the imported idea of secularism has become increasingly incompatible and, as it were, uncomfortable with the somewhat fluid definitions of the self with which many South Asian cultures live out. Such a self, which can be conceptually viewed as a configuration of selves, invokes and reflects the configurative principles of religion-as-faith. It also happens to be a negation of the modern concept of selfhood acquired partly from the West and partly from a rediscovery of previously recessive elements in South Asian traditions. Religion-as-ideology, working with the concept of well-bounded, mutually exclusive religious identities, on the other hand, is more compatible with and analogous to the definition of the self as a well-bounded, individuated entity clearly separable from the non-self. Such individuation is taking place in South Asian societies at a fast pace and, to that extent, more exclusive definitions of the self are emerging in these societies as a byproduct of secularization.[3]

A more fluid definition of the self is not merely more compatible with religion-as-faith, it also has—and depends more upon—a distinctive set of the non-self and anti-selves (a neologism analogous to 'anti-heroes'). At one plane these anti-selves are similar to what the psychotherapist Carl Rogers used to call, infelicitiously, the

[3] See Miller (1987).

'not-me'—and to what others call rejected selves. At another plane the anti-selves are counterpoints without which the self just cannot be defined in the major cultures of South Asia. It is the self in conjunction with its anti-selves and its distinctive concept of the non-self which together define the domain of the self. Religion-as-faith is more compatible with such a complex self-definition; secularism has no inkling of this distinct, though certainly not unique, form of self-definition in South Asia. For, everything said, secularism is, as Madan (1987) puts it, a 'gift of Christianity', by which he presumably means a gift of post-medieval, European Christianity to this part of the world.

It is in the context of these four processes that I shall now discuss the scope and limits of the ideology of secularism in India and its relationship with the new forms of ethnic violence we have been witnessing.

II. *The Fate of Secularism*

I must make it clear at this point that I am not a secularist. In fact, I can be called an anti-secularist. This is because I have come to believe that the ideology and politics of secularism have more or less exhausted their possibilities and that we may now have to work with a different conceptual frame which is already vaguely visible at the borders of Indian political culture.

When I say that the ideology and politics of secularism have exhausted themselves, I have in mind the standard English meaning of the word 'secularism'. As we know, there are two meanings of the word current in modern and modernizing India and, for that matter, in the whole of this subcontinent. One of the two meanings is easily found by consulting any standard dictionary. But there is difficulty in finding the other, for it is a non-standard, local meaning which, many like to believe, is typically and distinctively Indian or South Asian. (As we shall see below, it also has a western tail, but that tail is now increasingly vestigial, at least in the popular middle-class cultures of South Asia.)

The first meaning becomes clear when people talk of secular trends in history or economics, or when they speak of secularizing the state. The word 'secular' has been used in this sense, at least in the English-speaking West, for more than three hundred years.

This secularism chalks out an area in public life where religion is not admitted. One can have religion in one's private life; one can be a good Hindu or a good Muslim within one's home or at one's place of worship. But when one enters public life, one is expected to leave one's faith behind. This ideology of secularism is associated with slogans like 'we are Indians first, Hindus second', or 'we are Indians first, then Sikhs'. Implicit in the ideology is the belief that managing the public realm is a science which is essentially universal and that religion, to the extent that it is opposed to the Baconian world-image of science, is an open or potential threat to any modern polity.

In contrast, the non-western meaning of secularism revolves around equal respect for all religions. This is the way it is usually put by public figures. Less crudely stated, it implies that while the public life may or may not be kept free of religion, it must have space for a continuous dialogue among religious traditions and between the religious and the secular—that, in the ultimate analysis, each major faith in the region includes *within* it an in-house version of the other faiths, both as an internal criticism and as a reminder of the diversity of the theories of transcendence.

Recently, Ali Akhtar Khan has drawn attention to the fact that George Jacob Holyoake, who coined the word secularism in 1850, advocated a secularism accommodative of religion, a secularism which would moreover emphasize diversities and co-existence in the matter of faith. His contemporary Joseph Bradlaugh, on the other hand, believed in a secularism which rejected religion and made science its deity.[4] Most non-modern Indians (i.e. Indians who would have brought Professor Max Weber to tears), pushed around by the political and cultural forces unleashed by colonialism still operating in Indian society, have unwittingly opted for the accommodative and pluralist meaning, while India's westernized intellectuals have consciously opted for the abolition of religion from the public sphere.

In other words, the accommodative meaning is more compatible with the meaning a majority of Indians, independently of Bradlaugh, have given to the word 'secularism'. This meaning has always disconcerted the country's westernized intellectuals. They

[4] See Khan (1986).

have seen such people's secularism as adulterated and as compromising true secularism. This is despite the fact that the ultimate symbol of religious tolerance for the modern Indian, Gandhi, obviously had this adulterated meaning in mind on the few occasions when he seemed to plead for secularism: as much is clear from his notorious claim that those who thought religion and politics could be kept separate understood neither religion nor politics.

The saving grace in all this is that while the scientific, rational meaning of secularism has dominated India's middle-class public consciousness, the Indian people and, till recently most practising Indian politicians, have depended on the accommodative meaning. The danger is that the first meaning is supported by the accelerating process of modernization in India. As a result, there is now a clearer fit between the declared ideology of the modern Indian nation-state and the secularism that fears religions and ethnicities. Sociologist Imtiaz Ahmed euphemistically calls this fearful, nervous secularism the new liberalism of the Indian elites.[5]

Associated with this—what South Asians perceive as the more scientific, western meaning of secularism—is a hidden political hierarchy. I have spelt out this hierarchy elsewhere but I shall, nevertheless, restate it to make the rest of my argument. This hierarchy makes a four-fold classification of political actors in the subcontinent.

At the top of the hierarchy come those who are *believers* neither in public nor in private. They are supposed to be scientific and rational, and they are expected, ultimately, not only to rule this society but also to dominate its political culture. An obvious example is Jawaharlal Nehru. Though we are now told, with a great deal of embarrassment, that he believed in astrology and *tantra*, Nehru rightfully belongs to this rung because he always made modern Indians a little ashamed of their religious beliefs and ethnic origins, convincing them that he himself had the courage and rationality to neither believe in private nor in public. By the common consent of the Indian middle classes, Nehru provided a perfect role model for twentieth-century citizens of the flawed cultural reality called India. It is the Nehruvian model which informs the following charming letter, written by a distinguished

[5] Ahmad (1987).

former ambassador, to the editor of India's best-known national daily;

M. V. Kamath asks in his article, 'Where do we find the Indian?' My dear friend and colleague, the late Ambassador M. R. A. Beg, often used to say: 'Don't you think, old boy, that the only Indians are we wogs?' However quaint it may have sounded 30 years ago, the validity of this statement has increasingly become apparent over the years.[6]

On the second rung of the ladder are those who choose not to appear as believers in public, despite being devout believers in private. I can think of no better example of this type than Indira Gandhi. She was a genuine non-believer in public life, dying at the hands of her own Sikh guards instead of accepting security advice to change them. But in private she was a devout Hindu who had to make her seventy-one—or was it sixty-nine?—pilgrimages. Both the selves of Indira Gandhi were genuine and together they represented the self-concept of a sizeable portion of the Indian middle classes. A number of other rulers in this part of the world fit this category—from Ayub Khan to Lal Bahadur Shastri to Sheikh Mujibur Rahman. Though the westernized literati in South Asian societies have never cared much for this model of religious and ethnic tolerance, they have been usually willing to accept the model as a reasonable compromise with the 'underdeveloped' cultures of South Asia.

On the third rung are those who are believers in public but do not believe in private. This may at first seem an odd category, but one or two examples will make clear its meaning and also partially explain why this category includes problematic men and women. To me the two most illustrious examples of this genre from the Indian subcontinent are Mohammed Ali Jinnah, an agnostic in private life who took up the cause of Islam successfully in public, and D. V. Savarkar, an atheist in private life who declared Hinduism as his political ideology.

Such persons can be dangerous because to them religion is a political tool and a means of fighting one's own and one's community's sense of cultural inadequacy. Religion to them is not a matter of piety. Their private denial of belief only puts those

[6] Singh (1986).

secularists off guard who cannot fathom the seriousness with which the Jinnahs and the Savarkars take religion as a political instrument. On the other hand, their public faith puts the faithful off guard because the latter never discern the contempt in which such heroes hold the common run of believers. Often, these heroes invoke the classical versions of their faiths to underplay, marginalize or even delegitimize the existing ways of life associated with their faiths. The goal of those holding such an instrumental view of religion has always been to homogenize their co-believers into proper political formations and, for that reason, to eliminate those parts of religion which smack of folk ways and threaten to legitimize diversities, inter-faith dialogue and theological polycentrism.

At the bottom of the hierarchy are those who are believers in the private as well as public domains. The best and most notorious example is Gandhi, a believer both in private and public, who gave his belief spectacular play in politics. This category has its strengths and weaknesses. One may say that exactly as the category manifests its strength in someone like Gandhi, it shows its weakness in others like Ayatollah Khomeini in Iran or Jarnail Singh Bhindranwale in the Punjab—both of whom ended up trying to fully homogenize their communities in the name of faith. The category can even throw up grand eccentrics. Chaudhuri Rehmat Ali fifty years ago used to stand on Fridays outside King's College gate at Cambridge and chant like a street hawker, 'Come and buy *Pakistan*—my earth-shaking pamphlet'.[7]

These four categories are not neat and in real life rarely come in their pure forms. Often the same person moves from one to the other. Thus, the writer Rahi Masoom Raza, being also a script-writer for commercial Hindi films and at home with spectacular changes of heart, comfortably oscillates between the first two categories thus: 'This Babari Masjid and Ram Janambhoomi temple should be demolished. We as Indians are not interested in Babari Masjid, Rama Janambhoomis . . . as secular people we must crush the religious fanatics.'[8] Only ten months earlier Raza had, with as much passion, said: 'I, Rahi Masoom Raza, son of the late Mr. Syed Bashir Hasan Abidi, a Muslim and one of the direct descendants

[7] Anand (1985).
[8] Raza (1987).

of the Prophet of Islam, hereby condemn Mr. Z. A. Ansari for his un-Islamic and anti-Muslim speeches in Parliament. The Quran nowhere says that a Muslim should have four wives.'[9] For the moment I shall not go into such issues. All I shall add is that in India we have been always slightly embarrassed about this modern classification or ordering in our political life, for we know that the Father of the Nation, Gandhi, does not fare very well when the classification is applied to him.

Fortunately for some modern Indians, the embarrassment has been resolved by the fact that this classification is not working well today. It is not working well because it has led neither to the elimination of religion and ethnicity from politics nor to greater religious and ethnic tolerance. This is not the case only with us; it has been the case with every society that has been put up to Indians as the model, at various times, of the secular ideal.

Thus, problems of ethnicity and secularization today haunt not merely the main capitals of the world, Washington and Moscow, they even haunt England, the country which older South Asians have been trained to view as remarkably free from the divisiveness of ethnicity and religion. For some 150 years Indians have been told, as part of their political socialization, that one of the reasons why Britain colonized and dominated India was that the natives were not secular whereas the British were. This is given as the reason why Indians did not know how to live together, whereas Britain as a world power was perfectly integrated and fired by the true spirit of secular nationalism. Now we find, after nearly 300 years of secularism, that the Irish, the Scots and the Welsh are together creating as many problems for Britain as are some of the religions and regions for us in India.

Why is the old ideology of secularism not working in India? There are many reasons; I shall mention only a few, confining myself specifically to the problem of religion as it has become entangled with political process in the country.

First, in the early years of Independence, when the national elite was small and a large section of it had face-to-face contacts, one could screen people entering public life—specially the upper levels of the public services and high politics—for their commitment to secularism. Thanks to the growth of democratic participation in

---

[9] Raza (1986b).

politics—India has gone through eight general elections and innumerable local and state elections—such screening is no longer possible. We can no longer make sure that those who reach the highest levels of the army, police, bureaucracy or politics believe in old-style secular politics. To give one example, two ministers of the present central cabinet in India and a number of high-ups in the ruling party have been accused of not only encouraging, organizing and running a communal riot, but also of protecting the guilty and publicly threatening civil rights workers engaged in relief work. One chief minister has been recently accused of importing rioters from another state on payment of professional fees to precipitate a communal riot as an antidote to violent inter-caste conflicts. Another organized a riot three years ago so that he could impose a curfew in the state capital to stop his political opponents from demonstrating their strength in the legislature. Such instances would have been unthinkable only ten years ago. They have become thinkable today because India's ultra-elites can no longer informally screen decision-makers the way they once used to; political participation in the country is growing, and the country's political institutions, particularly the parties, are under too much strain to allow such screening. Religion *has* entered public life but through the backdoor.

Second, it has become more and more obvious to a large number of people that modernity is now no longer the ideology of a small minority; it is now the organizing principle of the dominant culture of politics. The idea that religions dominate India, that there are a handful of modern Indians fighting a rearguard action against that domination, is no longer convincing to many Indians. These Indians see the society around them—and often their own children—leaving no scope for a compromise between the old and new, and opting for a way of life which fundamentally negates the traditional concepts of a good life and a desirable society. These Indians have now come to sense that it is modernity which rules the world and, even in this subcontinent, religion-as-faith is being pushed to the corner. Much of the fanaticism and violence associated with religion comes today from the sense of defeat of the believers, from their feelings of impotence, and from their free-floating anger and self-hatred while facing a world which is increasingly secular and desacralized.

This issue has another side. When the state makes a plea to a minority community to be secular or to confine itself to secular politics, the state in effect tells the minority to 'go slow' on its faith, so that it can be more truly integrated in the nation-state. Simultaneously, the state offers the minority a consolation prize in the form of a promise that it will force the majority community also to ultimately dilute its faith. What the state says to a religious community, the modern sector often indirectly tells the individual, 'you give up your faith, at least in public; we also shall give up our faith in public and together we shall be able to live in freedom from religious intolerance.' I need hardly add that however reasonable the solution may look to people like us, who like to see themselves as rational non-believing moderns, it is not an adequate consolation to the faithful, to whom religion is what it is precisely because it provides an overall theory of life, including public life. For them life is not worth living without a theory of transcendence, however imperfect.

Third, we have begun to find out that, while appealing to believers to keep the public sphere free of religion, the modern nation-state has no means of ensuring that the ideologies of secularism, development and nationalism themselves do not begin to act as faiths intolerant of other faiths. That is, while the modern state builds up pressures on citizens to give up their faith in public, it guarantees no protection to them against the sufferings inflicted by the state itself in the name of its ideology. In fact, with the help of modern communications and the secular coercive power at its command, the state can use its ideology to silence its non-conforming citizens. The role of secularism in many societies today is no different from the crusading and inquisitorial role of religious ideologies. In such societies, citizens have less protection against the ideology of the state than against religious ideologies or theocratic forces. Certainly in India, the ideas of nation-building, scientific growth, security, modernization and development have become parts of a left-handed technology with a clear touch of religiosity—a modern demonology, a *tantra* with a built-in code of violence.

This can be put another way. To many Indians today, secularism comes as a part of a larger package consisting of a set of standardized ideological products and social processes—development, mega-science and national security being some of the most prominent

The table admits that the western concept of secularism has played a crucial role in South Asian societies, it *has* worked as a check against some forms of ethnic intolerance and violence; it *has* contributed to humane governance at certain times and places.

By the same token, however, the table also suggests that secularism cannot cope with many of the new fears and intolerance of religions and ethnicities, nor can it provide any protection against the new forms of violence which have come to be associated with such intolerance. Nor can secularism contain those who provide the major justifications for calculated pogroms and ethnocides in terms of the dominant ideology of the state.

These new forms of intolerance and violence are sustained by a different configuration of social and psychological forces. The rubrics in the table allude both to these forces as well as to the growing irrelevance of the broad models proposed by a number of important empirical social and psychological studies done in the fifties and sixties—by those studying social distance in the manner of E. Bogardus, by Erich Fromm (1941) in his early writings, by Theodor Adorno (1950) and his associates working on the authoritarian personality, by Milton Rokeach (1960) and his followers exploring dogmatism, and by Bettelheim (1979). The stereotyping, authoritarian submission, sado-masochism and heavy use of the ego defences of projection, displacement and rationalization which went with authoritarianism and dogmatism, according to some of these studies, have not become irrelevant.[13] There are persistent demonologies which divide religious communities and endorse ethnic violence. These demonologies, however, have begun to play a less central role in such violence. They have become, increasingly, one of the psychological identifiers of those participating in the mobs involved in rioting or in pogroms, not of those planning, initiating or legitimizing mob-action.

This is another way of saying that the planners, instigators and legitimizers of religious and ethnic violence can now be identified as secular users of non-secular forces in society. There is very little continuity between their motivational structures and that of the street mobs which act out the wishes of the organizers of a riot.

[13] See the essay by Kakar in this volume.

Only the mobs now represent, and that too partially, the violence produced by the predisposing factors described in the social-science literature of earlier decades. In the place of these factors have come a new set of personality traits and defence mechanisms, the most important of which are more 'primitive' defences such as isolation and denial. These defences ensure, paradoxically, the primacy of cognitive factors in violence over the affective and the conative.

The involvement of these newly-important ego defences in human violence were also first noticed in the fifties and sixties. But those who drew attention to these defences did so in passing, for instance, Fromm (1973) and Bettelheim (1979); and from outside the ambit of empirical social sciences there were Conrad (1973) and Arendt (1963 and 1969). Moreover, these early analyses of the 'new violence' were primarily concerned with 'extreme situations', to use Bettelheim's term, and not with the less-technologized and less extreme violence of religious feuds or riots. Even when the violence did not directly involve genocide and mass murders, it involved memories of genocide and mass murders, as in the well-known book by Alexander and Margarete Mitscherlich (1984).

Only now have we become fully aware of the destructive potential of the once low-grade but now persistent violence flowing from objectification, scientization and bureaucratic rationality. The reasons for this heightened awareness are obvious enough. As the modern nation-state system and the modern thought machine enter the interstices of even the most traditional societies, those in power or those who hope to be in power in these societies begin to view statecraft in fully secular, scientific, amoral and dispassionate terms.[14] The modernist elites in such societies then begin to fear the divisiveness of minorities and the diversity which religious and ethnic plurality introduces into a nation-state. These elites then begin to see all religions and all forms of ethnicity as a hurdle to nation-building and state-formation and as a danger to the technology of statecraft and political management. The new nation-states in many societies tend to look at religion and ethnicity the way the nineteenth-century colonial powers looked at distant cultures which came under their domination—at best as 'things' to be

[14] That is, in terms of what Banuri (1986) calls the impersonality postulate. See also Nandy (1987).

studied, 'engineered', ghettoed, museumized or preserved in reservations; at worst as inferior cultures opposed to the principles of modern living and inconsistent with the game of modern politics, science and development, and therefore deservedly facing extinction. No wonder that the political cultures of South Asia have begun to produce a plethora of official social scientists who are perfect analogues of the colonial anthropologists who once studied the 'Hindoos' and the 'Mohammedans' on behalf of their king and country.

This state of mind is the basic format of the internal colonialism which is at work today. The economic exploitation to which the epithet 'internal colonialism' is mechanically applied by radical economists is no more than a byproduct of the internal colonialism I am speaking about. This colonialism validates the proposal—which can be teased out of the works of a number of philosophers such as Hannah Arendt and Herbert Marcuse—that the most extreme forms of violence in our times come not from faulty passions or human irrationality but from faulty ideologies and unrestrained instrumental rationality. Demonology is now for the mobs; secular rationality for those who organize, instigate or lead the mobs. Unless of course one conceptualizes modern statecraft itself as a left-handed, magical technology and as a new demonology. Thanks to a few secretly taken photographs, one image that has persisted in my mind from the days of the anti-Sikh pogrom at Delhi in 1984 is that of a scion of a prominent family, which owns one of Delhi's most exclusive boutiques, directing with his golf club a gang of ill-clad arsonists. I suspect that the image has the potential to serve as the metaphor for the new forms of social violence in modern India.

As I have already said, this state-linked internal colonialism uses legitimating core concepts like national security, development, modern science and technology. Any society, for that matter any aggregate, which gives unrestrained play or support to these concepts gets automatically linked to the colonial structure of the present-day world and is doomed to promote violence and expropriation, particularly of the kind directed against smaller minorities, such as the tribals, and the less numerous sects who can neither hit back against the state nor any more live away from the modern market.

Secularism has become a handy adjunct to this set of legitimating core concepts. It helps those swarming around the nation-state, either as elites or as counter-elites, to legitimize themselves as the sole arbiters among traditional communities, to claim for themselves a monopoly on religious and ethnic tolerance and on political rationality. To accept the ideology of secularism is to accept the ideologies of progress and modernity as the new justifications of domination, and the use of violence to sustain these ideologies as the new opiates of the masses.

Gandhi, an arch anti-secularist if we use the proper scientific meaning of the word 'secularist', claimed that his religion was his politics and his politics was his religion. He was not a cultural relativist and his rejection of the first principle of secularism—the separation of religion and politics—was not a political strategy meant to ensure his political survival in an uniquely multi-ethnic society like India. In fact, I have been told by sociologist Bhupinder Singh that Gandhi may have borrowed this anti-secular formulation from William Blake. Whatever be its source, in some version or the other this formulation is becoming the common response of those who have sensed the new forms of man-made violence unleashed by post-seventeenth-century Europe in the name of Enlightenment values. These forms of violence, which have already taken a toll of about a hundred million human lives in this century, have come under closer critical scrutiny in recent decades mainly because they have come home to roost in the heart of Europe and North America, thanks to the Third Reich, the Gulag, the two World Wars, and the threat of nuclear annihilation. Many modern Indians who try to sell Gandhi as a secularist find his attitude to the separation of religion and politics highly embarrassing, if not positively painful. They like to see Gandhi as a hidden modernist who merely used a traditional religious idiom to mobilize his unorganized society to fight colonialism. Nothing can be more disingenuous. Gandhi's religious tolerance came from his anti-secularism, which in turn came from his unconditional rejection of modernity. And he never wavered in his stand. Note the following exchange between him and a correspondent of the *Chicago Tribune* in 1931:

'Sir, twenty-three years ago you wrote a book *Hind Swaraj*, which stunned India and the rest of the world with its terrible onslaught on modern western civilization. Have you changed your mind about any of the things you have said in it?'

'Not a bit. My ideas about the evils of western civilization still stand. If I republish the book tomorrow, I would scarcely change a word.'[15]

Religious tolerance outside the bounds of secularism is exactly what it says it is. It not only means tolerance of religions but also a tolerance that is religious. It therefore squarely locates itself in traditions, outside the ideological grid of modernity. Gandhi used to say that he was a *sanatani*, an orthodox Hindu. It was as a *sanatani* Hindu that he claimed to be simultaneously a Muslim, a Sikh and a Christian and he granted the same plural identity to those belonging to other faiths. Traditional Hinduism, or rather *sanatan dharma*, was the source of his religious tolerance. It is instructive that the Hindu nationalists who killed him—that too after three unsuccessful attempts to kill him over the previous twenty years—did so in the name of secular statecraft. They said so explicitly and declared Gandhi to be an enemy of the nascent Indian nation-state.

It is that very secular statecraft which now seeks to dominate the Indian political culture, sometimes in the name of Gandhi himself. Urban, westernized, middle-class, Brahmanic, Hindu nationalists and Hindu modernists often flaunt Gandhi's tolerance as an indicator of Hindu catholicity but contemptuously reject that part of his ideology which insisted that religious tolerance, to be tolerance, must impute to other faiths the same spirit of tolerance. Whether a large enough proportion of those belonging to the other religious traditions show *in practice and at a particular point of time and place* the same tolerance or not is a secondary matter. Because it is the imputation or presumption of tolerance in others, not its existence, which defines one's own tolerance in the Gandhian worldview and praxis.

That presumption must become the major source of tolerance for those who want to fight the new violence of our times, whether they are believers or not.

REFERENCES

Adorno, T. N. *et al.*, 1950: *The Authoritarian Personality*. New York: Norton.

Ahmad, I., 1987: 'Muslims and Boycott Call: Political Realities Ignored'. *Times of India*, 14 January.

Anand, M. R., 1985: 'New Light on Iqbal'. *Indian Express*, 27 Sept.

Ananthu, T. S., 1981: *Going Beyond the Intellect: A Gandhian Approach to Scientific Education*. New Delhi: Gandhi Peace Foundation, mimeo.

Arendt, H., 1963: *Eichmann in Jeruslam*. New York: Viking Press.

————, 1969: *On Violence*. London: Allen & Unwin.

Banuri, T., 1986: 'A Critical Review of Modernization Theories'. Paper presented at the meeting on Technological Transformation in Traditional Societies. Helsinki.

Bettelheim, Bruno, 1979: *Surviving and Other Essays*. London: Thames and Hudson.

Chatterjee, P., 1986: *Nationalist Thought and the Colonial World: A Derivative Discourse?* New Delhi: Oxford University Press.

Conrad, J., 1973: *Heart of Darkness*. Harmondsworth: Penguin.

Fromm, E., 1941: *Escape from Freedom*. New York: Farrar and Rinehart.

————, 1973: *The Anatomy of Human Destructiveness*. New York: Holt, Rinehart and Winston.

Kakar, S., 1989: 'Some Unconscious Aspects of Ethnic Violence in India'. See within this volume.

Khan, A. A., 1986: 'Secularism and Aligarh School'. *Times of India*, 2 December.

Khan, A. Q., 1987: 'Pak a few steps from bomb'. *Times of India*, 29 January.

Lokhandwala, S. T., 1985: 'Indian Islam: Composite culture and integration'. *New Quest*, March-April, pp. 87–101.

Madan, T. N., 1987: 'Secularism in its Place'. Distinguished Lecture at the Annual Meeting of the Association of Asian Studies, Boston.

Miller, D. F., 1987: 'Six Theses on the Question of Religion and Politics in India Today'. *Economic and Political Weekly*, July, pp. 57–63.

Mitscherlich, Alexander and Margarete, 1984: *The Inability to Mourn: Principles of Collective Behaviour*. New York: Grove.

Nandy, A., 1987: *Traditions, Tyranny, and Utopias: Essays in the Politics of Awareness*. New Delhi: Oxford University Press, pp. 95–126.

Patel, Raojibhai C., 1986: 'Building Secular State, Need to Subordinate Religion'. *Times of India*, 17 September.

Raza, Rahi Masoom, 1986: 'In Favour of Change'. Letter to the editor, *Illustrated Weekly of India*, 16 March.

———, 1987: "How to Resolve the Babri Masjid-Ramajanma Bhumi Dispute'. *Sunday Observer*, 18 January.
Rockeach, M., 1960: *The Open and Used Mind*. New York: Basic Books.
Singh, G., 1986: 'Where's the Indian?' *Times of India*, 21 Sept.

Chapter Four

The Colonial Construction of 'Communalism': British Writings on Banaras in the Nineteenth Century[1]

GYANENDRA PANDEY

Communal strife—conflict between people of different religious persuasions—was represented by the British colonial regime in India as one of the most distinctive features of Indian society, past and present. The communal riot narrative was perhaps the most important colonialist statement on the nature of politics in this society. In this paper I seek to investigate the making of that narrative.[2]

In a colonialist reading of history that had become dominant by the end of the nineteenth century, 'communalism' was seen as the special mark of the Indian section of the 'Orient'. This particular reading of Indian history was distinguished not only by its periodization in terms of the European experience ('ancient', 'medieval', 'modern'), nor simply by its use of communal—more specifically, religious—categories to differentiate these periods of Indian history (or, at least, the first two of them: the 'Hindu' and the 'Muslim'). This historical reconstruction was characterized also by an emptying out of all history—in terms of the specific variations of time, place, class, issue—from the political experience of the people, and the identification of religion (or the religious community) as

---

[1] The paper is reproduced from R. Guha, ed., *Subaltern Studies VI* (Delhi, OUP, 1989) by permission of the editor and publishers.

[2] An elaboration of some of these themes will be found in my forthcoming book *The Construction of Communalism in Colonial North India* (Delhi, OUP, 1990).

the moving force of all Indian politics. The communal riot narrative served to substantiate this reading of history.

Towards the end of the 1920s the Government of India drew up elaborate lists of Hindu-Muslim riots that had occurred in the country in the recent past. From one of these, we learn that there were 112 serious 'disturbances' between 1923 and 1927 which left approximately 450 people dead and 5000 more wounded; 1929 produced a carnage in Bombay, 1931 one more in Kanpur. Official statistics put the number of casualties in Bombay at 184 killed and 948 wounded. In Kanpur, several hundreds were killed (for a casualty list of the same order, a government memorandum observed, one had to go back to the 'grave Benares riots' of 1809) and about 80,000 people are said to have left the city by rail alone on the first day of conflagration that raged for three days.[3]

The record of Hindu-Muslim strife was also extended further back, to the beginnings of colonial rule, as one can see from Table 1.

It is not difficult to add to these official lists. For the period 1800 to 1920 alone, a recent study speaks of 'riots and communal conflicts in many North Indian cities in the 1830s and again in the 1850s' and refers to Hindu-Muslim strife in Lucknow, for instance, in 1843, 1853 and 1856.[4] There are records of clashes between Hindus and Muslims in Bareilly in 1837 (in addition to the riots of 1871–2 mentioned in Table 1); in Faizabad-Ayodhya in 1856; and, to take the two most important cloth-producing centres of Azamgarh district as another example, in Mubarakpur in 1813, 1834, 1842 and 1904, and in Maunath Bhanjan (or Mau) in 1806 and on several occasions from the 1860s onwards.

Again, the bloodshed at the Baqr'Id in 1893 in Azamgarh and other districts of eastern UP and western Bihar led to violent conflict between groups of Muslims in Bombay, Junagadh and Rangoon as well.[5] Bombay was witness to another round of fight-

[3] L/P 8 J/7/132, 'Communal Disorders', memorandum prepared by the Government of India for the Indian Statutory Commission, 1928, and Notes of 19–20 May 1931, in India Office Library and Records, hereafter IOL.

[4] See Bayly (1985).

[5] Burma was administered by the Government of India until 1935; hence, reports of riots in Rangoon appear together with reports of riots in different parts of India.

TABLE 1

Government Statement of
Major Hindu–Muslim Riots, 1800–1920

Year	Place	Observations by officials
1809	Banaras	'Grave Benares riots'; several hundred persons killed, some 50 mosques destroyed.
1871–2	Bareilly	'Serious riots'.
1885	Lahore & Karnal	
1886	Delhi	'The great riots'.
1889	Dera Ghazi Khan	
1891	Palakod	
1893	Azamgarh	'Grave outbreaks over a large area of country'.
	Bombay	'Very serious Muharram riots'; 80 persons killed.
1910	Peshawar	
1912	Ayodhya-Faizabad	
1913	Agra	
1917	Shahabad	'Baqr'Id disturbances which recalled the Azamgarh disturbances of 1893 and which are among the most serious which have occurred at any time since the British connection with the country'.
1918	Katarpur village (Saharanpur district)	30 Muslims killed, 60 or more injured; all Muslim houses in the village burnt.

SOURCE: L/P&J/7/132; Report of the Indian Statutory Commission, volume IV (1930), pp. 96–7.

ing between Hindus and Muslims at the Muharram of 1911, and there was a serious riot in Calcutta in 1918—partly it appears in retaliation for the Hindu attacks on Muslims in Shahabad district the year before.[6]

If this is the sometimes neglected history of Hindu–Muslim strife

[6] See McLane (1977), pp. 320–1, Masselos (1976), and Macpherson (1974), pp. 39, 40.

before the 1920s, evidence of Hindu-Muslim 'riots' can also be found for the pre-colonial period. Scholars have written of riots in Gujarat in the seventeenth and eighteenth centuries, and again of 'sporadic' local conflict in Banaras, for example, from the 1750s.[7] Indeed the list of Hindu-Muslim riots in colonial and pre-colonial India lengthens all the time with lengthening research—as indeed it must if 'riots' are what one is looking for.

It is possible for the researcher, however, to do more than just look for riots or simply delineate their differing contexts (though colonialist historiography was not particularly guilty of the latter crime). It is possible, and necessary, also to ask how reports of communal strife were received by contemporary and subsequent observers, what meanings were derived from them, what place they were assigned in different representations of the changing colonial world. How did colonialist observers 'read' the history of Hindu-Muslim strife that they dug up in the course of their attempts to come to grips with Indian society? This is the question that I take up in this paper through a close examination of the evidence relating to the 'grave' Banaras riots of 1809 which figure prominently in colonial diagnoses of the social and political condition of India in the nineteenth and twentieth centuries.

II

The District *Gazetteer* of Banaras compiled in 1907 introduces the 1809 riots as follows:

The only disturbance of the public peace in [in Banaras during the first half of the nineteenth century] occurred in 1809 and the following year, when the city experienced one of those convulsions which had so frequently occurred in the past owing to the religious antagonism of the Hindu and Musalman sections of the population.

This comment is followed by a one-and-a-half page description

[7] See Rizvi (1980), p. 197, Subramanian (1985) and Bayly (1985). In regard to Banaras, however, it is worth pointing out that officials making detailed enquiries after the 1809 outbreak reported that there had been no notable outbreak of violence between Hindus and Muslims in the city for the previous hundred years.

of the events of 1809, after which the compiler of the *Gazetteer* remarks:

A curious sequel of the riots was a feud that sprang up between the military and the police. This originated, no doubt, in religious differences, but these appear to have been dropped in the course of time and a long succession of affrays ensued, with Hindus and Musalmans indiscriminately mingled on either side.

The entry goes on as follows:

The trouble subsided with a partial reorganization of the city police in October 1810; but before peace had been restored fresh riots arose with the introduction of the house-tax under Regulation XV of 1810, and it was again found necessary to station troops throughout the city to repress the popular disorder till the withdrawal of the obnoxious measure in the ensuing year.[8]

This was the distilled account as it were of the history of Banaras in the troubled days before the soothing influence of British rule and their sense of fair play had 'civilized' the city. It was an account that was carried into the assessment of the constitutional and political condition of India in the 1920s and 1930s, and it has found its way into the history books.[9] Thus, a memorandum drawn up for submission to the Indian Statutory Commission of 1928 pointed to the 'grave Benares riots' of 1809 as evidence of the usual state of Hindu-Muslim coexistence, describing them as 'one of those convulsions which had frequently occurred in the past owing to the religious antagonism of the Hindu and Moslem sections of the population.'[10]

The particular description is of course lifted straight from the account contained in the Banaras *Gazetteer* of 1907, quoted above. Notice that scarcely a word is altered in the text; and yet the change of context completely transforms the statement. What applied to a *particular* city—the experience of 'convulsions' in the past and the 'religious antagonism' of the local Hindus and Muslims—now applies to the country as a whole. Banaras becomes the essence of

[8] Nevill (1921), pp. 207–9.
[9] See for instance McPherson (1932), p. 29, Coupland (1944), Altekar (1937), pp. 67–8, and Shukul (1974), pp. 281–2.
[10] L/P & J/7/132, 'Communal Disorders'.

India, the history of Banaras the history of India.[11]

What makes Banaras stand in India is not the 'typical' character of Banaras as a habitation, nor the 'representative' character of the strife of 1809. It is the magnitude of the riots of 1809—the 'grave Benares riots', paralleled we are told only after a century and a quarter, in the Kanpur outbreak of 1931—and the fact that they are among the first to be recorded in the colonial period, i.e. most nearly contiguous to pre-colonial times. This is a point to which we shall return.

Let us first examine how the Hindu-Muslim strife of 1809—that significant 'fragment' of the history of India—was reconstructed in some of the earliest accounts of the Banaras riots of 1809. One can construct an interesting table by putting together the information regarding some of the basic features of the 1809 riots as these are presented in the contemporary reports of colonial officials and the major published accounts up to the *Gazetteer* of 1907 (see Table 2).

Plainly there is not a great deal of agreement here even about the bare 'facts' of the incident, although every one of these accounts (barring the first, which is in a special category) was authenticated by the claim that it was based on the original government records or information supplied by officials who were in Banaras at the time. Heber notes that he obtained his information from the Acting Magistrate, W. W. Bird, himself, who gave Heber 'a far more formidable idea of the tumult than I had previously formed'.[12] Mill's *History* refers to his use of 'personal information and manuscript records'.[13] William Buyers' description of the 'War of the Lat', as he calls it, is based on Heber's account which, he writes, 'is no doubt more authentic than the common native reports of it . . . as he had the facts from Mr Bird, and other gentlemen, who were at that time in office at Benares, and had, themselves, the difficult task of quelling the tumult.'[14]

However, the purpose of the comparisons presented in Table 2

[11] Sherring (1868) makes this equation explicitly: 'The history of Benares . . . is to a great extent the history of India.' (p. 34).
[12] Heber (1929), p. 323.
[13] Mill and Wilson (1858), p. 335.
[14] Buyers (1848), p. 273, emphasis added.

TABLE 2

1. Ms. Colonial Government records (1809–10)	20–24 October 1809	Lat Bhairava	Pollution of Lat Bhairava following dispute over attempted conversion of a Hanuman shrine at the site	28–29 killed; 70 wounded	Connivance and 'highly criminal' conduct of police; military alone preserves order	Brahmans and 'superior orders' of the Hindus fast at riverside from evening 20 Oct. Persuaded to abandon fast on 23rd. 24th morning, Gosains assemble in protest at Ghats.
2. Heber (1824)	?	Lat Bhairava	Breaking down of the Lat	—	Temper of the sepoys was 'extremely doubtful' but they held true	Fasting at the riverside by all the Brahmins in the city, 'amounting to many thousands' for 2–3 days after the 'tumult' was quelled.
3. Prinsep (1825–30)	1805	Lat Bhairava	Frenzy excited by Muharram lamentations	—	—	—
4. Mill (1845)	21–23 Oct., 1809	Lat Bhairava and Imambarah in close proximity to it	Alteration between Hindu and Muslim worshippers, leading to injury to the Imamb, and demolition of a makeshift Hanuman temple in the same precinct	About 20 Muslims killed; 70 people wounded	'The Sipalis, although of both persuasions, discharged their duties with perfect impartiality and military steadiness: the police, equally mixed, had early	'The Brahmans and principal inhabitants' fasted at the riverside 'night and day', during the continuance of the disorder'; persuaded with some difficulty to abandon this on 23 Oct.

5. Buyers (1848)	—	?Lat Bhairava	Clash between Holi 'procession' of Hindus and Muharram procession of Muslims	—	taken part in the conflict according to their respective creeds. 'Difficult . . . to trust the native soldiers; but, they did their duty well'.	'After the riot had been suppressed, the worst difficulty still remained': 'all the Brahmans in the number', fasted for 2–3 days.
6. Gazetteer (1907)	Oct. 1809	Aurangzeb mosque on the site of the old Vishwanath temple	Friction over the mosque leads to a 'sudden' outbreak	Several hundred killed	Nothing worthy of special note during the 'riots'. But 'a curious sequel' was a feud between the military and the police, which 'originated, no doubt, in religious differences'.	—

SOURCES: India Office Library and Records, London, Bengal Criminal Judicial Proceedings for 1809 and 1810; R. Heber, *Narrative of a Journey through the Upper Provinces of India, from Calcutta to Bombay, 1824–25*, vol. I (London, 1828); J. Prinsep, *Benares Illustrated (3 series of drawings)* (London, 1831, 1832, 1834); J. Mill (and H. H. Wilson), *The History of British India* (in ten volumes), vol. VII (London, 1858); W. Buyers, *Recollections of Northern India* (London, 1848); H. R. Nevill, *Benares: A Gazetteer, Being vol. XXVI of the District Gazetters of the United Provinces of Agra and Oudh* (Lucknow, 1922), Preface, dated Dec. 1907. Among other major colonial writings of the period, the Rev. M. A. Sherring, *Benares, the Sacred City of the Hindus* (1868; reprinted Delhi, 1975), and E. B. Havell, *Benares, the Sacred City* (London, 1905) agree in almost every particular with Buyers' account of 1848.

is not simply to point out the discrepancies existing in the earliest
and most 'authoritative' accounts of the 1809 outbreak, although
these are striking enough. It is to suggest that even the 'bare facts'
of the situation were constructed—and constructed out of the
prejudices, biases and 'common sense' of the writers.

What I propose to do in the remainder of this paper is to examine
the principal features of this construction. I shall go about this task in
two ways. First, I shall try to trace the steps whereby differences
on major points of fact may have crept into the colonial accounts
of the Banaras events of 1809. How did figures of 28 or 29 people
killed and 70 wounded, which Mill put at about 20 Muslims killed
and 70 wounded,[15] get inflated so dramatically in the *Gazetteer*
of 1907 and the government memorandum of 1928 to 'several
hundred' killed? How did the site of the initial outbreak shift from
the Lat Bhairava, in the open area a mile outside the limits of the
city, to the Bisheshwar (or Vishwanath) temple in the very heart
of it? What accounts for the displacement of the 'cause' of the
conflict from the pollution and breaking down of the Lat Bhairava,
to the 'frenzy' excited by Muharram lamentations, to a clash
between Holi and Muharram processions, to 'friction' over
the mosque built by Aurangzeb at the Gyanvapi, the site of the
Vishwanath temple?

Secondly, I shall argue that the reconstruction of the Banaras
riots in colonialist discourse, in its successive recessions spread
over a hundred years or so, amounts to the making of a narrative
form of strategic importance for the analysis of Indian politics.
This is a form of representation of communal riots which assumes,
over time, the importance of a master narrative and acts as a sort
of model for all descriptions, and hence evaluations, of communal
riots in official (and, I might add, nationalist) prose. In the colonial
case, this communal riot narrative, as we have called it, is simultaneously and necessarily a statement on the Indian 'past'.

---

[15] See Mill and Wilson (1858). Mill apparently took note only of casualties
reported during the worst phase of the violence on 22 Oct. 1809.

III

In order to examine the basic features of this narrative, we may analyse the colonial accounts of the 1809 Banaras riots under three broad headings: (1) the question of 'origins' or 'causes'; (2) the identification of rival crowds and the description of collective actions; (3) the reduction of these actions to a law-and-order problem, a part of the history of colonial administration. The concern with 'origins' is evident from some of the earliest reports of the Banaras riots. This is how the matter is dealt with in a detailed letter written by the local Magistrate, W. W. Bird, to the government less than a week after the suppression of the violence.

At the site of the Lat Bhairava where, according to this report, a mosque and Imambarah[16] had been erected in the days of Aurangzeb, there was also a mud construction which housed an image of Hanuman. A Nagar Brahman tried to convert this shrine into one of stone in fulfilment of a vow. This was resisted by Muslim weavers who worshipped there on the ground that the stone construction would be an encroachment on 'the *masjid* which surrounds the Laut'. The Hindus and Muslims involved in the dispute agreed to wait until after the Dasehra holidays, which ended on 19 October 1809, and then refer the matter to the court. However, on the evening of 20 October, 'the Joolahirs [Julahas, Muslim weavers], instead of referring, assembled suddenly at the Laut to decide their differences in person' committed 'those indignities' (that is, the pollution of the Lat Bhairava) that led to the riots of 21 October.

Early on the morning of the 21st, the report goes on to say, large numbers of Hindus 'of all cast[e]s, especially Nagirs, Goshaieens, and Rajepoots' gathered and, after some hesitation, did some damage to the Imambarah that stood adjacent to the Lat. Upon this, Muslim weavers from the vicinity marched to the Lat and upset some of the images erected round about it. Tempers rose and the local police, both Hindus and Muslims, 'partook of the infection'. The *kotwal*, a Muslim, succeeded through his personal exertions, in holding off both the Muslim and the Hindu party for a while. How-

[16] Other reports speak of a mosque that extended into an Idgah, and that is what exists on the site today.

ever, 'at length the Joolahirs collecting in considerable numbers armed with swords and clubs, hoisted a standard, and exclaiming Imam Hoosein and beating their breasts, marched towards the city.' They were reported to be heading for the Bisheshwar or Vishwanath temple, 'the principal place of Hindoo worship in the city.' But they were defeated on the way in a battle at Gai Ghat where a very large crowd of Hindus had assembled: here two or three Muslim Julahas were killed or wounded. Upon this, assembled Julahas 'with great precipitation' retraced their steps and threw down and broke the Lat Bhairava. 'The effects of this outrage on the minds of the Hindus will be readily conceived.'[17]

This account, which we need pursue no further for the moment, perhaps provides a few clues as to where the later colonial writers got their ideas about the origins of the 1809 outbreak. Heber's view that the breaking down of the Lat was the immediate provocation for the riots comes naturally enough, for this was perhaps the moment of maximum fissility when things might have gone in any direction: after this, what was a fairly localized clash became a general fight over large parts of the city, and this moment may well have stood out in Bird's recollections when he talked to Heber fifteen years after these events.

Prinsep seems to have been the originator of the view that Muslim lamentations at the Muharram were responsible for the tension that led to the outbreak (see Table 2). It is possible that he obtained this idea from the report that, on 21 October 1809, a large body of Julahas marched towards the Vishwanath temple 'armed with swords and clubs, (carrying) a standard... exclaiming Imam Hoosein and beating their breasts'.[18]

Muharram refers to the ten-day period of mourning in the first month of the Muslim year which Muslims, especially Shias, observe in memory of the martyrs Imam Hasan and Imam Husain who lost their lives in battle at the Karbala. While orthodox Sunnis are supposed to take no part in this ritual, in the past Muslims of all persuasions, and indeed large numbers of Hindus too, in

---

[17] IOL, Board's Collections, vol. 365, F/4/365, no. 9093, W. W. Bird, Acting Magistrate, Benares—Dowdeswell, Secretary to the Government, Judicial Dept., 30 Oct. 1809, Consultn no. 23 of 5 Dec. 1809.

[18] Loc. cit., para 4.

villages and small towns all over India joined in the processions of *tazias* (replicas of the graves of the martyrs) and participated in the recitations of the story of their sacrifice. This public statement of community grief reaches its height on the last two or three days of the mourning period, when the processions become larger, the competition between different groups (each presenting their own laments and recitations) sharper, and the exhibition of sorrow takes on an extreme physical dimension. 'One of the most impressive religious spectacles in India', Crooke writes in the 1890s, 'is . . . the long procession of Tazias and flags which streams along the streets, with a vast crowd of mourners, who scream out their lamentations and beat their breasts till the blood flows, or . . . sink fainting in an ecstacy of sorrow.'[19]

Prinsep described these same proceedings from what he had seen of the 'Procession of the Tazeeas' in Banaras in the late 1820s. For ten days in Muharram, Muslims clad in green and black, 'their trappings of woe', commemorate the martyrdom of Hasan and Husain, he observed. 'The piteous tale is chaunted in the current language by people hired, apparently, for their strength of lungs, who work themselves and their audience by degrees into a phrenzy of grief; tearing their hair, beating their breasts, and crying "Hoosyn, Hoosyn", until quite exhausted.' This was not unlike the Banaras Magistrate's description of the Julahas' march towards the Vishwanath temple on 21 October 1809, 'armed with swords and clubs, (carrying) a standard . . . exclaiming Imam Hoosein and beating their breasts.'

It was perhaps this superficial resemblance that led Prinsep to conclude: 'It was under such a state of excited zeal [owing to Muharram lamentations] that a congregation at the Lat'h Imam-bareh, in 1805 [*sic*], was urged by some fanatic preacher to over-throw and defile the pillar and images of Hindoo worship at that place.' In any event, we have no other evidence of a Muharram procession having been taken out at this time. A Muharram procession, in any case, there could not have been, for Muharram on this occasion happened to come three-and-a-half months later, in early February 1810.

Here, in Prinsep's hands, 'Muharram' becomes a metaphor for

[19] Crooke (1897), pp. 263–4.

the representation of the other. This public exhibition of grief, like its obverse the carnivalesque celebration of joy, is the kind of dramatized and ritualized behaviour that stands for the primitive—once found in the West, still widespread in the Orient. It is that aspect of Oriental life that is furthest removed from the restrained, privatized, 'civilized' life of modern Europe. It is volatile as well: insurgency and violence lurk just beneath the surface here; it is all too easy for the primitive to get out of control. As Crooke (1897) put it:

One of the most difficult duties of the Indian Magistrate is to regulate these [Muharram] processions and decide the precedence of its members. The air rings with the cries of these ardent fanatics, and their zeal often urges them to violence directed against Hindus or rival sectaries. But the English Gallio is no judge of such matters, and his anxieties do not end until he has steered without conflict or disturbance the howling crowd of devotees through the stifling city lanes into the open fields beyond, where the mimic sepulchres of the martyrs are supposed to be flung into a tank or buried.

Or the Rev. C.P. Cape (n.d.):

The annual celebration of the death of Husain undoubtedly helps in some Indian cities to accentuate the differences between the Shiahs and the Sunnis; and the Deputy Commissioner congratulates himself [again the singular form, testimony to the universality of the statement] if Muharram has passed off peacefully. In Bombay, British artillery and infantry have been requisitioned [when? every year?] to keep the excited crowds in order and to patrol the streets at night. . . . When this festival occurs at the same time as the Holi, the authorities in certain towns know that, unless great care is taken, there may be serious disturbance.[20]

Thus: Muharram (Muharram/Holi)→ Excitement→ Violence. Since these are the steps, an outbreak of violence such as that in Banaras in 1809 makes the colonial observer look for 'Muharram' as the 'cause'—and find it! Prinsep finds 'Muharram' in his search for the origins of the riot, Mill and Buyers the compound 'Holi-and-Muharram'.

A similar metaphorical function is performed by the religious

---

[20] Cf. Masselos (1982), who notes (p. 48) that nineteenth century colonia-list observers looked at Muharram as a 'grand spectacle of religious passion'.

sites of the Hindus and Muslims. All the nineteenth-century accounts of the Banaras events of 1809 point to the significance of such sites and the 'irrational' attachment of the 'natives' to them (as to idols, cows, rivers, trees, what have you). Heber's account of the *dharna* that followed, or in some versions accompanied, the riots of October 1809, provides adequate illustration:

The holy city had been profaned; the blood of a cow had been mixed with the purest water of Gunga, and salvation was to be obtained at Benares no longer. All the brahmins in the city, amounting to many thousands, went down in melancholy procession, with ashes on their heads, naked and fasting, to the principal ghats leading to the river, and sate there with their hands folded, their heads hanging down, to all appearance inconsolable, and refusing to enter a house or to taste food. . . .[21]

In the same way, colonial accounts dwell on the double sanctity—to Hindus and to Muslims—of the sites over which the disputes of October 1809 are supposed to have arisen. The Kapal Mochan ground, where the Lat Bhairava stood, was one of several places in the city where buildings sacred to the Hindus and the Muslims respectively stood adjacent to one another. Aurangzeb, they tell us, had ordered the demolition of a number of temples and the construction of mosques 'with the same materials and upon the same foundations', in Prinsep's words, 'leaving portions of the ancient walls exposed here and there as evidences of the indignity to which the Hindoo religion had been subjected.'[22]

Among these constructions, perhaps the most widely talked about was the Gyanvapi mosque built under Aurangzeb's instructions at the site of the old Vishwanath temple. Colonial observers in the nineteenth century were agreed that this spot was 'the chief source of friction'[23] between the Hindus and Muslims of the city; 'a constant source of heart-burnings and feuds both to Hindus and Mohammedans',[24] 'a monument of Moslem pride and intolerance and of Hindu humiliation in former times.'[25] The extraordinary sanctity accorded to the Vishwanath temple was

[21] Heber (1828), p. 325.
[22] See Prinsep (1831), p. 11 of the chapter titled 'Benares 1830'.
[23] *Benares Gazetteer, 1907*, p. 207.
[24] Sherring (1868), p. 52.
[25] Buyers (1848), p. 256.

testified to by the interesting observation in the Magistrate's report of 21 November 1809 that the rumour of an intended Muslim attack on the Vishwanath 'was at first not credited. It was too extravagant for belief'.[26]

These assessments regarding the destruction of temples and the construction of mosques in their vicinity at several places in Banaras, the resulting bitterness and friction, and the special sanctity attached by the Hindus to the principal temple of Vishwanath perhaps help to explain both the shifting of the initial site of the 1809 outbreak in some of the later colonial writings and the *Gazetteer's* exceptional account of its proximate cause. Mill, who obliquely suggested some link between the violence of October 1809 and the coincidence of the 'moveable feasts' of the Hindus and Muslims, went on further to write of friction at the sites where Muslim religious buildings had been erected near old temples as the context for the conflict in 1809.[27] The semantic field from which one could draw for an explanation of Indian politics—'riots'—had been laid out: it was upto the individual writer to pick out the mixture of elements that best fitted a particular case.

The Rev. C. P. Cape, a less careful historian than Mill, referred to the clash of the Muharram and Holi 'festivals', and then proceeded to write with such vagueness about the site of the outbreak that it becomes impossible to tell the exact location of even the buildings he specifically names; indeed it becomes clear that in his reckoning one place was as good as any other as an excuse for the violence. The Muslims were defeated in 'some street fighting' that broke out owing to the alleged clash of Holi and Muharram processions, Cape wrote. They then 'revenged themselves by retreating into a courtyard of Aurangzeb's mosque and broke down the Lat of Shiva, which the Hindus held in high esteem. The Hindus pulled down a mosque, and then the military intervened'.[28]

There is no way of knowing from this account whether 'Aurangzeb's mosque' refers to the mosque built adjacent to the Lat Bhairav (which no one referred to by this name), or whether Cape believed that the Lat was in fact located in the great mosque built at the

---

[26] F/4 41365, E. Watson, Magistrate—Government, 21 no. 1809.

[27] Mill (1858), vol. vii, pp. 336–73.

[28] Cape (n.d.), p. 110.

Madhavrai ghat with its minarets towering over the city (which is still called the Alamgiri masjid) or in the Gyanvapi mosque built by Aurangzeb at the site of the Vishwanath temple (which was in fact the mosque attacked and partly demolished by Hindu rioters on 22nd October after the felling of the Lat Bhairav the day before). But the point is that for Cape's purposes it really does not matter. Processions clash: street-fighting follows: the defeated party retreats and despoils a sacred structure: the other party pulls down a mosque: the military intervenes. This is the structure of a tale. Evil clashes with evil. Good intervenes. Order is restored.

It is not very difficult to see, in this light, why the compiler of the Banaras District *Gazetteer*, writing around the same time as Cape, and more directly concerned to make a general statement regarding the benefits of British rule, should suppose that the worst instance of Hindu-Muslim strife in Banaras in the nineteenth century must have originated at the site of their most obvious quarrel, i.e. the spot where the Vishwanath temple and the Gyanvapi masjid stood cheek by jowl; or again why he should assume that such an instance of fighting over such a sensitive spot amongst such a fanatical people must, inevitably, have claimed 'several hundreds' of lives.[29]

What the colonial accounts sought to do was to give the violence of 1809 a cause and the cause a name (fanaticism, irrationality), thus emptying it of all other significance, including, as we shall see, its dangers for the colonial state. For the point of the exercise was a deeper one: it was to describe the 'native' character, establish the perverse nature of the population and the fundamental antagonism between 'Hindus' and 'Muslims'. This may be inferred from a glance at certain other features that recur over and over again in the colonial writings on the Banaras events of the early nineteenth century: the emphasis on ethnic and doctrinal signs for the identi-

---

[29] Since then this colonial account, considerably amplified, has been widely accepted. K. N. Shukul speaks of major riots both in 1805 and 1809, accepting the dates given in both Prinsep and the *Benares Gazetteer* (see Shukul 1974, p. 281). Diana Eck attributes the 1809 riots to the attempted construction of a shrine between the Gyanvapi mosque and the Vishwanath temple, the clash of the Holi and Muharram festivals *and* the destruction of Lat Bhairav (see Eck 1982, p. 197).

fication of rival crowds; the construction of a diachrony into which these events fitted; and the description of violence as a means of describing native character.

IV

The colonial obsession with ethnic and doctrinal signs for the identification of rival crowds is perhaps best illustrated by the Banaras *Gazetteer's* remarks on the military-police feud that followed the riots of 1809. We have already noted the *Gazetteer's* contention that this feud 'originated, no doubt, in religious differences'. There is nothing, however, in the original correspondence of the Magistrate, the military commanders and other people in Banaras at the time, to suggest even remotely that the clashes between military and police personnel in 1810 had anything to do with religious matters.

If there was a connection with October 1809, it was that the behaviour of the police at that time had rendered the name of the police, in Bird's words, 'generally obnoxious, but particularly to the Sepoys, whose meritorious conduct entitled them in a manner to feel contempt for the cowardice of the police.'[30] When the military guard was finally withdrawn in 1809 and the police restored to their normal functions in Banaras, sepoys going into the city reportedly poked fun at the police. Some of them also persistently defied a magisterial order against the carrying of arms in the streets of Banaras. The incidence of disputes between military and police personnel on account of these pin-pricks increased in August and September 1810. As the season of *melas* associated with the Dasehra celebrations approached, the civil authorities were understandably perturbed about the possible consequences of such quarrels between the two arms of the law and the state, and they urged their military counterparts to ensure strict discipline.

That—the approach of an important religious festival and the apprehensions aroused by it—was the extent of the 'religious' dimension to this feud, which degenerated in the course of time,

[30] IOL, Bengal Criminal Judl. Progs., Range 130, vol. 22, Bird—Dowdeswell, 13 Oct. 1810, Consultation no. 46 of 24 Oct. 1810. The rest of the paragraph is based on the same consultation.

as the District *Gazetteer* has it, into 'a long succession of affrays . . . with Hindus and Muslims indiscriminately mingled on either side.' The failure of the indigenous population to conform to the colonial stereotype of Hindu and Muslim crowd (or for that matter, individual) behaviour could only be 'indiscriminate'.

Such compulsive thinking in stereotypes is evident also in the earliest colonial writings on the events of 1809–11, as we can see from the contemporary official reports of the great anti-house tax *hartal* of December 1810–January 1811: This extraordinary act of protest was described as follows in a letter from the Banaras Magistrate, dated 28 December 1810:

An oath was administered throughout the city both among the Hindus and the Mohommedans, enjoining all classes to neglect their respective occupations [until the tax was withdrawn]. . . . The Lohars, the Mistrees, the Jolahirs, the Hujams, the Durzees, the Kohars, the Bearers, every class of workmen engaged unanimously in this conspiracy . . . during the 26th, the dead bodies were actually cast neglected into the Ganges because the proper people could not be prevailed upon to administer the customary Rites.[31]

To which Mill added, colourfully: 'although the shops and houses were left without protection—the people deserting in a body.'[32]

In trying to make sense of this staggering popular protest, the officials turned to their experience of 1809 and their 'common sense' about the dynamics of the local society. 'Men of all classes and description, from the highest to the lowest, whether Mohammedans or Hindus, Jolahirs, Rajpoots and Goshains included, were all of one mind, and engaged by oath to promote the common cause', Bird wrote in January 1811.[33] The echoes of 1809 are clear. Then Brahmins, Rajputs and Gosains were seen as being the most active elements on the Hindu side, and Julahas on the Muslim side. Now, those who have risen are described as 'Muhammedans (and) Hindus, Jolahirs, Raujpoots and Goshains included'. 'Following the same logic, the commander of the troops stationed at

[31] See Board's Collections, vol. 323, F/4/323, no. 7407, Bird—Dowdeswell, 28 Dec. 1810. Many of the letters and documents from this volume referred to here are reprinted in Dharampal (1917).

[32] Mill and Wilson (1858), vol. VII, p. 334.

[33] F/4/323, no. 7407, note on verbal communication made by Bird to MacDonald at conference held at Mr Brooke's house on 13 Jan. 1811.

Banaras expressed the fact that the Rajputs, Gosains, "Muslims" and other "fighting casts" [sic] might take up arms, especially if the blood of Brahmans or other "religious orders" were spilt.'[34] The Magistrate spoke of how the 'religious orders' had exerted their full influence in favour of the agitation and 'men of rank and respectability' encouraged the huge crowds;[35] and Heber later wrote of *dharmpatris* issued by 'the leading Brahmins' as being central to the process of mobilizing the people.[36]

In all this, the colonial observers neglected the evidence that they had before them of the very different sections of local society that formed the vanguard of the rising in 1810–11 as compared to 1809. The Rajputs, who are described as the 'moving spirits' behind the Hindu actions in 1809,[37] hung back in 1810–11: indeed, on the latter occasion, many Rajput landowners assisted the colonial authorities in their attempts to disperse the crowds.[38] And while many of the 'leading native inhabitants' and 'religious orders' of Banaras were certainly involved in the anti-house tax agitation, they appear to have conceded the leadership, at least in the earlier stages of the protest, to artisans, skilled workers and other sections of the lower classes.

I have quoted earlier the first detailed report regarding the crowds that had assembled, which listed the Lohars, Mistris, Julahas, Hajjams, Darzis, Kohars and Kahars as the 'seven classes of people' who, '*attended by multitudes of others* of all ranks and descriptions', gathered in the vicinity of the city. The Lohars, in particular, were singled out as prime movers of the uprising. 'The Lohars, who originally assembled for another purpose, soon took a principal part in the conspiracy, and have collected herein great numbers from all parts of the (Banaras) province', Bird reported on 2 January 1911.[39]

W. O. Salmon, the Collector, confirmed this in a communication to the government on the same day:

[34] Ibid., MacDonald—Bird, 12 Jan. 1811, and note on conference held at Mr Brooke's house on 18 Jan. 1811.

[35] Ibid., Bird—Dowdeswell, 4 Jan., 8 Jan. and 28 Jan. 1811.

[36] See Heber (1882), vol. 1, p. 327.

[37] See *Benares Gazetteer*, p. 207.

[38] F/4/323, no. 7407 Bird—Dowdeswell, 8 Jan. 1811, and Dowdeswell—Bird, 11 Jan. 1811.

[39] F/4/323, no. 7407, Bird—Dowdeswell, 2 Jan. 1811.

If one party be more obstinate and more determined upon extending the mischief than another, the Lohars, or blacksmiths, may be so charged, for they were not only the first to convoke the assembly of their near brethren, but they have far and wide called upon other Lohars to join them with the intent that no implement of cultivation or of harvest (which is fast approaching) be either made or mended, and thus that the zeminders and royots may be induced to take part with the malcontents, in short that the whole of the country shall directly or indirectly be urged to insist on the repeal of the tax. *With these Lohars almost all other caste[s], and sects and persuasions are in League*, and I am informed under a most binding oath amongst each other.[40]

Many of the most familiar features of Orientalist knowledge are already in evidence here: the typecasting ('fighting castes' like 'Rajputs', 'Gosains', 'Muslims'!), the centrality assigned to the 'religious orders', the charge of manipulation by elite groups or 'leading native inhabitants'. This reductionist tendency naturally influenced colonial descriptions of crowd action as well. Consider once more Cape's matter-of-fact statement on the 1809 riots: Holi and Muharram clash. There is 'some street fighting'. The defeated 'Muhammadams' revenge themselves by retreating into 'Aurangzeb's mosque' and breaking down the Lat Bhairava. 'The Hindus' pull down a mosque. And then, the military intervenes. The message is transparent: *this* is the natural order of things in this kind of society. The sequential order is fixed—as an order of mimesis; and it is accepted by all colonial writers in their description of local politics.

It is the same understanding that informs the Banaras *Gazetteer's*, and thence the Government of India's 1928 remarks on what followed the breaking down of the Lat Bhairav in Banaras in October 1809:

Great crowds of Hindus attacked the mosque of Aurangzeb, set it on fire and put to death every Muhammadan of the neighbourhood who fell into their hands. The entire city was given up to pillage and slaughter; and order was not restored by the troups until some fifty mosques had been destroyed and several hundred persons had lost their lives.[41]

Another expression of the essentializing process noticed above is

---

[40] Ibid., Salmon, Secy., GOI, Revenue Dept., 2 Jan. 1811 (emphasis added).
[41] *Benares Gazetteer*, pp. 207–8.

found in the colonial writers' historicization of the Banaras events of 1809. Given the nature of 'Hindus' and 'Muslims', 'Hinduism' and 'Islam', a violent conflict between the two was always on the cards. The riots of 1809 are represented as part of a continuum, a tradition: 'one of those convulsions which had frequently occurred in the past owing to the religious antagonism of the Hindu and Moslem sections of the population'. Or as Francis Younghusband put it in a book entitled *Dawn in India*, published in 1930, 'the animosities of centuries are always smouldering beneath the surface.'[42]

Judging by the colonial accounts of the strife in Banaras, 1809 sees only a development in degree, an intensification. 'Towards the close of 1809 an open rupture could no longer be delayed,' says Mill, while Nevill states that, 'The ill-will between the rival religions [*sic*] culminated in a sudden outbreak of great intensity in October 1809.'[43] In certain instances, the tradition of conflict is seen as growing out of an actual historical experience—in the Banaras case, Aurangzeb's iconoclasm. Thus in a 'Handbook' on Banaras published in 1886, the Rev. J. Ewen notes that the Lat Bhairav stands on a site appropriated for Muslim worship in Aurangzeb's time but continues to be used by Hindu worshippers as well. He then simply adds: 'The dispute between the parties reached a climax at the end of the last century [*sic*].'[44]

An 'ill-will' exists from the mid-seventeenth century, if not earlier, 'culminates' for no obvious reason, 'reaches a climax' in a 'sudden' outbreak of rioting in 1809. In this kind of history, 'violence' always belongs to a pre-colonial tradition: the imposition of British rule, the displacement of an earlier balance of power, the raising of new hopes and fears, has nothing to do with it. This 'tradition' of strife becomes, indeed, the justification for colonial rule. By the later nineteenth century it is no longer the power of the English sword, nor simply the superiority of English science and commerce, but also the argument that the 'natives' are hopelessly divided, given to primitive passions and incapable of managing

---

[42] Younghusband (1930), p. 144.

[43] See Mill and Wilson (1858), vol. VII, p. 336, and Nevill (1921), p. 207.

[44] See Ewen (1886), p. 40.

their own affairs, that legitimizes British power.[45] Hence the Rev. James Kennedy, after his sojourn in northern India in the 1870s and 1880s, observed: 'The antagonism [between Hindu and Muslim 'systems'], though generally latent, every now and then breaks out into fierce strife, which but for the interposition of Government would lead to civil war.'[46]

V

I have left to the last what is possibly the most striking feature of the colonial writings under discussion and also perhaps the least investigated, in part because it has passed without great change into nationalist writings and a good deal of recent historiography. This is the reduction of Indian history to the history of the state. In colonialist writings, a distinction was first made between the history of local society—wild, chaotic, liable to unexpected explosions—and the history of the state. The impressive efforts at state building in the past were noted, and the early British rulers of India self-consciously modelled themselves on their claimed 'predecessors', the Mughal emperors (and, to some extent, different Hindu ruling dynasties in southern India). But above all in these writings it was the new, colonial state that stood out in contrast to the primitive, pre-political, one might even say proto-historic, character of the local society.

The Rev. M. A. Sherring put the case unambiguously in 1868 with reference to the history of Banaras which was, in his view, 'to a great extent the history of India'. 'While its career has been of long duration', he wrote, 'it has not been of a character to awaken much enthusiasm or admiration. It cannot be said that either the moral, or the social, or even the intellectual, condition of the people residing here is a whit better than it was upwards of two thousand years ago. . . .' In other words, they had no history. But: 'while I look with profound regret on much of the past history of India, I look forward to its coming history with strong hope and confidence.'[47]

---

[45] This line of argument is, of course, already put forward for the annexation of Awadh and other such cases, even earlier.

[46] Kennedy (1885), p. 335.

[47] Sherring (1868), pp. 342–4.

The *Gazetteer* of 1907 also set off this 'past' history of Banaras against what Sherring called its 'coming' history. Thus, the history of Banares during the first part of the nineteenth century, according to him, was mainly a record of administrative development under British rule with the only disturbance of the public peace occurring in 1809. James Mill had made the same point much earlier, when he wrote that the maintenance of peace and order in that city was 'for some time' a 'troublesome' and 'imperfectly' accomplished task. But the 'unrelaxing firmness' of British rule, a 'better knowledge of the British character' and the 'improving intelligence' of the Indians (no less!) 'lightened the labour'—presumably the divinely ordained British task of bringing 'law and order' to these domains—so that ten years after 1809 'Benares was regulated with as much facility as any other city in the territories of the Company'.[48] The altered speed of time here is striking. The 'pre-history' of Banaras, like the history of all India before the coming of the British power, is chaos. And then, within ten years, 'history' supervenes, order is established.

The representation of all popular politics as a problem of 'law and order', and their assimilation thereby to the history of the state, is a commonly observed feature of colonialist writings on India. In Banaras 1809, it is worth noting in this context, the origins of Hindu-Muslim strife were seen as lying not only in the peculiar religious sensibilities of the people but also in an 'unwarranted' act of assembly on the part of the Muslim weavers. The dispute over the consolidation of a Hanuman shrine at the Kapal Mochan was apparently followed by an agreement between local Hindu and Muslim leaders to wait until the Dasehra holidays ended on 19 October 1809 and then refer the matter to the court. However, on the evening of 20 October, the Magistrate's report tells us, 'the Joolahirs, *instead of referring, assembled* suddenly at the Laut *to decide their differences in person*' and took those actions that led to riots on the following day.[49]

Nine months later, while discussing measures that might be adopted to prevent a recurrence of such disturbances, the Magistrate wrote to the government: 'The disturbance (of October 1809) is

---

[48] Mill and Wilson (1858), vol. VII, pp. 338–9.
[49] F/4/365, Bird—Dowdeswell, 30 Oct. 1809, para 7, emphasis added.

found to have originated in the abuse of that privilege which the Natives have been permitted to enjoy, of *assembling among themselves to deliberate on questions of common interest.* I found it expedient to prohibit all assemblies of this nature without previous application to the police. . . . '[50] So that along with its disarming of the population of Banaras in 1809, the colonial regime also at this very early stage imposed strict limitations on the right of assembly of the subject people.

A similar obsession with law and order is discernible in the colonialist accounts of the anti-tax agitation of 1810–11. We find a great deal of writing on the extraordinary caste solidarity, the diversity of castes involved and, as we have noticed, the 'leadership' of the religious orders and the use of religious injunctions, that went into the making of this remarkable *dharna* and *hartal.* Having established the ethnic identity and the religious motivation of the crowd to their own satisfaction, the officials then turned to their other major concern—the question of law and order. One official observed that 'instead of appearing like a tumultuous and disorderly mob, the vast multitudes came forth in a state of perfect organization: each caste, trade and profession occupied a distinct spot of ground, and was regulated in all its acts by the orders of its own punchayet.'[51] But the dispersal of the assembly, an active assertion of people's power, was nevertheless a matter of the greatest urgency. The Magistrate's report of 20 January 1811 is couched in familiar terms: 'It becomes every day an object of greater importance to disperse the people, and compel them *to put an end to their seditious and unwarrantable* proceedings.'[52] There is a return here to precisely that sequential order that we mentioned earlier. Law and order is indeed the only 'order' that is allowed to emerge out of the colonial writing up of the Banaras events. The appropriation of all history to the history of the state proceeds by glossing over, underplaying, even omitting significant areas of the people's and of course the state's experience and activities. Of the two parts that make up the story of a 'riot' in the colonial account—the circumstances and manner

[50] Ibid., Bird—Dowdeswell, 20 Jan. 1811.

[51] See *Selections of Papers from the Records of the East India House Relative to Revenue, Police, Civil and Criminal Justice Under the Company's Government in India,* vol. 2 (London, 1820), p. 89.

[52] F/4/323, Bird—Dowdeswell, 20 Jan. 1811.

of its outbreak, and the process of its suppression—it is only the first that survives as a major presence, an example, in later colonial writings. The significance of the second part increasingly resides in its very brevity—in what appears as the clinical efficiency of the colonial administration. Notice, for example, the Banaras *Gazatteer's* silence over police inefficiency and the possibility of military disloyalty in 1809. The contrast in this respect with the earlier colonial writings is remarkable (see Table 2).[53] The immediate reports from the front in 1809 and 1810 expressed serious concern over the collapse of the police force and the possible repercussions on the military. The police were pronounced guilty of a 'most culpable neglect of duty' and 'highly criminal conduct'; 'both Hindus and Mahomedans composing it . . . exerted themselves to inflame the passions' of their co-religionists.[54] The military sepoys luckily held firm: but there was considerable anxiety among civil and military officials in Banaras at the time as to which way the wind would blow.

For about twenty days in October and November 1809 the sepoys were not allowed time off to bathe, dress, or prepare their food. 'It was deemed advisable', wrote the Magistrate,

considering the delicate nature of the service they were engaged in, to *prevent them* as much as possible *from communicating with the people*. For this purpose they were provided with *mithai* [local sweetmeats] that they might be at all times within the control and observation of their officers.

On 21 November 1809, when a reinforcement of troops arrived from Danapur, the authorities withdrew a good many sepoys from the city, but it was still thought advisable to retain the entire contingent of European officers 'to prevent all intercourse between the Seapoys and the people'.[55]

It was as if all this had been completely forgotten by the end of the century. Nevill's *Gazetteer* of 1907 referred to the sepoys in passing as having restored 'order' in Banaras after some fifty

[53] See also John Malcolm's discussion of the 'alarming' nature of the opposition to the government in Banaras in '1812', as in Dacca, Bareilly and other places a few years later. Malcolm (1826), vol. 1, pp. 577–80.

[54] F/4/365, Bird's letters of 6 and 11 Nov. 1809.

[55] Bengal Criminal Judl. Progs., Range 130, vol. 19, Bird—Dowdeswell, 11 July 1810, emphasis added; F/4/365, Watson—GOI, 21 Nov. 1809, para 15.

mosques had been destroyed and several hundred people killed. Nevill did not so much as mention the police in his description of the events of 1809. There was not the faintest suggestion here that these forces could have done anything but obey orders, that they were—even in the earliest years of British rule—anything more than cogs in a well-oiled colonial machine that arrived fully assembled and functioned with perfect efficiency from the moment of its installation. ('The history of Benares during the first part of the nineteenth century is mainly a record of administrative development'.)

Mill had of course admitted otherwise; the maintenance of peace and order in Banaras was 'for some time' a 'troublesome' and 'imperfectly' accomplished task. But the 'unrelaxing firmness' of British rule, a 'better knowledge of the British character' and the consequent improvement in the intelligence of the 'natives' had cured all that. Here Mill and Nevill occupy the same ground. Firmness, Character, Intelligence. These are the hallmarks of British rule; this is the history of the 'perfect' state that is the colonial regime in India. What the nineteenth century colonial writings on Banaras seek to do, almost without exception, is to promote a picture of the colonial state as a wise and neutral power, ruling almost without a physical presence, by the sheer force of its moral authority. By the end of the nineteenth century, this is established with the aid of a few blind spots: the colonial regime pretends to have no allies, no local collaborators (Mill, by contrast, had mentioned the opportune intervention of the Maharaja of Banaras in 1810–11) and a minimal armed force.

These blind spots are of course nothing compared to those that came to mark the history of the political activities of the colonized as told by the colonizers. One gets some idea of the extent of the distortion of that history from the omission of any meaningful reference to the dharna of 1810–11 from the *Gazetteer's* summary of the history of Banaras in the early nineteenth century. I have earlier quoted Heber's account of the 1809 dharna involving 'all the brahmins in the city, amounting to many thousands', the Gosains, and so on. According to Heber, Bird who was 'one of the ambassadors [of peace]' on this occasion, recalled that

the scene was very impressive and even aweful. The gaunt squalid figures of the devotees, their visible and apparently unaffected anguish and dismay, the screams and outcries of the women who surrounded them, and the great numbers thus assembled, altogether constituted a spectacle of woe such as few cities but Benares could supply.[56]

In his account of the Banaras events of 1809, Heber devotes nearly as much space to this dharna as he does to the incidents of violence and rioting, and his account is followed closely by later colonial writers like Mill and Buyers, Sherring and Havell. Not so by the compiler of the *Gazetteer* of 1907, who does not mention the dharna at all. The *Gazetteer* is equally dismissive of the anti-house tax agitation of 1810–11, during which (by Heber's account) Banaras witnessed a dharna 'exceeding', as 'spectacle' even the dharna of 1809.[57]

Heber is sufficiently moved by what he learns of the popular protest in 1810–11 to devote several pages of his journal to a discussion of the agitation against the house tax. He writes without reservation of the strength and unity of the rising. After elaborating what he understands of the traditional Indian practice of dharna, the Bishop notes: 'Whether (or not) there is any example under their ancient princes of a considerable portion of the people taking this strange method of remonstrance against oppression [*sic*]...in this case it was done with great resolution, and surprising concert and unanimity.'[58] Heber's comments on the apprehensions of the government also merit quotation:

The local government were exceedingly perplexed. There was the chance that very many of these strange beings would really perish, either from their obstinacy (in fasting), or the diseases which they would contract in their present situation. There was a probability that famine would ensue from the interruption of agricultural labours at the most critical time of the year. There was a certainty that the revenue would suffer very materially from this total cessation of all traffic. And it might even be apprehended that their despair, and the excitement occasioned by such a display of physical force would lead them to far stronger demonstrations of discontent than that of sitting dhurna.[59]

Even in this 'sympathetic' colonial account, however, it is the

[56] Heber, vol. 1, p. 325.
[57] Ibid.
[58] Ibid., p. 326.
[59] Ibid., pp. 326–7.

colonial regime that emerges as the hero of the tale. Of the two sides involved in this confrontation, one is made up of an emotional population—'strange (obstinate) beings' with 'strange. methods'—seething with 'anguish', 'dismay', 'despair', but ultimately passive. In comprehending protest as despair, Heber aligns the expression to existential and, at bottom, passive categories; for protest, unlike despair, is deliberate and constitutes a programme of action—Heber relates the event to 'being' rather than to social and political circumstances. In his account the dharna has the potential of leading to more dangerous protest.

The active part in this confrontation is performed by those who make up the other half of Heber's history. The point is best made in the Bishop's own words. The 'wise and merciful' conduct of the officials stationed in Banaras who refused to do anything to provoke the crowds into violence, and the 'wisdom' of the 'Supreme Government' in repealing the 'obnoxious tax'—nothing said here about who imposed the tax and what made it 'obnoxious' in the first place—'ended [the disturbance] which, if it had been harshly or improperly managed, might have put all India in a flame.'[60]

In the less sympathetic colonial account contained in the Banaras *Gazetteer* of 1907 and carried into the reports of the Indian Statutory Commission and other authorities, the colonial regime becomes the exclusive subject of modern Indian history. The *Gazetteer* devotes precisely five lines to the anti-house tax movement of 1810–11, less than one complete sentence. Here they are:

... before peace had been restored fresh riots arose with the introduction of the house-tax under Regulation XV of 1810, and it was again found necessary to station troops throughout the city to repress the popular disorder till the withdrawal of the obnoxious measure in the ensuing year.[61]

It will be noticed that the history of the state makes its entrance here almost bashfully. What we are presented with is a caricature of all that belongs to the history of the community which succeeds in assimilating the life of the community to the development of

[60] Heber, vol. 1, pp. 328–9.
[61] *Benares Gazetteer*, p. 209.

the colonial administration—'peace', 'law' and 'order'. The reduction of the history of society to the history of the state is
complete.

Let us quickly re-read the *Gazetteer's* summary of the history of
Banaras for the first half of the century. 'The only disturbance of
the public peace occurred in 1809 and the following year.' Notice
'and the following year'. Does this refer to a conflict that lasted
from 1809 well into 1810? Or, what is more likely in the circumstances, to a more extended state of being? 'A curious sequel' to
the 1809 strife was a military–police feud that 'originated, no doubt,
in religious differences, but these appear to have been dropped in
the course of time and a long succession of affrays ensued, with
Hindus and Muslims indiscriminately mingled on either side.'
'Curious' perhaps because Hindus and Muslims had got so confused
about their identities as to mix with one another; but of course
this made no difference whatsoever to the essential 'irrationality'
of their feuds, nor to their form which could only be 'affrays',
'riots', 'convulsions'.

'The trouble subsided with a partial reorganization of the city
police in October 1810; but before peace had been restored fresh
riots arose. . . .' Surely a novel understanding of the term 'riots'
and how they occur or, rather, 'arise. . . .' Nothing remains in
the five-line entry on the 1810–11 events of the great crowds that
gathered, the manner of their gathering, the remarkable mode of
their protest, the consultation and decision-making, the perplexity
and fears of the Government and, one need scarcely add, the feelings
of the people of Banaras when they were confronted with the new
house tax. The entry reverts, instead, to the theme of violence and
disorder as the normal state of affairs and the consequent need for
British intervention to establish peace and orderly behaviour.

Here, all political action undertaken outside the domain of
British administrative initiative is represented as a 'convulsion'.
Politics before the era of English-style constitutions in India is
banished to the domain of the irrational, indeed the pre-political—
'spontaneous', 'un-conscious', 'fanatical'. It is a tradition that
historians are still struggling to relinquish.

We may read on: 'Nothing' occurred in Banaras after 1810–11
that was 'worthy of record' until the 'riots of 1852', when some
Nagar Brahmans organized protests against an alleged proposal

to introduce common messing arrangements for prisoners in the jail, and clashes occurred with the police.[62]

Astonishingly, given the record of its ability to smell out a 'riot' in the most unlikely places, the *Gazetteer* has nothing to say about the events of 1891 in Banaras; perhaps the entry on the history of the city had already become too long. But Crooke, writing a general account of the North-Western Provinces of India in 1894, made up for this lacuna: 'Only three years ago, the weavers of Benares, always a turbulent, fanatical class, took advantage of a quarrel over an almost deserted Hindu shrine, with which they had no possible concern, to spread rapine and outrage through the city.'[63] Once again, this remark is made in the course of a discussion of Hindu-Muslim conflict, and it is worthwhile to note what some of the other surviving evidence from this period tells us about 1891.

The agitation in this instance appears to have begun with the opposition of several municipal councillors and other prominent Hindus of the city to the proposed demotion of all or part of a temple dedicated to Ram, in order to clear the ground for a water-pumping station. A Temple Protection Committee was apparently set up, the Sujan Samaj (or 'Respectable People's Society') also took up the cause, 'thousands' of applications were sent to the Collector and numerous meetings held between November 1890 and April 1891 to protest against these plans. There is some suggestion that this protest was connected, at the start, with the desire to ward off further taxation, and that it got mixed up in time with a more widespread fear about the threat to religious buildings, Hindu as well as Muslim, posed by the system of colonial rule.

That is one part of the story. Another is that the large community of Muslim weavers in Banaras was in exceptionally straitened circumstances in this period owing to the fall in the demand for their rich fabrics and the prevalent high prices of all kinds of food-grains. They had therefore approached the Collector to ask for some relief. There is nothing in the official records to suggest a Hindu-Muslim clash over this or any other issue in Banaras at this

---

[62] IOL, NWP, Criminal Judl. Progs., Range 233, vol. 36, no. 1466 of Aug. 1852.

[63] Crooke (1894), p. 187. See also Shukul (1974), pp. 289–94, and L/P and J/6/301, no. 907 of 1891; also Mall (1958), pp. 410–13.

particular juncture. On the contrary, the Magistrate of the city spoke of the 1891 outbreak as the result of a 'league or covenant' between Muslims and Hindus for the future 'mutual protection' of their religious buildings which might be threatened by the extension of water-works and drainage schemes.

Even this suggestion of the Magistrate was questioned by the Acting Commissioner in his report on the riots. He acknowledged that the Muslim weavers were in difficult circumstances and had protested against high prices. 'But the remonstrance of the Julahas about the high prices, though made by a large crowd', he wrote, 'was not made in any spirit of lawlessness'. And

there is no evidence whatsoever to connect them as a body (emphasis original) with these outbreaks. Muhammadans were undoubtedly to be found in the crowd of rioters, as is only natural; but we may safely assert that had the Julahas as a body joined the Hindus, the results would have been far more serious. An excited Muhammadan mob is one of the most dangerous elements in society, and bad as things were in the late disturbances, experience tells us what fearful scenes might have been enacted had the industrious but poverty stricken Julahas joined the well-nourished lazy crowd of 'budmashes' who live on the pilgrims and toil not. . . .[64]

Here, the senior official reveals a marvellous ability to challenge the facile logic of his subordinate without throwing away any of the underlying assumptions—the elements—of colonialist knowledge about Indian society: those 'most dangerous' Muslim mobs that create 'fearful scenes', the badmash or criminal elements that abound in cities like Banaras, 'rumours' such as are always afloat throughout the length and breadth of Indian cities.[65] It was out of such ingredients, found in all official reports, and out of official 'common sense' about the people they governed, that Crooke concocted his statement regarding the 'turbulent and fanatical' weavers of Banaras who spread 'rapine and outrage through the city' in 1891.

One could go on. But this much of the writing on nineteenth-century Banaras should suffice to indicate that a methodical recons-

[64] L/P & J/6/301, no. 907 of 1891, Z. H. Wright, Off. Comm.—Chief Secy., Govt. of NWP and Oudh, 28 Apr. 1891, para 9.

[65] Loc. cit., para 8.

truction of Indian history was in process as the colonial regime set out to systematize its knowledge and consolidate its power.

VI

It is perhaps unnecessary to multiply instances to show how widely this process of the re-writing of Indian history occurred. However, I shall briefly cite two other examples from the Bhojpuri region and one from outside to illustrate how the structure of the master narrative appears again and again in the writing up of the history of Hindu-Muslim relations, which is taken to be the history of the community *tout court*—the Indian 'past'—at least in northern India. The first of these examples comes from the Shahabad district of Bihar. It is one of the 'Notes' contained in a 'Supplementary Report (Secret) to the Government of India regarding the Origin of the Bakr-Id Disturbances of 1917' in that district.[66] The note is dated 31 May 1919 and is written by an official who was posted in Shahabad for a few months in 1893 on special duty in connection with the anti-cow-killing agitation.

The author invites attention to the 'curious parallel' between the events of 1893 and 1917. In both years,

the riots began in the Patna district, but though they were sufficiently formidable there, they never reached anything like the widespread violence and rapid extension of these in Shahabad . . . on both occasions, the Dumraon Raj, alone of all the great Baronial families of Bihar, was deeply implicated to the point of moral conviction, though short of actual proof. . . . Though the disturbed area during 1893 was comparatively small in Shahabad itself, the disturbances covered all the territories of the Dumgraon Raj on the north bank of the Ganges in the districts of Ballia and Azamgarh of the United Provinces.

He notes further that the great zamindars of Tirhut, Darbhanga, Ramgarh, Bettiah, Hathwa, Tikari, and so on, who were acquitted of complicity in the riots of 1893, 'are either Brahmins or Bhumihar Brahmins. Dumraon on the contrary is a Rajput.'

In 1893, the official goes on to say, the Maharaja of Dumraon's

[66] Bihar State Archives, Patna, Pol. Science Dept. file no. 223/1919.

involvement was partly accounted for by personal interest. Brahmans and Cow-Protectionists were said to have persuaded him that 'his inability to beget a son was due to "the complaint of the cow".... The Maharajah of Rewa (since dead), who married the late Maharajah [of Dumraon]'s daughter, was a fanatical supporter of anti-kine-killing propaganda, and had even made himself conspicuous within British territory in this connection. It is believed that he has since blackmailed the present [Dumraon] Zamindar.'[67]

In the events of 1917, however, Dumraon may have been moved more by his ambition to be the undisputed leader of the zamindars of South Bihar. 'The late Maharajah of Dumraon was utterly uneducated and boorish, a man of very limited knowledge and intellect. The present man is of a far superior type [*sic!*], socially and intellectually, and it may well be believed that his thoroughly experienced European Manager, Mr Wilson, was able to do a good deal to steady him and to open his mind to the reality of facts.' But in 1917, the War was not going too well for Great Britain, and Dumraon may well have feared that his traditional rivals, the Jagdishpur zamindars, might not only enrich themselves but add considerably to their status by taking a leading part in the anti-cow killing agitation.

On the whole, therefore . . . there is every ground to believe that the [Dumraon] Raj played exactly the same part as in 1893, i.e. every facility was given to the movement, and the Raj sowars and officials not only did not obstruct but took an underhand part in it, while at the same time every precaution was taken to keep the Maharajah's personality out of the matter. . . .

Finally, the note suggests, in both 1893 and 1917 'extremist politicians' had a hand in the agitation. The Nagpur Congress of '1892 or 1893 [*sic*] . . . was followed immediately by a meeting in the same Pandal in support of the agitation against kine killing, and the riots of the following year were consequently attributed to the decision then taken.' In 1917, as in 1893, Extremist politicians used

[67] Though no larger than Dumraon and other similar zamindaris in Bengal and Bihar, Rewa was a small princely state in Central India (now Madhya Pradesh).

'the unquestionably genuine feeling among Hindus on the subject of the cow, as well as . . . the lawless instincts of the disorderly portion of the population, notably in districts like Shahabad and Saran which had formerly been favourable recruting grounds for the Army.' Ras Bihar Mandal, an important local Extremist, 'headed a large organisation of Goalas, of whom there are many in the affected areas, and who are notoriously as prone to dacoity and rioting as the Rajputs of that area.'

The history of the 1917 strife in Shahabad is here reduced to the machinations of big zamindars and a few 'extremist politicians'. The motives of these 'ringleaders' are to be found not only in their personal ambitions, but also in their *essential character* as a caste or community. Ras Bihar Mandal is a man of 'rascally private character and low birth'. The present Maharaja of Dumraon, in spite of his western education and the steadying influence of a thoroughly experienced European manager, is after all 'a Rajput'.

The circumstances, the consciousness, the aspirations of the people of western Bihar, disappear without a trace, except in so far as the Hindus in general have an 'unquestionably genuine feeling' about the cow, which can be fanned into flames at will; and certain communities are congenitally prone to lawlessness: 'the disorderly portion of the population', notably in districts like Shahabad and Saran which had formerly been favourable recruiting grounds for the army,[68] and the Ahirs or Goalas 'who are notoriously as prone to dacoity and rioting as the Rajputs of that area'.

The specificity of the historical experience of 1917 is also wiped out: 1917 was no different from 1893. In both these instances, the riots began in Patna district (it is not at all clear why this is taken to be so significant) and spread in a far more virulent form to Shahabad. In both, the Dumraon Raj was deeply implicated (although the 'disturbed area' in 1893 was 'comparatively small in Shahabad itself'). In exactly the same way, the organization and activities of extremist nationalist politicians were behind the riots on both occasions.

A very similar line of argument is put forward in a comparison

---

[68] Cf. the Bihar governments's observation in 1942 on the notoriously . . . criminal district of Saran, in Mansergh (1971), p. 789.

of the 1874 and 1893 riots in Bombay, in a despatch of 26 October 1893 from the Bombay Judicial Department to the Secretary of State for India in Council. On both occasions, the despatch notes, the first group to turn to violence was the Muslims and the scene of the outbreak was near the Jama Masjid. However, the outbreak of 1893 was on a much larger scale. On 13 February 1874, officials dispersed the gathering with comparative ease, and the crowd broke up with apparently no plans of further violence, for it was not till the 15th that further trouble occurred near the Muslim cemetery.

The outbreak in 1893 was more 'serious', 'widespread' and 'uncontrollable' than that of 1874. The dispersal of the crowd that initially attacked the Hanuman temple would appear 'to have had the effect of arousing the Muhammedan population of the city generally; and, as will always happen on such occasions, the criminal classes . . . were not slow to avail themselves of the confusion. Much of the looting, and probably some of the deaths, are due rather to the depredations and violence of these classes than to religious excitement.' And so on.[69]

Before discussing these accounts further, it may be well to take up our final example of colonialist writings on communal riots in the nineteenth century. This piece of writing relates to a small habitation, not far from Banaras, and like it a centre of handloom production conducted in the main by Muslim weavers, but in every other respect vastly different from that great Hindu pilgrimage centre. Established probably in the eighteenth century at the instance of some Sheikh Muslim zamindars of the neighbourhood, the weaving *qasba* of Mubarakpur in Azamgarh district was a place of no special sanctity or great renown. The parallels between the colonialist writing up of the history of the people of Mubarakpur and their reconstruction of the history of Hindu-Muslim relations in Banaras, are, therefore, all the more striking.

The two-page entry on Mubarakpur in the 1909 *Gazetteer* of Azamgarh district records that the *qasba* had a population of 15,433 people in 1910, of whom 11,442 were Muslims and 3991 Hindus. It then proceeds to sum up the 'past' history of social relations in the locality as follows:

[69] IOL, L/P & J/6/326, no. 10, Judl. Dept., Bombay—Secretary of State in Council, 26 Oct. 1893.

The Muhammadans [of Mubarakpur] consist for the most part of fanatical and clannish Julahas, and the fire of religious animosity betwen them and the Hindus of the town and neighbourhood is always smouldering. Serious conflicts have occurred between the two from time to time, notably in 1813, 1842 and 1904. The features of all these disturbances are similar, so that a description of what took place on the first occasion will suffice to indicate their character. In 1813 a petty dispute about the inclosing within the grounds of a Hindu temple of a little piece of land near a Muhammadan takia [tazia] platform was followed first by the slaughter on the spot of a cow by the Muhammadans and then by the defiling of the platform and of a neighbouring imambara with a pig's blood by the Hindus. The Muhammadans retaliated by cruelly murdering a wealthy Hindu merchant of the place named Rikhai Sahu, by plundering and burning his house and by defacing a handsome temple which he had erected. Hereupon the whole Hindu population of the vicinity rose and a sanguinary battle ensued in which the Muhammadans were overpowered after many had been killed and wounded on both sides. The inhabitants of the town fled and the place was given up to plunder for some days till a magistrate arrived with troops from Gorakhpur and restored order. Similar disturbances occurred in 1893–94 and punitive police were quartered on the town for several months.[70]

Let us note first that this history of Mubarakpur appears as part of a notice on a small and fairly 'ordinary' place in a district gazetteer or handbook; whereas the history of Hindu-Muslim strife in Banaras that we have examined earlier in this paper appears not only in the District *Gazetteer* and other histories of Banaras but in more general historical statements on British rule and on continuing Hindu-Muslim 'disturbances'. As regards the entry on Mubarakpur, I have written elsewhere[71] of the fact that the alleged 'disturbances' of 1893–4 in the *qasba* exist nowhere except in the imagination of the writer of this notice (they are, in this respect, not unlike the 'Hindu-Muslim' riots of 1891 and the 'undoubtedly religious' origins of the military-police feud in Banaras in 1810, which I have referred to earlier). In another paper, I have also dealt at some length with the figure of the 'fanatical (or bigoted) Julaha' that appears in this passage as in Crooke's comments on Banaras.[72] Here I shall refer only to the common structure of the colonial argument on

[70] Drake-Brockman (1911), pp. 260–1.
[71] Pandey (1984).
[72] Pandey (1983).

the history of Indian society, whether this is represented in the qasba of Mubarakpur òr the populous city of Banaras or, for that matter, the rural areas of Shahabad.

The first, and perhaps most obvious, point to note is the characterization of the 'past', the pre-British period, as essentially chaotic and unruly. In Mubarakpur, as in Banaras/India, as in 'districts like Shahabad and Saran' (with their 'disorderly... population(s)... notoriously prone to dacoity and rioting'), that was what the British administration—'enlightened', 'orderly', 'rational', 'experienced'—was up against from the beginning. The communal riot narrative, as exemplified in these instances, ranges freely through time and space, unfettered by either. In it, all riots are the same—simply the reflexive actions of an irrational people ('fanatical and clannish' Julahas/Muslims, riot-prone Ahirs and Rajputs, 'the whole Hindu (or Muslim) population' that rises blindly when a religious building is attacked, or such an attack is beaten back, 'criminal classes' who take advantage of this; and so on). The geographical location of an outbreak does not appear to make very much difference, as I have already remarked in connection with Cape's identification of the site of the Banaras riot of 1809; the principal features of the narrative are the same for the *qasba* of Mubarakpur as they are for a *mohalla* in the city of Banaras or Bombay, as they will be for Shahabad or Kanpur or Calcutta. Nor does the date of a clash very significantly alter the plot: the changing conditions of state power are scarcely noticed after the early nineteenth century, the rise of new social identities and aspirations is practically inconceivable, the emergence of new social and political movements appears only to feed into pre-existing loyalties and tendencies. It is well after the end of the nineteenth century that the stubborness of colonialist historiography gives even a little in this respect.

Throughout the nineteenth century and for long afterwards, the colonial narrative on communal strife tends to proceed by identifying the 'first' major riot, that is, usually the first recorded after the establishment of British rule (1813 in the case of Mubarakpur, 1809 in that of Banaras), and then tracing a straight line through to the 'last'—which of course keeps changing with the date of the writing (1904 in the case of the entry on Mubarakpur in the Azamgarh *Gazetteer* of 1909; Kanpur 1931 in the Government of

India file on 'Communal Disorders' prepared in the early 1930s).

In this mode of history writing one may take any two 'serious riots' and they will stand in for one another, irrespective of conjuncture or locale. All that can be usefully compared is magnitude. For a casualty list of the same order as that in the Kanpur riots of 1931, one has to go back to the 'grave Benares riots' of 1809, even though, the official 'Note' adds, 'conditions were *presumably* so different then as to make the two cases not really comparable'.[73] 'Presumably' is a significant word. In such a long time, a good deal ought to have changed. In this slow-moving country, however, it is remarkable how much goes on being just the same.[74] So a description of the 'first' outbreak—1813 in Mubarakpur—suffices to indicate the character of all subsequent strife, just as 1893 more or less adequately explains what happens in Shahabad in 1917, and 1874 what happens in Bombay in 1893 (or 1911, or 1929).

Metaphoric interventions make up for the lack of overt metonymic connections in the 'mature' communal riot narrative, and one might suggest that the frequency of these interventions increases with the passage of time from the 'first' events described.[75] In the absence of detailed description, it is the essentialist signs that represent Mubarakpur/Shahabad/Banaras/India that enable the narrative to move along. Thus, 'fanatical and clannish' entities,

[73] L/P & J/7/132, 'Notes' of 19–20 May 1931, emphasis added.

[74] Hence the same note compares the pattern of rioting in Bombay and Calcutta and Kanpur. The Bombay riots of 1929, it says, 'originated in fights between oil-strikers and Pathans employed in their places and gradually developed into murderous assaults by Moslems on Hindus. *As in Calcutta in 1926* there was a second phase [of rioting in Apr.-May 1929, after the initial outbreak in February] and *a further resemblance with those riots (and those at Cawnpore)* lies in the fact that the disturbances consisted of murders in side lanes rather than riots in the ordinary sense of the word.' Loc. cit., emphasis added.

[75] Cf. Guha's (1983), comments on 'primary', 'secondary' and 'tertiary' discourse in his study of the prose of counter-insurgency. The metaphorical charge is high, as we have seen, even in 'primary' colonial discourse, the 'battle front' reports of officials on the spot at the time of a 'riot'. But indexical interventions increase significantly as the history is written up for a wider public even if this is done within days of the outbreak in question. For an extraordinary example of such writing-up see Reade (1858), who was Commisioner of Benares.

'disorderly sections of the population', communities 'prone to dacoity and rioting', 'fires of religious animosity', 'indiscriminate affrays'—these are the phrases that make for the history of Mubarakpur or Banaras or Shahabad in the nineteenth century as told by colonialist writers at the beginning of the twentieth.

This is of course *not* a history, to repeat a point already made, for evidently *nothing* ever changes in this community. The communal riot narrative cannot but be a history of the state, first because everything in it revolves around the question of 'law and order', and equally because if any change occurs in the local society it will occur (by this accounting) as a result of the efforts and the influence of the colonial state (for example, the education of the young Maharaja of Dumraon and the 'steading influence' of his English manager).

An outstanding feature of this discourse is its distancing of 'us' and 'them'. In the communal riot narrative, as in colonialist discourse more generally, 'rioting', 'bigotry', 'criminality' are of a piece—the marks of an inferior people and a people without a history. Naturally, even the violence of the subject population is distinguished from the often unacknowledged but, in any case, 'controlled', 'rational' and 'legitimate' violence of the colonial state. 'Native' violence has parallels with the violence of the eighteenth-, and even nineteenth century, European mob—hungry, displaced, turbulent—which also on occasion turns to rioting. (Happily, as the promoters of this view at the turn of the century might have said, Europe was fast 'civilizing' its lower classes.) But the violence of the 'native' has other, specifically Oriental, characteristics. It is a helpless, instinctive violence, it takes the form of 'convulsions' and, in India, these are more often than not related to the centuries' old smouldering fire of communal strife. That is all there is to the politics of the indigenous community. That is the Indian past. In the twentieth century a new name would be found for the past: that name was 'communalism'.

REFERENCES

Altekar, A. S., 1937: *History of Benares: From Pre-historic Times to the Present Day*. Benares: Culture Publication House.

Bayly, C. A., 1985: 'The Pre-history of "Communalism?"' Religious Conflict in India, 1700–1860. *Modern Asian Studies*, vol. 19, no. 2, pp. 177–204.

Buyers, W., 1848: *Reflections of Northern India*. London.

Cape, Rev. C. P., n.d.: *Benares: The Stronghold of Hinduism*.

Coupland, R., 1944: *The Constitutional Problem in India*. London: Oxford University Press.

Crooke, W., 1897: *The Northwest Provinces of India*. Reprinted Karachi, 1972.

Dharampal, 1971: *Civil Disobedience and Indian Tradition: With Some Early Nineteenth Century Documents*. Varanasi: Sarva Seva Prakashan.

Drake-Brockman, D. L., 1911: *Azamgarh: A Gazetteer being vol. XXXIII of the District Gazetteers of the United Province of Agra and Oudh*. Allahabad: Government Press.

Eck, D. L., 1982: *Banaras: City of Light*. New York: A. A. Knopf.

Ewen, J., 1886: *A Handbook for Visitors*. Calcutta.

Guha, Ranajit, 1983: 'The prose of counter-insurgency', in *Subaltern Studies II* (ed. Ranajit Guha). Delhi: Oxford University Press.

Heber, R., 1829: *Narrative of a Journey Through the Upper Provinces of India from Calcutta to Bombay, 1824–1825*. London: John Murray.

Kennedy, J., 1884: *Life and Work in Benares and Kumaon, 1839–1877*. London: T. Fisher Unwin.

Macpherson, K., 1974: *The Muslim Microcosm: Calcutta, 1918–1935*. Wiesbaden: Franz Steiner Verlag.

Malcolm, J., 1826: *Political History of India from 1784–1823 in Two Volumes*. London: John Murray.

Mall, Vijayshankar (ed.), 1958: *Pratapnarayan Granthavali*. Kashi.

Mansergh, N. (ed.), 1971: *The Transfer of Power, 1942–47: vol. II, 'Quit India'*. London: Her Majesty's Stationery Office.

Masselos, J., 1976: 'Power in the Bombay "*Mohalla*", 1904–1915'. *South Asia*, vol. 6.

———— 1982: 'Change and Custom in the Format of the Bombay Mohurrum during the 19th and 20th centuries'. *South Asia* (n.s.). vol. 2.

Mcpherson, H., 1932: 'The Origin and Growth of Communal Antagonism, especially between Hindu and Muhammadans, and the Communal award' in J. Cummings (ed.), *Political India*. London: Oxford University Press.

McLane, J., 1977: *Indian Nationalism and the Early Congress*. Princeton: Princeton University Press.

Hill, J. and H. H. Wilcon, 1858: *The History of British India*, vol. VII. London: James Madden.

Nevill, H. R., 1921: *Benares: A Gazetteer*. District Gazetteers of the United

Provinces of Agra and Oudh. Lucknow: Government Press.

Pandey, Gyanendra, 1983: 'The Bigoted Julaha'. *Economic and Political Weekly* (15th Jan.).

————, 1984: 'Encounters and Calamities: The History of a North Indian Qasba in the Nineteenth Century' in *Subaltern Studies III* (ed., R. Guha). Delhi: Oxford University Press.

Reade, E. A., 1858: 'The disturbances at Benares—August 1852' in E. A. Reade, *Benares City*. Agra. Govt. Press. (Originally published in 1852 in *Benares Recorder*.

Sherring, M. A., 1868: *The Sacred City of the Hindus: An Account of Benares in Ancient and Modern Times*. London: Trubner & Co.

Shukul, K. N., 1974: *Varanasi Down the Ages*. Varanasi: Bhargava Bhushan Press.

Subramanian, L. 1985: 'Capital and Crowd in a Declining Asian Port City: The Anglo Bania Order and the Surat Riots of 1795'. *Modern Asian Studies*, vol. 19, no. 2, pp. 205–38.

Younghusband, F., 1930: *Dawn in India*. London.

Chapter Five

Some Unconscious Aspects of Ethnic Violence in India

SUDHIR KAKAR

The need to integrate social and psychological theory in the analysis of cultural conflicts, i.e. conflicts between ethnic and religious groups, has long been felt while its absence has been equally long deplored. Though everyone agrees on the theoretical questions involved—how do these conflicts originate, develop, and get resolved; how do they result in violent aggression—a general agreement on the answers or even on how to get these answers moves further and further away.

A large part of the problem in the study of these questions lies with the nature of and the crisis within the social sciences. The declining fortunes of logical positivism, hastened in the last twenty years by the widespread circulation and absorption of the views of such thinkers as Gadamer, Habermas, Derrida, Ricouer and Foucault, has led to a plethora of new models in the sciences of man and society. The dominant model of yesteryears—social science as social physics—is now only one among several clamouring for allegiance and adherents. It incorporates only one view among many on the nature of social reality and of social science knowledge. Anthropology, sociology, political science, psychology and even economics are all becoming more pluralistic and scattering into frameworks. In such a situation, the calls for a general theory of ethnic violence or indeed (as Clifford Geertz has remarked) of anything *social*, sound increasingly hollow, and the claims to have one science seem megalomaniacal.[1] Thus, without taking recourse to other disciplines and even ignoring the grand

[1] See Geertz (1983).

theories of human aggression in psychology itself—those of animal ethology, sociology, Freudian Thanatos and so on—I would like to present some limited 'local knowledge' observations on ethnic violence in India from a psychoanalytic perspective.

In the manner of a clinician, let me begin with the concrete date on which I base my observations on the first question, namely the origins of ethnic conflict. The data for these observations, and those which follow, come from diverse sources: spirit possession in north India, dreams of psychotherapy patients, eavesdropping on group discussions at the Golden Temple complex in July 1984, and finally, personal participation in large religious assemblies.

The Other in Ethnic Conflict

Some years ago, while studying the phenomenon of possession by spirits in rural north India, I was struck by a curious fact.[2] In a very large number of cases, 15 out of 28, the *bhuta* or malignant spirit possessing Hindu men and women turned out to be a Muslim. When, during the healing ritual, the patient went into a trance and the spirit started expressing its wishes, these wishes invariably turned out to be those which would have been horrifying to the patient's conscious self. In one case, the Muslim spirit possessing an elderly Brahmin priest vigorously insisted on eating kababs. The five women surrounding the man who had engaged the *bhuta* in conversation were distinctly disheartened that he had turned out to be a *Sayyad* and one of them lamented: 'These Mussulmans! They have ruined our *dharma* but they are so strong they can withstand our gods.' In another case, the *bhuta* inhabiting a young married woman not only expressed derogatory sentiments towards her 'lord and master' but also openly stated its intentions of bringing the mother-in-law to a violent and preferably bloody end.

Possession by a Muslim *bhuta*, then, seemed to reflect the afflicted person's desperate efforts to convince himself and others that his hunger for forbidden foods and uncontrolled rage towards those who should be loved and respected, as well as all other imagined transgressions and sins of the heart, belonged to the Muslim destroyer of taboos and were furthest away from his 'good' Hindu

[2] See Kakar (1985).

self. In that Muslim *bhutas* were universally considered to be the strongest, vilest, the most malignant and the most stubborn of the evil spirits, the Muslim seemed to symbolize the alien and the demonic in the unconscious part of the Hindu mind.

The division of humans into mutually exclusive group identities of tribe, nation, caste, religion and class thus seems to serve two important psychological functions. The first is to increase the feeling of well being in the narcisstic realm by locating one's own group at the centre of the universe, superior to others. The shared grandiose self, maintained by legends, myths and rituals, seems to demand a concomitant conviction that other groups are inferior.

India has not been exempt from this universal rule. Whatever idealizing tendencies we might have in viewing our past history, it is difficult to deny that every social group in its tales, ritual and other literature, has sought to portray itself nearer to a purer, divine state while denigrating and banishing others to the periphery. It is also undeniable that sharing a common ego-ideal and giving one's own group a super-individual significance can inspire valued human attributes of loyalty and heroic self-sacrifice. All this is familiar to students of culture and need not detain us further here.

For the psychoanalyst it is the second function of division into ethnic groups, namely the need to have other groups as containers for one's disavowed aspects, which is of greater significance. These disavowed aspects, or the demonic spirits, take birth during that period of our childhood when the child, made conscious of good and bad, right and wrong, begins to divide himself into two parts, one that is the judge and the other that is being judged. The unacceptable, condemned parts of the self are projected outside, the projective processes being primitive attempts to relieve pain by externalizing it. The expelled parts of the self are then attached to various beings—animal and human—as well as to whole castes, ethnic and religious communities. This early split within our nature, which gives us a future license to view and treat others as if they were no better than the worst in ourselves, is normally completed by the time the child is six to seven years old. The earliest defenses for dealing with the unacceptable aspects of the self—namely their denial, the splitting from awareness and projection onto another group—require the active participation of the members of the child's group-parents and other adults who must

support such a denial and projection. They are shared group
defenses. The family and extended group of a Hindu upper-caste
child, for instance, not only provides him with its myths and rituals
which increase his sense of group cohesion and of narcissism in
belonging to such an exalted entity, but also help him in elaborating
and fleshing out his demonology of other ethnic and religious
groups. The *purana* of the Muslim demon, for instance, as elabora-
ted by many Hindu groups, has nothing to do with Sufi saints,
the prophet's sayings or the more profound sentiments of Islam.
Instead, its stories are of rape and pillage by the legions of Ghazni
and Timur as well as other more local accounts of Muslim mayhem.

The Muslim demon is, so to say, the traditional container of
Hindu conflicts over aggressive impulses. It is the transgressor of
deeply-held taboos, especially over the expression of physical
violence. Recent events in Punjab, I am afraid, are creating yet
another demon in the Hindu psyche of north India. Over the last
few years, tales of Bhindranwale's dark malevolence and the lore
of murderous terrorists has led to a number of reported dreams
from patients where Sikhs have appeared as symbols of the patient's
own aggressive and sadistic superego. A group of Sikhs with raised
swords chasing a patient who has broken into an old woman's
shop, a Nihang stabbing a man repeatedly with a spear on the street
while another patient as a frightened child looks down upon the
scene from an upstairs window—these are two of many such dream
images. Leaving aside the role played by these images in the
patients' individual dramas, the projection of the feared aggressive
parts of the self on the figure of the Sikh is an unhappy portent
for the future relationship between the two communities. The
fantasy of being overwhelmed by the frightening aggressive
strength of the Sikhs can, in periods of upheaval and danger—
when widespread regression in ego takes place and the touch
with reality is weakened—lead to psychotic delusions about
Sikh intentions.

Sikh Militancy

Until this point I have used some psychoanalytic, especially
Kleinian, concepts of splitting and projective identification to
understand data that bears on the question of ethnic conflict. More

specifically, I have outlined the origins of certain pre-conscious attitudes of Hindus towards Muslims and Sikhs. These attitudes reflect the psychological needs of the child, and the adult, to split off his bad impulses, especially those relating to violence, and to attach them to other communities, a process supported and reinforced by other members of the group. Let me now use another set of analytical concepts of group identity and narcissism, narcisstic hurt and rage, to understand the phenomenon of Sikh militancy. To avoid any misunderstanding let me state at the outset that I am primarily talking about the militant Sikh youth of Punjab, not of all Sikh youths, and certainly not of the Sikh community as a whole. Also, the word narcissism in psychoanalysis is not used in a pejorative sense but, together with sexuality and aggression, as the third major and fundamental motivational factor in human beings which is concerned with the maintenance of self-esteem. The data for these observations comes from being an observer of heated and anguished discussions among randomly formed groups which were being spontaneously held all over the Golden Temple complex in Amritsar, five weeks after Operation Blue Star. As I have said elsewhere,[3] the aftermath of Blue Star, which heightened the awareness of their cultural identity among many Sikhs, also brought out in relief one of its less conscious aspects. I have called it the Khalsa warrior element of Sikh identity which, at least since the tenth guru and at least among the Jats, has expressed itself in images of 'lifting up the sword' against the 'oppression of a tyrannical ruler', and whose associated legends only countenance two possible outcomes—complete victory (*fateh*) or martyrdom (*shaheedi*) of those engaged in the battle. The surrounding society has of course reinforced this identity element over the years by its constant talk of Sikh martial process and valour. The Sikh youth's acceptance of these projections of heroic militancy made by the Hindu can lead to his overestimation of this aspect of his identity as he comes to feel that it is his very essence. All other qualities which may compromise heroic militancy, such as yearnings for

---

[3] See Kakar (1985). Operation 'Blue Star' was the code name for the army action to clear the Golden Temple of Sikh militants in June 1984, in which the militant leader Bhindranwale died. The operation resulted in extensive damage to the sacred site.

passivity, softness and patience, will tend to be denied, split off and projected onto other, despised groups. The damage done to the Akal Takht—as much a symbol of corporate militancy as of religious piety—reinforced the two M's—militance and martyrdom—the inner counterparts of the well-known five K's which constitute the outer markers of the Khalsa warrior identity. The exaggerated value placed on martyrdom is hard to understand for Hindus since oppressors in *their* mythology—the Hindu equivalent of Sikh legendary history—tended to be destroyed by divine intervention rather than by the sacrifice of martyrs.

The army action was then a hurt to Sikh religious sentiments in a very different way from the sense in which a Hindu understands the term. It was an affront to group narcissism, to a shared grandiose self. The consequent feelings were of narcisstic hurt and rage. This was brought home to me again and again as I listened to groups of anguished men and women in front of the ruins of the Akal Takht. Most men stood in attitudes of sullen defeat, scorned and derided by the women with such sentences as 'Where is the starch in your moustache now?'

Given the collective need for the preservation of this core of the group identity, the Golden Temple action automatically completed a circle of associations. The army action to clear Akal Takht from desperadoes became an attack on the Sikh nation by a tyrannical 'Delhi durbar'. It was seen as an assault designed to wipe out all its traces, its *nishan*—since this is how it was in the past. The Sikhs killed in the attack were now defenders of the faith and martyrs—since this too is a pattern from the past. The encounter was viewed as a momentous battle, an oppressive empire's defeat of the forces of the Khalsa. The relatively heavy army losses are not a consequence of its restraint but a testimony to the fighting qualities of the Khalsa warrior. Paradoxically, the terrorist losses were exaggerated to simultaneously show the overwhelming strength of the army and the Khalsa readiness to die in martyrdom when victory is not possible.

Bhindranwale, in dramatically exemplifying the two M's of militancy and martyrdom, has touched deep chords. His status with much of the Sikh youth today is very near that of an eleventh guru. Initially, Bhindranwale may have been one of many *sants*, though more militant than most, who dot the countryside in Punjab. What began the process of his elevation was his successful defiance of the government—echoes, again of Sikh history, of defiant gurus contesting state authority. In setting the date and terms of his arrest ('*Santji* gave arrest', and not 'He was arrested', is how the people at the Temple complex put it),[4] and predicting the day of his release, Bhindranwale began to be transformed from a mortal preacher to a 'realized' saint with miraculous powers. (And the reputation of being able to work miracles is, we know, essential for those aspiring to enter the portals of gurudom in all religious traditions.) His 'martyrdom' has now cemented the transformation and made his elevation into the Sikh militant pantheon irreversible. The tortures and murders in the Temple complex or outside are no longer his responsibility, being seen as the doings of deluded associates, acts of which Santji was, of course, unaware.

It is obvious that after the army action there was a threat to the cultural identity of at least a section of the Jat Sikh youth. This led to regressive transformations in the narcisstic realm, where reality is interpreted only as a balm to narcissistic hurt and as a coolant for narcissistic rage. It needs to be asked what precisely constituted this threat. I would tend to see the threat to the Jat Sikh group identity as part of a universal modernizing process to which many groups all over the world have been and continue to be exposed. This group though has preferred to change a social-psychological issue into a political one. The cultural decay and spiritual disintegration talked of in the Anandpur resolution are then viewed as an aspect of majority-minority relations rather than as an existential condition brought on by the workings of a historical fate. A feeling of inner threat is projected outside as oppression, a conflict around tradition and modernity as a conflict around power.

Narcissistic rage, then, is the core of the militancy of Sikh youth and Sikh terrorism. As Kohut (1972) says about this rage: 'The need for revenge, for righting a wrong, for undoing a hurt by whatever means, and a deeply anchored, unrelating compulsion in the pursuit of all these aims, gives no rest to those who have suffered a narcissistic injury.' For the analyst, this becomes paramount in the understanding of youthful militancy, the foreground, while

---

[4] This referred to the arrest of Bhindranwale in 1981, after the murder of Lala Jagat Narayan in Punjab.

political, social and other issues recede into the background.

Let me now make a few observations on the question of ethnic conflict resulting in violent aggression, i.e on mob violence. My data for these remarks is, paradoxically, personal participation in largely peaceful and loving groups engaged in religious and spiritual endeavours. Yet many of the psychological processes are common to the two kinds of groups. Both emotionally charged religious assemblies and mobs on the rampage bring out in relief the vulnerability of human individual ego functions confronted with the power of group processes. In the face of these, the 'integrity', 'autonomy', and 'independence' of the ego seem to be wishful illusions and hypothetical constructs. Mobs, more than religious congregations, provide striking examples of the massive inducement, by group processes, of individuals towards a new identity and behaviour of the sort that would ordinarily be repudiated by a great majority of the individuals so induced. They illustrate, more clearly than in any other comparable social situation, the evanescence of rational thought, the fragility of internalized behavioural controls, values, and moral and ethical standards.

The most immediate experience in being part of a crowd is the sensual pounding received in the press of other bodies. At first there may be a sense of unease as the body, the container of our individuality and the demarcator of our boundaries in space, is sharply wrenched away from its habitual way of experiencing others. For, as we grow up, the touch of others, once so deliberately courted and responded to with delight, increasingly becomes a problem. Coming from a loved one, touch is deliciously welcomed; with strangers, on the other hand, there is an involuntary shrinking of the body, their touch taking on the menacing air of invasion by the other.

But once the fear of touch disappears in the fierce press of other bodies and the individual lets himself become a part of the crowd's density, the original apprehension is transformed into an expansiveness that stretches to include others. Distances and differences—of class, status, age, caste hierarchy—disappear in an exhilarating feeling that individual boundaries can indeed be transcended and were perhaps illusory in the first place. Of course, touch is only one of the sensual stimuli that hammers at the gate of individual identity. Other excitations, channelled through vision, hearing and smell, are also very much involved. In addition, there are exchanges of body heat, muscle tension and body rhythms which take place in a crowd. In short, the crowd's assault on the sense of individuality, its invitation to transcend one's individual boundaries and its offer of a freedom from personal doubts and anxieties is well nigh irresistible.

The need and search for 'self-transcending' experience, to lose one's self in the group, suspend judgement and reality-testing, is, I believe, the primary motivational factor in both religious assembly and violent mob, even though the stated purpose is spiritual uplift in one and mayhem and murder in the other. Self-transcendence, rooted in the blurring of our body image, not only opens us to the influx of the divine but also heightens our receptivity to the demonic. The surge of love also washes away the defences against the emergence of archaic hates. In psychoanalytic terms, regression in the body image is simultaneous with regression in the superego system. Whether the ego reacts to this regression in a disintegrated fashion with panic that manifests itself (in a mob) in senseless rage and destructive acts—or in a release of love encompassing the group and the world outside—depends on the structure provided to the group. Without the rituals which make tradition palpable and thus extend the group in time by giving assurances of continuity to the beleaguered ego, and without the permanent visibility of leaders whose presence is marked by conspicuous external insignia and who replace the benign and loving functions of the superego, religious crowds can easily turn into marauding mobs. Transcending individuality by merging into a group can generate heroic self-sacrifice but also unimaginable brutality. To get out of one's skin in a devotional assembly is also at the same time to have less regard for saving it in a mob.

Some Implications

The implications of my remark, I know, are not too comforting. The need for communities, our own to take care of our narcissistic needs and of others to serve as recipients for our hostility and destructiveness, are perhaps built into our very ground-plan as human beings. Well meaning educative efforts in classrooms or in national integration seminars are for the most part too late and too little in that they are misdirected. They are too late since most of the evidence indicates that the communal imagination is well entrenched by the time a child enters school. They are misdirected in that they never frankly address the collective—and mostly preconscious—fears and wishes of the various communities. Demons do not much care for 'correct' interpretations of religious texts by scholars, nor are they amenable to humanist pleas of reason to change into good and loving beings. All we can do is accept their existence but reduce their potential for causing actual physical violence and destruction. The routes to this goal, the strategies for struggle with our own inner devils, are many. One strategy strives for the dissolution of small group identities into even large entities. Sikhs and Hindus in Punjab can move towards a group identity around 'Punjabiyyat', in which case the despised demon shifts outside to the *Purubia* or the *Madrasi*. One can go on to progressively larger identities of the nationalist Indian whose *bete-noire* can then be the Pakistani or the Chinese. One can envisage even larger groupings, for instance of the 'Third World', where the sense of narcissistic well being provided by this particular community needs a demonic West as the threatening aggressor.

A second strategy is, in a certain sense, to go the opposite way. By this I mean less the encouragement of various ethnic identities than in ensuring that all manifestations of ethnic group action—assemblies, demonstrations, processions—are given as much religious structure as possible in order to prevent the breakout of archaic hate. Vedic chants and Koranic prayers, *mahants, pujaris* and *mullahs* in their full regalia and conspicuous by their presence are fully encouraged to be in the forefront of religious processions and demonstrations. Traditional religious standards, flags and other symbols are liberally used to bind the religious assemblies.

Yet another strategy (and let me note that none of these are exclusive) is to concentrate all efforts at the containment of the communal demon on the dominant community. We know that the belief of the dominant party in a relationship often becomes a self-fulfilling prophecy, involuntarily changing the very consciousness of the weaker partner. In India the Hindu image of himself and of other communities is apt to be incorporated in the self image of non-Hindu minorities. Even when consciously accepted, the denigrating part of the image is likely to be a source of intensive unconscious rage in other communities. Their rage is stored up over a period of time, till it explodes in all its violent manifestations whenever historical circumstances sanction such eruptions.

REFERENCES

Geertz, C., 1983: *Local Knowledge*. New York: Basic Books.

Kakar, S., 1982: *Shamans, Mystics, and Doctors*. New York: Knopf.

———, 1985: 'Myths as History'. *Times of India*, 30 April, Bombay.

Kohut, H., 1972: 'Thoughts on Narcissim and Narcisstic Rage'. *Psycho-analytic Study of the Child*. New York: International University Press.

Chapter Six

Communal Riots and Labour: Bengal's Jute Mill-hands in the 1890s

DIPESH CHAKRABARTY

I

On 26 April 1895 the Indian Jute Manufacturers Association (I.J.M.A.)—the organization of employers in the jute industry of Bengal—wrote to the Bengal government asking for 'additional police supervision in the Riverine Municipalities stretching from Cossipire to Naihati', covering a distance of twenty-five miles, for controlling the 'riotous combination' of mill-hands.[1] In the same year the European assistants[2] employed in the jute mills near Barrackpur organized a Cossipore Voluntary Artillery Force to meet labour unrest 'with arms'.[3] During the following three years the I.J.M.A. and the Bengal Chamber of Commerce coerced the Bengal government into reorganizing and reinforcing the police force in the mill areas of Calcutta itself, and of Hooghly, Howrah and 24-Parganas—the three districts containing the industrial belt around Calcutta.[4] A special Fourth Company of the Bengal Military Police was formed in 1897 at Barrackpur, 'whence they could be easily and rapidly moved to any disturbed spot... for employment

---

[1] Indian Jute Manufacturers Association (hereafter I.J.M.A.), *Report*, 1895 (Calcutta, 1896), pp. 4–6.

[2] The owners and managerial staff in the industry were all Europeans, mainly Scotsmen.

[3] *I.J.M.A. Report*, 1895, appendix, pp. 76–80.

[4] Ibid., pp. 32–9, West Bengal State Archives (hereafter W.B.S.A.), Judicial (police), Sept. 1897, A no. 85, Apr. 1899, A nos. 39–42.

COMMUNAL MAP
AREAS AFFECTED BY MILL DISTURBANCES 1894-1897

HOOGHLY

NAIHATI

KANKINARA

SHAMNAGAR

Marked portion shows roughly the area
of ' occurrence of the 1897 riot

– – – Calcutta boundaries as in 1911

– ∙ – District boundary

RIVER

BARRACKPUR
TITA GARH

24-PARGANAS

RISHRA

N

KAMARHATI

BARANAGAR
KASHIPUR (COSSIPORE)
CHITPUR
TALLA
SHYAMBAZAR

0   5
miles

HOWRAH
HOOGHLY

Chitpur Road

Harrison Road

SEALDAH

GARDEN
REACH   CALCUTTA

METIABRUJ

on the occurrence of disturbance among the numerous up-country operatives' working in the mills on the two sides of the river Hooghly.[5]

This was a dramatic change from even the recent past when, in 1892, in reply to a labour commission inquiry, both the Bengal government and the I.J.M.A. had made extremely confident statements about industrial peace in Bengal.[6] The I.J.M.A. in fact stated that it took 'no notice of such disputes' as occurred in the jute mills, and that no strikes or lock-outs 'of general interest or importance' ever took place there.[7]

The events that caused such a sudden reversal of official attitude in 1895 are the subject of this essay. They took the form of a series of riots and disturbances that broke out unexpectedly among the jute mill operatives of Bengal between the years 1894 and 1897.[8] Interestingly, most of these riots turned around religious and community sentiments and not around purely economic issues. The riots show strong communal (Hindu-Muslim) divisions existing among the workers. Some of the riots, those of 1896, were in fact caused by disturbances between Hindus and Muslims. A prominent example of the issues involved in such communal riots is seen in the Muslim worker's desire to kill cows on the occasion of festivals such as Bakr-Id,[9] and in the active opposition to this sacrifice by Hindu workers. But there were also instances— some in 1894–5 and in the Talla riot of 1897—when only Muslims or Hindus rioted against the authorities over essentially communal demands. The period, it seems, saw the growth of 'community consciousness' among significant sections of the mill workers.

The official finger pointed to 'the masses of ignorant up-country

[5] *Bengal Administration Report, 1897–8* (Calcutta, 1899), pp. 8–9 ('Summary'), p. 41. National Archives of India, New Delhi (hereafter N.A.I.), Home Pol., June 1898, A nos. 133–47.

[6] N.A.I., Home Judl, Sept. 1892, A no. 280. See also *Report of the Royal Commission on Labour*, Parliamentary Papers 1892 (*c.* 6795–XI), XXXVI, pt. 5 (ii), *The Colonies and the Indian Empire*.

[7] *I.J.M.A. Report, 1892* (Calcutta, 1893), p. 17.

[8] After 1898 the labour market was disrupted for some time, when there was an outbreak of plague in Calcutta: *Census of India 1911*, v, pt. 1, p. 72.

[9] The Bakr-Id festival commemorates the patriarch Abraham's sacrifice of his son Isaac.

mill hands [who] . . . evince now-a-days a greater tendency to combine readily than was formerly the case' as the main source of trouble.[10] The up-country men referred to were the Hindi- or Urdu-speaking migrant workers from the areas now covered by Bihar and Uttar Pradesh (previously called North-West Provinces and Oudh, and later the United Provinces or U.P.). They were indeed the main participants in the riots; from all available evidence this appears to be true, though official thinking about them obviously involved a lot of racist stereotyping.[11] It is difficult to know exactly how many up-country operatives there were at the jute mills in 1900. The census data do not help. However, an inquiry in June 1895 by one Mr Pratt, a deputy commissioner of police, revealed that out of about 70,000 jute mill workers surveyed, between 35,000 and 40,000 were 'inhabitants of the congested districts of the North Western Provinces and Bihar'.[12] Another estimate for 1901 put the up-country share of the mill labour force at more than 60 per cent.[13] This would have been mainly a male labour force, as the female- and child-labour component in the jute mills was always small (never more than 25 per cent).[14]

The sources used here are conventional: mainly government documents, police reports and newspaper accounts. The evidence is scrappy, and therefore much that I say is conjectural in nature.

II. *Early 1890s—A Communal Culture Emerges*

Calcutta and its surburbs appear to have enjoyed a fairly peaceful history of communal relations over large parts of the nineteenth century.[15] But from the early 1890s onwards a communal culture

[10] W.B.S.A. Jdl. Pol., Sept. 1897, A no. 92; Bengal Chamber of Commerce (hereafter B.C.C.), *Report, Feb. 1895-Jan. 1896*, 2 vols. (Calcutta, 1896), II, pp. 695–6.

[11] By 1898, up-country men were described as having 'unknown antecedents . . . extremely excitable at times and . . . likely to act together.' N.A.I., Home Pol., June 1898, A nos. 133–47.

[12] Cited in *The Report of the Labour Enquiry Committee* (Calcutta, 1896), para 10.

[13] See Das Gupta (1976), p. 296.

[14] See Mukherjee (1948), p. 210.

[15] S. N. Mukherjee's current research on the social history of Calcutta in the period 1806–66 confirms this impression: personal communication to me.

grew in the northern parts of Calcutta and its northern suburbs, areas which had concentrations of immigrant merchants and labourers.[16] The first recorded Muslim riot broke out at Shyambazar in north Calcutta in 1891. The issue was the demolition of a building alleged to be a mosque.[17] Interestingly, the 5000 strong crowd in the riot had a very large up-country component, mostly Jolahas, members of a Muslim weaving caste from Bihar and U.P.[18] Immediately after the Shyambazar riot several incidents of conflict between Hindus and Muslims took place in the area loosely described as Chitpur, especially at Machuabazar which had a large settlement of immigrant Muslims.[19] The Urdu press of the city reported in detail the Hindu-Muslim 'kine-killing riots' of Bihar and U.P. of the early 1890s.[20] In 1894 the Muslim leaders of the city—most of them Urdu-speaking—memorialized the government on the subject of its circular restricting cow-killing in the Bengal municipalities.[21] Earlier, in October 1893, the Muslim butchers of Calcutta were complaining about 'the conduct of the Hindus in not selling cows to them'.[22] About the same time, a

[16] Compare the surprise in the contemporary Bengali press by the Muslim riot of 1891, the first in the city: 'No riot of this nature ever occurred in Calcutta. Why were the Mahomedans so excited?' *Report on Native Press (Bengal)* (hereafter R.N.P.B.), week ending 23 May 1891. For a description of the social and cultural aspects of life in the northern parts of the city (the area covered by Burrabazar, Chitpur and Kashipur), see Broomfield (1968), pp. 10–14.

[17] This was to become a frequent issue for rioting in north Calcutta throughout the 1890s. The Talla riots of 1897 discussed below fall into this pattern.

[18] N.A.I. Home Public, June 1891, A nos. 63–7. By 1900, weavers in the jute mills were usually Jolahas, a 'notoriously ignorant and superstitious people [who] took the lead... in the Calcutta plague riots [of 1898]'. W.B.S.A., Gen. Misc., June 1900, A nos. 1–8; S. H. Freemantle, *Report on the Supply of Labour to the United Provinces and Bengal* (Nainital, 1906), para. 40.

[19] See, for example, *Amrita Bazar Patrika*, 21 July 1983, 'Editorial'; R.N.P.B., 29 Apr. 1893, 6 July 1895. By 'Chitpur' I refer to the area through which the Chitpur Road ran.

[20] See R.N.P.B., vols. for 1893, especially for the months of June and July; *Muhammadan Observer*, 1894, *passim* (only the 1894 vol. seems to be available in India).

[21] *Muhammadan Observer*, 11 Jan. 1894, p. 13.

[22] R.N.P.B., 14 Oct. 1893

Gorakshini Sabha (Cow Protection Society), apparently formed by the north Calcutta Marwaris (about whom more later), started distributing strongly anti-Muslim leaflets in the suburbs. The leaflets created 'some excitement', and 'the Police Commissioner had to stop . . . [their] distribution'.[23]

A significant rumbling of communal demands was also heard in the years 1894–5 in the jute mills. Sections of the mill workers became extremely assertive about observing their religious festivals, including those of Id, Bakr-Id, Muharram and Rath Jatra.[24] Disturbances occurred over demands for paid leave during these festivals. There was a Bakr-Id riot, for instance, at Baranagar Jute Mills in 1894, and 'a little disturbance' at Kamarhati Jute Mills where the Muslim workers were refused leave.[25] In 1895 similar riots took place at the mills in Titagarh, Baranagar and Kamarhati. At the Gourepore Jute and Oil Mills, Muslims demanded holidays for the Id, Bakr-Id and Muharram festivals, while Hindus asked for leave on the day of Rath Jatra.[26] The Empress of India Cotton Mills granted such leave, and so did the Victoria Jute Mills in Hooghly, where the Hindus also 'were given half a day for Rath Jatra'.[27] At the cotton mills at Shamnagar no holidays were given for Rath Jatra or Muharram. The mill-hands therefore took them 'forcibly' by 'threatening' the mill with a strike. At the adjoining Shamnagar Jute Mills, where only three hours' leave had been granted for Id

[23] R.N.P.B., 2 Sept. 1893. The leaflet had 'pictures representing a cow with the names of the Hindu deities inscribed on its body, and about to be attacked by a butcher, knife in hand', who represented the Muslims. The leaflet bore a remarkable similarity to those distributed by Hindus during the cow-killing riots in Bihar and UP at this time. See N.A.I., Home (Public), Dec. 1893, A no. 212.

[24] The Id festival occurs at the end of Ramadan, the ninth month of the Muslim year during which strict fasting is observed during daylight hours. The Muharram festival celebrates the end of the period of fasting and public mourning observed during the first month of the Muslim year in commemoration of the deaths of Hassan and Husain. Rath Jatra is the chariot festival of the Hindus.

[25] W.B.S.A., Jdl. (Pol.), Jan. 1896, A nos. 6–11.

[26] *I.J.M.A. Report*, 1896 (Calcutta, 1897), appendix, pp. 76–80. The Hindus were probably too divided by caste to have the same festivals for all. This may explain the Muslim preponderance in the area.

[27] W.B.S.A., Jdl. (Pol.), Jan. 1896, A nos. 6–11.

and Bakr-Id, the 'coolies determined to take, and took, a whole day at the Muharram'.[28] 'A day', therefore, was given at Rath Jatra. Similarly, 'holidays were claimed and taken this year [1895]' at the mills in Kankinara, whereas at the Lower Hooghly Jute Mills, where holidays were 'given liberally', there was 'no discontent at present'.[29]

The most interesting point about these demands is of course their novelty—'Last year [1894] and in the former years they were never demanded'.[30] This new accent on religious and community festivals revealed to the authorities 'quite a new attitude on the part of the mill coolies'.[31] Thus the Baranagar Jute Mill workers in 1895 were reportedly 'more exacting than they had been hitherto. . . . Last year they had no Muharram holidays at all, but this year they took them'.[32]

The demands also reveal a new community consciousness on the part of the workers. The Muslim worker was emphasizing the Muslim part of this identity, while the Hindu emphasized the Hindu part. In 1894–5 this did not yet lead to communal (that is Hindu-Muslim) conflicts,[33] but the 1896 Bakr-Id riots in the jute mills were indeed communal. As our discussion of these and the 1897 riot will show, such community consciousness on the part of the mill worker, especially the migrant, was only to grow over time both in its depth and spread.

III. *The Mill Riots of 1856*

The Bakr-Id riot at Titagarh in 1896 started when Mahomed Hossain, an up-country bricklayer working at the construction site of the Standard Jute Mills, brought in a heifer to be sacrificed. The heifer was stolen by a group of four men—Ganesh Lalla,

[28] *I.J.M.A Report*, 1896, pp. 76–80.
[29] Ibid.
[30] Ibid.
[31] Ibid.
[32] Ibid.
[33] The statement needs to be qualified. According to *Englishman* (27 May 1896, p. 5), there had been 'for sometime past . . . bad blood between the Hindu and the Mahomedan employees on both sides of the river in the vicinity of Barnackpore and Serampore.'

Ganesh Misr (both *durwans* or watchmen at the construction site), Chowki (a Hindu bricklayer), and Ghamundi (a caterer employed by a firm of contractors, Anderson Wallace and Company).[34] These men (Lalla and Misr suggesting up-country origin) were opposed to the sacrifice of cows on Bakr-Id. In the ensuing riots, however, workers of the neighbouring Titagarh Paper Mills and the Titagarh Jute Mills joined in, taking sides according to communal allegiance. Word had spread from the 'Titaghur mosque', where about 300 Muslims from neighbouring areas congregated on the morning of Bakr-Id and where Mahomed Hossain and other Muslim brick-layers had gone to say their prayers. About '300 or more Hindus and 180 Mahomedans' took part in the riot where slogans like 'Mar Hindu sala log (Beat up the blasted Hindus!)' were frequently shouted in frenzied outbursts.[35] A newspaper account of some of the principal Muslims accused (and later convicted) in the case gives an idea of the kind of people involved in the riot: 'Dhanuk [Sheik] is a boiler maker ["the second boiler sirdar" in the Titagarh Paper Millsl], Shamad Ali a labourer but [who] now sells vege-tables; Roja [Sheikh] is a coolie in the old Jute Mills; Ramjan [Sheikh] used to work in the paper mills, but now works in the Jute Mills'—where Sukur, another of the accused, was also emp-loyed.[36] These men fought for their right to sacrifice cows on Bakr-Id. Obviously a feeling of community embraced them all— the relatively skilled, the unskilled and the former factory worker.

The Bakr-Id riot at the Lower Hooghly Jute Mill also witnessed conflict between Hindu and Muslim immigrants. Here too, on the day of Bakr-Id, the Muslims sacrificed a cow, and in revenge some Chamars and Dosadhs (low-caste up-country Hindus) killed a pig within the mill premises.[37] It was reported that the 'low-caste Hindus gave out that they [too] would have a . . . porab [festival] as well as the Muhammadans'. The night 'passed quietly', and 'the men all came to work the next morning about 5 a.m.'. The mill was short of yarn on this particular day, so the weavers, all

---

[34] W.B.S.A., Jdl. (Pol.), Aug. 1896, A nos. 4–5.
[35] Ibid., nos. 13–14; *Englishman*, 2 June 1896, p. 3.
[36] *Englishman*, 2 June 1896, p. 3; Ibid., 26 June 1896, p. 6.
[37] W.B.S.A., Jdl. (Pol.), July 1896, A nos. 36–8; *Englishman*, 2 May 1896, p. 3.

Muslims as was quite usual, were given a three-hour break. 'During the interval the Muhammadans were talking together, and they asked the manager what he was going to do with the men who had killed the pig'. Passions rose and the Muslims refused to resume work 'till the business of the pig had been settled'. Thereafter the riot started; the Muslim mill-hands were aggrieved that while they had been forbidden to hold their sacrifice within the mill premises, the low-caste Hindus had actually been permitted to do so.[38]

As in the Bakr-Id riot at Titagarh, here also Muslim mill-hands from neighbouring areas showed a readiness to come to help their co-religionists. 'Some outside Muhammadans' were reportedly already inside the mills, and made a demand jointly with the Muslim workers that the Chamars and Dosadhs be made over to them. On the evening of the same day the Hindu employees raised the alarm, saying that a large Muslim force was coming down 'to beat the Hindus at the mill'. At the same time, about 300 Muslims arrived, probably from the Garden Reach and Metiabruj area, in order to 'protect their co-religionists living in the [coolie] lines' who feared a big Hindu attack on them.[39] Finally, when 'a number of Muhammadan employees of the Upper Hooghly Jute Mills at Garden Reach left work [on 26 June 1896] with the object of helping friends in the lower mills', the managers made peace by dismissing the *durwans*. Work was resumed but communal discontent continued to smoulder. A 'large number of Mahomedans' of the Lower Hooghly Jute Mills appeared on 29 June before the joint magistrate of Alipore and complained against the Hindu employees, 'charging them with killing a pig in their presence while they were engaged in their prayers on the occasion of the Bakr-Id, and thereby wounding their religious feelings'.[40]

Communal passions were similarly aroused to a high pitch in the Bakr-Id riot at Rishra (in Serampore, Hooghly district), where Hindu and Muslim employees of the Hastings Jute Mill were involved.[41] The Muslim had made it known in the locality that

[38] *Englishman*, 2 May 1896, p. 3.
[39] **Ibid**.
[40] *Englishman*, 1 July 1896, p. 6.
[41] This account is based on W.B.S.A., Jdl. (Pol.), July 1898, A nos. 52–7; *Englishman*, 29 May 1896, p. 6; R.N.P.B., 13 June 1896.

they would be sacrificing a cow that year, and a petition in protest of the sacrifice was made to Mr Lister, the sub-divisional officer, by Hindu mill-hands as well as shopkeepers, 'mainly . . . telis'[42] of the 'Rishra Bustee', headed by a 'rich Marwari shopkeeper'. One of the petitioners said: 'Eight days ago I heard Buna Mian, a worker in Hastings Mill, say that they would kill cows. He also heard Khuda Mian, a weaver, say [that] three days ago'. This was on 18 May, six days before Bakr-Id. On 21 May Lister received a petition from Muslim workers, headed by one Multan Mian, asking for permission to kill cows, whereupon a counter-petition was submitted by fifty Hindus saying that '*Korbani* [animal sacrifice] at Rishra should be forbidden'.

Lister immediately arrested 'some eight to ten persons who were heard to consult' on the question of sacrificing a cow 'within [the Rishra] musjid [mosque]', and so he also placed the building under police guard. Nazir Mian, the imam of the mosque, who was regarded by local Muslims as a *fakir*, had reportedly been to Barrackpur to organize help from the Muslim workers of Titagarh in case of any riot with the Hindus. He had also sent a letter to Calcutta asking for men to fight the Hindus. The letter was intercepted and Nazir Mian was arrested when he returned on the eve of Bakr-Id. Cow sacrifice was forbidden. On 24 May, the first day of Bakr-Id, the whole area was tense. Both Hindu and Muslim mill-hands refused to go to work and spent the day keeping an eye on each other. Only measures which included a strong police detachment near the mosque forced stoppage of 'Ingress of Mahomedans into the town', and bands of constables patrolling all over the town succeeded in preventing a riot.

IV. *Cow Killing: An Imported Issue*

What is the import of this sudden emphasis placed by mill-hands on communal issues such as cow-killing?

The very fact that cow-killing became such an important issue in the 1894–6 riots strongly suggests the up-country social origins of the rioters. For cow-killing riots had never been seen in Bengal to any significant extent,[43] whereas they raged in districts of Bihar

---

[42] *Teli*, literally 'oil pressers', traditional money-lenders in Bengal.

[43] Compare the reaction of a Bengali newspaper to the mill riots of 1896:

and U.P. such as Ballia, Benares, Azamgarh, Arrah, Saran, Gaya and Patna throughout the years 1888–93, i.e. the period just preceding the troubled years at the Calcutta jute mills.[44] The districts affected were also typically the supply areas for immigrant labourers in Bengal's jute mills and other industries. 'Cow-killing' thus seems to have been an 'imported' issue. Some observations of contemporary officials confirm this. For instance, during the Rishra riot (1896), Mr J. Laing, the magistrate of Hooghly who had his 'own personal experience in the kine-killing [riots at] . . . Gaya, Arrah and Saran', observed that 'the disturbing element at Rishra was composed of the very same low-class, ignorant, religious fanatics whom I had to deal with in those districts . . .'.[45]

As is known, until the years 1885–6, 'all the hands [in the jute mills] were Bengalis'.[46] Later they were gradually 'displaced by Hindusthanis from the United Provinces and Bihar', and by 1916–18 Bengalis formed 'only about a tenth of the jute mill labour force'.[47] It is precisely this immigrant labour force that took part in communal disturbances, and we have to look at the different waves in which they came.

Between 1891 and 1900–1, the number of workers in the jute mills rose from 61,698 to 111,272, of whom by 1900 more than 60 per cent were up-country labourers.[48] If we correlate this with the figures available for the increase of looms in the jute mills (see Table 1), we can see that until the year 1894 there was probably very little addition to the number of up-country men who had been employed in the jute mills in 1890. In 1894 a major expansion

---

'This is the first year in which cow-killing quarrels have taken place in Bengal, and that in the vicinity of the metropolis': R.N.P.B., 27 June 1896. But there were a few minor and individual cases of Hindu zamindar oppression of Muslim peasants over this question, especially in the eastern districts of Bengal (now Bangladesh): R.N.P.B., for the years 1893–6.

[44] See N.A.I., Home (Public), Jan. 1894, B nos. 309–414.

[45] W.B.S.A., Jdl. (Pol.), July 1896, A nos. 55–6.

[46] B. Foley, *Report on Labour in Bengal* (Calcutta, 1906), para. 29.

[47] A.R. Murray, 'Note on the Industrial Development in India', in *Report of the India Industrial Commission*, 6 vols. (Calcutta, 1918–19), VI, pp. 103–13. The story of this replacement is not yet fully told, far less explained, but a good summary of the available data is in Das Gupta (1976).

[48] Freemantle, *Report on the Supply of Labour to the United Provinces and Bengal*, para. 39; Das Gupta (1976), p. 297, Table 6.

took place in the employment capacity of the mills, for the first time in that decade. The process of expansion continued through 1896–7 with the setting up of six new mills.

TABLE 1: Increase in the Number of Looms in Bengal Jute Mills 1889–97★

Name of mill	1889	1890	1891	1892	1893	1894	1895	1896	1897
Champdani	358	358	358	358	358	430	430	430	480
Wellington	260	260	260	260	260	276	277	277	277
Howrah	500	500	500	500	551	551	646	646	646
Shamnagar	458	458	458	458	458	560	560	560	560
Titagarh	260	260	260	260	260	400	435	600	707
Victoria	168	168	168	168	168	340	374	374	374
Kamarhati	320	320	320	320	320	320	459	459	508
Kankinara	310	320	320	420	420	420	420	420	436
Hastings	515	515	515	515	515	521	521	521	522
Budge Budge	460	460	460	460	460	460	460	762	780
Union	350	350	350	350	350	351	375	375	390
Baranagar	769	769	769	769	769	799	809	944	1053
Clive	150	150	150	150	150	162	162	272	272
Shibpur	300	300	300	300	300	500	500	735	850
Ganges Manuf.	403	403	403	403	403	412	413	550	550
India	300	300	300	300	300	300	300	300	354
Gourepore	286	286	286	300	300	415	415	415	665
Fort Gloster	253	253	253	253	253	370	397	500	500
Hooghly						815	815	815	829
Gordon							1848	1848	1280
Anglo-Indian								352	353
Alliance								300	320
Standard								240	240
Khardah								300	300

★NOTE AND SOURCE: Indian Jute Manufactures Association, Reports for 1889–97 (Calcutta, 1890–8). Where no figures are given, the relevant mills were not in operation.

Thus in 1894–7 we have a sizeable component of up-country mill-hands, a number of whom were, in addition, entirely new to industrial work. It was natural that their past attitudes, memories and prejudices would also form 'fresh recruits', as it were, in the formation of a social outlook of this group of people. A telling piece of evidence is the argument which a worker at Rishra gave to Mr Lister as his reason for insisting on killing a cow on Bakr-Id, claiming that 'he should not now be prohibited from so doing, merely because he had changed his residence'.[49] There was thus an 'immigrant mind' at work.

V. *Community Consciousness and the Labour Market*

What was happening, however, was not just a mere transfer of past attitudes into a new situation of industrial work. Life in industry had elements which helped such attitudes to persist and grow.[50] To explain that phenomenon, we now turn to a discussion of the jute mill labour market. In the absence of any significant growth of other industries in the narrow industrial belt around Calcutta, especially in the absence of any significant engineering industry,[51] the jute mills were the most important employers of industrial labour in a market where supply of labour always outstripped demand. In 1911, for example, jute mills employed more than 73 per cent of the factory labour force in the industrial areas of Hooghly, Howrah, 24-Parganas and Calcutta. (See Table 2.)

TABLE 2: Factory Labour in Bengal 1911*

	Number of factories	Number of workers
Jute mills	50	200,446
Brick and tile factories	161	22,019
Jute presses	109	13,842
Printing presses	103	12,171
Cotton mills	18	11,752
Machinery and engineering factories	37	11,714

*NOTE AND SOURCE: Adapted from Das Gupta (1976, p. 284, Table 2), which is based on census data for 1911. The above table underestimates the proportion of workers employed in jute mills, as some of those mentioned would have been situated outside the industrial region of Calcutta.

[49] W.B.S.A., Jdl. (Pol.), July 1896, A nos. 55–6.

[50] Cow-killing riots, for example, were to break out in the jute mill labour milieu even in 1898, while such rioting in the labour supply areas ceased after 1893–4: N.A.I., Home (Public), July 1898, B nos. 80–1.

[51] The slow growth of the engineering industry is traced in Bagchi (1973), pp. 302–31.

Work in the jute mills required a low degree of skill and little rigorous training.[52] Workers therefore were highly replaceable, and since the mills had a pull on the entire labour market of Bihar, U.P. and Orissa, the industry could easily afford to change the social composition of its work-force whenever this was to its advantage.[53] Stability of labour was not in itself a crucial concern to the industry as, over the long run, labour supply was abundant, though there were some periods of temporary scarcity.

What concerned the industry most, then, was a steady supply and control of labour. Also, being a labour-intensive industry where labour alone accounted for more than 50 per cent of the 'cost of conversion',[54] the jute had to find a relatively less expensive means of recruiting and controlling its labour force. For instance housing, which involved capital expenditure, was never thought of as a means of control: in 1897 only 13.5 per cent of the work-force lived in company-built coolie lines.[55] The industry's answer to its problem of supply and control was the *sardari* system.

Sardari, or 'jobbery' as it was called in English, is probably an example of a pre-colonial, pre-capitalist institution being made an essential feature of the process of industrialization in a colony.[56]

[52] The labour process in the mills was simple and repetitive. See Barker (1935).

[53] Thus it is interesting to observe that the replacement of Bengalis by up-country workers in the mills in the mid-1890s took place at a time when mill work was becoming more onerous and Bengali workers had started complaining. Electric lighting was introduced to the mills in 1895. The 'working day was increased to 15 hours, Saturdays included, which involved an additional amount of clearing and repairing work on Sundays', but not everywhere with a corresponding increase in wage. A witness before the 1908 Factory Commission stated that this was the time when the Bengalis came to dislike mill work. See Wallace (1909), pp. 49–50; *Indian Factory Labour Commission*, 2 vols. (London, 1909), II, p. 271.

[54] Buchanan (1934), p. 250.

[55] W.B.S.A., Jdl. (Pol.), Sept. 1897, A nos. 95–9. Calculated from a list submitted by the inspector-general of police, Bengal.

[56] Ashin Das Gupta has encountered jobbery in his research on pre-British Surat: personal communication to me. For an instance of jobbery in Bengal, in the pre-factory days of the early nineteenth century, see Chakrabarty and Das Gupta (1974), pp. 73–5. For a discussion of jobbery as a ubiquitous form of labour recruitment and control in Indian industrialization, see *Report of the Royal Commission on Labour in India*, 2 vols. (London, 1931, hereafter R.C.L.I.), I, pp. 22–4.

Simply put, the *sardar* was both a recruiter and supervisor of labour. He was of the same social origin as the ordinary worker. He had the power also to effect dismissal. He·indulged in all kinds of financial extortions, which included taking a dastoory (commission) from each of his recruits. In the jute mills he was also the workers' money-lender and landlord, and his major economic instrument of control was debt-bondage.[57]

The *sardar's* mode of operation had some crucial pre-capitalist elements. For one thing, he always recruited on the basis of the often overlapping networks of community,[58] village and kin, making such links extremely valuable to the worker. The basis of the *sardar's* social control of the work-force lay in manoeuvring these relationships, and the ideologies and social norms associated with them. *Sardars* would thus have dominated the caste panchayats of up-country Hindu workers which were already in existence in 1890 and which the contemporary Factory Commission reported on.[59] Muslim *ulama* (priests), whose influence over up-country Muslim workers was so visible during the riot at Rishra in 1896,[60] must have had the *sardars* as their patrons and cohorts. For the *ulama* were attached to mosques, and mosques in working-class localities situated in jute mill districts are still named after important *sardars*.[61]

Thus the *sardari* mode of recruitment and control went hand in hand with the retention of community consciousness and other forms of pre-capitalist ideology in the working-class milieu.[62] In

[57] R.C.L.I., I, pp. 22–4.

[58] 'Sirdars [*sardars*] in the jute mill, engineering works, and other concerns recruit in their own native villages and surrounding areas; hence, there is a tendency for people from the same village or the immediate neighbourhood to congregate in the same industrial area in Bengal'. R.C.L.I., v, pt. 1, p. 11.

[59] *Report of the Indian Factory Commission of 1890* (Calcutta, 1890), p. 85.

[60] An *alim* (Muslim priest), for example, declared Rishra during the 1896 riot to be a '*dur-ul-harb*' i.e. 'a country of kafirs [unbelievers] against whom it is lawful to make war of jihad': R.N.P.B., 13 June 1896.

[61] This information is based on my own fieldwork, including an interview (on 5 Aug. 1976) with a ninety-year-old up-country *sardar* in the Bhatpara area, called Ishaque Sardar, who has a mosque in his own name in that area. Note also how mosques figure in all the riots of 1896.

[62] We do not know to what extent local Bengali workers were recruited by *sardars*, but from twentieth-century evidence it would seem they were less amenable to *sardari* control than the migrant as they often lived in their own

the mid-1890s, as demand for jobs grew, the *sardar's* powers increased, and with that the worker's community consciousness became more manifest.

The 1890s were a period of over-supply in the jute mill labour market, when immigration from U.P. into Bengal reached its peak.[63] Between 1891–2 and 1901–2, the net increase in Hooghly, Howrah, 24–Parganas and Calcutta of migrants from Bihar, U.P. and Orissa was 182,536.[64] Even if we assume that the entire intake (48,492) in the jute mill work-force in this decade consisted only of migrants, and that other factories (see Table 2) had an absurdly high rate of growth, employing in this period as many people (all of them migrants) as they did in 1911 (i.e. 71,498), we would still be left with more than 50,000 unemployed migrants in the jute labour belt. When we add to this figure the number of Bengalis[65] who may have sought work in the same areas of occupation, we have a high number of unemployed, surely exceeding 100,000.[66]

The operations of *sardars* could only have added to the actual physical competition in the labour market, as *sardari* corruption (i.e. the taking of bribes for every recruit) usually led to a higher turnover in the mills.[67] The growing crisis of the jute mill labour force in the mid-1890s shows in some of the events of the time. In October 1893 at a Howrah jute mill, 'old and new workmen' fought with each other. 'The former struck work as their pay had been reduced'.[68] There were strikes, and managers were attacked in a few mills. Workers were essentially fighting wage cuts. The Kanki-

---

houses and had their own small plots of land to cultivate. For the migrant worker the sardar, besides being the money-lender, was often the landlord as well. This point has been touched upon in Stuart (1978).

[63] Das Gupta (1976), p. 290, Table 3.

[64] Ibid. The Orissa component was extremely small, so that figure mainly relates to people from Bihar and UP. These people migrated mostly without their families: *Census of India*, 1901, VI, pt. I, p. 142. We may therefore reasonably take this to be the figure for migrant job seekers. For these people categories such a 'dependents' and 'unemployed' coalesce.

[65] The Bengali population of this district increased by 265,613 between 1891–2 and 1901–2.

[66] Some of them would have been absorbed in the tertiary sector, but employment in that sector was usually of a temporary and casual nature.

[67] See Mukerjee (1948), pp. 37–9.

[68] W.B.S.A., Jdl. (Pol.), Jan. 1896, A nos. 6–11.

nara Jute Mills, Dunbar Shamnagar Cotton Mills and Champdani
Jute Mills were some of the sites involved.[69] The scramble for
jobs (especially when the mills were expanding in the mid-1890s)
and the consequent weakening of the workers' bargaining power
is reflected in the wage data. The index of the average real wage
(taking the average for 1890–4 as the base) for the jute mill workers
fell first from 108 in 1895 to 105 in 1896, and then to 91 in 1897.[70]

In such a scramble for work, the *sardar* in his capacity of recruiter
would undoubtedly have been crucial to the worker's life.[71]
Communal connections through which the *sardar* found his
recruits, and therefore community consciousness (which *sardari*
control fostered anyway), would have become extremely important to the worker, especially to the migrant in search of work.
Such community consciousness was indeed revealed in the demand
for holidays in 1894–5. In fact the new accent on cow-killing
in 1896[72] shows a recent tightening of communal bonds, for the
price of a cow was such that it could not be bought without raising
subscriptions from the community.[73]

Community consciousness was then, in a sense, the migrant
worker's substitute for closed-shop trade-unionism.[74] Yet surely
it was much more than just that. In a life characterized by the

[69] Ibid. See also *Bengal Administration Report, 1895–6* (Calcutta, 1897),
pp. 135–6; N.A.I., Home (Jdl.), Dec. 1896, A no. 241.

[70] K. L. Datta, *Report on Enquiry into the Rise in Prices in India*, 8 vols.
(Calcutta, 1914), ii, pp. 194–5.

[71] Indeed from 1893 onwards we hear increasingly of powerful and oppressive *sardars* in the jute mills: W.B.S.A., Jdl. (Pol.), Jan. 1896, A nos. 6–11;
Bengal Administration Report, 1895–6.

[72] Goats seem to have been customarily sacrificed in mill areas in earlier
years, at least since 1892: W.B.S.A., Jdl. (Pol.), July 1896, A nos. 55–6.

[73] In the Bakr-Id riot at Titagarh in 1896, for example, the heifer was bought
for five rupees four annas, while the weekly wage of the weaver fluctuated
between Rs 3 and Rs 6, approximately. The weaver was usually the highest
paid worker in a jute mill. See W.B.S.A., Jdl. (Pol.), Aug. 1896, A nos. 4–5,
Report of the Labour Enquiry Committee, para. 49.

[74] We can now see why the first organization of mill workers, formed at
Kanikinara in 1895, would call itself the Mahomedan Association and have
as its principal objectives the recruiting of more Muslims to jute mill work and
the renovating of mosques: *Indian Factory Labour Commission*, ii, pp. 263–4.

preponderance of men, unstable marriages,[75] precarious living conditions,[76] and desperate gambling in years of rising prices,[77] socialization usually took place along communal lines. Hindus and Muslims often lived in separate *bustis* (slum dwellings).[78] The caste panchayats of the Hindu migrants, or the Muslim *ulama* acting as communal figureheads for the Jolaha weavers from U.P.,[79] would all serve the same function: to fulfil the immigrant's need to hold on to certain constants in a hostile and changing environment. Community consciousness thus also gave to these socially marginal people psychological comfort and security.

This is what made Muslim workers receptive to the politics they received at the hands of the city's Muslim leaders who controlled the Muslim (especially Urdu) press, and from the itinerant 'maulavis and oolamas' who naturally spoke a religious language.[80] This is not to suggest that the Hindu migrant was any less (or more) communal. It was just that for the Hindus, as the following discussion will show, such organized leadership was not available.

[75] In the 24-Parganas in 1890, 'cases relating to marriage rose from 164 to 211'. The joint magistrate of Sealdah observed 'that these are generally instituted by up-country Mahomedans working in the mills, etc., who form *nikah* [marriage] connections with women whose previous history affords no guarantee for their future conjugal fidelity': [Govt. of India], *Report on the Administration of Criminal Justice in the Lower Provinces of Bengal during the Year 1890* (copy at N.A.I.), p. 11. A jute-mill manager, when asked in 1893 if there was any family life at all among his workers, replied, 'Practically there is not': *Dundee Advertiser*, 28 Jan. 1893, p. 6. (I am indebted to Carmel Grammal for this reference.) For the fast-declining female/male ratio in the mill areas, see R.C.L.I., v, pt. 1, p. 10.

[76] Fire and diseases such as cholera and malaria were constant hazards. I have examined the minute books preserved at the Bhatpara municipal office which confirm the point. See also W.B.S.A., Municipal Progs., Dec. 1899, A nos. 242–5; *B.G.G. Report, 1894–5* (Calcutta, 1895), pp. 278–9, 312–13.

[77] See W.B.S.A., Jdl. (Pol.), Jan. 1896, A nos. 6–11; W.B.S.A., General Misc., May 1901, A nos. 34–6; *Bengal Administration Report, 1896–7* (Calcutta, 1898), p. 39.

[78] Hence the expression 'Muslim *busti*'. See, for example, W.B.S.A., Jdl. (Pol.), Aug. 1896, A nos. 6–8.

[79] On the traditionally strong *ulama* influence on Jolahas from UP, see Robinson (1974) and Crooke (1896), p. 70.

[80] *Maulavi* (or *maulvi*) is usually the title of an *alim* (Muslim priest; plural: *ulama*, '*oolamas*').

VI. *Workers and Communal Leadership: A Document*

The character of the social leadership that these community-conscious working men often sought in this period is remarkably brought out in a letter written by the imam of Rishra, Nazir Mian, to Haji (*Hadji*) Nur Muhammad Zakaria, an important Muslim trader living in north Calcutta, asking for help during the *Bakr-Id* riot of 1896:

It is informed that in village Rishra, police station Serampore, district Hooghly, the Hindus are going to create a row during the *Bakr-Id* (cow) slaughter; they say they do not sacrifice here, if you do so, we [Hindus] will create row. Therefore, I request that you assist us. We are poor people and work in mills. You better give this information to Muhammadans in the Friday prayers that it is religious act and everybody should assist as possible.[81]

The letter is significant. Part of it merely shows the poor man's sense of his position ('We are poor people and work in mills'), but the invocation of a 'religious act' and the whole purpose of writing the letter clearly bring out my point about the growth of community consciousness.

The letter, further, suggests a situation. We have here at the end of the nineteenth century a group of up-country workers, acutely conscious of being Muslims, approaching a wealthy Muslim of the city for his support of their communal demands. The haji must have appeared in their eyes as a community leader.

VII. *The Talla Riot of 1897*

Evidence is lacking on the question of how, or what sort of, connections were formed between the haji and the Muslim mill-hands. But we may use the Talla riot of 1897 in Calcutta and the events connected with it to prove indirectly a basic point: a person like Haji Zakaria was accepted by the poor Muslims in and around the city as their protector and guide. It is to men of this sort that they repeatedly turned for leadership in trying to solve their problems.

The Talla riot was the first ever large-scale riot to break out in Calcutta. It started on 29 June over the issue of the eviction by court

[81] W.B.S.A., Jdl. (Pol.), July 1896, A nos. 55–6.

order of a Muslim mason named Himmat Khan from a piece of land at Talla in north Calcutta. Maharaja Jotindra Mohan Tagore held a life interest in the plot of land. Himmat Khan, faced with the court order, declared his hut to be 'a Masjid of long standing'. The 'mosque' was subsequently demolished by the police, and this sparked off the riot.[82] It blazed in the northern parts of the city until 2 July—Circular Road, Machua Bazar, Halliday Street, Bhabani Charan Datta Lane, Thanthania, Harrison Road and Rajabazar being the areas affected—while the mill-hands in the outskirts were reported to be restive as on the 6th.[83] Eighty-seven people were ultimately sent up for trial on charges of rioting, and eighty-one were convicted.[84]

Throughout the history of the riot Haji Zakaria and other leading Muslims of Calcutta figure as the people involved in the events leading up to the outbreak of the riot, as in those which finally culminated in its quelling.[85] In fact as soon as the police had pulled down Himmat Khan's 'mosque', Himmat with two of his Muslim neighbours, Nabbi Bux and Abdul Ghani, 'came to the Nakhoda's mosque in Chitpore Road, and failing to find Haji Nur Mohamed [Zakaria], went over to his house at Amratolla Street, where they informed him of what had happened'. The haji contacted Golam Ariff, a wealthy silk merchant in the city from Gujarat, and the next morning they both went with the 'Talla men' to the house of Maulvi Shams-ul-Huda, where they were joined by Khan Bahadur Seraj-ul-Islam, Maulvi Jowad, Abdur Rehaim and Jowad-ul-Rahim, all of them practising advocates except Abdur Rahim who was a barrister. 'On consultation they came to the conclusion that the land in dispute must be taken possession of and a new hut built on it'. 'The Talla Mahomedans were therefore advised to

[82] Ibid., Nov. 1897, A nos. 12–13, 39–43; *Amrita Bazar Patrika*, 2 July 1897; R.N.P.B., 17 July 1897.

[83] W.B.S.A., Jdl. (Pol.), Nov. 1897, A no. 22.

[84] N.A.I., Home (Public), Jan. 1898, A nos. 55–7; Oct. 1897, A no. 150.

[85] For some days the city was agog with all kinds of rumours about the number of people killed during the riot. *Sulabh Dainik*, 10 July 1897, reported that 'The public belief is that more than a thousand men have been killed'. *Indian Daily News* had the number at 300, while *Englishman* put it at 900: R.N.P.B., 17 July 1897, but see also entries for *Dacca Prakash*, 11 July 1897, suggesting the doubtful character of these reports.

rebuild their mosque [and] to resist any attempt to dispossess them; acting upon this advice the ignorant Mahomedans of Talla, Chitpur, Baranagar and Nikaripara assembled at the spot on the night of Tuesday, the 29th June'—the fateful night when the riot started.[86]

The haji and Shams-ul-Huda were the only two gentlemen ever to appear at the actual scene of the riot, where they addressed a large assembly of the rioters at a Muslim *busti* 'on the west of the demolished mosque'.[87] The haji also tried negotiating on behalf of the rioters with the Tagores, the owners of the plot of land at Talla,[88] but this failed. The haji's importance to the rioters is finally illustrated in the manner in which the riot ended. It was necessary for the haji to issue a religious *fatwa* (decree) before the rioters would calm down. The *fatwa* was to the effect that 'no one could build a mosque on another's land, and that no mosque could be built on a land which is not wakf (Charitable Trust) and if a landlord did not give his permission, then it was not lawful to offer Friday prayers on his land'.[89] The *fatwa* was signed[90] not only by the haji but also by Shams-ul-Huda, Haji Rahim Buksh, Sayed Mahmed Tahir, Haji Abdul Razaq and Sheikh Buksh Elahi, the last two being 'prosperous Delhi merchants trading in Calcutta'.[91] Two other groups of Muslim gentlemen—one of them representing the Muhammadan Literary Society—also issued leaflets to this effect, but '[Haji] Nur Mahomed and others' were the ones officially described as the men 'who seem to have the confidence of the rioters'.[92]

It is true that the physical involvement of Muslim mill-hands in the Talla riots remained mostly marginal,[93] being confined mainly

[86] This paragraph is based on a confidential note by Mr James, Calcutta police commissioner, appended to C. W. Bolton's letter, 1 Aug. 1897: N.A.I., Home (Public), Oct. 1897, A nos. 124–57.

[87] *Amrita Bazar Patrika*, 2 July 1897, p. 4.

[88] Ibid., 7 July 1897, p. 4.

[89] See Ahmed (1974), pp. 201–2.

[90] W.B.S.A., Jdl. (Pol.), Nov. 1897, A nos. 39–43.

[91] See Bolton's letter, 1 Aug. 1897: N.A.I., Home (Public), Oct. 1897, A nos. 124–57.

[92] Bolton's letter, 7 July 1897: ibid.

[93] This is partly to be explained by police precautions and military measures taken very early during the riot to prevent any mill-hand from entering the

to the few mills that were situated either within or very close to the city, including those at Sealdah, Garden Reach and Baranagar. But certain events which occurred some days after the riots had subsided in the city served to bring out the importance and esteem in which the haji was held by some sections of Muslim mill-hands. It seems that they would not come and help the Talla rioters without the haji asking them to do so. That was the extent of the hold Haji Zakaria had on their minds. Babu G.C. Mukherjee, assistant superintendent of police, 24–Parganas, has left a graphic account of the events:

On the morning of the 6th ultimo [July] a letter in Bengali, purporting to be under the signature of Hazi Nur Mohomed [Zakaria] of Calcutta, reached some of the mill operatives of the Kankinara Jute Mill, requesting all true Muhammadans to join the Talla rioters in rescuing the Masjid-Ground and calling those, not complying, 'sons of Muchis [cobblers]'.

The letter . . . created great excitement, and the Muhammadan employees of the Jute Mill applied for an obtained leave from the Manager, Mr Clark, for the day at 9.00 a.m. The mill-hands struck work and marched downwards, shouting and beating a romtom. Some had sticks. They numbered over a thousand. . . .

These operatives came down at the gate of the next mill, viz. the Kankinara Paper Factory, but as there were only 75 adult Muhammadans . . . employed, the Manager Mr Boon somehow managed to make them work on; and so this mill was not closed.

The Kankinara Jute Mill coolies next marched down to the Anglo-Indian Jute Mill, at Jag[ad]dal, a mile off.

The Manager, Mr Thompson . . . allowed his coolies a holiday when asked for, and closed his mill for the day. There were 816 Muhammadan coolies here, including females and children.

The few Muhammadan coolies employed in the adjoining Jute Mills, also were allowed by the Astt . . . to join their brethren of the Mills. At the Gordon only 76 Muhammadans were employed.

This large body, numbering about 1,500, arrived at the gate of the last mill at Jag[ad]dal, viz. the Alliance. The operatives inside, who had evidently been informed of the plans of the operatives of the other mills named above, applied for leave, but having been refused communi-

---

city. For example, 'the Kankinara and Shamnagore Railway clerks were instructed not to issue tickets to any large number of muhammadan passengers to Calcutta by rail'. W.B.S.A., Jdl. areas, see W.B.S.A., Jdl. (Pol.), Nov. 1897, A nos. 16–22.

cated . . . what had happened to the coolies who had collected outside the gate and began creating disturbances.[94]

'A row then occurred', in which the coolies used brickbats in response to the European assistants opening fire on them, and a few were killed. The news of the disturbance spread to the two mills at Shamnagar, the Dunbar Cotton Mills and the Shamnagar Jute Mills, where more than 6000 operatives were employed. The Muslims in the former struck work after midday, 'evidently on receipt of information of the state of things at the other mills of Jag[ad]dal and Kankinara', while some of the 2000 Muhammadan coolies at Shamnagar Mills came out and 'collected on the road close to their busties. . .'. The entire mill-hand crowd was later dispersed by the police.[95]

In retrospect it does seem very significant that all this unrest of the Muslim mill-hands was over a mere letter which had reached them requesting their help, and which was purported to be from Haji Zakaria. The letter being in Bengali, the Muslim mill-hands doubted its genuineness as they knew that the haji 'could neither speak nor write Bengali'.[96] The police later ascertained that the march of the Muslim mill-hands from one mill to another was caused by their anxiousness 'to meet on a maidan and discuss the propriety of accepting the call, and deciding on some plan of action'.[97]

Such then was the influence of Haji Zakaria's name among poor Muslims, both of the city and of the suburban jute mills. Whoever wrote the letter that reached the mill-hands must have relied on this.

VIII. *Zakaria, His Audience and Community Consciousness*

Haji Zakaria was an important member of the Kutchi Memon community living in the Chitpur quarters of the city. The *Amrita Bazar Patrika* described him in 1897 as a 'respectable merchant of

[94] W.B.S.A., Jdl. (Pol.), Sept. 1897, A nos. 101–3.
[95] Ibid.
[96] Ibid.
[97] Ibid.

Amratolla [street]'.[98] The Memons were a trading community from Gujarat who had started to migrate to Calcutta in 1770 following the decline of Surat.[99] In Calcutta they traded mainly in traditional items such as 'hide and skin, [the trade of] which they virtually controlled', and exported 'gums, spices, indigo, tobacco and rice'.[100] Out of this community came many of the Nakhoda merchants of Calcutta in the nineteenth century, and a government document of 1881 describes the haji as their leader.[101] It is this community which later gave its name to the biggest mosque in the city—the Nakhoda Mosque, which evolved out of an earlier mosque the haji had founded, named the Zakaria Mosque.[102] In the 1870s we see the haji running his own firm called Haji Jackariah Mahomed and Company[103] when he was secretary of the Indian Trades Association in Calcutta. In this latter capacity he was considered important enough to be consulted by the government for his views on the first Factories Act proposed for India,[104] which was passed in 1881.

What might otherwise have only been conjectured from the letter of Nazir Mian, the imam of Rishra, can now be seen as reality. In 1897 we have a wealthy Muslim trader who is at the same time a 'religious' man (as evidenced by his founding a mosque) and who enjoys a great deal of social importance, commanding a following from among the more indigent Muslims in the city. The haji's followers were a motley crowd, men of different labouring occupations. In the absence of court documents it is indeed difficult to depict the people who constituted the 'crowd' in the Talla riot. Besides, motives for joining the riot varied widely.[105] But looking

---

[98] *Amrita Bazar Patrika*, 2 July 1897, p. 4.

[99] See *Statesman*, 5 May 1929, p. 10; *Gazetteer of the Bombay Presidency*, 23 vols. (Bombay, 1876–1901), IV, pt. 2, p. 51.

[100] See McPherson (1972), pp. 1–4.

[101] See Shukla (1973), p. 176 and Meilink-Roelofz, in *Asian Trade and Europen Influence* (The Hague, 1962).

[102] Interview on 15 Aug. 1976 with Abdur Razzak, a descendant of Zakaria. The family is still represented on the board of trustees of the Nakhoda Mosque.

[103] N.A.I., Home (Public), Feb. 1878, B no. 215.

[104] W.B.S.A., General Misc., May 1879, A no. 1.

[105] There were the obvious hangers-on who were quick to join the rioting. One such person mentioned in the reports is a Jew called E. M. Cohen, who

through some newspaper reports on rioting at Talla near the site of the mosque, we do indeed catch glimpses of the mob, and can identify some faces—few in number, but they may be indicative of the social composition of the men who fought to save the demolished mosque. There was for example Sheikh Chadi, a fifty-year-old rioter killed by the police, who was a 'thatcher by profession'.[106] So was Gajadhar Kurmi, a fifteen-year-old boy, also killed by police firing.[107] Natra Abdul, another of the rioters, was a 'coolie' who declared in court that 'he and several others kept away from work' during the riot on 30 June.[108] Another accused, Nanku Khan, 'worked in Jetty' and lived in Subedarpara, an area of rioting.[109] One Nabijan was identified as having been among a group of labourers accused of assaulting a certain Mr Slotter, engineer in the Ashcroft Jute Press at Chitpur[110]—Chitpur and Kashipur (Cossipore) being two places where many of the local jute presses were located.[111] Himmat Khan, the man at the centre of events in the Talla riot, was himself a mason; the newspapers[112] carried reports on the 'hundreds of masons and coolies' who fought a see-saw battle with the police throughout the two days of rioting.[113] The commissioner of police later reported that the rioters were composed mostly of 'low class' Muslim weavers, perhaps Jolahas, and 'bricklayers, who were joined by bad characters of the disturbed area',[114] while another newspaper identified

---

was unemployed and dependent on his father: *Amrita Bazar Patrika*, 6 July 1897, p. 4. A part of the disturbance was also created by Marwari grain-gamblers, who gambled on whether, or who, were lately getting 'strict' with the crime: N.A.I., Home (Jdl.), Mar. 1897, A nos. 31–42; May 1897, B nos. 297–308.

[106] *Amrita Bazar Patrika*, 16 July 1897, p. 4.

[107] Ibid., p. 5.

[108] Ibid.

[109] Ibid., 25 July 1897, p. 5.

[110] Ibid., 22 July 1897, p. 5.

[111] Indian Central Jute Committee, *Report on the Marketing of Jute and Jute Products* (Calcutta, 1941; repr. Calcutta, 1952), pp. 166–7.

[112] *Amrita Bazar Patrika*, 2 July 1897, p. 4.

[113] The police 'demolished the mosque as often as the Musalmans built and rebuilt it': R.N.P.B., 17 July 1897.

[114] W.B.S.A., Jdl. (Pol.), Nov. 1897, A nos. 39–43.

the bulk of the rioters as 'up-countrymen'.[115]

These, then, were the poor up-country Muslims of the city who made up the Talla rioters and accepted the social leadership of Haji Zakaria—the mason, the thatcher, the bricklayer, the coolie, the jetty worker and the labourer from a jute press in north Calcutta.[116] These and many other up-country Muslims working in mills north of the city shared certain communal bonds and were, in other words, community conscious. This is reflected in their acceptance of the leadership of Haji Zakaria and in the fact that on the first night of the Talla riot Muslims came over from different places such as Chitpur, Kashipur, Baranagar and Nikaripara to fight the police,[117] and that mill-hands at Garden Reach felt restive on the same night.[118] This is why Nazir Mian of Rishra had earlier thought that his appeal for help from Muslims in fighting Hindus during the Rishra riots would find a receptive ear in the city.

IX. *Pan-Islamism, the Plague and the Poor in 1897*

Haji Zakaria was one of the earliest and most confirmed pan-Islamists in Calcutta. His allegiance dated from the time when the first wave of pan-Islamism reached the city during the Russo-Turkish war of 1876–8.[119] In the pro-Turkish agitation he was regarded as one of the 'most active of Muhammadans at present' in Calcutta, another one being 'Hajee Ahmad of Burra Bazar'.

---

[115] *Mihir-O-Sudhakar*, 24 July 1897, said that the Talla rioters were 'men who had come from up-country to make a living in Calcutta': R.N.P.B., 31 July 1897.

[116] The community consciousness of these men was strengthened by the fact that they were all, locationally, in the same labour market. Thus Sheikh Chadi, the thatcher killed in the Talla rioting, had a son called Sheikh Abdul who worked in the jute mill at Sealdah. At 2.00 p.m. on 30 June, when the son heard that 'his father had been shot by some *goras* [whites] at the Moonshi Bazar', he left the mills with '200 or 250 workmen and went to the scene of the riot' to join the mob: *Amrita Bazar Patrika*, 16 July 1897, p. 4.

[117] See the Confidential Note by Mr James, Calcutta police commissioner: N.A.I., Home (Public) Oct. 1897, A nos. 124–57.

[118] W.B.S.A., Jdl. (Pol.), Nov. 1897, A no. 9.

[119] See Bamford (1925), p. 110, Shukla (1973), pp. 96, 100, 176, and Hardy (1972), p. 118.

The government of Bengal warned that 'the Government of India might perhaps obtain valuable intelligence by directing the Telegraph Department to give information of the messages received by these two men. They are in constant communication with Bombay and the North-West Provinces. They have been appointed as treasures to transmit to Bombay the money raised in Calcutta.'[120] The haji's dedication to the pan-Islamist cause is also shown by frequent meetings held at his house[121] or at his mosque. Such gatherings would be addressed either by himself or someone famous like Amir Ali.[122] Syeed Atreah, the Arab *muttawallee* (custodian) of the mosque, would read prayers for the Turkish sultan's welfare,[123] and delegates from Mecca would be received and heard.[124] On these occasions sums of between Rs 40,000 and 60,000 could easily be raised for the Turkish Relief Fund.[125]

Apparently many of the earlier enthusiasts dropped out of the pan-Islamist group when the second wave of the movements reached the city during the Greco-Turkish war of 1896. In Calcutta a proposed 'illumination programme' on the occasion of the Turkish victory was not celebrated 'except at four mosques', and a proposed message of congratulation never got sent to the sultan. 'A small fund was collected for the relief of Mahomedans who had suffered in Crete, but it has not been remitted, and is not now likely to be'.[126] The lack of response is perhaps explained by the fact that, unlike the years 1876–8 when Great Britain supported Turkey, pan-Islamism in 1896–7 had an anti-British corollary.[127] Most Muslim leaders in the city played a fairly safe and compro-

---

[120] N.A.I., Home (Public), Feb. 1878, B no. 217.
[121] Ibid.
[122] N.A.I., Home (Public), Feb. 1878, B no. 216.
[123] N.A.I., Foreign (Secret), Apr. 1878, A nos. 230–1.
[124] N.A.I., Home (Public), Feb. 1878, B no. 218.
[125] Ibid., B no. 216.
[126] Bolton's letter, 1 Aug, 1897: N.A.I., Home (Public), Oct. 1897, A nos. 124–57.
[127] Cf. the following: 'We have a new element of intrigue and commotion introduced into India by the Pan-Islamist Council in Constantinople, and the closer connection which is being established between the Sultan and Indian Mahommedans': Hamilton to Elgin, 30 July 1897: India Office Library (hereafter I.O.L.), Elgin Papers, MSS. Eur. F 4/15 (microfilm copy at N.A.I.)

mising politics, avoiding mass contacts and concentrating their efforts on demands for more jobs and education for Muslims.

Even in these lean years of pan-Islamism in the city, Haji Zakaria remained a consistent follower of the creed. People who stood by him in this were also the men who had signed his religious *fatwa* during the Talla riot, the men who were described officially as enjoying the confidence of the rioters: Shams-ul-Hunda, 'Haji Mahomed Abdur Rezak, Sheikh Buksh Elahi, Syed Mahomed Tahir and others'. Of course they were not anti-British as such, and showed 'every disposition to please the authorities'.[128] But in their pan-Islamism they did form a 'party', which was described as having been

active in holding up the Sultan as the head of Islam, in representing him as being unjusty harassed by Great Britain and the European powers, and in magnifying his might as manifested by victories over the Greeks. The leaders are Haji Nur Mahomed Zacharia, Shams-ul-Hunda, Seraj-ul-Isalam and Abdul Hamid, the Editor of the *Moslem Chronicle* which has been their organ. All the men who signed the compromise leaflet[129] besides Haji Nur Mahomed and Shams-ul-Huda, belong to the party.[130]

Thus if the men who gave social leadership to the Tall rioters were pan-Islamist, it is interesting to observe that pan-Islamism also formed an important part of the feelings that circulated during the riot. The Talla incident, wrote a correspondent to the *Amrita Bazar Patrika*, 'has its origin in a current of feeling which was inspired by the manner in which the news of the victory of the Sultan over the Greeks were so freely circulated among the Mahomedan population in the country'. 'The educated Mahomedans were the agents in circulating the news', so much so that the Talla rioters often thought that they were fighting 'the cause of the Sultan and the [Afghan] Amir'.[131] The *Hitavadi* concurred in the opinion that the Greco-Turkish war did rouse Muslim feeling in the city:

[128] Bolton's confidential letter, 7 Sept. 1897: N.A.I., Home (Public), Oct. 1897, A nos. 124–57.

[129] The reference is to the religious *fatwa* issued during the Talla riot.

[130] Bolton's letter, 1 Aug. 1897: N.A.I., Home (Public), Oct. 1897, A nos. 124–57. It should be noted that the 'party' consisted mainly of traders and professionals (pleaders), who may have enjoyed a patron-client relationship.

[131] *Amrita Bazar Patrika*, 11 July 1897, p. 5, letter from 'K'.

War news began to be picked up by ignorant Musalamans from their semi-educated brethren, and by the latter, from their educated co-religionists. . . . Ignorant Musalmans now began to talk to one another in this strain—'The Sultan has defeated the Christians. He can now, if he chooses, drive the English out of Egypt at any moment. English fear him and the Amir of Afghanistan.'[132]

Rumours current during the Talla riots also point to the pan-Islamist content of the riot. The *Amrita Bazar Patrika*, in an editorial after the Talla events, wrote of the 'very many' stories circulating on the subject of the rioters. One such story held 'that they sent telegrams to the Sultan and the Amir asking for help, and received favourable replies'. 'Of course, there is no truth in the above', the *Patrika* commented, 'but it is certain that the rioters were led to believe that telegrams were actually sent and that their appeals have extorted favourable replies'. 'This stupid rumour' invigorated the rioters, some of whom were even 'telling yesterday [6 July] . . . [that] the Sultan . . . got very angry with the Indian authorities, and that in order to punish them, he immediately ordered ten thousand troops to start for our city [and] that they are expected here in seven days.'[133]

It was not only the distant reality of the Sultan that came to be looked upon with pan-Islamist eyes by the poor Muslim; the ideology of pan-Islamism seems to have gone deeper. Even things nearer to the daily lives of the city poor often received a pan-Islamist interpretation. The mid-1890s were problem years as much for the city poor as they were for the jute mill workers. There had been, first of all, a very sharp drop in real wages. (See Table 3.) The city had suffered a bad attack of cholera that began in March 1897.[134] Besides, at the end of 1896 fear of plague had gripped the city.[135] This fear, and resentment of attempts by the government to effect

[132] *Hitavadi*, 9 July 1897; R.N.P.B., 17 July 1897.

[133] *Amrita Bazar Patrika*, 7 July 1897, p. 4. Cf. also R.N.P.B., 17 July 1897: 'So great is the credulity of the ignorant Musalman masses, that they readily believed the rumour set going by mischief makers that the Amor of Afghanistan had sent artillery and the Sultan of Turkey an army in aid of the Musalman rioters'.

[134] Elgin to Hamilton, 17 Mar. 1897: IOL, Elgin Papers, MSS. Eur. F 84/15.

[135] See Catanach (n.d.). I am grateful to Dr Catanach for allowing me to read and refer to this paper.

'plague regulations', were assuming alarming proportions by early 1897. Hamilton, the secretary of state for India, wrote to Lord Elgin: 'I am surprised, in looking through the Vernacular Press, to [see] the strong opinions expressed against the plague regulations. Though such reading is not conclusive evidence still its practical unanimity gives one a sense of the deep seated aversion to house to house visitation and segregation.'[136]

TABLE 3: Index of Average Real Wages
in Calcutta 1896–7*

	1896	1897
Industrial workers	105	95
Artisans	101	94
General labourers	102	100
Domestic servants	100	88

*NOTE AND SOURCE: K. L. Datta, *Report on Enquiry into the Rise in Prices in India*, 8 vols. (Calcutta, 1914), II, p. 204. All figures derive from a base of 1890–4—100.

Early in the year, Calcutta was 'restive with rumours about plague regulations', and the 'wildest possible notions' were being 'freely supported'. The Muslims especially disliked the restrictions the government had put on haj pilgrimage; in April 1897 the pilgrimage had been temporarily stopped by the government under the Epidemic Diseases Act.[137] This was interpreted by the Muslim labourers as an action which ran counter to pan-Islamism. The *Amrita Bazar Patrika* wrote:

To say that the dispute about a cotta of land is the cause of the Talla riot. . . is to show ignorance of human character. The feelings had been simmering long before the present riot occurred; and the reason which offended the Musalman community, or rather the lower class of the community, was openly proclaimed by the rioters during the hottest part of their work at

[136] Hamilton to Elgin, 7 May 1897: IOL, Elgin Papers, MSS. Eur. F 84/15.
[137] See Elgin to Hamilton, 17 Feb., 10, 24 Mar., 21 Apri. 1897: I.O.L., Elgin Papers, MSS. Eur. F 84/15. For a background to the pilgrimage restriction policy, see Hamilton to Elgin, 19 Feb. 1897: I.O.L., Hamilton Papers, MSS., Eur., Collection C-125. See also, N.A.I., Home (Public), Oct. 1897, A nos. 124–57, for further official correspondence on the matter.

Talah. This was heard by our reporters and hundreds of other. They said that the plague regulations were a myth, and the Government had an ulterior object in view in preventing them from going to Mecca. The Government, they said, feared that if the Musalmans of India went to Mecca, they would come in contact with the soldiers of the Sultan; and the result would be that the Indian Musalman would come to this country, re-enforced by the Sultan's men, and thus the British-raj would come to end![138]

On top of everything, there was surely the urge of an immigrant community to settle down. For, behind every protest against the demolition of 'illegal' *masjids*, there must have been an objective demand for land and settled habitation. And if some of those alleged mosques were performing the roles of real ones, then their demolition would only upset the life of a settled community.

Thus, fear of plague, resentment of plague regulations, a drop in wage rates, the predicament of a migrant labouring population, the Sultan, the British raj—all these issues were becoming one. This in the end lent the Talla riot an anti–British character that worried the authorities.[139] Feeling at times ran so deep that when a young boy injured in the Talla riot was asked by a 'native gentleman', 'if he would like to be conveyed to hospital for treatment', he replied by saying, 'What! To be taken to a sarkari [government] hospital? That will never do Babu Sahib.'[140]

It would appear that such sentiments also spread into the mill areas and influenced the immigrant Muslims there. The *Samay* described some of the 'up-country', 'low–class' Muslims who had come into the Howrah mill areas in search of jobs: 'These men are generally addicted to ganja [hashish] and bear a turbulent character . . . Musalmans, in particular, seem very fond of idle talk. Whenever a number of them sit down together, the only subject they chat upon is the Sultan.' The sultan appeared to them to be all-powerful:

[138] *Amrita Bazar Patrika*, 2 July 1897, p. 4.

[139] Hamilton to Elgin, 26 Aug. 1897: IOL, Elgin Papers, MSS. Eur. F 4/15. This is better read together with Elgin to Hamilton, 16 Sept. 1897, in *ibid.*, where Elgin cautions against magnifying the anti–British significance of the Talla riot.

[140] *Amrita Bazar Patrika*, 2 July 1897, p. 4.

The usual tenor of their talk is that the Sultan is supreme over all the kings of the world not excepting the British, that he can appoint or remove kings at his pleasure; that the English Government in India pays him a regular tribute. In this they are supported by some uneducated or half-educated man who pretends to be a Maulvi. . . .[141]

The *Samay* concluded that 'the Talla riot was created by men of this stamp'.[142] Thus the poor migrant Muslims of the city and the mills had indeed received and accepted the politics of the pan-Islamist Muslim elites in the city.

X. *The Communal Question and Problems of Social Leadership in the 1890s*

Why were the immigrant Muslim traders of the Chitpur area so interested in linking up with the Muslim poor? After the Shyam-bazar riots of 1891 over the issue of the Nikaripara mosque, Kasim Ariff (father of the wealthy Gujarati silk merchant Golam Aritt) purchased the disputed piece of land for Rs 4500 and made it over to the rioters so that they could have their *masjid*.[143] These Muslim merchants did the same when two other decrees were issued by the civil court in 1893, 'for possession of plots of land held by Mahomedans on which there were huts alleged to be mosques.'[144] Additionally, 'the Haji had subscribed largely for the defence, in court, of the Shambazar rioters', whom the *vakil* (pleader) Shams-ul-Huda defended.[145] Haji Zakaria, Kasim Ariff, Shams-ul-hads,

[141] *Samay*, 3 Sept. 1897: R.N.P.B., 11 Sept. 1897.

[142] Ibid. At the present level of knowledge it is difficult to fathom deeper than this the mental world of the Muslim labourer, the deep psychological sources in the poor man's mind from where 'religious feelings' could spring. Such feelings were indeed expressed by a Muslim rioter who said that 'they [the Talla rioters] are simply trying to get beaten', since 'in the masjid one cannot, without imperilling one's interest in the life to come, avoid being beaten': R.N.P.B., 24 July 1897.

[143] Bolton's letter, 1 Aug. 1897, in 'Notes': NAI, Home (Public), Oct. 1897, A nos. 124–57, and James's report appended thereto. On the Arums, see [I.G. Chumming?], Review of Industrial Position and Prospects in Bengal (Calcutta, 1908), p. 11.

[144] Bolton's letter, 1 Aug. 1897: N.A.I., Home (Public), Oct. 1897, A nos. 124–57.

[145] *Amrita Bazar Patrika*, 2 July 1897, p. 4. This was also promised by the merchants to the Talla rioters if they would calm down.

Seraj-ul-Islam, Abdur Rahim and Muhammad Yusuf were also involved as early as 1894 in protesting against the 1893 circular of Sir Carter Elliott concerning cow sacrifice.[146] Abdur Rahim and Muhammad Yusuf had also tried to help the Muslim mill workers of Rishra during the 1896 riot.[147]

Muslim charity or factional politics[148] may have been important factors in these developments, but a police document of 1910 suggests an interesting alternative explanation. Such an explanation can again only be speculative in the absence of hard data.

The document in question relates to the anti-cow-killing agitation in Chitpur in 1910.[149] The agitation was led by immigrant Marwari traders from Rajasthan, Hindu or Jain by religion, who were to dominate much of Calcutta's business history in the twentieth century. The document shows that by 1910 Marwaris were pushing into the residential areas of Muslim traders and labourers, and were prepared to use communalism to displace them. The marwaris, who were deeply entrenched in the trade of rice and jute, the two principal twentieth century crops in Bengal, brought with them new chains of retail and wholesale trade connections.[150] Their entry into the Chitpur area, the central business district of the city, may have been of importance to their interests.

Though a digression, a brief description of this agitation may be worthwhile. On 29 October 1910, the Marwari Association of Chitpur petitioned the police, requesting the forced stoppage of a cow sacrifice on *Bakr-Id* at a mosque on Amratolla Street (where the haji, apparently dead by 1910, had once lived). The Marwaris argued that 'they had never heard of any such sacrifice taking

[146] See *Muhammadan Observer*, 1 Jan. 1894, pp. 36–7; 25 Jan. 1894, p. 41; 1 Mar. 1894, p. 99.

[147] See *Englishman*, 27 May 1896, p. 5; W.B.S.A., Jdl. (Pol.), July 1896, A nos. 52–3.

[148] The Kutchi Menons had, a charity fund which possessed 'properties worth Rs 1,000,000' in 1906: *Statesman*, 10 May 1929, p. i. For factions in the world of Muslim elites in Calcutta, see Ahmed (1974), pp. 180–1.

[149] W.B.S.A., Home Pol., Special Branch, confidential file no. 290/1910, nos. 1–3. I am grateful to Pauline Rule and Stephen Gourlay for drawing my attention to this document.

[150] Pauline Rule is working on some of these points for her Ph.D. thesis at the University of Melbourne. See also her 'Goonda Raj in Calcutta, 1919–1923' (forthcoming).

place before'. The police found this allegation totally untrue.[151]

The history of the mosque and its locality shows how the Muslims had been gradually yielding ground to the incursions of the Marwaris throughout the second half of the nineteenth century:

The mosque in question is a small building. . . . It was built by a man named Din Mahomed, a coachman in the employ of the late Haji Jakeria [Zakaria], and some other syces and coachmen. At that time [the 1850s] the inhabitants of the locality were rich Momins [Memons? 'momins' were weavers, never 'rich'] and Sartis [Surtis, from Surat?] of Bombay. These people have now lost most of their means and are being displaced by wealthy Marwaris and Hindus who are overflowing from . . . the surrounding quarters . . . it is natural enough that the marwaris, who . . . have a very strong aversion to . . . [cow] sacrifices, feel the existence of the mosque as a grievance.[152]

However, 'the immediate cause of the . . . agitation' is even more suggestive. Opposite the mosque there used to be a Muslim *basti*, 'a little over three bighas [approximately one acre] in extent'. In about 1903 or 1904 this plot of land was sold, half of it to a Marwari firm, Gopi Ram Bhagat Ram and Company, and the other half to a Muslim gentleman, A. M. Isabhai. Bhagat Ram evicted the busti dwelling Muslims on his side and built himself a large house there, whereas the 'land belonging to Isabhai remained a *basti*.' In January 1910 Bhagat Ram purchased Isabhai's part too, for twice the selling price of 1903–4:

The [Muslim] *basti* has now been cleared and the Marwari appears to intend to build, but so long as the [cow] sacrifices continue he will be unable to let or sell the house to one of his religion. Land anywhere near Harrison Road [a street close by] is very valuable, and if there were nothing to offend the marwaris, Gopi Ram Bhagat Ram & Co., would probably make a large profit.[153]

Thus, 'it is the general opinion of everyone that Bhagat Ram started

[151] 'Sacrifice of cows has taken place at the mosque every year for at least forty years': W.B.S.A., Home Pol., Special Branch, confidential file no. 290/1910, nos. 1–3.

[152] Ibid.

[153] Ibid. Note the 100 per cent increase in land price in just seven or eight years, as also the huge amount of money involved. In 1903–4 the land was sold for Rs 110,000.

and did his best to keep up the present agitation'. The Marwaris were also importing hundreds of strong men from Bikanir and were obviously preparing for a communal fight.[154]

Such Marwari incursions into the Muslim residential areas of Chitpur and Burrabazar did not start in 1910. Indirect evidence points to an earlier beginning. The formation of a Marwari-inspired Cow Protection Society in Burrabazar in 1894, or Marwari gambling that was particularly rife in 1896 in Chitpur,[155] suggest a growing Marwari presence in these areas in the 1890s. If this is true, then it would partly explain why in the decade the poor migrant Muslims were often fighting the demolition of 'alleged mosques'. Their settlements were under pressure from developments in the local land market. The residential areas of the old Muslim traders were being invaded by the Marwaris. They may have faced business competition, too, from the Marwaris.[156] The Zakarias and Ariffs were probably on the defensive and therefore keen to link up with the poorer migrant Muslims so as to be able to use their own 'communalism' against that of the Marwaris. In this, a pan-Islamist ideology could be a very good bond to cement the Muslim rich and poor.

The leadership of the up-country mill-hand, by contrast, went by default. His communalism may have received occasional support from Hindus important in the locality—the shopkeepers' role in the Rishra riot, or that of Annapurna Devi (a Titagarh zamindar),[157] or of Hindu-Bengali mill-clerks during the Titagarh riot[158] being cases in point. But the chain of patronage would hardly go beyond the locality.[159]

[154] Ibid.

[155] See 'Proceedings of the General Committee of the Calcutta Corporation for 21 Aug. 1896', pp. 243–6 (copy at Calcutta Corporation Archives).

[156] It is interesting to observe that the Nakhoda Mosque and the Marwari areas of Burrabazar remained the two focal points for organization in the command riot of 1918: see Broomfield (1968), pp. 196–224.

[157] She owned slums in the Titagarh mill area, and used to insert 'a clause in the *patta* [contract] granted tenants making it a condition of the lease that Musalman tenants should not slaughter cows on the estate'. R.N.P.B., 10 June 1896.

[158] Three Hindu-Bengali mill clerks gave evidence in support of up-country Hindus during the trials following the Titagarh riot of 1896: W.B.S.A., Jdl. (Pol.), Aug. 1896, A nos. 13–14.

[159] Organized Marwari (and up-country Hindu) patronage for communal

The Bengali *bhadralok* ('respectable person' of the middle class) in the nineteenth century, with his 'education, clean clothes, and hands unsoiled with manual labour',[160] perhaps felt distant from the world of men who worked in the mills. In the 1890s, with a large number of immigrant mill-hands, the gulf between the *bhadralok* and working men was only to grow wider. The Bengali *bhadralok* were not sufficiently equipped culturally to communicate with such groups. Their premier political organization, the Indian Association, reacted to the Talla riot by petitioning the viceroy to 'open a volunteer crops and train the Bengalis in the use of arms... [which] would... help them to resist the rowdy rioters'.[161] In healthy contrast to this, Rabindranath Tagore showed a much better grasp of the *bhadralok's* problems when, in a very perceptive essay written in 1898, he referred to the Talla riot thus:

Recently a group of lower class ignorant Musalmans, brickbats in hand, tried to create trouble on the streets of Calcutta. What was surprising about their attempt was that the English were made special targets of it. They [the Muslims] were adequately punished. It is said that if you start throwing stones at others, some will be thrown back at you. These fools threw stones but were hit back with much harder stuff. We understand that they committed a crime, and were punished; but the whole affair is still not sufficiently clear. These lower class Musalmans neither read newspapers nor do they write in them. What happened was after all a matter of some importance, yet we know nothing went on in the minds of these inarticulate people.[162]

It was in this context of a social and cultural hiatus between the *bhadralok* and the migrant workers that the community consciousness of Hindu mill-workers found foster-parents in the idiosyncratic communalism of an Annapurna Devi or a Hindu mill babu, while Muslim migrants found similar support in the broader community politics of someone like Haji Zakaria. Bengal did not provide them with any alternative social leadership.

---

riots was to become really important in the twentieth century.

[160] The description is from Sarkar (1973), p. 509.

[161] See Bagal (1953), p. 129.

[162] Rabindranath Thakur [Tagore], 'Kanthorodh' [The Throttling of Our Voice], in *Rabindra Rachanabali* [Collected Works of Rabindranath], 15 vols. (Calcutta, 1961), xii, p. 961 (my italics).

XI. *Conclusion*

The mid-1890s saw intense competition in the jute mill labour market, caused by an over-supply of cheap migrant labour. Real wages dropped, and workers were largely on the defensive, as some of the strikes of the period suggest. But at the same time strong communal divisions surfaced, especially among the migrant workers. In this the method of recruitment and control of labour, the sardari system, seems to have played a crucial role. It effectively shielded the workers from viewing in other than community terms what was potentially a situation of conflict between labour and capital.[163] The working class as a result remained fragmented.

The picture was complicated by the cultural distance between the Bengali *bhadralok*, the main political group in the city, and the workers. The only elite group interested in taking their politics to the poorer, working-class and up-country Muslims was a group of wealthy Muslim traders. Their ideology was provided by pan-Islamism, and this ideology did indeed achieve considerable success among these men. However, it only reinforced the community consciousness and fragmentation which the labour market tended to produce in the working class.

Some of the beginnings of twentieth century mass-communal politics in Calcutta may be discerned in this story. The cultural gap between the mill worker and the Bengali intelligentsia remained.[164] The Marwaris and the Hindu Mahasabha party were to become in time the chief patrons of Hindu communalism in the city. The tradition of Haji Zakaria or Golam Ariff found twentieth century

---

[163] The institution of jobbery in India thus distanced the worker from the 'political facts' of his life. A contrasting but instructive case is that of central Africa (Rhodesia) where, owing to factors unique to colonialism there, recruitment (and control) of labour was not left in the hands of the jobber. Instead, there was visible and violent state intervention on the side of the capital on both these matters, and this contributed to a fairly quick rise in worker consciousness. See Arrighi (1970), pp. 197–234: van Onselen (1976).

[164] This is not to belittle the heroic efforts of leftist and communists in Bengal to bridge the gulf, but their organizational basis, down to the 1950s, remained somewhat limited to a minority of mills having a mainly Bengali workforce. See Indrajit Gupta (1953), p. 42.

successors in men like H. S. Suhrawardy or Y. C. Ariff (a descendant of Golam Ariff) who organized 'black' Muslim trade unions
in the jute mills and the Calcutta docks in the 1920s and 1930s.[165]
The crucial continuity was of course in the labour market—where
the migrants were to grow in number—and in the sardari system
which grew much stronger. The labour market thus continued to
churn out human material that communalist-minded politicians
in the city were only too happy to use. The Calcutta riots of 1918
and 1926, and to some extent the Great Calcutta Killings of 1946,
bear gruesome testimony to this.[166]

REFERENCES

Ahmed, F. S., 1976: 'Muslim thought and leadership in Bengal in the
    nineteenth century', in Barun De, *et al.* (ed.), *Essays in Honour of
    Professor S. C. Sarkar.* Delhi.
Ahmed, Sufia, 1974: *Muslim Community in Bengal, 1884–1912.* Dacca:
    Oxford University Press.
Arrighi, G., 1970: 'Labour Supplies in Historical Perspective: A Study of
    the proletarization of the African peasantry in Rhodesia'. *Journal of
    Development Studies,* vol. VI, pp. 197–234.
Bagal, J. C., 1953: *History of the Indian Association, 1876–1951.* Calcutta.
Bagchi, A. K., 1972: *Private Investment in India, 1900–1939.* London:
    Cambridge University Press.
Bamford, P. C., 1925: *Histories of the Non-Co-operation and Khalifat
    Movements.* Delhi: Govt. of India Press. Reprinted: Delhi, Deep Publi-
    cations, 1974.
Barker, S. G., 1935: *Report on the Scientific and Technical Development of the
    Jute Manufacturing Industry in Bengal with an Addenda on Jute, its Scientific
    Nature and Information Thereto.*
Broomfield, J. H., 1968: *Elite Conflict in a Plural Society: Twentieth Century
    Bengal.* Berkeley: University of California Press.
Buchannan, D. H., 1934: *The Development of Capitalist Enterprise in India.*
    New York: Macmillan.

[165] See McPherson (1976), pp. 41, 160.

[166] This is a revised version of a paper prepared at the Centre for Studies in
Social Sciences, Calcutta. Thanks are due to several friends and colleagues
for comments, especially to Partha Chatterjee, A. K. Bagchi, R. Das Gupta,
Majid Siddiqi, Diana Tonsich, Stephen Henningham and Roger Stuart. I am
also grateful to E. P. Thompson for detailed, helpful criticism. My greatest
debt, however, is to Barun De.

Cartes, C. and van Onselen, 1976: *Chibaro: African Mine Labour in Southern Rhodesia*. London.

Catanach, I. J., n.d.: 'Plague in India in the Late Nineteenth and Early Twentieth Centuries'. (Unpublished typescript.)

Chakrabarty, D. & B. Das Gupta, 1974: 'Functions of nineteenth century Banias: A document'. *Economic and Political Weekly*, vol. IX, no. 35, pp. M 73–5.

Crooke, William, 1896: *The Tribes and Castes of the North Western Provinces and Oudh*. Calcutta.

Das Gupta, Ranajit, 1976: 'Factory Labour in Eastern India: Sources of Supply, 1845–1946: Some Preliminary Findings'. *Indian Economic and Social History Review*, vol. XIII, no. 3, pp. 277–31.

Gupta, Indrajit, 1953: *Capital and Labour in the Jute Industry*. Delhi: Orient Longman.

Hardy, P., 1972: *The Muslims of British India*. London: Cambridge University Press.

Meilink-Roelofz, M. A. P., 1962: *Asian Trade and European Influence in the Indonesian Archipelago between 1500 and about 1630*. The Hague: Nijhoff.

Mcpherson, K. T., 1972: 'The Muslims of Calcutta, 1918–1935: A Study of the Society and Politics or an Urban Minority Group in India. Unpublished Ph.D. dissertation of the Australian National University.

———, 1976: 'Muslims of Calcutta, 1918–1935', in Barun De *et al., Essays in Honour of Professor S. C. Sarkar*. Delhi.

Mukherjee, Radhakamal, 1948: *The Indian Working Class*. Bombay.

Robinson, Francis, 1974: *Separatism among Indian Muslims*. London: Cambridge University Press.

Sarkar, Sumit, 1973: *The Swadeshi Movement in Bengal, 1903–1908*. Delhi: Orient Longman.

Shukla, R. L., 1973: *Britain, India, and the Turkish Empire 1853–1882*. Delhi.

Stuart, Roger, 1978: *The Formation of the Communist Party in India*.

van Onselen, Charles, 1976: see Cartes, above.

Chapter Seven

The Karachi Riots of December 1986: Crisis of State and Civil Society in Pakistan

AKMAL HUSSAIN

Introduction[1]

The violence that erupted in Karachi during December 1986, both in scale and sheer brutality, was unprecedented since the partition of the subcontinent in 1947. What we saw were bands of men armed with Kalashnikov rifles charging into the homes of people belonging to other communities, with whom they had lived for a generation, killing men, women and children without mercy, burning and looting, until entire housing localities were left in charred ruins. There were counter-attacks against the homes of the invaders, and the battles engulfed the streets of Karachi. For two days there was random killing on the roads by armed marauders on fast motorbikes and cars, machine-gunning innocent bystanders. Subsequently, a curfew was declared and the army moved in, but even then there were scattered scenes of violence, and open violation of the curfew for a week afterwards.

The events of December 1986 have been labelled 'ethnic riots' between the Pathan community and the Muhajirs (immigrants from India at the time of partition in 1947, and later Bihar, or from Bangladesh in 1971). Yet even in the Karachi case what appears as 'ethnic violence' is symptomatic of a deeper malaise in the relationship between the state and civil society. What we saw in Karachi

[1] I am grateful to Mr Amer Shahzad, Mr Muhammad Arshad and Mr Maqbool Hussain Toor of Sayyed Engineers (P.) Ltd, Lahore, for their help in compiling data on the Karachi riots.

highlighted the trajectory of a crisis of the state.

In this three-part paper, the first section provides a snapshot picture of the environment of violence in December 1986. The second indicates some of the major psychological, social and political factors underlying the so-called ethnic violence in Karachi. In the third I discuss the polarization of civil society in Pakistan as well as the structural crisis of state power.

I. *The Bloodshed in Karachi: 12 to 17 December 1986*

The spark that lit the fires of December 1986 in Karachi was the now famous Sohrab Goth operation.[2] Sohrab Goth is the name of a locality on the outskirts of Karachi where the drug market is concentrated. A largely lumpenized population associated with the storage of heroin, its local distribution and transfer abroad for export, resides here. The locality is equipped with tunnels in which drugs and weapons are stored. The lumpen residents of the area are mostly Pathans from the NWFP, and some Afghan migrants. Legally, these people in Sohrab Goth are squatters, for most of the land which they occupy has been sold to big real-estate dealers of Karachi. The authorities decided to launch Operation Clean-Up at Sohrab Goth, and on 12 December the area was surrounded by army trucks. Then security forces moved in, bulldozing the homes of the residents, and arranged for them to move out to a new locality. By the evening the authorities recovered only a token amount of drugs and guns— 150 kgs of heroin, 5 pistols and 2 rifles. The drug operators had apparently been tipped off about this operation in time for them to remove their stocks to safer storage points.

Meanwhile, in another operation in Orangi township on Thursday night, just before the Sohrab Goth operation, the police raided the homes of Muhajirs to seize home-made bombs and explosive material. Whatever the reason for this action, it effectively weakened the ability of the Muhajirs to defend their homes in subsequent attacks by the Pathan community.[3]

[2] For a detailed description, see 'Karachi: Apocalypse Now?', *Herald*, Annual Number, Jan. 1987. Karachi: Pakistan Herald Publications.
[3] See the daily *Dawn* from 13 to 18 December 1986.

The drugs mafia instituted an organized campaign to mobilize the Pathan community along ethnic lines soon after the Sohrab Goth operation. Hand-bills were distributed claiming that the attack on the home of Pathans in Sohrab Goth was launched at the behest of the Muhajirs, and that this was part of a conspiracy to evict Pathans from Karachi.

Early on 13 December there were scattered incidents of rioting, and a number of roads were blocked by minibus operators (mostly Pathans) in protest at the Sohrab Goth operation. Then, just after 10.00 a.m., in response to a call from the Pirabad Masjid, several hundred Pathans armed with Kalashnikovs charged down the hills overlooking the Muhajir residential areas of Qasba, Aligarh and Sector I-D. The call to attack was couched in highly emotive language provoking the pride and dignity of Pathan manhood. Under the cover of a hail of machinegun fire the invaders, using kerosene tanks, set the houses of Qasba and Sector I-D afire. The invaders were careful to leave non-Pathan homes untouched. The police and army failed to intervene for five hours, during which the carnage continued unabated. By 4.30 p.m. hundreds of homes were burnt to the ground. According to official estimates the death toll was forty; it was hundreds by unofficial accounts.

In the days that followed, the violence spread all over Karachi. The homes of Biharis in Orangi came under attack by Pathans. In retaliation non-Pathan mobs went on the rampage, killing and burning people and property on the streets of Karachi. The killing by frenzied mobs of Pathans and Muhajirs continued until 17 December 1986.

II. *The Major Factors Underlying the*
'Ethnic Violence' in Karachi

What we have observed in Pakistan in recent times is not just ethnic violence between Pathans and Muhajirs but also a conflict between the Shia and Sunni sects in Lahore during August 1986 and the tension between Sindhi nationalists and Punjab in the since-aborted movement of 1983. It can be argued that these are manifestations at the level of civil society of the underlying crisis of the state in Pakistan. Before I characterize the crisis in the next section, let us briefly look at the more immediate factors underlying the Karachi violence.

(i) Since 1977, with the steady inflow into Pakistan of Afghan refugees and the use of Pakistan by the USA as a conduit for arms for the Afghan War, two trends have emerged which have had a direct impact on the Karachi situation. First, a large proportion of weapons meant for Afghan guerrillas has filtered into the illegal arms market. This has pushed down, for example, the price of a Kalashnikov from Rs 40,000 in the 1970s to Rs 10,000 today. Second, there has been rapid growth in the heroin trade. Powerful mafia-type syndicates have emerged which produce, transport and export heroin. These syndicates have pulled into their orbit some senior government officials as well as several officers of the armed forces. At the same time, many Afghan refugees who now have a significant share of inter-city private overland cargo services have also been integrated into the drug syndicates. Thus, Karachi is now a city with a polarized community, and one in which opposing social factions have a high level of fire power. The syndicates, when threatened by the Sohrab Goth affair, retaliated by mobilizing the Pathan community on the basis of primordial emotions. If the purpose was to show the power of the mafia bosses by paralyzing Karachi, it was achieved.

(ii) The question that arises is: in the immediate context of Karachi, why were the Pathan and Muhajir communities vulnerable to being emotionally manipulated into an ethnic conflict? One of the most important proximate factors is the nature of the transport problem in Karachi.

Most of the private minibuses linking the various districts of Karachi are owned and operated by Pathans. The big owners who buy fleets of minibuses then lease them out at high rates to individual drivers who are poorer members of the Pathan community. The driver pays the lease in instalments and is under heavy pressure to make money quickly. Consequently, he grossly overloads the minibus, oblivious of the consequent acute discomfort to passengers, and drives at breakneck speed to reach the next bus stop before his competitors to pick up passengers. This results in frequent accidents. Manslaughter on the roads, combined with the humiliation suffered by passengers, has caused acute resentment amongst the public. This has reached a stage whereby there is usually a spontaneous riot following an accident on a busy road. The Pathan driver is often killed by the mob and the minibus set on fire. Such incidents, combined with demands by the Muhajir Qaumi Mahaz that the government should take stern measures against transporters, fuelled the Pathan-Muhajir tension.

(iii) With the staggering growth of Karachi's population, the basic public services such as water, housing and transport are in a state of virtual collapse. Scarce public services in a situation of a highly unequal distribution of income has resulted in the elite acquiring a disproportionate share of these services through bribery, thereby making the shortage for the poorer population worse still. For example, while in some parts of Karachi there is an acute shortage of drinking water, Karachi Municipal Corporation (KMC) tankers are 'purchased' by the elite to water their front lawns. Consequently, much of the lower-middle classes and impoverished sections of the population live on a razor's edge of anxiety and a sense of outrage at the breakdown of law and public services. For most citizens the emotional trigger is easily pulled. Thus, even relatively minor incidents can spark off a riot: a traffic accident, a murder, a kidnapping. Evidence for this phenomenon is offered in Table 1, which shows that in the short period between January 1986 and August 1987 there were 242 incidents of rioting. These were sparked off by a range of events, varying from electricity breakdown to politically motivated bomb explosions. The

TABLE 1: Karachi—Frequency of Rioting/Violence by Cause and Number of Casualties, January 1986 to August 1987

Cause		
Electricity Breakdown	1	—
Water Shortage	4	1
Transport Problem	17	78
Politically Motivated Banditry	80	34
Politically Motivated Bombing	76	188
Others	102	—
Total	242	403

SOURCE: Compiled from these daily newspapers: *Dawn, Star, Muslim, Jang*

largest number of deaths has occurred as the result of the rioting that ensued (188 deaths) after a bomb explosion, followed by 78 deaths due to riots caused by the transport problem. Social existence, having been deprived of the institutions through which problems are resolved in an orderly way, has been brutalized and brought close to a state of anarchy.

III. *The Crisis of State Power in Pakistan*

The current crisis of the state in Pakistan originates in a state structure inherited from the colonial period in which the military bureaucratic oligarchy is overdeveloped relative to the institutions of civil society. This dominance of the military bureaucratic oligarchy has systematically constrained the development of the political process, thereby preventing the emergence of issue-oriented political parties with institutionalized grass-roots support.

The predominance of the army and bureaucracy in Pakistan's state structure was due to the form of the freedom struggle in the pre-partition period on the one hand, and the nature of the Muslim League on the other. Since the freedom struggle was essentially constitutionalist, the state apparatus of the colonial regime remained largely intact at the time of independence. Thus, the bureaucracy and the army, which constituted the 'steel frame' of the Raj, continued after the emergence of Pakistan to determine the parameters within which political and economic change were to occur.

The other factor is the failure to subordinate the army and bureaucracy to the political system, and the reason for this lies in the two basic characteristics of both the Muslim League before partition and the Pakistan People's Party during the 1970s (the only two parties with mass popular support in the respective periods). The Muslim League in the pre-partition period as well as the People's Party during the 1970s were *movements* rather than parties. They were therefore unable to establish an organizational structure on the basis of which the power of the people could be institutionalized and used to subordinate the army and bureaucracy to the political system. Second, the Muslim League in the decade before partition[4] and the People's Party during the early 1970s

---

[4] For a detailed analysis of the establishment of the hegemony of the landlords over the Muslim League, see Ali (1975).

were taken over by landlords whose political interests lay in constraining the process of political development within the confines specified by the military bureaucratic oligarchy.

In the post-independence period the nature of economic growth which occurred in an economy dominated by landlords and the industrial bourgeoisie generated acute economic inequality between rich and poor social strata on the one hand, and between various regions on the other. These economic contradictions manifested themselves in growing political tensions between social groups' and regions.

Hamza Alavi (1984) has attributed a relative autonomy to the military bureaucratic oligarchy on the basis of which it could mediate conflicting political forces for the preservation of the status quo. However, during the last two decades, as political tension between social groups and the regions has intensified, the relative autonomy of the military bureaucratic oligarchy has also been eroded due to internal politicization.[5] Thus, while the task of mediating conflicting political forces became increasingly difficult, the ability of the military bureaucratic oligarchy to do so, became weaker.

As civil society became polarized, the state increasingly used coercive forms of control. Unlike the earlier martial law governments, for example, the Zia regime was unable to effectively hand over power to its civilian facade. Thus, in spite of formally declaring the end of martial law, the posts of Chief of Army Staff and President continued to be held by Zia till his death in September 1988. This system made possible the presence of the military in the daily affairs of the state. It has also created the institutional basis of short-circuiting the civil administration by the military chain of command whenever this was felt necessary. It is in this perspective that several major elements that comprise the crisis of the state and civil society can be understood.[6]

First, the state, till recently dominated by a repressive apparatus, was highly centralized and unable to recognize, let alone grant, the rights of the various nationalities. This enhanced sub-national

[5] For a detailed discussion of this phenomenon, see Hussain (forthcoming).

[6] This paper was written before Zia's death and the subsequent political events.

tendencies given the fact that the army is drawn predominantly from the province of Punjab. Second, the state's interpretation of religion was seen by the people as sanctifying particular class interests and justifying repression against those who dared to question it. The state was, therefore, bereft of a legitimizing ideology. For this reason the army, unlike in the past, could not withdraw behind a civilian facade.

Third, the prolonged military rule and the demise of the 1970 constitution eroded the balance between the various institutions of the state, i.e. the armed forces, the bureaucracy, the judiciary, etc. There was, therefore, an institutional crisis of state authority.

Fourth, the fragmentation of civil society along various groups on religious, ethnic, *biradari* and sub-regional lines, and the rapid arming of conflicting groups weakened the basic function of the state, which is the protection of citizens. This has accentuated the tendency of the individual to seek security in the most proximate identity, and to assert with militancy this parochial identity as an emblem of his membership within a parochial group.

Conclusion

The Karachi riots of December 1986 are symptomatic of a deeper crisis of state and civil society. These symptoms have been evident both before and after the December 1986 riots.

During the last decade, protracted military rule has progressively weakened the political and social institutions through which people experience themselves as a political community, and through which problems are expressed and resolved politically.[7] At the same time, an inequitable and dependent economic growth process has enriched a few at the expense of the many. Economic disparities between regions and social groups have grown, while public services such as health, education and social welfare which could cushion the worst aspects of inequity have been undermined. For example, only 62 per cent of the population has access to piped drinking water, almost 45 per cent of the population lives below the calorific poverty line (i.e. they are unable to afford 2300 calories

---

[7] For a detailed analysis of the crisis of state power in Pakistan, see Hussain (1985).

per day per person), literacy levels are among the lowest in the world at 24 per cent, housing conditions are so inadequate that out of the total housing units in the country 81 per cent have on average 1.7 rooms inhabited by an average of seven people.[8] Finally, and perhaps most important, with the daily bombings in the NWFP, resulting from America's Afghan war, and the collapse of state authority in large parts of Sind, confidence in the basic functions of the state has been undermined.

In these circumstances, it is not surprising that an increasing number of people are seeking alternative support mechanisms in their communities to seek redress against injustice as well as to secure themselves against a physical threat to their persons and families. The proximate identity or group membership through which the individual seeks such security can be an ethnic, sub-religious, sub-nationalist or *biradari* group. Thus, the crisis of state power has engendered a crisis in civil society in which the polity is polarized along various vertical lines. Each group whether ethnic, sub-religious, sub-nationalist or *biradari*, has an intense emotional charge rooted in primordial loyalties and a high degree of fire power derived from the contemporary arms markets.

REFERENCES

Alavi, Hamza, 1984: 'Class and State in Pakistan', in *The Unstable State*, ed. H. Gardezi and J Rashid. Lahore: Vanguard Books.

Ali, Imran, 1975: *Punjab Politics in the Decade Before Partition*. Research Monoraph Series no. 8, South Asian Institute. Lahore: Punjab University.

Hussain, Akmal, 1985: 'Origins and Nature of the Crisis of the State', in *Islam, Politics, and the State*, ed. Asghar Khan. London: Zed Publications.

———, 1987: 'Behind the Veil of Growth: The State of the Pakistan Economy'. Paper presented at UNESCO Regional Research Seminar, Bangkok, July.

———, forthcoming: 'The Crisis of State Power', in *Challenge in South Asia: Development, Democracy and Regional Co-operation*.

---

[8] For a detailed presentation of data on these issues, see Hussain (1987).

Chapter Eight

The Pathan–Muhajir Conflicts, 1985–6: A National Perspective

FARIDA SHAHEED

Introduction

The widening and intensifying cycle of violence witnessed particularly, but not solely, in Karachi in the last three months of 1986
leaves no doubt of the urgent need in Pakistan, as in other South
Asian countries, to devise a meaningful response to the repeated
occurrence of ethnic confrontations that threaten the very fabric
of society. In order to curtail the level, spread and frequency of
such violence in the immediate future and to move towards a
resolution of the underlying tensions in the long term, it is necessary
that the response be based upon a solid foundation of understanding. But understanding may not be enough. The roots of
ethnic riots are often complex and deeply embedded. The ability
to defuse a particular situation, and to unwind the spiral of violence,
depends on the strength that those who intervene can muster
against the sources of ethnic militancy. Frequently, the odds appear
to be so heavily stacked in favour of the militants that they seem
to render futile any attempt at resolving the situation. Yet the
dimensions of the problem are so devastating and the likely
repercussions of inactivity so depressing that inaction is no choice
at all.

This paper examines reasons for the Pathan–Bihari riots of 1985,
leading to the subsequent and more intense confrontations of 1986.[1]

---

[1] The violence in Karachi has intensified as this paper goes to press. Between
January and September 1987 the Punjabi community was pulled into the
conflict on the Pathan side under the aegis of the Punjabi Pakhtoon Ittehad

However, to put these in perspective, a brief review is offered of the types of violent outbursts that have occurred in Pakistan where at least one of the groups involved has been ethnically or religiously identifiable. Ethnic riots cannot be understood separately from either other types of violent outbursts and confrontations or from the general environment in which they take place—including the social, economic and political developments of the country.

A Review of Other Riots

Broadly speaking, ethnically coloured violence in Pakistan can be divided into religious or sectarian conflicts, and those involving ethnic groups within the same religion. In the former category, three types of confrontations have occurred. Firstly, there are the annual clashes between members of the two major sects of Islam, the Shias and Sunnis. Secondly, starting in the fifties, there have been periodic instances of anti-Ahmadi violence. Thirdly and more frequently, there have been sectarian confrontations without precedence, and so far sequel, between variously paired groups.

Religiously inspired riots, or pogroms, appear to have a very long history. While the immediate reason for a particular outburst can often be identified, the roots of the problem appear to defy socio-economic analysis. Certain social and economic conditions intensify the likelihood of violence, while others promote harmony between religious groups. What is common in these conflicts is a social construction by which the adherents of one religion put those outside it as being 'beyond the pale'. In a sense this reduces the 'humanity' of the 'infidels', making it easier to perpetrate violence against them. The infidel, the heretic and the savage are all, in such constructions, less than human and therefore beyond the considerations of common humanity. Religious groups who are willing to lend their 'divine' backing to such acts—in order to consolidate their own power—always seem available. In Pakistan, three categories of religiously defined violence have happened.

(Punjabi-Pakhtoon Union), while some Sindhis in Hyderabad sided with the Muhajirs. On 1 October 1988 more than 200 people died in ethnic clashes in Karachi and Hyderabad.

Dating back to soon after the birth of Islam, the division of Sunnis and Shias has historically created tensions between the two groups, and clashes pre-date Independence. Shia-Sunni confrontations occur in Karachi with almost ritualized regularity during the religious month of Moharrum, on the occasion of Ashura, when both sects take out processions. While there are clear indications that historical differences between the two are used by local leaders to strengthen or consolidate their hold in a localized power game, the very durability and historical basis for the antagonism necessitate a scope of analysis which is beyond this paper.

On the other hand, the anti-Ahmadi riots can be traced directly to the actions of religious political parties, in particular the Majlis-e-Ahrar and the Jamaat-e-Islami. During the pre-Independence period, these parties mobilized support by claiming that Islam and the Muslim minority were endangered by the predominantly Hindu majority. In an overwhelmingly Muslim Pakistan, such a platform was meaningless. Adapting to the changed circumstances, such parties averred to 'Islamize' the country (although they themselves had opposed the creation of Pakistan) and one tactic used to mobilize public support was proclaiming that a small indigenous sect of Muslims, the Ahmadis, were not in fact Muslims but *munafiqeen* (those who act as fifth columnists), and therefore a source of great danger. These parties capitalized on latent anti-Ahmadi sentiments, which assumed an aura of religious sanctity and culminated in rioting in the fifties. This was particularly in Punjab where most Ahmadis live. The Ahmadis, who did not and have not related in kind, became the victims of violence; their mosques and buildings were objects of attack. Even in this early instances of ethnic rioting, the administration was slow to act, allowing the seeds of violence to spread and take root. Subsequently a tribunal was set up to investigate the matter, but it dealt with the problem exclusively in terms of 'law and order'. The more fundamental question of providing religious approval to anti-Ahmadi sentiment amongst the public was dismissed summarily. Unsettled, the Ahmadi issue retained its potentially combustible nature and provided religious parties—devoid of mass support—with an ideal means of exerting pressure on any government in power by whipping up religious feelings and creating law-and-order situations. A cumulative pressure resulted in the Ahmadis being declared non-Muslims during Bhutto's tenure, and more recently other such measures were taken by Zia's regime.

There is no easy answer to the question of why anti-Ahmadi sentiments should exist in the first place, but they obviously do; and coloured as they are by religion, they appear to explode into violence at the least provocation.[2] The Ahmadi issue in Pakistan points to several factors. Firstly, since the essential issue was not dealt with when the initial violence broke out, it created a precedence for subsequent occurrences. Thus, the breaking of law and order was condemned whenever violence occurred, but the underlying hostility and mistrust towards the Ahmadis did not come under censure from any authority. Secondly, the place of religion and religious sentiments at the popular level and its implications in politics were never comprehended by those acceding to power after Independence. The 'modernist' approach of both politicians and bureaucrats made them eschew religion, which over time was monopolized by right-wing forces. (The consequences of this have been most clearly demonstrated during Zia's government.) Thirdly, the Ahmadi issue is only one proof that religion has been used in the pursuit of power by both—those in and out of office. The role of religion in political processes and people's consciousness merits greater attention than it has received.

The more recent clashes, opposing different pairs of sects, stem directly from Zia's policy of Islamization. With its promise of greater power for amenable religious persons and groups, the emphasis in Islam and Muslim jurisprudence has provided a new impetus to the numerous schools of religious thought. In the absence of any democratic institutions or processes that could provide a channel for achieving consensus, the general debate has sharpened the differences between various sects. Fearing the imposition of a particular school or brand of Islam with which they differ, and vying with each other for the mantle of absolute truth, members of different sects have not only come to blows in mosques, but

---

[2] The leadership of the Ahmadiya sect was regarded as suspect just after Independence because they had always adopted a pro-British stance. However, that the problem is deeper is shown by the reservations expressed, for instance, by Allama Iqbal at the turn of the century about the Ahmadiyas being Muslims.

also, at least on one occasion, have fought pitched battles with firearms across the main street of Lahore. These occurrence reflect the lack of tolerance and the increasing acceptability of violence in society. The processes of public debate and discussion are rapidly being replaced by armed confrontation as a means of self-expression as well as of the expression of differences.[3]

Unlike sectarian conflicts, the anti-Pathan riots following the 1965 elections, the Urdu-Sindhi language riots of 1972, and the more recent Pathan-Bihari clashes (all of which occurred in Karachi) can be directly related to political and socio-economic developments in the country.

Seeking legitimacy for his six-year-old dictatorship, Ayub Khan held in 1964, a limited form of elections designed to maximize his chances of winning. This was the first opportunity for the political parties in Pakistan to oust a military dictatorship. They could, therefore, sink their differences to form the Combined Opposition Party. In Karachi, the COP candidate, Fatima Jinnah, was staunchly supported by the numerically strong Muhajir (refugee) community (i.e. immigrants from India), whereas Ayub Khan, himself a Pathan, was widely supported by the Pathans. Fatima Jinnah lost the elections, generating frustration and disappointment amongst the opposition. Widespread allegations of rigging transformed this disappointment into anger. Since the targets of the anger, i.e. Ayub Khan and his family, were beyond the reach of the people, it turned against Ayub Khan's community, the Pathans. A victory march in Karachi led by Gohar Ayub resulted in bloody clashes between Ayub's Pathan supporters and the poorer sections of the Muhajir community, which culminated in general attacks against all Pathans.

The 1972 language riots opposing Muhajirs and Sindhis have to be understood in the context of historical developments within the country. At Independence, the bulk of non-Punjabi migrants who came to West Pakistan from India arrived in Sind and settled

---

[3] It is not only the *people* who increasingly take resort to violence: so does the state. The repeated use of violence by the state through its agency increases the tolerance of society towards violence. Moreover, when groups opposed to the government are repeatedly silenced by the use of force, they feel they have no alternative but to arm themselves for self-protection and self-expression.

in the urban centres of Hyderabad and Karachi. Largely from urban backgrounds, these Muhajirs were better placed to compete for jobs, and to start businesses or industries, than were the indigenous people of Sind. The Muhajirs were culturally distinct from the Sindhis and, though composed of various ethnic groups, gravitated towards the Urdu-speaking culture of central India, so that Urdu became the *lingua franca* of Karachi. The situation in Sind was further complicated by land policies. To compensate for their losses in India, refugees were given land, while the government also continued the British policy of allotting land to armed-forces personnel. Since there are virtually no Sindhis in the armed forces, both policies resulted in the province's land being progressively acquired by non-Sindhis. Finally, unbalanced economic policies discriminated against all provinces in favour of Punjab and the city of Karachi. The latter, though situated in Sind, was dissociated from the province and monopolized by non-Sindhis (and initially dominated by Muhajirs). Sind was thus deprived of its greatest asset: Karachi. By the time Bhutto, himself a Sindhi, acceded to power, there was a sizeable Sindhi educated class, well able to compete with Muhajirs, which resented the usurpation of their land and employment opportunities by outsiders.

It should be added that the Muhajir community retained a separate identity; it did not integrate itself with the Sindhi population. Also, there was a political difference between the two. Although many Muhajirs supported Bhutto's Pakistan People's Party, the middle-class Muhajirs of Karachi had traditionally been strong supporters of the urban-based Jamaat-e-Islami that has never had any support amongst the Sindhis. Consequently, Bhutto's domicile-quota policy, differentiating between Muhajirs and Sindhis in the province, was the spark that ignited Urdu-Sindhi riots. These expressed years of rivalry between the two communities for the same educational seats, job opportunities and development benefits.

The Roots of Muhajir-Pathan Conflict

Ethnic riots are, therefore, not new to Pakistan. What is being witnessed today is in many ways a continuation of the past. The fact that riots are erupting at shorter intervals and are spreading geographically reflects the deepening crisis in the country as a whole. The underlying causes of the 1964 and 1972 riots were never resolved and in the intervening years the grievances described earlier have become more acute. The frustration of a people denied any means of participating in the decision-making processes of their country, and the total lack of any accountability of those whose decisions have to be suffered, is stronger today than in 1964. Unbalanced economic and political policies have continued to widen the gulf between different groups and between the provinces. As a result, sub-state nationalities have become so important that the multi-ethnic Muhajirs have been declared a nationality by the recently formed Muhajir Qaumi Mahaz (Refugee People's Front). It is against this background that the more recent riots have to be seen, and questions asked. Two major questions which need answering are: why have ethnic identities become so important in people's existence after almost forty years of Independence? Second, why does violence erupt between any two given communities at a particular time and place? In the context of Pakistan, and in the light of recent events, one also has to ask why the anger gene-rated by state action—which is initially directed against the government—transforms itself repeatedly into ethnic riots.

In three separate incidents in Karachi, which I shall describe, riots occurred in the wake of either demonstrations against the government or as a direct consequence of a particular course of action followed by the government. In April 1985 this happened when a road accident and police mishandling of the situation sparked off general riots and demonstrations that culminated in the first Bihari-Pathan clashes in Orangi. In October 1986 the same sequel of events was repeated when, in response to an accident at an unmanned railway crossing, what started as anti-government demonstrations ended up as Muhajir-Pathan confrontations. Finally, in December that year the government decision to evacuate Pathans living in Sohrab Goth, ostensibly to clean up narcotics and arms dens, led to the worst bout of rioting in nearby Orangi township, again between Pathans and Muhajirs. Incidentally, a Muhajir-Pathan clash had already taken place in the same area in November. Clearly, between April 1985 and December 1986 the original differences between Pathans and Biharis that crystallized in April had solidified into a Pathan-Muhajir (including Bihari) conflict.

At first glance this may seem surprising since the earlier underlying tensions between Sindhis and Muhajirs have a longer history and reflect the kind of contradictions described. However, the configuration of the current ethnic conflict is less surprising in view of the fact that Karachi is not populated by Sindhis alone, and that the ethnic mix is tilted in favour of, firstly, the Muhajirs, and secondly, and increasingly, the Pathans. (There are more Pathans in Karachi than in the Provincial capital of Peshwar.) Pakistan's only seaport, Karachi, has become its trading, banking and industrial centre. Roughly 40 per cent of Pakistan's industry is located in greater Karachi, accounting for approximately 90 per cent of Sind's industrial labour force. Another 40 per cent is located in Punjab, with the result that the remaining provinces of Baluchistan and NWFP are not in a position to offer employment opportunities for large sections of their populations. If the problem is less acute in Baluchistan it is only because of its sparser population. In the more densely populated North West Frontier Province, large numbers of Pathans have been forced to migrate in search of employment and have gravitated, like other migrants, to the country's largest industrial centre, Karachi. Furthermore, as job opportunities opened up in the Middle East, Karachi, as a conduit to the West, has collected significant numbers of transitory migrants en route to the Middle East. In recent years the Middle East has no longer been able to absorb labour, and returning migrants have swollen the ranks of the unemployed. Among them Pathans have figured prominently. As a result the matrix of Karachi's population has shifted. In the words of one journalist:

The Pashtuns (Pathans) came as shoeshine boys, but they worked hard and, in time, monopolized the transport and trucking sector . . . [and] took over the new grocery and fruit and vegetable markets as Karachi grew. The Muhajirs [found that] employment opportunities were narrowed down to the services sector and middle trading, in which expansion could not be unlimited. They developed a seize mentality and an identity crisis (Bulleh Shah, 1987).

Socio-cultural differences also underwrite the Pathan-Muhajir divide. There are two important differences between the Muhajir and Pathan communities in Karachi. First, the Muhajirs are city dwellers of long standing, and it is their culture which has coloured life in Karachi. In contrast Pathans are rural tribal people who remain tied to their tribal culture except for a minority of older families settled in Karachi. Secondly, Muhajirs have no province or hinterland with which they identify, where they leave their families, own land, or send remittances. For the mixed ethnic Muhajirs, there is no one code of conduct, nor is there a particular social entity or organization which incorporates them all. The Pathans continue to adhere to their own codes, and the social organization of the tribes maintains its hold. Consequently, the value systems, codes of honour and lifestyles of these two communities divided by language (Pathans speak Pushto while the *lingua franca* of Karachi is Urdu) are frequently at variance.

Alienated by the urban culture, Pathan migrants, like those of other provinces, seek out their own community members. The state has neglected to provide institutions that would allow individual citizens to become assimilated into the urban environment, and the access of newcomers to basic amenities like accommodation and employment is determined by the earlier contacts that they have. For the poor who do not have the advantage of either old school ties or money, such contacts are limited to their own communities. Clan, tribal, village and regional loyalties are thereby strengthened and ghetto mentalities develop. Amongst Pathans these affiliations are very strong. Given that influential Pathans are connected with the transport and smuggling racket, poorer Pathans who frequently depend on them for a livelihood became inextricably linked to the transport and smuggling nexus even when their own work is not involved in the trade. Where tribal differences and rivalries exist in the Frontier, these are erased in Karachi where Pathans present a united front to all the 'others', to the extent that the intense conflict between the Pathans and Afghan refugees in the Frontier is glossed over in the context of Karachi.[4]

The discriminatory economic policies of the Government have

[4] Haji Sher Khan, President, Pakhtoon Mettehads Mahaz explained this in the following terms: 'They say that the Afghans are creating this situation... we are against their being brought here. . . . But though it is true . . . that we have our problems with them, we just can't throw them out. And in the

given rise to separatist feelings in Baluchistan, the Frontier and Sind, which has in turn created insecurity amongst the Muhajirs who have no province to call their own and whose strength in the administration and military has decreased over time. This insecurity is responsible for the formation of the 'Muhajir Quami Mahaz' (MQM), led by young men who broke away from the Jamaat-e-Islami because they felt it was not answering the specific needs of the Muhajir community. Although relatively recent in origin, the MQM has severely undermined the support of the Jamaat and other religious parties amongst the Muhajirs, and today it provides the Muhajirs with the ethnically defined social organization that they previously lacked. For their part the Pathans in Karachi have formed the Pukhtun Mutahida Mahaz (United Pathan Front). Backed by these formal organizations, the riots in 1986 and 1987 were qualitatively different from those of 1985.

Non-Party Elections, Heroin and Urban Development

Other than the formation of ethnically defined organizations, three separate factors have contributed to the present crisis. The first of these is the disruption of the political process and a prolonged period in which all political parties and political activities have been banned, followed by a non-party-based election. Whereas political moratoriums have often been imposed in Pakistan, the holding of non-party elections is a new phenomenon. In this context, candidates devoid of a political platform resorted to mobilizing votes, largely, and sometimes exclusively, on the basis of sectarian, caste and ethnic identities. This was the case in Orangi—site of the first clash between Pathans and Biharis—where for the first time Biharis opposed and defeated Pathan candidates for both the provincial and national seats. Constituencies and therefore favours were distributed along ethnic lines, and whereas this was true throughout the country, Karachi's ethnic mix sharpened the dividing lines with explosive results.[5]

present circumstances in Karachi, when Pakhtoons are being identified as the culprits along with the Afghans, we have a common cause'. *Herald*, December 1986.

[5] Details of the specific problems in Orangi have been discussed in Azam Ali and Shaheed (1985).

The second factor is more complex, but is visibly identifiable in the predominance of Pathans in the transport business. The lack of state subsidized and adequate transport facilities has generated a flourishing business of private transporters. Run on highly competitive and exploitative lines, the transport trade is linked to the police and administration through a complex system of graft. Private carriers are manned by underpaid and overworked drivers who frequently resort to narcotics for stamina, and to overloading so that they can pocket the extra fare. It makes little difference whether vehicles are run on a commission basis or whether owners demand a fixed sum of money, for fierce competition makes for reckless driving and frequent accidents. As in other instances, what is a mere problem for the rest of the country is amplified into a veritable nightmare in the sprawling city of Karachi. Private carriers who well deserve the nickname of 'yellow devils' are a daily bane for Karachites, and are greatly hated. Anger is directed both at the government for failing to provide transport facilities and for refusing to check the recklessness on the roads, as well as against those who run the business, the majority of whom are Pathans. (The Pathan monopoly dates back to Ayub Khan, who rewarded Pathan support in Karachi during the 1965 elections by issuing the majority of route permits to his community.) It should be added that Pathans have traditionally accounted for many of the country's drivers, but, until transport became such a problem, this did not matter. Then, too, for most of the older residents of Karachi, unfamiliar with the different faces of the north, Kashmiris, Baluchis and other northerners are often mistaken for Pathans.

A more sinister complication, precipitated by the Afghanistan war, has been the development of narcotics and arms smuggling in Karachi. This depends upon transport as well as the connivance of police and administration for its survival.

Heroin arrived with the Afghan refugees and the lucrative profits of the trade rapidly transformed the traditional poppy-growing areas of Pakistan's north into the golden crescent of heroin. The massive aid provided to the Afghan refugees by the United States in the form of arms and ammunition quickly found its way into the local markets to provide narcotics dealers with armed backing. The two are inextricably linked, and recent years have seen the emergence of a powerful narcotics-arms mafia, accompanied by the growth of a smuggling-transport-police nexus. The fact that the arms and heroin flow into Karachi from the Frontier, combined with the high profile of Pathans in the transport business, creates the impression that the Pathans are in the forefront. While the mafia has no particular ethnic identity, there is also no doubt that Pathans, best placed to receive arms from Afghan refugees and heroin from both sides of the border, are involved in the trade at all levels. Thus:

Hence certain Pathan settlements in Karachi have become centres of mafia operation. Most of these settlements grew out of the transport trade and as such are strategically placed on the entry points to various areas of the city. In recent years the mafia . . . has created Sohrab Goth . . . at the entrance to Karachi and become a major slum landlord in Quaidabad, thus controlling [Karachi's other exit] as well (Hassan , 1986, p. 76).

The third factor which has deepened the present crisis has been the criminal inadequacy of urban development schemes in Karachi. Karachi's population increases at an annual rate of 6 per cent, but civic amenities provided by the state grow at the rate of 1.2 per cent. The vast bulk of Karachi's poor, especially incoming migrants, are forced to fend for themselves. Officially developed land is too expensive for most of the poor, who end up in squatter settlements; these *katchi abadis* now account for close to 40 per cent of Karachi's population. In the sixties, Ayub's crusade against illegal settlements intensified the problem. A solution was found by enterprising state officials who backed unofficial operators to illegally occupy, subdivide and sell the land to the poor. In return, state officials received a commission and profited by speculating on important plots. This connection between illegal developers and the administration allowed the developers to service the settled populations by lobbying with officials for amenities and protection from eviction. Developers were also instrumental in providing or arranging loans for building. Critical at the local community level, these 'developers' acquired political power, and during the seventies many were replaced or joined the PPP. Ethnically mixed, the developers were dominated, however, by the Muhajirs and Punjabis. According to a reporter: 'The influx of heroin money into Karachi's economy in the late seventies and early eighties changed all this. New patterns of illegal land development emerged; new systems of informal banking came into being; the transporters' mafia expanded to control the city roads and the older squatter settlements came under attack.'[6]

Backed by heroin money and high-powered arms, the mafia is now in a position to hold Karachi to ransom, and a strike of private transporters paralyses the city, doing immense economic damage.[7] Having been unable to provide its citizens with the basic needs of life, the administration in Karachi is no longer in a position to assert its authority over that of the underground, which effectively controls the city. In the first riots in Orangi, a number of residents—irrespective of ethnic identity—stated that the trouble in Orangi had been contrived by the drugs-arms smuggling leaders to intensify their control over the population and to make their point to the administration, which had been talking of increasing control over transporters and of 'cleaning up' the Sohrab Goth dens.[8] (Orangi, Baldia and Sohrab Goth are neighbouring areas that lie at Karachi's main exit for the north.)

From the Khyber in NWFP the heroin trail leads down to Karachi—its vital connection· for the international market—entering through Sohrab Goth. For several years now, the administration has been aware that the area houses a thriving narcotics and arms trade, but has ignored it; undoubtedly mafia connections with highly placed officials—that at the national-international level seems to be largely non-Pathan—ensured inaction. Even after the Orangi riots of April 1985, which clearly indicated that arms were being smuggled into the township from Sohrab Goth, the administration limited itself to making ineffectual statements in the press (announcing for instance that a raid would take place). When the government finally decided to act and launched 'Operation Clean-up', the timing was such that it was bound to instigate rather than abate the riots.

Breaking Point, 1986

From April 1985, when the first Pathan-Bihari confrontation took place, to October 1986, violent confrontations between the people

---

[6] Hassan (1986), p. 77.

[7] It was estimated that millions of rupees worth of losses were sustained due to the inactivity for three days in the SITE area in Karachi.

[8] See Azam Ali (1986).

and law-enforcing agencies occurred regularly. Curfews had continuously to be imposed in some area or the other of the city, though
without exception in crowded and poor localities, and frequently
in the squatter settlements. In the face of state inaction, the public
increasingly took the law in its own hands and sporadic violence
against transporters continued. But the causes of violence were
diverse. Riots occurred because of water and electricity shortages,
but also due to localized confrontations with the police. In one
instance the death of an anti-narcotics social worker at the hands
of the police set off a bout of violent protest. But these eruptions were mainly spontaneous. In late October, an accident at
an unmanned railway crossing that left dozens dead similarly
ignited spontaneous rioting as well as demonstrations against the
failures of the government to provide protection to citizens.
This time, however, the intervention of the MQM converted this
into an anti-Pathan campaign. Then, on 31 October, a group of
MQM members leaving via Sohrab Goth to attend a party rally in
Hyderabad became embroiled in a skirmish that quickly gave way
to an armed combat in which several MQM members died.

It remains unclear why this group of MQM members was
leaving via Sohrab Goth since the tension between the Muhajirs
and Pathans had convinced the MQM to route its procession
through the less hostile point of Quaidabad. In the event, the
government reacted by arresting MQM leaders and workers on
their return from Hyderabad later that day, provoking what at
the time was the worst bout of communal rioting since Independence, only subsequently overshadowed by the December carnage.
Spreading from Sohrab Goth, the riots affected a number of
localities, but the worst violence occurred in Orangi, where non-
Pathans were the victims, and in Liaquatabad, where Pathans
were the victims. For the first time the trouble also spilled over
into Hyderabad in a now familiar pattern. A journalist investigating
the event discovered that hostilities could be traced to specific
causes in affected localities.[9] In many localities people died and
were injured by the law-enforcing agencies, and not because of
inter-ethnic conflict—bringing into question the role of the state.
These events took place in Karachi during the same week that

9. Ibid.

Quetta witnessed the worst sectarian riots to date, Peshawar the biggest bomb blast, and in Lahore the police killed two students leading to a renewed bout of violent protest. Instead of trying to bring about a reconciliation of the two communities in Karachi, the government launched its 'Operation Clean-up' in Sohrab Goth.

Whether it was deliberately planned or simply intended to pacify the immediate and widespread public protest, the timing of the operation made it clear that action against this Pathan stronghold would have repercussions. When they moved into Sohrab Goth the authorities did nothing to protect the residents of the nearby Orangi township, while information about the raid was leaked to the relevant people. The result was that the raid produced precious few guns, ammunition, or heroin, and certainly no mafia leaders. Instead, by treating all Sohrab Goth residents alike, i.e. as criminals, bulldozing all homes and evacuating everyone, Afghans and Pathans alike, the government succeeded in further alienating the Pathan community as a whole. Pathans felt victimized and blamed the Muhajir community and its contacts in the administration for the humiliation inflicted upon them. They also reacted by executing a swift and savage reprisal on the defenseless inhabitants of Orangi. For six long hours, armed bands swept down from the Pathan-dominated hills and wreaked havoc in the township, without let or hindrance from the administration. During this time, in the most vicious display of brutal savagery yet, houses were destroyed, people fired upon indiscriminantly and killed, and individuals dragged from their homes and burnt alive. When the armed forces and police finally intervened, many more, mostly innocent, people died at their hands. As in the past, the government provided no succour to the victims at all. As before, most aid— from ambulances to food and subsequent rebuilding work, as also clothes, medications and blood—came from non-governmental organizations, and from concerned citizens, particularly from Sattar Edhi and his foundation. The state had nothing to offer. In the wake of the December carnage, the riot victims began demanding guns and revenge.

In the deepening crisis, the response of political parties was disappointing. More ominous was the fact that political parties seemed to be on the verge of splitting along provincial lines. Many parties in Pakistan are provincially based and consequently side with whichever community forms the bulk of their supporters. Others who have scattered constituencies, including the only party enjoying nationwide support (the PPP), were reluctant to take any stand that might alienate either community. Other than the standard condemnation of martial law, and the demand for the existing government to hand over power, parties had little to offer. Although they were unanimous in their call for an end to the violence, for conciliatory talks and for the restoration of democracy with immediate elections, none of the parties proposed any measure that would indicate more than a surface analysis. It was certainly true that long periods of martial law had obstructed the growth of political parties and democratic processes, eroding the relevance of parties in the present political context, but it also seemed to be beyond their capabilities to devise appropriate measures or strategies to deal with the present situation.

In the intervening years of martial law, few political parties made any attempt to continue or initiate grassroots activities enabling supporters to cope with or to understand the multitude of problems they face in their daily existence. Springing into action mainly to demand the restoration of democracy—largely equated with the electoral process—political parties, who rarely practice what they demand for the nation within their own party structures, have failed to achieve their main objective. This has eroded their credibility, and they have proved irrelevant in the crisis of today. Inter-provincial contradictions have narrowed political conscious-ness to provincial borders. Hence in the Karachi-Hyderabad scenario, instead of the older political parties who have national aspirations even when they are provincially based, it is the leaders of MQM and PMM, with constituencies restricted to specific communities, who have emerged as the relevant partisan forces. The displacement of political affiliations by community loyalties suggests the need to examine the role of sub-state entities in the relationship of the state and its citizens.

States and Sub-state Nationalities

From the point of view of nationhood, most ex-colonial countries have not had the advantage of the evolutionary process witnessed in Europe, where national borders were determined over long periods of time, power politics were played out, and matching administrative support systems evolved. Logically, smaller communities only relinquish their independent existences for the sake of a larger state if either community members or leaders see some direct benefit being derived from the change in status (these are certainly financial, but also social—such as education and health—or political—such as protection from a larger hostile neighbour). In the gestation period, different communities were accommodated, to a lesser or greater but always acceptable degree, in the state structure. On the other hand, after colonization, most countries gained Independence as nation-states composed of various communities whose common point of reference was sometimes only the colonizer. Such sub-state entities had their own social structures, whose legitimacy at the popular level pre-dated Independence. In Pakistan, these were institutions such as the *jirgas* and *lashkars* of the tribal north and *panchayats* in Punjab, the autonomous administrations of the nawabs, princes and *pirs*, etc. In many instances the legitimacy of the newly formed nation-state depended on and was negotiated by those leaders of these sub-state structures who had a more immediate hold over the people.

Paradoxically, having initially borrowed legitimacy from smaller entities, the ability of a country to make the transition to a nation-state depends on how successfully national institutions replace the fragmentary legitimacy of smaller social groups. This requires direct contact and interaction between the state and its citizens, and also that the benefits of the state, in the form of social, economic and political rights, reach the people. Only by inducting its citizens into decision-making and by evolving democratic institutions can the state hope to reduce or eliminate the authority of sub-state entities. This has notably not happened in most ex-colonial states which have maintained the administrative structure inherited from the colonial power almost intact, and which, though declaring universal rights for citizens, have dealt and negotiated primarily with the leaders of traditional structures of power.

After Independence, these leaders or local elites frequently became the state's representatives and in their own context continued to negotiate the state's legitimacy. Whether state representatives or not, as the local power these elites tend to prevent development processes/benefits from reaching the masses since such benefits have the potential of undermining their own control. When benefits are made available, in the form of schools, roads or medical facilities, for instance, they are often presented at the local level as the 'gifts' of the local elites rather than as emanating from the state. In contrast the less attractive aspects of the state apparatus—the bureaucracy, taxes and law-enforcing agencies—remain identified with the central state system. Moreover, with a large number of the state's citizens dependent on the local tribal chief or feudal landlord for livelihood, this system cannot be challenged through an electoral process unless the state affords some measure of protection to those who oppose the local power structure. However, since the state depends on these very powers and is often represented by them (as reflected in the composition of Pakistan's legislators), it is not willing or able to do this. Industrialization and urbanization could also serve to weaken the power of local elites, but in Pakistan these processes have been so uneven that, with the exception of Punjab, the power of non-state organizations remains intact or has been strengthened.

This lack of state credibility and the supra-level legitimacy of autonomous sub-state structures and societal organizations manifested itself after the Pathan-Bihari clashes of 1985, for example. Although the government set up a tribunal to investigate the trouble, the Pathans appealed to their own community members in the Frontier to initiate a parallel investigation by a *jirga*. It was the verdict of the latter and not the former which carried weight.

Where state benefits only discriminate between classes, it is to be expected that class contradictions will be foremost. When there is an additional layer of provincial or ethnic discrimination, local elites who mediate between the state and the individual can easily manipulate the resentments of a people along ethnic lines and provide the necessary backing for a movement. In the end, provincial demands usually benefit the elites more than the masses; nevertheless, they normally encompass genuine grievances. Until these grievances are resolved, the distance between the state and the individual citizen is conducive to the belief that benefits derive from the local elites, and that the state is only a coercive force. The independent state of Pakistan has tried to use and/or pacify local elites without instituting measures that would allow it direct contact with all its citizens. Taking its cue from British colonial policy, it has, for instance, drawn up agreements with the tribal leaders of the Khyber Agency, thereby recognizing and abetting their independent authority. In a number of places in Baluchistan, the Frontier and Sind, the state apparatus has never penetrated; these have been ruled exclusively through the local structures of power that pre-date Pakistan, where even the law of the land is not the law of the state.

If the state seeks to use sub-state authority, it remains uncomfortable with the arrangement, its central power threatened by any popularly backed demand for real autonomy. This fear is exemplified in the refusal of each successive government to concede something as simple as the long-standing demand of the Pathans to change the name of the North West Frontier Province to one that reflects its people's identity (Pakhtunistan). This fear has grown in direct proportion to the rising nationalism of the smaller provinces which springs from the unequal distribution of the state's assets and a drain of provincial resources to support this inequality. In turn, provincial inequalities originate in the predominance of Muhajirs and Punjabis (now increasingly only the Punjabis) in the state apparatus, particularly the bureaucracy and military. The main recipients of state benefits, the Punjabis have come to rely less on sub-state structures than do people in other provinces. The ethnically disparate, uprooted Muhajirs had no single structure to bind them together and, as refugees, they placed their trust in the central state, where initially they had considerable representation. This trust was shaken during the Bhutto era and since then, in the face of increasing provincial nationalism, particularly that of Sind, this has now collapsed altogether.[10] In the changed circumstances, Muhajir insecurity has created the MQM.

Conclusion

In the course of its forty years of existence, the Pakistani state has not been able to evolve any system of accountability to, or participation of, its citizens. Elections have been rare and sporadic; the

---

[10] For a discussion of similar issues in a cross-cultural perspective, see Batallion (1977).

democratic process has been still-born. When elections have taken place, they have been used by local elites to consolidate their own power. On acceding to power, every government has equated itself with the state and ruthlessly put down opposition, whether class- or province-based, as anti-state. The judiciary has been systematically eroded of its autonomy, educational institutions have been straitjacketed, the media silenced through censorship, political parties and activities banned so often as to render them irrelevant in today's context, and the state apparatus and coffer frequently used as an extension of individual power and privilege. All this, accompanied by blatantly discriminatory practices *vis-a-vis* the smaller provinces, has led to the present crisis in which, having abandoned its citizens to all intents and purposes, the state itself is endangered. Consequently, to look at the recent ethnic riots in isolation is to see the symptoms and not the disease.

The depth of the crisis can be gauged from a decision taken in 1987 to grant each member of the assemblies with a quota of arms licenses to be issued at their discretion. Tacitly acknowledging that the state could no longer offer protection to its citizens, the then prime minister justified this by saying that every citizen had the right to feel secure. With the state encouraging its citizens to arm themselves, with virtual anarchy in interior Sind, increasingly violent chaos in Karachi and an explosive situation simmering in the Frontier, finding solutions to the underlying causes of tension amongst different communities is not easy and will take considerable time. Even to ease the tension, several steps need to be taken simultaneously to deal with the different levels of antagonism and conflict of interest.

Thanks to the Hyderbad-Karachi riots, the connection between the Afghanistan war and the arms/narcotic mafia was brought home to the people of Pakistan with a force that left them reeling. It made clear the necessity of stopping the growth of heroin and arms, and of finding a resolution to the Afghanistan issue. The solution of the problems generated by the easy availability of sophisticated weaponry, however, is going to be difficult. A responsible government, if it comes to power, will have to immediately reduce the use of arms in the conduct of life within the volatile regions ruled by Pakistan's leaders.

REFERENCES

Azam Ali, Ameenah, 1986: 'Frontline City', *Herald*, Karachi. December.
——, and Shaheed, Farida, 1985: 'Karachi Riots—April 1985: A Report on the Pathan-Bihari Clashes in Orangi'. Paper written for International Centre for Ethnic Studies. Colombo.
Batallion, C., 1977: *Etat, pouvior et espace dane le tiers monde*. Paris: PUF.
Bulleh, Shah, 1987: 'The Sinners Go Scot Free', *The Star*, Karachi, 1 January.
Hassan, Arif, 1986: 'Karachi's Godfathers', *Herald*, Karachi, December.

Chapter Nine

Reflections on the
Reservations Crisis in Gujarat

UPENDRA BAXI

The anti-reservations movement in Gujarat in 1985, with the attendant violence and repression, was in many ways a repetition of the 1981 violence encountered in the anti-scheduled-caste agitations, as well as earlier in the Nav Nirman Movement of 1974. These violent episodes stand as a stark negation of the claim that Gujarat is Gandhi's state, his first *karmabhumi*. The dramatic episodes of violence during the agitations should be understood against the background of a normal, structural violence embodied in everyday life in Gujarat.

Unlike its image, society in Gujarat is very violent. Gujarat is the home of patriarchal violence against women, and India's central site of dowry murders. National statistics on rape show it as being among the first five states. The atrocities, including the burning alive of untouchables in the course of the 1981 agitation, were a dramatic manifestation of the deep-seated repression of untouchables. Gujarat does not make shocking, one-shot-headline atrocities, as do Bihar and Tamil Nadu. It institutionalizes tolerance to violence, as in the case of hostile caste-based discrimination, at the level of everyday life. For example, 68 per cent of the untouchables are denied access to potable water from high-caste Hindu wells. The cities of Ahmedabad and Baroda are pre-eminent theatres of communal carnage, with annihilating violence directed against Muslims. The exploitation of Adivasis, in terms of deprivation of land, low wages and indebtedness, is comparable to the worst regions of India. The 'Gandhian tradition' of trade-union leadership allows unmitigated exploitation of unorganized industrial and migrant labour; this is acute enough to help us re-live Marx's descriptions in *Capital*.

Over the decades, Gujarat has also developed its own patterns of lawlessness. Political corruption is as widespread as in the rest of India; but it is, like everything else in Gujarat, extremely well managed. There is virtually no public movement against corruption, unless the Nav Nirman Movement in 1974 can be so regarded. The emerging social-action litigation and developments in administrative law have brought to light, in numerous ways, the patterns of governmental deviance in Gujarat. And the police brutalities in crisis management are not exceptions; they merely represent the heightened extensions of normal repressive behaviour by the colonial police force of India.

The crisis of 1985 cannot be adequately grasped without keeping in mind such everday forms of violence in Gujarat. It seems that the groups which have come to acquire positions of dominance precisely on account of distorted developmental patterns, perceive in the demand for increased reservations for the Scheduled Castes and Tribes and Backward Classes a threat to their own position. It is not that there are well-defined classes engaged in class war; it is that demand for increased opportunities of participation in modern institutions, such as medical colleges, on behalf of groups as ill-defined as 'Backward Classes', can lead to an anticipatory class war. In these, the high castes can signal the extent to which they are willing to use violence in order to prevent any serious questioning of their hegemonic positions.

As distinct from the category of Scheduled Castes and Scheduled Tribes, the category of Backward Classes is amorphous. It is ill defined and therefore subject to varying interpretations and manipulations. In some states, such as Karnataka, Andhra and Tamil Nadu, the prosperous peasant castes have appropriated these categories for themselves. In other cases, there are attempts to define this category so as to allow better prospects to less prosperous groups to benefit from educational and occupational opportunities. In the case of Gujarat, reservations for Backward Classes were introduced only in 1978, and only by a 10 per cent quota.[1]

---

[1] This is distinct from reservations for Scheduled Castes and Scheduled Tribes for which Gujarat has 21 per cent reservations, 14 per cent for Scheduled

As we shall see, the lack of accepted criteria to define Backward Classes made it a contested site. It gave the character of Absurd Theatre, with tragic consequences, to the entire agitation of 1985.

Even in the midst of the orgy of death and devastation, it was acknowledged on all sides, including the government, that the increase for reservations by 18 per cent for the Backward Classes would not have any substantial impact for a long time to come. For example, in 1984, out of a total of 675 seats in medical colleges, 7 per cent (47 seats), 14 per cent (94 seats) and 10 per cent (67 seats) were reserved, respectively, for the Scheduled Tribes, Scheduled Tribes and Socially and Educationally Backward Classes. In fact, only 3.4 per cent for the Socially and Educationally Backward Classes was filled in 1984; the rest of the seats went to the high castes. The position as regards engineering colleges was not markedly different. Therefore, even if the total reservation quota may have been as high as 31 per cent up to 1984, and 49 per cent under the present revised policy, the actual utilization did not, at the very most, exceed 15 per cent. The underutilization of the quota is directly related to the material conditions of existence of the impoverished strata of Gujarati society, on which no effective assault has been launched through planning.

Reservations in employment have somewhat affected the base. Low-level administrative people—peons and clerks—tend to have an increasing representation from the better-off among the depressed classes. The system of promotions through the roster procedure has had some visible impact on promotion for government employees who belong to the lower and middle classes. But job reservations do not extend to the private sector, nor do they extend rigorously to government companies or statutory corporations.

In this sense, the passionate espousal and opposition to enhanced reservations constituted an exercise in symbolic or rhetorical politics. The state, more under the compulsions of electoral politics than under the imperatives of the Constitution, has had to create and manage a contradictory reality. It has initiated, slowly and with wayward implementation, a process of pro-poor policies

---

Castes and 7 per cent for Scheduled Tribes as is consistent with the Constitution and national policy.

and programmes. Since these policies are not designed to bring about any immediate change in the material conditions of the impoverished, this exercise in rhetoric has generated the potential for delegitimation on all sides. The impoverished know that the policies addressed to them are not really meant for them; the dominant classes know this too, but fear that if they do not constrain the state now, they may be the losers in the long run.

This certainly explains the fact that people in the ideological professions (lawyers, doctors, university and college teachers) came next only to students in constituting the vanguard of the movement against reservation. These professions were able to articulate the ideologies of the dominant classes rather persuasively, and were successfully able to generate a debate for diversionary issues like 'merit', 'efficiency' and 'equality'. The real issue was, of course, the emancipation of the impoverished, for which reservation policies and programmes are only minor instrumentalities in any case. As brokers of the dominant and privileged classes, these professions were strategically placed to exploit the ambiguous commitment of the government on the issue of reservations.

Immediate Background of the Crisis

Gujarat did not have reservations for Socially and Educationally Backward Classes (SEBC) or Other Backward Classes (OBC) till 1 April 1978. It is true that the Janata government introduced 10 per cent reservations for these classes for the first time; but contrary to the propaganda, the A. R. Bakshi Commission (Panch) was appointed by the Congress government on 8 August 1972. The Bakshi Panch took four years to identify 82 castes/groups as backward; its report was submitted on 27 February 1976. Even during the height of the Emergency's feverish concern for the downtrodden, the Bakshi report was not implemented. Indeed, it was left to a successor government to implement it.

The implementation of the Bakshi Panch recommendations did not provoke any resistance, a fact which needs to be histori- cally underscored as well as understood. On 20 April 1981 another Commission, headed by yet another retired High Court justice, was constituted to specifically consider 'representations for being considered as belonging to socially and educationally backward classes from two sources', namely: (a) those castes/groups which had failed to get themselves favourably considered by the Bakshi Panch; and (b) other groups which had made fresh representations for inclusion. The Rane Panch started its work on 6 May 1981 and submitted its report to the government of Gujarat on 31 October 1983. As far as I am able to ascertain, no agitation greeted the announcement of the Rane Panch. It had certainly not needed high political imagination to forecast that the Rane Panch would end up by suggesting extended reservations. No parents, students, or political association was formed to articulate anti-reservation views for consideration by the Rane Panch.

This fact is significant because the Rane Panch was constituted almost in the wake of the withdrawal of the agitation of 1981, which was specifically directed at post-graduate reservations for the Scheduled Castes in medical faculties. Perhaps the proponents of 'meritocracy' were expecting that the Rane Panch, like its predecessor, would take its own time to report. They might also have expected that the Congress government would take at least as much time considering the report as it did with the Bakshi Panch.

This was not to be. The Rane Panch report, put in cold storage for well over fourteen months, was suddenly activated on 11 January 1985, as elections were announced. The Rane Panch did, predictably, suggest extension of reservations for OBC by 18 per cent, thus bringing the total reservations to 49 per cent. But it did so in a unique manner, for this was the first Backward Classes Commission to take the Indian Constitution seriously. It based its recommendations on 'class' and not 'caste', taking the view that when the Constitution employs the phrase 'Other Backward Classes', and 'Socially and Educationally Backward Classes', it legitimizes special provisions which are class-based and not caste-based.

The Rane Panch provided very many good reasons for shifting from 'caste' to 'class', aside from the basic argument of Constitutional intent. First, it maintained that the provision of special benefits by castes would perpetuate all 'the evils of the caste system', for the 'stigma' of backwardness would attach to a person 'till his death' if caste were to be the basis of identification. Classification by occupation and income would achieve a more secular and equalizing result, since a beneficiary could, as it were, step out of backwardness. Second, caste identification for backwardness had the tendency to create a vested interest in backwardness, as was evident in the case of Gujarat. The Panch found that the 'very castes which were at one time... showing progressive trends' were now aggressively competing for recognition as 'backward' castes. Third, caste criteria had the natural tendency to exclude from ESBC and OBC 'all such classes amongst non-Hindu communities, which do not recognise caste in the conventional sense known to Hindu society.' Fourth, caste-based classification suffered from many inherent defects, especially from the 'want of exact and complete information in regard to castes and sub-castes.' This lack could not be redressed as the Census of India had abandoned caste enumeration since 1931. The process of representation concerning backwardness would therefore be a continuing one and, indeed, a never-ending one.

For all these ideological, constitutional and practical reasons, the Rane Panch identified, in all, 63 occupations for the benefit of reservations. These occupations were divided into three classes: agriculture and cattle-rearing groups (4 occupational categories); occupations involving manual labour (24 categories), including hand-cart-pullers, rickshaw-pullers, porters, *beedi* workers, grave-diggers, cooks, and unprotected workers; occupations involving elements of manual labour as well as trade (29 categories), inclusive of carpenters, blacksmiths, copper-smiths, tailors, *jari* workers, tanners, *charkha* weavers or spinners, butchers, hawkers, peddlers, street vendors, waste-recycling workers, and 'victims of adverse circumstances or adversity' such as destitute persons, mendicants and inmates of orphanages.

In order to derive benefits on the grounds of educational and social backwardness, the Rane Panch fixed a maximum of family income of Rs 10,000 per annum. They further suggested the adoption of schemes specifically designed to help the poorest of the poor, such as development programmes for small and marginal farmers, the integrated rural development programme, and *antyodaya*.

A few days after the announcement of assembly elections in March 1985, the government announced the new reservations policy. It accepted the Rane Panch's proposal for raising the quota of reservations for OBC to 28 per cent. The recommendation that the income limit for eligibility be raised from Rs 7500 to Rs 10,000 was also accepted. The government, however, did a bypass surgery on the report by insisting that 'caste', not 'class', should be the basis of the identification of backwardness. This left the government in a curious situation. While the quota was raised, the beneficiaries still remained to be identified. It promptly set up a committee of six (including three MLAS), headed by a leading advocate and an MP, Haroobhai Mehta, to identify the beneficiary castes within ten to fifteen days. There was urgency because the decision was announced as having come into operation with immediate effect, but it could not achieve its purpose without an identification of the new beneficiaries. It was overlooked that the same task took the Bakshi Panch abour four years and the Rane Panch about two years, to complete. This report is still awaited.

The Rane Panch report was not made available simultaneously with the announcement of the new policy. The release of this report became a major demand of the anti-reservation campaign. It was finally released on 19 March 1985, by which time the protest was entering its most intense phase. There was no room for reasoned debate on the vital changes suggested by the Panch.

It is of some importance that we understand the implications of the government's refusal to accept the criterion of 'class' (defined by income and occupation) suggested by the Rane Panch, and its insistence upon a hasty return to 'caste' criteria for identification of backwardness. The government maintained that in offering the criterion of class as an appropriate measure of backwardness the Rane Panch had gone beyond the terms of its reference.

There was, however, no basis to assume (except on grounds of political expediency) that the Rane Panch exceeded its terms of reference. Indeed, the Panch was asked to 'make such other recommendations germane to the main terms of reference as may be deemed necessary by it'. The four main terms of reference constantly referred to socially and educationally backward classes. The Panch was also asked to deal with the problem of exclusion of sub-castes from OBC because of the 'ambiguity' prevailing in the 'names of sub-castes'. The Panch did, as noted briefly earlier, no more and no less than to interpret its task as it 'deemed necessary'.

That the government did not expect such an approach (replacing 'caste' by 'class') was understandable. But then it could and should have rejected the Report in its entirety on that ground, rather than publicly undermine and question even the IQ of the eminent members of the Rane Panch.

The confused actions of the government—the insistence that the Rane Panch had exceeded its terms of reference, yet the acceptance of the recommendation of enhanced reservation quotas without the means to identify the beneficiaries of this policy— make sense only in the context of a political rhetoric geared towards the securing of electoral advantage. There were other similar announcements, such as the introduction of the midday-meal scheme (costing the state exchequer close to Rs 110 crores per annum) and free women's education from kindergarten to doctoral studies. Barring an occasional minor political statement, the opposition parties could ill afford to protest at the new reservation policy: their prospects of returning to power were in any case not exciting and it would have been suicidal to have expressed any conscientious opposition to the policy. The Congress-I strategy was invincible; and in the event the Solanki-led party returned with a massive absolute majority, unprecedented since the formation of the state of Gujarat.

The ruling party reaped the rewards of the new reservation policy at the hustings. These were, however, shortlived. For soon political mobilization took place around the anti-reservation issue, and it was now the opposition which began to make political capital out of the issue. Consistent with the respective traditions of amorality in power politics, the reservation issue was essentially a political game on both sides; social justice and constitutional goals were only incidental to the pursuit of power.

It may appear curious that, soon after its massive electoral victory, the Congress-I government had to face such massive opposition in the streets. Clearly, political rhetoric does not translate itself into legitimacy very easily. The strength of the anti-reservation movement showed the potential of political mobilization of 'forward' castes and classes round the issue. It also showed the lapses in the internal organization of the Congress-I. Tickets had been denied to at least six sitting cabinet ministers, and there had been a systematic exclusion of the socialist leadership within the party in the distribution of tickets. These senior leaders were now conspicuous by their absence in the public domain. Meanwhile the integrity of Chief Minster Solanki was not above question. During the anti-reservation movement itself Solanki was alleged to have links with a leading industrialist in Surat who was facing an investigation for major criminal charges. Then there was the much publicized Mirkesh Jaykrishna affair, involving charges of corruption, collusion, and state patronage by the chief minister. Disclosures of this kind weakened the authority of the chief minister within the party and the credibility of his public performances.

The Course of the Anti-Reservation Movement

When the new policy was announced on 10 January 1985, Devjibhai Vanai, the minister for social welfare, confidently announced that 'there would be no agitation'. He gave the correct theoretical reason that even after the extension of quota to 49 per cent, 30 per cent of the high-caste population still enjoyed a *de facto* reservation of 51 per cent. The minister's perception would have been justified if the new policy had been announced with due deliberation and an attempt at multi-party consensus. But it was announced for immediate political advantage. While he was and is right in theory, he was proved totally wrong in his prognosis.

Any unilateral decision to increase reservation for OBC at any time would probably have generated anti-reservation agitation and students would have been the activators of dissent and protest. In Gujarat, for reasons which await analysis, neither the peasantry not the industrial working force is easy to mobilize. Students as well as young men generally have always been in the forefront of political dissidence in Gujarat. And the timing of the announcement of the new policy was a perfect gift to those who would wish to oppose the government, for close to five lakh high-school students were to appear on 18 March for higher secondary examinations in April–May. Disruptions of examinations could thus signal a dramatic protest against the reservation policy. This contest formed the pre-election backdrop.

Localized, small-scale student protests commenced within three weeks of the announcement of the new policy. An All-Gujarat Education Reforms Committee (AGERC) was formed in early

February. Protest took the form of burning buses, organizing rallies which violated prohibitory orders, boycotting classes in schools and colleges, and token fasts before Gandhi statues in various cities. In response, the Higher Secondary Board ordered closure of schools and colleges. The universities followed suit. In the thirty-odd incidents of the burning of state transport buses, the most gruesome was the burning incident in Nadiad, forty kilometres from Ahmedabad, where (on 27 February 1985) a passenger was also burnt alive. The conscience of Gandhiji's Gujarat was not shocked. The political parties conducted their campaigns as usual; this period saw no hostile press editorials. A single atrocity was of no major significance in a subcontinent full of atrocities. Soon there were to be many more, but the early warnings were not heeded.

The protestors received unexpected encouragement from the extempore remarks of Rajiv Gandhi on 2 March at Hyderabad. He told newspersons that the whole business of reservations 'is going a little out of hand' and announced that they would 'go over the entire matter' after the elections were over. Leaders of the anti-reservation movement construed this as a sign of their might and a signal that, if they persevered, they could achieve their objective of a total reconsideration of the reservations policy. As the agitation intensified in late March and through April, the union home minister clarified that reservations for Scheduled Castes and Tribes were non-negotiable and that there were no immediate plans for a review of reservations for OBC. Enough ambiguity had, however, already been created around the issue.

The movement also received support from the judiciary when the Gujarat High Court ordered a stay restraining the government from enhancing the quota for OBC. What was stayed is not very clear since the government had as yet to identify the beneficiaries of backwardness. In an astute move, the High Court extended the stay until 11 March, by which time the new ministry would have been sworn in.

The new ministry, which began functioning from 10 March, was not wholly sure in its handling of the agitation. The Home and Education Minister[2] insisted that the Higher Secondary Board

---

[2] A combination of portfolios unique to Gujarat!

examinations would be held as scheduled on 18 March; at a rally of Congress youth the chief minister was reported to have said that the government would be steadfast in its stand and would not yield to anti-poor agitations. He was reported to have gone even so far as to say that he preferred justice to power, and that his government would rather go out of power than participate in an exploitation of the inarticulate majority, the poor.

This was, even if sincerely felt, extravagant rhetoric, understood by his opponents to indicate a possibility of the ouster of the government through continued agitations. The rhetoric was soon swallowed when the cabinet decided on 16 March to keep the new policy in 'abeyance' for a year and to work out a new policy. Why was this done? The chief minister stated that the decision was taken in view of the student agitation, the High Court stay, the prime minister's announcement, and representations received from various sections of society. While the education minister and others were announcing that examinations would take place on schedule, the chief minister was engaged in extensive discussions with many associations to find a via media. In the event, the chief minister also announced that the examinations would be postponed by a week.

Instead of pacifying the anti-reservationists, this decision encouraged them to intensify their movement. The very next day the AGERAC announced its decision to go ahead with the movement until the government eliminated all forms of reservation. This was a demand which no constitutional government in India can possibly accept and was later to be modified and equivocated upon by the leaders of anti-reservation movement. The government's display of anxiety over the conduct of examinations on time was allowed to be misconstrued as a sign of weakness.

The anti-reservationists were convinced that the see-saw postures of the government on the reservations issue were based upon sheer political expediency. The decision about the postponement to implement the policy simply reaffirmed this view. The student leaders also became anxious that the support which they had gathered in their long six-week struggle should not be allowed to wither away. They also suspected that the new extensions would once again be announced from the next year. Thus they propagated the view that it was better for high-caste students to lose a year than to lose their privileges for generations to come. An 'All Vali Mandal' now came into being, under the leadership of a college professor of sociology, Shankarbhai Patel. A 'Gujarat Navarchna Samiti' was also formed. The anti-reservationists succeeded yet once again in creating conditions under which examinations could have been held only under the supervision of the armed forces. In many places, door-to-door campaigns were undertaken to persuade parents and wards against participation in the examinations. Bonfires of examination scripts were also organized. The examinations were indefinitely postponed by the government and the universities followed this. Once again, the Backward Classes were not strong enough, in leadership or organization, to bring enough political pressure in favour of the holding of examinations along the revised schedule.

It was here that the internal weakness of the Congress-I surfaced sharply. Its lack of cadres, its inability to bring exiled leaders into united action, its own vacillating commitment to the cause of the downtrodden—all these contributed to a situation where the large masses for whom the reservation policies were devised remained unmobilized and inarticulate. The state was left only with the arsenal of repression and the intelligent manipulation of the inherent organizational weakness of non-institutional politics conducted by assorted *mandals* and committees. The latter could not prevent violence and damage to state property in the course of the agitation. From mid-March to mid-May they were not even able to prevent their movement from being hijacked by communal forces and criminal elements.

A heavy propaganda warfare was inaugurated swiftly on all sides. The opposition was quick to say that the hijacking was masterminded by senior, ousted personalities in the Congress-I. The latter was quick to respond and to identify the opposition, especially the BJP, as the source of the violence that ensued. Even the prime minister and the home minister of India had no compunction pointing an accusing finger at the Opposition. In Parliament, the union home minister hinted at 'forces of destabilization' operative in Gujarat, although he discreetly declined to elaborate the thesis.

Embedded Violence in the Anti-Reservations Movement

The course of the movement, even before the 19–30 March communal violence in Ahmedabad, did involve considerable violence. We have already noted the burning alive of a passenger with the bus in Nadiad. In Rajkot a bus conductor was sprinkled with kerosene, tied and thrown into the burning bus.

The movement claimed that such violence was the work of anti-social elements—a category of concealed multiple reference. Alas, we will never know the truth as there is no investigation or prosecution. Gandhi, incidentally, would have suspended his civil disobedience movement and gone on an indefinite fast in such circumstances. The leaders of the movement, who claimed to follow the path indicated by Gandhi (*Gandhi chindhya marg* was their favourite phrase), were made of sterner stuff; the shedding of innocent blood was no one's responsibility.

There is no doubt that the movement till 18 March was hospitable to organized violence. For example, the burning of buses and government vehicles was an accepted strategy. It was accomplished by trained hands of youths, numbering up to fifteen persons. The bands were usually unarmed but they were highly skilled. There were very few incidents of accidental injury in these operations, and there was little reason to suppose that the youth involved had much experience or knowledge about the mechanisms of buses and other vehicles, or of arson. To my mind, most of the young people involved had been trained by 'elders' supporting the anti-reservations movement.

In addition to training, it was also clear that people had been supplied with materials. Groups of fifty to a hundred people had no difficulty in engaging the police in systematic combat, showing that organization and procurement of materials must have taken place.

The same holds true of *kakadas* or lit rags thrown at human beings, buildings and vehicles. The union home minister, on his visit to Ahmedabad in March was astonished; 'does Gujarat have a huge industrial production of *kakadas*', he is reported to have asked. Undoubtedly, for these required prior manufacture, chains of distribution, a choice of targets and manifold skills. These issues need authoritative investigation, in Gujarat and elsewhere, if the phenomenon of urban guerrillas propagating caste hegemony is not to take root in India.

The destruction of Government property, including the burning of offices, banks and post offices, was an important aspect of the movement. When I asked some young men for their view of such destruction, their answer was unequivocal: 'It is true that they are destroying property. But what is Government property? It comes from the taxpayer's money. It is *our* property and we are entitled to do what we feel with it.' The *sarkar* had made them angry, but it was the very sarkar the majority of voters had recently installed in power.

Whatever one's analysis of or judgement upon this kind of attitude, it is clear that the Gujarat middle and upper-middle class (including the leaders of social action, the press, intellectuals, and members of the ideological professions) voiced no powerful objections against such violence. But their restraint extended only in relation to the destruction of public property. When private property was hit by communal violence in Ahmedabad in late March, everyone was outraged. Suddenly the law-and-order machinery had failed, the government had failed to protect citizens. It was overlooked that if a popular movement systematically creates disregard for property, it is only a matter of time before other groups learn the same lesson. A student of the middle class becomes a hero by burning a bus; others learn how to become heroes by looting shops. At this point it is too late for anyone to credibly condemn violence.

Indeed, the objections by the leaders of the movement to the hijacking of their movement by 'anti-social' elements, and the complaints against consequent repression by the police, lose much of their credibility and legitimacy in view of their own encourage-ment to violence against public property. Gandhi was no fool when he stressed the relevance of non-violence in civil disobe-dience. He knew that if state power is to be successfully challenged or overthrown, citizens must, in addition to the strength of numbers, have the moral strength that comes from non-violence which puts the state on the defensive when it uses its might upon people. Even if one has qualms about the *morality* of non-violence,

Gandhi certainly demonstrated its superior virtue as a *technology* of people's movements.

Communal Conflagration: The Cost of Propaganda Warfare

The Gujarat Bandh called by the AGERC on 18 March was relatively peaceful. But it was followed by a series of incidents of violence inside the walled-city areas of Ahmedabad. According to Asghar Ali Engineer, the toll of communal violence was the highest since the 1969 Ahmedabad riots. Among the 19 persons killed, 14 died as a result of police firing and 5 of stabbings; 52 were severely injured; 115 shops were set ablaze. The total damage was estimated to be in the neighbourhood of Rs 3 crores. Such communal violence was unusual because there was no characteristic build-up of the tensions which usually precede carnage. Equally striking were the incidents of looting and arson in a variety of areas, such as Navarangpura, Ashram Road, Sharda Society, Ambavadi, Ghee Kanta Road, Jhaverivad, Panpur Naka, Shahpur and Relief Road—beyond the traditional conflagration points, such as Khadia or Shahpur. The actual details of violence are difficult to assemble from contemporary accounts. But all sorts of 'weapons' were used. Stabbing and stone-throwing produced the largest casualties. Pipes, cycle chains, and special cement stones with nails were also used. Hospitals reported injuries caused by police action, including multiple fractures owing to lathi-charges, teargas-shell injuries, bullet injuries.

Despite the fact that the army was called in on 19 March, violence and arson continued unabated in most areas for two days. It is clear that, on the first three days of the violence, the police proved both inadequate and somewhat indifferent. *The Times of India*, reporting on the situation on 19 March, pointed to the 'passive role played by the police' which provided ample opportunity for arson and violence.

This failure to manage the riot is reminiscent of what happened in the wake of Indira Gandhi's assassination. The law-and-order authorities appeared passive in relation to what are colloquially

called 'anti-social' elements. In addition, communal conflagra-
tion occurred in areas which were not usually involved in com-
munal tensions. All this gave scope for rumours that disgruntled
Congress-I people had encouraged and even instigated the riots.
In turn, the ruling party escalated the propaganda war against the
Opposition, especially the BJP.

Even in the face of such a virulent situation, there was no ethic
of responsibility in the public utterances of those who held high
public office. For instance, the prime minister visited Ahmedabad
on 23 March and attacked the Opposition as the organizers of agitations and riots. He said that those who build their strength on
casteism and communalism would have to be destroyed. Yet, in
rejecting the Rane Commission's principal recommendation that
reservations be based upon 'class' and not 'caste', the ruling party
had shown its own vested interest in caste. Even at the highest
level it was thought that a propaganda offensive would solve the
underlying problems. Thus, a politics of dialogue had to give
way to a management of dissent by the use of crude force by the
state. This constituted a serious crisis of legitimacy not only for
the majority party but even for bourgeois liberal democracy.

The most disturbing fact about the nature of such propaganda
politics was that it identified the anti-reservations movement
completely with the opposition parties. Whatever one's views
about the movement (and I consider it devoid of any constitutional morality), this straightforward identification denied the
movement any autonomy of its own. A reckless reiteration of
propaganda led many to believe that what was being propagated
as reality was indeed real. Thus the ruling party came to believe in
its own myths by sedulously blinding itself to social realities; the
identification of the movement with opposition parties limited the
scope of mature social intervention and peace-keeping initiatives.
New demands began to be generated. Thus, the governmental
secretarial staff registered its demand for the abolition of the roster
system and for the publication of the Sadhwani Committee
Report—all this on 21 March, when anti-reservations movement
had already led to widespread violence. The escalation of demands
and the complete inability to manage dissent within democratic,
constitutional confines led to repression and, finally, to unprecedent

police brutalities on the peaceful agitation by the government staff in May.

Police Violence in April

It is not possible to describe the violence perpetrated by the police against civilians in the month of April 1985 in anything other than broad outline. The violence was widespread; our descriptions are confined to Ahmedabad.

Asarwa was the first site of police violence in Ahmedabad. It had been a quiet area. But when the Government issued orders for resumption of teaching in schools from 1 April, students became available as targets for police violence. Two students were picked up outside the Asarwa Vidyalaya, and were threatened and assaulted. They were coerced into naming two other students who were then picked up for interrogation. All four spent the night in police lock-up.

Upendra Patel, a fifteen-year-old student, narrated to his mother, Pramilabehn, the story of beatings and harassment. He also narrated, what was perhaps his first lesson in legal education, that the police had threatened to frame him for violation of prohibition laws after forcing him to drink liquor. Pramilabehn Patel took four days to muster enough courage to file a representation on behalf of residents of the area against the high-handedness of the police. When she returned from the Commissioner's office she was beaten up by a group of policemen, whom she named. Thereafter the police went on a campaign of terror. They made people open houses and beat up everyone in sight. This included an old woman of 65, Sharadabehn; Avina Shah, wife of a 26-year-old shopkeeper and his two sisters; Hitendra Shah, who was attempting to return home after buying ice-cream; Narendra Mistry, a mill-hand who had just returned home after a day's hard work; and a widow, Indumatibehn Patel. It was also alleged that a notorious bootlegger was let loose in the area, threatening people with dire consequences if they reported against the police.

Clearly, this was the beginning of a deliberate 'get tough' policy. Although attempts were made to dismiss the complaints as 'minor incidents', these could not gain any credence. A protest fast was held on 6 April and Chief Minister Solanki apologized 'for the instances of beating up some women in Asarwa area'. The chief minister further stated that he was issuing instructions to the police 'not to mete such treatment to women and children'. A departmental enquiry was ordered.

Khadia, the site of many pre-Independence struggles and post-1950 communal conflagrations, was another trouble-free area until it became the theatre of police violence on 9 April. Police atrocities here were merely a bloody variation on those in Asarwa. A police officer later explained that ever since Indira Gandhi's assassination the force had been heavily deployed and, in their desperation, wanted to quell the anti-reservations agitation by methods they knew best.

Overall, the attempt to terrorize the population by the police may be understood as a calculated use of state force to batter people into submission. Yet, if this was a rationally calculated strategy, it was neither well conceived nor well managed. The police seem to have overlooked the fact that such naked use of force could not go uncondemned in a system within which the judicial process was in operation, and where there was relative press freedom. The police could not have assumed that their terror would not come under judicial scrutiny. It seems that, more than a rational and calculated use of force, these acts of the police may be better understood as the acts of a desperate and fatigued people.

Meanwhile, the police behaviour *had* come under judicial scrutiny. The High Court of Gujarat, in dealing with a petition filed by a BJP leader, constituted a panel to report on police excesses, to which the Government of Gujarat agreed. The High Court's intervention was unprecedented and therefore likely to be misunderstood. The Delhi High Court had, somewhat disgracefully, earlier declined a petition for the appointment of a commission to probe the post-Indira Gandhi Delhi riots. Of course, the High Court was entitled to its opinion, but the manner in which benches were changed mid-hearing was disgraceful. Some of the remarks made by a justice, expressing his contempt for social-action litigation, investigative journalism, and citizen action, did not do great credit to the judiciary either.[3] The Gujarat High Court,

---

[3] Justice Dayal of the Delhi High Court made several hostile observations

progressive as it has always been, had no hesitation in taking human suffering seriously.

When the High Court ordered this enquiry on 19 April, there was demoralization among the police and para-military forces. There were signs of panic in the government for there was a strong possibility of the police immobilizing itself to signal its silent protest. It was decided, therefore, to withdraw the police and hand over certain areas to the army. This, in turn, must have added to the dangerous demoralization of the force. It is not surprising that for the first time the Solanki sarkar held a conclave with Opposition parties on 19 April. The chief minister issued a joint appeal for restoration of peace and normalcy with two former chief ministers, Babubhai Jasbhai Patel and Chimanbhai Patel (of Janata and BJP respectively), signing it. But this display came too late in the day.

The police rebellion did happen. The immediate provocation was the killing of a police head constable by irate people. This incident broke all inhibitions. Prevented by the army from storming Astodia, policemen rushed to the hospital where lay the body of the head constable, where they went berserk. They set fire to buildings, the press and journalists being special targets of attack. The worst victim was the *Gujarat Samachar* building, which had highlighted police atrocities. The entire building was gutted. The *Indian Express* and *Western Times* offices were also attacked. The police surrounded fire stations and prevented the fire brigade from responding to distress calls for well over an hour. The total loss to property was estimated to be close to Rs 7 crores. There were also sporadic incidents of looting by policemen in the city. By the evening the rioting policemen were persuaded to return to the fold. However, the following two days saw an outburst of virulent communal violence in Bapunagar. Close to 25 people were killed while nearly 3000 were rendered homeless.

Despite all this violence, the chief minister denied that there was a police revolt. Instead, he attributed the police behaviour to

---

about the role of civil-rights workers and called journalists and university professors 'worse than wretched' in the course of hearings about the demand to set up a judicial enquiry on the 1984 riots. These remarks were not part of the judgment.

'resentment spreading through the ranks' which was aggravated due to the anti-police stand of the press.[4] In other words, policemen were not held to be accountable in law for their actions. As a strategy of riot control this may have had short-term advantages, but its long-term costs will be to the legitimacy of bourgeois democracy itself. Further, the relation between the police and para-military forces on the one hand, and the armed forces on the other, worsened. And, finally, the violence spread to as many as eight towns, with the army being called out in every one of them, including Surat. The number of people killed all over Gujarat, and the number of people injured, has yet to be estimated.

Karamchari Strike: The Wages of Ineptitude

The fall in violence in the first week of May was followed by a strike of about 800,000 government *karamacharis* (employees). They had, as noted earlier, articulated their demand for the publication of the Sadhwani Committee Report on the Roster System on 21 March in a meeting with Chief Minister Solanki. The report was submitted to the government on 10 September 1981. Two years after this, Shashikant Lakhani, a Congress-I MLA, had demanded the release of this report in the Congress legislators' meeting, but to no avail. Government employees decided, not without reason, that a show of strength was most likely to provide results. The response of the government to this demand on 21 March was to declare the secretariat staff as a part of 'essential services' under the Essential Services Maintenance Act. When the employees went to present a memorandum of their demands on 29 April to the secretariat, they were severely lathi charged. The lathi-charge was so brutal that governor, B. K. Nehru, publicly expressed shock and indignation. To the initial demand for the publication of the Sadhwani Committee Report were now added two additional demands: a judicial enquiry into police excesses and the punishment of policemen guilty of brutality. These

---

[4] The panic reaction of the chief minister was evident in the announcement granting Rs 1 lakh as compensation to the family of the Head Constable who was killed. No policy issues about normal compensation to be paid to policemen killed in action were discussed.

demands were rejected on 7 May. Consequently, nearly 300,000 *Panchayat Karamcharis* also joined the strike. As many as thirty-five associations were involved in the decision, creating an unprecedented solidarity across associations. The only exception to this solidarity was provided by employees of reserved categories, who were the prime beneficiaries of the Roster System.

Why was a report available to the government since 10 September 1981 not released for three and a half years? This secrecy supported the dominant view that the Committee had in fact recommended abolition of the Roster System, including the carry-forward system. Even so, the report was probably not unanimous, for a different view may have been articulated by members of the groups who were beneficiaries of the reservations system. Finally, the report was released at a meeting between the representatives of the karamcharis and the government on, 17 May 1985, when an accord was announced. The accord was rejected by the bulk of the karamcharis after two days.

The entire manner in which the strike was managed shows the conduct of politics today. In my opinion, the demand for the abolition of the Roster System cannot be conceded as it is anti-constitutional. However, in order to take a principled stand on the matter the Sadhwani Committee Report should have been released and then rejected. Instead, it seems that the state government thought it could 'kill' the report, without having to reject it explicitly. It showed again how the manner of doing politics is based upon domination via the concealment of information. This modality of politics is clearly not acceptable to the articulate urban populations of modern India.

A Darkening Landscape

We leave the narrative at this point of time to raise some issues regarding the nature of political processes in Gujarat, to which the anti-reservations movement can be related.

The most important question that clearly needs to be addressed is the future of the reservations policy itself. At one stage in May 1985 an announcement was made by the union government to the effect that states should await the formulation of a national consensus on the reservations issue. This, again, seems like an exercise in the kind of rhetorical politics that we have been describing. The effort to evolve a national consensus would create an explosive situation for it would require an unequivocal policy declaration by the union on the Mandal Commission Report. In the absence of proper mobilization of the *dalits*, and a wavering commitment towards translating the radical politics of the Indian Constitution into state action, a national consensus on reservations would only create the kind of movement that we have been discussing here, on a wider scale.

It is important to remember that even if we arrived at a national consensus, we cannot accomplish a reversal of history. As a result of the political mobilization of the Backward Classes in the pre-independence era in South India, the southern states have well exceeded the national policies, beyond 10 per cent. But to transpose southern policies on the Backward Classes to the northern states, where reservations policies began to emerge after 1950, would be to create chaos.

Finally any national policy would have to make a conscious choice between class and caste as the basis for reservations. As the Gujarat case shows, the acceptance of class as a criterion for reservations can create enormous enforcement problems. Retaining caste, on the other hand, will only perpetuate discontent with irreversible quotas, and lead to a permanent investment on the part of such castes into backwardness. The emergence of divisive and authentic terrorist forces in Indian society and polity do not offer any prospects of consensus on such deep-seated emotional issues. The ease with which protest movements may be hijacked into criminal violence is directly related to methods of political management that have been evolved and cannot be regarded as accidental. It would be a mistake to think that the crisis in Gujarat is only about the reservations policy. It is also about the crisis of state in Gujarat. The politics of backwardness and the backwardness of politics fused together to perpetuate the crisis.

The backwardness of Gujarat politics is, I trust, writ large in the foregoing text. To put it crudely, people in power in Gujarat do not seem to understand that they are not the rulers of Gujarat, and that a nascent bourgeois liberal democracy can only produce an elective oligarchy or 'managers' of the people. And even oligarchy and 'managers' cannot take their legitimacy for granted. The crude assertion of political will is likely to evoke resistance and deplete the legitimacy of power. It also threatens, or is perceived to threaten, the interests of the bourgeoisie who, as a social class, need the state but are always ambivalent to state power insofar as its exercise affects differentially the various forms and fractions of capital. Apart from the material interests at stake in any exercise of state power, the manner and form of its exercise has become increasingly important to these classes. A crude assertion of the will to power is generally not acceptable.

A second aspect of the backwardness of politics in Gujarat is the increasing tendency of the government to resort to brute force in the management of dissent. This is directly related to a arbitrary exercise of political power, for such arbitrariness leads to a crisis of legitimacy, which in turn makes it difficult to negotiate with protest movements without the police, para-military and armed forces. Ironically, this creates an illusion among the oligarchy and managers of the polity to the effect that the state is strong, whereas the opposite is true.

It is possible to go further and argue that the frequent use of the police to repress internal dissent poses very serious dangers to the legitimacy of the state. For members of the police force also share in world-views generated in society, especially on such emotive issues as reservations. If state action lacks legitimacy in the eyes of the police, the latter cannot be used to support such action without the risk of rebellion. This is why it has become a frequent practice to call in the army, with consequent tensions between army and police. The police feel publicly humilated and superseded, leading to a further deterioration of relations between the state and one of its important arms.

The role of 'anti-social elements' always surfaces into conscious-ness during politically turbulent periods. Yet it is often forgotten that state power is frequently secured in normal times on the strength of such 'anti-social elements'. The political patronage that they enjoy gives them immunity against the criminal justice system. At the micro-level of political management, criminal inti-midation is carried on with impunity by such elements. Breaking strikes in industry or inhibiting movements for minimum wages are other examples of their activities. Given the colonial structure of the Indian law and its policing, anti-social elements have become necessary as police informers as well.

The crisis of legitimacy is starkly visible in the case of Gujarat in the lack of party cadres that could propagate policy at the grassroots level. For example, the Congress-I as a *party* was nowhere visible in the whole crisis. The absence of intra-party democracy, common to most political parties in Gujarat and in India, has simply encouraged the oligarchic practice of politics, which has in turn brought about a spectacular dissociation between the party and its leadership.

Unfortunately, the politics of protest in Gujarat is also enveloped by the backwardness of politics. While three or four associations mushroomed during the agitation, a disciplined control over strategy and tactics was never contemplated. The movement, like the government and the Opposition, simply blamed anti-social elements for the violence. No effort was made to take responsibility for those who suffered the violence, or to launch an effective protest against communal violence.

The anti-reservations movement could achieve cohesion only on this one issue of opposition to reservations. The lack of an ideology blunted the protest against the autocratic and arbitrary exercise of power on the part of the government. This arbitrariness was visible at every point in the management of dissent. Yet the movement could not develop into one that could seek a transformation of the very practices of politics which accommodate such absolute will to power.

The most tragic aspect of the backwardness of politics is the passive role of the Scheduled Castes, Scheduled Tribes, and Other Backward Classes in Gujarat. They have strength of numbers, but the practice of *savarna* politics has turned them into the subjects of the dominant classes. Unless the beneficiaries of the reservations policies can emerge as a political force, these policies can only be partially implemented.

In general, thus, the arbitrariness of the state and unaceptable political practices have created the broad social crisis of which such violence is a manipulation. The transformation of political practices is not the issue. The issue is the containment and elimination of political practices which are perceived as destroying the structure of bourgeois politics.

From this standpoint, history will not repeat, *contra* Marx, first time as tragedy and second time as a farce. Time and time again it shall repeat itself as a tragedy until the elected oligarchs and managers begin to appreciate that they cannot become rajas.

The *ati-sudras* of Gujarat too will learn from all this. What is today a struggle for the restoration of practices for bourgeois politics may itself be the portent for a struggle against the repressive practice of politics against the *ati-sudra*.

Chapter Ten

Noise as Cultural Struggle: Tom-Tom Beating, the British, and Communal Disturbances in Sri Lanka, 1880s–1930s[1]

MICHAEL ROBERTS

The blaring radio is an ubiquitous presence in any Asian bazaar. Westerners who have travelled in Asia will vouch for the fact that, generally speaking, Asians habitually accept decibel levels of music which most Westerners consider intolerable. It is not loud music alone that intrudes upon the Westerners' aural senses: fire-crackers, drumming and howling dogs penetrate and shatter their thresholds of tolerance.

This was forcefully brought home to me in March 1987 by an incident at the Unawatuna beach resort in southern Sri Lanka. Unawatuna is a 'low' beach resort and its two small hotels are cheek by jowl with the huts of fishermen and other villagers. At about 9.30 p.m. one night I emerged from the entrance of one hotel on the landside and headed for my vehicle to pick something up, passing a security guard who was tucking into his rice and curry in a watch hut. At this moment a German appeared on a balcony on the first floor. Speaking haltingly but fervently in broken English, he summoned the guard and commanded him to put an end to the howling of village dogs in the vicinity. Otherwise,

[1] This article was made possible by the support of the Alexander Von Humboldt Foundation and the International Centre of Ethnic Studies in Sri Lanka. I am grateful to Rohán Bastin, Chris Bayly, Rob Jones, John D. Rogers and George and Mona Stauth for their comments and/or assistance.

he stressed, he would come down personally and kill them. He spoke with feeling. He meant every word.[2]

British administrators, planters and merchants also responded in opposition to such 'disturbance of their repose'. I recall one occasion in Galle during the 1950s, when a retired planter complained about the tom-tom beating from a neighourhood temple which had disturbed his sleep the night before. He had, I think, telephoned the police and lodged a complaint. Likewise, about 120 years previously, in 1833, one learns that the privates in the 97th Regiment complained about the noise made by tom-tom beating and *chicoti* singing in their neighbourhood in Colombo.[3] The latter incident indicates that, at least in the colonies, the antipathy to loud drumming was not confined to upper-class Britons.

These temporally disparate incidents indicate the typical response of Britons to nocturnal noise or overpowering noise levels. As colonial masters, they were in a position to enforce their norms in British Ceylon, especially after a rudimentary police force had been established during the mid nineteenth century. Their regulations on this point were included within Ordinance No. 16 of 1865, the 'Police Ordinance' as it was widely referred to, the pertinent sections being clauses 69 and 90:

69. . . . All officers of Police shall and may keep order in the public roads, streets, thoroughfares and landing places and all other places of public resort; and prevent obstructions on the occasions of such assemblies and processions, and in the neighbourhood of places of worship during the time of public worship. . . . They may also regulate the use of music in the streets, when the same shall be allowed . . . 90. All persons who shall, at any time, *within any town* or limits, either within any house or building, beat drums or tom toms, or have or use any other music *calculated to*

---

[2] Sequel: the security guard proceeded to peer helplessly into the darkness beyond the hedge and then, wisely, returned to his dinner. When I returned a few minutes later, nevertheless, a remarkable silence resigned. The dogs, it seemed, understood English-backed-by-feeling! Cf. too, the recent complaint against Ginger Baker's son's practice sessions of drumming by an irate neighbour in London (*Daily Telegraph*, 5 Aug. 1987).

[3] *Colombo Journal*, 15 June 1833, p. 288. *Chicoti* refers to a form of music favoured by the so-called Portuguese Burghers or Topaz, which has since influenced the *baila* of the south-western littoral.

frighten horses, or who shall make any noise in the night *so as to disturb the repose of the inhabitants*, or shall, at any time, discharge fire arms, crackers or fireworks except under Military regulation, or unless they shall have obtained a license from the Police Magistrate of the district, or from the Chief Superintendent of Police . . . shall be guilty of an offence, and be liable to any fine not exceeding Five pounds, or to imprisonment . . . not exceeding Three months (emphasis added).

It is my contention that the principles encoded within this Ordinance were at variance with the life ways of the Sinhalese. In seeking to regulate the interaction between individuals or bodies of people in this manner, the Police Ordinance stimulated religious friction. Where such friction escalated into 'disturbances' or 'riots' (official nomenclature), the agencies of state then became involved as arbitrators or punishing arms. In this manner, by laying down rules about unacceptable noise, the British colonial state both 'promoted' and mediated specific forms of tension between neighbours or between religious communities in British Ceylon.

The most unacceptable form of noise from the British point of view was that of drumming, usually referred to in the literature as 'tom-toming'. Yet, to the Buddhists and Hindus, drumming was part of the fabric of life-crisis rites, whether celebrations, exorcisms, or community rituals seeking to ward off evil/disease. Indeed, even in funeral processions drumming was not out of place. While I have used the past tense here, these comments are pertinent to contemporary Sri Lanka even though the cultural practices today have been amended by the influence of Westernization. A shift into the present tense is therefore apposite for the speculations which follow. In the Sinhala Buddhist milieu, I suggest, drumming and appropriate forms of music act as an extension of self. They are at once existential and proclamatory. They function as commemorative and/or celebratory claims. They speak to the world at large, both sowing and reaping the wind. This is especially true of the sounds associated with large religious gatherings. The buzz, of people of the tom-tom, the flute, exude religious fervour.

These suggestions are founded upon my intuitive cultural knowledge rather than an analysis of 'native' exegesis. Some fragmentary support for this thesis is found within what is known as the Gampola Perahara Case (1912–18). When a lay trustee of

Walahagoda Devala petitioned against the government's application of the Police Ordinance in September 1912, he noted: 'Stopping tom-tom before any particular individual or place of worship is in our opinion a dishonour to that individual or place of worship.'[4] When this issue was eventually brought before the courts, it happened that the District Judge was Paul E. Pieris, a Sinhalese civil servant who was a scholar-historian of nationalist disposition. His judgement against the government contended, among other arguments, that music was 'a mark of honour', and a 'sacrifice of praise and thanksgiving'. He unfortunately weakened his case by giving it a universal cast; 'With every nation and at all times the accepted manner of showing particular honour is to make a noise'— the universality being illustrated by a reference to the firing of guns in salute.[5] Such a generalization ignored the valorization of silence in the context of worship within Islamic and Christian civilisations.[6] It relied on the language of universality when the case should have rested on the language of differentiated religious traditions.

The commemorative 'occupation' of space through sound which is part of the Sinhala Buddhist tradition, I further surmise, is not necessarily an exclusive claim. That is, a drumming sound from one Sinhala Buddhist corner can readily permit another drum from a neighbouring, 'opposed' corner to claim the same 'space'. It may seek to incorporate or subsume the other, but it will not deny its right to beat.

These speculations on the anthropology of drumming and music in traditional Sinhala Buddhist life ways are in line with Ashis Nandy's arguments about the character of South Asian religion until recent times. Nandy suggests that, before colonial times, South Asian society was marked by the pursuit of 'religion-as-faith', i.e. religion 'as a way of life, a tradition which was defini-

---

[4] Nugawella (1912). Nugwella wrote in his capacity as President of the Buddhist Temporalities Office, District Committee. Cf. the way in which the Hindus of Agra in the 1890s considered music and cries of 'jaikara' at their festivals to be part of their 'ancient rights' (Freitag 1980: 604).

[5] Thalgodapitiya (1963), pp. 56, 59.

[6] My comments on Islamic attitudes are based on Ameer Ali (1981), p. 11 and information provided by George and Mona Stauth (Egypt and Bielefeld).

tionally non-monolithic and operationally plural'—involving 'a confederation of a number of ways of life' and providing 'some theological space for heterogeneity'.[7]

In Nandy's argument it was not till the colonial experience that the more uncompromising face of religion, 'religion-as-ideology', came into prominence. This face of religion involved 'religion as a sub-national, national or cross-national identifier of populations contesting . . . or protecting specified interests'. In this view, religion-as-ideology is 'a by-product . . . of modernity' and 'a response to Western colonialism'.[8] This contention needs to be tested and recast in the light of the research on disturbances in pre-British India in the eighteenth and early nineteenth centuries. Chris Bayly has revealed that the prevalence of syncretic religious practices in the north Indian cities during this period did not prevent clashes occurring 'over the status that different religious traditions held in relation to the control of festivals or holy places'.[9]

The regulation of processions and noise in the Police Ordinance of 1865, therefore, falls within a general issue for South Asia: the clash of cultural principles. This clash was not simply the Western-Asian opposition with which I began this essay. The Asian world was split on this point insofar as the emphasis on silence as a mark of respectful worship was ingrained in the Islamic world as much as Judaeo-Christian civilization. The Hanafiite and Shafiite Muslim traditions of India, it seems, considered music to be abominable (*makruh*).[10] For the area of Indian civilization, therefore, we need to explore a whole series of questions relating to processional music in front of places of worship: What policies did the Mughul rulers pursue in this regard? What was the practice in other kingdoms where Muslim rulers governed Hindu majorities, such as

[7] Nandy (1987), p. 2. For some ethnographic support for this viewpoint, see Obeyesekere (1984), *passim*.

[8] Nandy (1987:2) and pp. 19–20. I have altered Nandy's phraseology by substituting 'specified' for 'non-religious'.

[9] Bayly (1985), p. 202 and *passim*. Bayly suggests that during the colonial era there was a clear focus for communal rivalry, whereas before 'the clashes were more diffuse'. But cautions that this is 'an unknown area' in the present state of knowledge (personal ommunication, 2 Aug. 1987).

[10] Ameer Ali (1981:11).

the Nizamate of Hyderabad and Tipu Sultan's kingdom in Mysore? What was the practice in pre-colonial times in Hindu states with Muslim minorities? Could Syrian Christians in the Hindu states on the Malabar coast seek or secure such a convention? Did Hindu processions in the kingdom of Jaffna and Buddhist processions in the kingdom of Kandy cease making music when they passed the mosques of Muslims in their midst?

I believe that the answer to the last question would be a firm negative. Furthermore, I assert that, speaking generally, music and noise have not posed a problem for either sleeping persons or worshippers in the Hindu and Buddhist world. The regulation of sound in the Police Ordinance, therefore, was at variance with indigenous customs, while its modalities were those of Roman law: the language of clear-cut boundaries and exclusive rights. These Western thought ways can be fleshed out by a survey of some revealing documents from the 1920s. These documents also show how pragmatic adjustments were made *during the 1920s* in the application of these regulations, both in 'country districts' and slums on the one hand and with reference to public religious cere-. monies in towns on the other.

The Regulations of Noise and Processions *during the 1920s*

The most significant set of documents contains the official responses to separate applications by Hindus in Matale and Colombo which sought licenses to beat tom-toms at wedding ceremonies till 2 a.m.[11] In reporting on one of these requests, the district adminis-

---

[11] One of the Hindus affected was S. Rajaratnam of 'Chisle Hurst' in Barnes Place, Colombo. He was a Member of the Legislative Council and promptly made the refusal to grant a music-making licence beyond 11 p.m. into a Legislative Council issue.

The Hindus in Matale were M. Raja and Sankaran Asari, persons who were regarded by the A. G. A., Matale, as 'ordinary inhabitants of the town with no claim to a special concession', in contrast to K. T. M. Markikar Tamby (a Muhandiram with 'a long . . . record of service under Government . . .' etc.) who had recently been given permission to beat tom-toms till 3 a.m. (J. L. Rogerson to I.G.P., 16 July 1927, in DNA 80/560).

trator at Matale, J. L. Rogerson, observed that in Matale town the police issued licenses which permitted music *at private ceremonies* only till 11 p.m. He was aware that at Hindu wedding ceremonies the *thali* was tied at about 1 or 2 a.m. He was ready to bend the rules and permit certain forms of music (e.g. clarionette, flute and cymbals) to be played after 11 p.m. 'provided they did not make sufficient noise to disturb the repose of others', i.e. of neighbours. As a general rule, however, this freedom would not be extended to tom-tom beating; and, indeed, one of the licensees had been prosecuted and fined for disregarding the time limit.[12] Rogerson point was that 'Tom-toms undoubtedly disturb the sleep of the neighbours'.

He noted that the licensing restrictions exercised by the police in this manner in the case of private ceremonies was 'in order that the town may be habitable at night to persons in need of repose, who have to work during the day'. It was singularly unfortunate that the auspicious hour and climactic moment at Hindu wedding ceremonies usually fell 'at an hour when the world's workers are enjoying a well-earned sleep, i.e. at 1 or 2 a.m.'. He added:

I also deny that the use of music at Hindu marriages is *religiously* imperative. There is no religious requirement that music should be played. It is entirely a matter of custom. I think it is desirable to permit such music as far as possible without discomfort and loss of sleep to the general community. As my predecessor stated in a letter to you (dated 8 July 1925) . . . private individuals usually prefer to suffer in silence rather than to incur the enmity of the offending party and the trouble of giving evidence in court. The night in a town is already sufficiently disturbed by noises and the people should in my opinion be encouraged to restrict their private festivities in the quantity of noise produced in the interests of the general population. Religious processions with music are always allowed. Church and Temple bells already make the daytime hideous and the community must be given reasonable protection during the hours of sleep.

The predecessor's letter was that by W. E. Hobday, one which describes the policies pursued towards 'private ceremonies', as distinct from 'Public religious ceremonies', in the following manner:

[12] Rogerson to I.G.P., 16 Jul 1927, in DNA 80/560.

It has always been the custom to impose some restrictions on nocturnal tom toming. In fixing the time limit at 11 p.m. I have, I believe, followed the practice obtaining in other towns. . . . It is evident that some such restriction is necessary if the town is not to be rendered uninhabitable.[13]

These letters are witness to specific, overlapping cultural premises attached to the industrial and bureaucratic order of modern times and its work ethic. Firstly, time was to be routinely and invariably perceived in terms of 'day' and 'night'. Secondly, in carving up time in this manner, a primacy was attached to the 'working day'. The night was preparatory to this end, a 'space' for repose and recuperation. And thirdly, it was taken for granted that one could not sleep through reverberating and penetrating noise (when, in fact, many Sri Lankans regularly achieve this feat as a matter of course).

This corpus of reasoning was not particular to Rogerson and Hobday, or to Matale. Letters and reports written by Dowbiggin, the Inspector General of Police, during the late 1920s make it clear that Rogerson's letter summed up the general lines of government policy;[14] while 'disturbing the repose' was a standard phrase in official literature (being, in fact, rooted in the Police Ordinance of 1865). The only thing out of the ordinary, perhaps, was the catholic sweep of Rogerson's definition of 'hideous' sounds. This encompassed the pealing of church bells. In Rogerson, clearly, one had a secularized Christian to whom church bells were neither uplifting nor edifying.

During the 1920s the restrictions encoded in this policy were, in practice, only held applicable to towns; and even in the towns were not enforced in the slum areas becuase in these localities, as in the villages, 'the neighbours did not mind or object to tom toming'.[15] As subsequent letters penned by Dowbiggin reveal, the *Ceylon Police Gazette* of 25 September 1918 had specified that the Police Ordinance was to be enforced 'in country districts only

[13] Hobday (A. G. A. O, Matale) to G. A., Central Province, 8 Jul. 1925 in DNA 80/560.

[14] Dowbiggin to Col. Sec., 22 Jul. 1927 in DNA/560. Also see Dowbiggin to Col. Sec. 12 Nov. 1927 in DNA 80/560 and Dowbiggin to Revd. A. F. Jessen, 4 Jan. 1935 in DNA 80/979.

[15] Note by police officer (signature indecipherable), 30 Jan. 1926 in DNA 80/560.

in exceptional circumstances'. In such areas 'the religious or other ceremonies of the people and their amusements were not to be unduly interfered with'. Accordingly, police officers at outstations were expected to 'act with discretion'; and the general rule was that they should not 'interfere with tom-toming in villages or processions to temples which did not cause obstruction, annoyance, a breach of the peace, etc'.[16] This decree nevertheless made it clear to all concerned that the Police Ordinance would be implemented in rural areas if offence was caused and some party presented complaints.[17]

Beyond the note that villagers did not object to such disturbance the reasoning behind these modifications in rural areas was not spelt out. It is conceivable that the police authorities were making a virtue out of necessity: they may not have had the personnel or the means to enforce such a policy in the outlying areas. However, one can surmise that three other considerations influenced this policy. Firstly, that in most rural areas the inhabitants were attached to one religion so that the possibility of friction between different religious groups in the course of processional activity was minimized, in contrast to the multi-religious environment of towns (see below). Secondly, that the characteristic spatial form of most villages in Sri Lanka, their dispersed and straggling spread of homesteads, made nocturnal disturbance a matter of lesser consequence in comparison with the situation in towns. Thirdly, that the working schedule of villagers was structured differently to that of office workers and shopkeepers in towns.

To the extent that such considerations guided the government's policy in rural areas, there appears to have been a welcome attentiveness to the life ways of what I will call 'the extra-bureaucratic domain'. However, these villagers were not only residing within such a domain, they were also Buddhist or Hindu (for the most part). Taking Buddhists as our illustration, this meant that a hamlet might arrange a series of ceremonies known as the *gammaduva*

[16] Dowbiggin to Col. Sec., 12 Nov. 1927, in DNA 80/566 as well as Dowbiggin to Revd. A. F. Jessen, 4 Jan. 1953 in DNA 80/979.
[17] T. P. Attygalle (Acting I.G.P.) to Attorney General, 29 Nov. 1926 in DNA 80/566.

(which took place, when performed in its complete form, over a period of five or six weeks) or a *pirit* chanting ceremony to ward off sickness. Individual households would sometimes arrange *pirit* ceremonies, ceremonies which traversed the night. Likewise, where an individual member of a household was deemed to be under the control of a demon, an all-night exorcist ceremony would be held. Exorcisms were to Sinhala Buddhists what psychiatrists are to contemporary Western households. But a Westerner usually sees his shrink privately and the cure is usually privatized. The success of exorcist rituals, in contrast, depends on each performative ritual being deemed successful by the kinfolk and the neighbouring folk who are witnesses to the curing act.[18] In that sense, it is a cure with community participation. When the *poya* days fall, moreover, Buddhist Sinhalese of religious disposition move into another time frame. The idea of a working day is (and was) at odds with this time frame. Rites at one's temple as well as religious processions sometimes occur in the late evening or night.

Such life ways were not restricted to rural folk. The Buddhists in urban localities, several of whom were, in any event, recent migrants from rural districts, partook of these practices. This, then, was the problem. The town:country dichotomy in British policy was fallacious, or partly so. However, the British were sufficiently alive to their situation to modify the implementation of the rule within slum areas and to draw a distinction between private and public ceremonies. As the quotation from Rogerson's letter would have made evident, licences were invariably granted for public religious ceremonies (whether *in situ* or involving processions). In effect, on these occasions tom-toming was permitted till later at night. Indeed, for such religious festivities as *Wesak* and *Theru*, tom-toming was allowed throughout the night.[19]

There were several critical qualifications attached to these licences, however, when they were granted for religious processions which involved tom-toming and music. The noise had to be stopped if the procession encountered horse-riders or carriages

---

[18] Kapferer (1983), pp. 55 and 59–60.

[19] Hobday to G.A., Central Province, 8 July 1935 and Note by a police officer, 30 Jan. 1926 in DNA 80/560.

on the road. It had to cease 'within one hundred yards of any place of Public Worship'.[20]

As far as I am aware, the first restriction was not productive of friction. During the inter-war years, of course, with motor transport replacing horse and carriage, this restriction became increasingly obsolete. The cessation of music and drumming in front of other religious sites, however, remained an issue which could generate confrontation or riotous disturbances. In the Jaffna Peninsula, these clashes were usually between the Vellarlar high castes and castes deemed low.[21] Elsewhere, such confrontations were between localized religious groups: between Sinhala Catholics and Sinhala Buddhists at Nakandapola in 1927–30, between Catholics and Hindus at Negombo in the years 1924–7, between Muslims (i.e. Moors) and Sinhala Buddhists at Vincent Street in the Pettah, Colombo, in 1933, between Moors and Sinhalese in the bazaar of Galle in 1936, for instance.[22]

These illustrative examples of communal clashes during the inter-war years should not be regarded as exhaustive. A careful search of official sources and the newspapers will probably produce more instances. In restricting my choice of examples to the inter-war period I have been mindful of the fact that, thus far, my outline of government policy has relied on sources from this period. A particularly significant document in this regard was the 'departmental order' embodied in the *Ceylon Police Gazette* of 25 September 1918, an order which modified the application of the Police Ordinance in 'country districts'.

The question that arises, now, is the nature of government policy before this notification, and especially before the 1915 communal riots. On that occasion, in May–June 1915, the Muslims (i.e. mostly the Moors) in the south-western and south-central parts of the

[20] See the standard 'Ceylon Police Procession Form' in DNA 80/560. In some of the official literature before 1915 a distance of 50 yards rather than 100 yards is stipulated.

[21] *Admin. Repts. 1924*, Police, III: 826 and Dowbiggin's Report in Correspondence associated with D. S. Senanayake's strictures against the militarization of the Police, 1927, in DNA 80/687, p. 25.

[22] See, respectively, DNA 80/566 (Nakandapola); 80/579 and 388 (Negombo); 80/1726 (Vincent Street); and 80/2181 (Galle bazaar).

island, were subject to widespread attacks by Sinhalese. The immediate provocation for this pogrom was a procession dispute at Castle Street, Kandy, which followed upon a protracted procession dispute at the neighbouring town of Gampola between 1907 and 1915 and a number of localized clashes in the early 1910s at Kurunegala, Balangoda, Badulla, Kandy and Hambantota.[23] The British responded to these riots with a heavy hand. The brutalities and indiscriminate punishments effected by the state agencies, in their turn, promoted a concerted nationalist campaign along constitutional channels against 'British injustice'.[24]

The ill feeling aroused in elite circles was such that the new governor, Sir John Anderson, took carefully conceived steps to assuage resentment. One of these measures was to consult M.T. Akbar, a Muslim judicial officer of Malay stock, before proceeding to Gampola on 17 August 1916.[25] There he set up 'throne' at the rest house, to which location the trustees of 'the town mosque' (Ambagamuwa Road) were 'summoned before His Excellency'. Having emphasized to them 'that British policy was to maintain an impartial attitude towards all communities and religions', Anderson delivered a sermon:

Hostile attitudes between communities could not be tolerated and must cease, giving way to peace and goodwill. The Sinhalese people had been good customers of Mahomedan traders from olden days, and it would be to their advantage to cultivate good relations with them. The annual Gampola Perahera was a religious function handed down from ancient times, and they ought to modify their objections.

He then ordered them to arrange specific hours of worship so that the Buddhist processions could take the usual route past the mosque by avoiding these hours. Whereupon the trustees 'expressed their pleasure to abide by whatever decision was arrived at by His Excellency' (in the words of a news report).[26] It was a command

---

[23] See Appendix IIc of *The Sinhalese Memorial*, encl. in CO 54/786; Woolf 1965–66: 241–42, and Ameer Ali (1981), p. 11. For the 1915 riots, see the references in fn. 94 below.

[24] See P. T. M. Fernando (1970) and D. D. Ranasinghe (1976).

[25] M. T. Akbar (1927). On some of Anderson's other measures, see Blackton (1970), p. 250 and *Sessional Paper XVI of 1916*.

[26] *Ceylon Morning Leader*, 18 Aug. 1916, and Akbar (1927).

performance: compromise by fiat. Anderson then consolidated this achievement by gracing the Asala Perahara of Gampola when it was revived after a six-year lapse on 10 December 1916.[27]

This agreement was a concession on the part of the Moors who controlled the destinies of the Ambagamuwa mosque, a concession that was presumably influenced by the experience of the 1915 riots as well as the force of Anderson's intervention. Both in the decades immediately before 1915 AD in the 1920s the standard Muslim (and Catholic) demand was that processional music should cease *at all times* in front of their places of worship, for they claimed that worshippers could be present at any time.[28]

The argument remained in force at Gampola in the 1920s. It was specific to Ambagamuwa mosque. Such a practice was not extended to other urban areas because the Inspector General of Police held that it was not practicable to either organize or monitor such an arrangement in urban localities where there were numerous places of worship, especially because processions rarely adhered to their intended schedule.[29]

It is against this background, and with retrospective advantage, that we can turn to a consideration of government policy towards the noise generated by processions in the period 1865–1915.

Pre-1915: Processions and the Preservation of Peace

The evidence on this subject which I have secured to date is fragmentary and incomplete. It appears that the town–country distinction was adhered to till the early 1900s. Readers would have noticed that section 90 of the Police Ordinance was specifically restricted to 'towns'. Even in towns its application appears to

[27] *Ceylon Morning Leader*, 11 Dec. 1916, p. 8. The Basnayake Nileme of Walahagoda Devala responded to Anderson's visit by invoking Kataragama Deiyyo to safeguard the governor. It is not clear whether this had any effect on Anderson's cycle of life: he died in Sri Lanka in 1917, the only governor to 'achieve' this.

[28] E.g. Akbar (1927); summary of statements by Mr Oorloff, F. Dominic Perera and others in the memo by M. D. M. Gunasekera (A.S.P., Western Province), 28 Jan. 1927 in DNA 80/566; and Thalgodapitiya (1963), p. 73.

[29] Dowbiggin to Col. Sec., 17 Oct. 1927 in DNA 80/566.

have been restricted and spasmodic. In 1884 the governor, A. H. Gordon, observed that in Kandy tom-toms were beaten every morning and evening and that it was only in Colombo that this aspect of the law was much enforced.[30] Other evidence from the previous year shows that even in Colombo unlicensed processions took place in the daytime and evening.[31]

Gordon was responding to a request from a spokesman for the Buddhists (the American Theosophist, Colonel Olcott) that all restrictions on music-making in the streets should be removed. He refused to go that far: the government had to retain the power to keep different processions apart. But he also observed that there had been unnecessary meddling by the police and expressed his opposition to the deployment of Western ideas in ways which interfered with the 'harmless usages' of the native peoples. Gordon's position on this point was in line with the attentiveness to native custom which he had revealed in Fiji. But it was not an attitude shared by the generality of British administrators, policemen or judges in British Ceylon, especially in reference to such a penetrating custom as tom-toming at night. Nor did Gordon delete sections 69 and 90 from the statute books. Thus institutionalized, the problem of clashing cultural premises remained. As long as they were part of the law these clauses could be activated by individuals and the state agencies could be mobilized against tom-tom beating or noises which 'disturbed the repose'. Printed judicial reports from the higher courts reveal that at least ten such cases reached appellate jurisdiction before 1915, four being instituted by Britons.[32] It would seem that some Ceylonese at least had imbibed the alien norms incorporated into the Police Ordinance, though one should not discount the possibility that they were using these clauses of the Ordinance as a rod against neighbours whom they disliked. The diffusion of the idea that tom-toming was a disturbing and disrespectful noise is illustrated in the manner in

---

[30] Gordon to Derby, 29 Aug. 1884, CO 54/554 (notes kindly provided by John D. Rogers).

[31] Memo by the S. P., Western province, 16 Mar. 1883 in the Riots Commission (1884), p. 9.

[32] See 1 *SCC* 90; 2 *SCC* 167; 2 *SCR* 160; 1 *NLR* 179–80; 7 *NLR* 126–27; 7 *NLR* 380–82; 8 *NLR* 74; 14 *NLR* 426–27.

which an English newspaper directed by Sinhala Protestants described the reasons for the Catholic-Buddhist fighting at Wattala on 26 February 1900, 'a party of Buddhists with tom-toms created a great noise and disturbed the service. This *naturally* infuriated the Catholics . . . '.[33]

These clauses could also be invoked by localized bodies of religionists to require processions to maintain silence in the immediate vicinity of their places of worship. Within the south-western and central parts of the island it appears that some Catholics and Muslim communities began to make such demands during the late nineteenth and early twentieth centuries. My initial surmise that Buddhists did not make similar demands against the chants which were characteristic of some Muslim and Catholic processions has since gained partial confirmation, 'the Buddhists have never raised any objection to the Muhammedans taking their pagodas and their Hobson Jobson festivals by the side of any Buddhist places of worship', said the trustee speaking on behalf of the Walahagoda Devala in 1912.[34]

The emergence of these localized struggles for symbolic space at a particular point of time can be attributed to the heightening of the Buddhist (and Hindu) revitalization movements in the island, a subject I will attend to in due course. These developments, I suggests, influenced the religiosity of Catholics and Muslims in the midst of the Buddhist or Hindu majorities. It is noteworthy that the Muslim insistence on this point appears to have gathered pace in the 1900s rather than earlier. This was because Muslim revivalism was a relatively late development (it did not have its roots in an anti-Christianization struggle, unlike the Buddhist and Hindu revivalisms). It appears that the Wahhabi movement in India and the development of Hindu-Muslim conflict on the

---

[33] *Ceylon Standard*, 26 Feb. 1900.

[34] P. B. Nugawela (1912). It is not clear whether these Muslim processions made noise. Nugawela's letter may be raising an issue of entry into symbolic space: the G.A., Central Province appears to have, at least at one point, denied the procession any right to pass the mosque at all (see a somewhat later communication, Procession Form License, dated 26 Sep. 1912 and sent to B. Elikewela, Basnayake Nilame, Walahagoda Devala in the same corpus of documents).

subcontinent were the forces which promoted Muslim zealotry in British Ceylon.[35] The vanguard of this line of Muslim revivalism appears to have been the Hanafiite seats among the Indian Moor traders residing within the island, migrants who were 12.3 per cent of the total Moor population in 1911 and who were known locally as Coast Moors, or Hamba (a derogatory term) in Sinhala. The Ambagamuwa mosque at Gampola seems to have been a Hanafiite mosque in which Coast Moors predominated.

The use of the Police Ordinance in this manner to create a convention of silent respect in the vicinity of another religion's seat of worship, it should be noted, was not a generalized phenomenon in the urban or urbanizing localities. There was local variation in the stance of Catholic, Protestant and Muslim communities. The spatial and temporal unevenness in demand made it all the more difficult for the Buddhists to adjust themselves to these innovatory claims. The Buddhists associated with the Walahagoda Devala procession in Gampola, for instance, were only too aware that the Muslim folk of the Kahatapitiya mosque in Gampola, an older seat of worship, continued to accept this practice without demur.[36]

The situation of the Buddhists was made more difficult by a hardening of British attitudes during the 1890s, 1900s and 1910s. One can sense the growth of a Curzonian rigidity, an attempt to maintain imperial authority at all costs.[37] Be that as it may, a majority decision of the Supreme Court in 1904 seems to have extended the application of section 69 of the Police Ordinance to villages as well as towns, though the dissenting judge argued that this clause was 'inapplicable to the circumstances and surroundings of the

---

[35] Ameer Ali (1981), pp. 5–13. Also see Samaraweera (1979).

[36] P. B. Nugawela (1912) and Ameer Ali (1981), p. 2.

[37] 37. E.g. I. M. Thurn to Chamberlain, 420, 7 Sep. 1902 as well as the G.A., NCPs letters in CO 54/677; and Rogers (1986). Contrast, too, the brusque letters from the G.A., Central Province, to the spokesmen of the Walahagoda Devala during the 1910s in comparison with a previous G.A.'s policy in the 1880s when the Ambagamuwa mosque had tried to raise the same issue (Appendix II in *The Sinhalese Memorial*, encl. In CO 54/786). My surmise on this point is supported by John Rogers, who refers to F. Saunders and H. L. Crawford (among others) as officials who developed a negative attitude to the Buddhists (personal communication).

villagers themselves, and would almost deprive them of the harm-less amusement of beating tom-toms'.[38] By this stage, moreover, the reach of the police force was being extended to some rural areas, albeit unevenly.[39] It is against this backdrop that we must assess the I.G.P., Herbert Dowbiggin's unequivocal statement on 3–4 February 1915 to the effect that the cessation of music was 'the rule universally in force throughout Ceylon and enforced by the police in accordance with Section 69 of Ordinance No. 16 of 1865'.[40]

One should not accept this general statement at face value. Take the grand pageant, the Asala Perahara, in Kandy as a point of illus-tration: though it would seem that the Buddhist dignitaries in Kandy had agreed in 1905 to curtail the music associated with the Asala Perahara in front of places of worship, a subsequent statement in 1927 indicates that it was normally held without a licence.[41] In other words, it is likely that the implementation of this law was as wide as the local police officer's foot. But where Catholic or Muslim dignitaries took up the issue one can be certain that the government decree was brought into force.

Dowbiggin's letter of 3–4 February was a response to the legal challenge to these regulations instituted by the Basnayake Nilame of Walahagoda Devala and upheld by Paul E. Pieris's judgement of 20 March 1914. In attaching weight to the rule emanating from section 69, his reasoning was as follows:

In my experience there has been trouble over this matter of processions tom-toming and using music when passing places of worship not only in Gampola, Kurunegala and Badulla (Kandyan Districts) but also in Colombo and Jaffna as between Buddhists and Catholics, Sivites and Mohammedans and Sivites and Roman Catholics. It is most important therefore that the Police Rule made in accordance with Section 69 . . . should be preserved and enforced throughout the Island.[42]

Composed on the eve of the Supreme Court's appellate decision

[38] 8 *NLR*: 164–73.

[39] Rogers (1987a), p. 7; Dep. 1969 and the *Admin. Repts.* 1900s.

[40] Dowbiggin (1915). Also see Rogers (1987a-c).

[41] Cf. de Sampayo in 18 *NLR* 205 with Letter from Akbar to Col. Sec., Confid, 8 Oct. 1927 in DNA 80/566.

[42] Dowbiggin (1915).

on the District Court judgement, Dowbiggin's initial draft held that a fundamental problem had been created by Pieris's decision: 'The matter to my mind is one of great importance from the point of view of *the preservation of order* in the island' (emphasis added).[43] It was Dowbiggin's hope that the Supreme Court would, in their impending decision in appellate jurisdiction, set the District Judge's verdict aside. 'If it is not it will generally be held that Kandyans can tom-tom and use music when passing places of public worship and *this will lead to serious rioting*' (emphasis added).[44]

There is irony here, a paradox which the opening segment of this essay has been designed to reveal. Dowbiggin and the other British authorities appear to have been totally oblivious to the possibility that their cultural premises and laws, as specifically embodied in sections 69 and 90 of the Police Ordinance, had created the conditions for such potentialities, had inadvertently encouraged inter-religious friction. It is my argument that if the British had held that music and noise in front of a place of worship was neither disrespectful nor disturbing a great deal of trouble would have been averted because such a stance would have been in step with local mores. This is not to say that there would have been no religious clashes over symbolic space, but that the occasions for such struggles would have been lessened.

There is yet another paradox however. Several Buddhists began to conceive of noise in the manner in which it was perceived by the British, the Catholics and the Muslims: namely as a disruptive force. John Rogers has perceptively made this point and suggested that several Buddhist-Catholic confrontations during the 1880s were the outcome of this realization.[45] Rogers provides several instances when Buddhist groups appear to have paused in front of Catholic churches and beaten tom-toms, shouted and clapped with extra vigour; (i) before St Lucia's Cathedral at Kotahena,

---

[43] Dowbiggin to Col. Sec., no. 72, 4 Feb. 1915 in DNA 80/1501.

[44] Dowbiggin (1915). The sentence which I have quoted was part of the original draft of this letter. But, evidently, the Supreme Court decision became public immediately after it was drafted. Whereupon Dowbiggin deleted this sentence and replaced it with the statement: 'I am glad to see that the judgment of the District Judge of Kandy has been set aside'.

[45] Rogers (1987a), p. 180; (1987b), pp. 589–90, and personal communication.

22 May 1883; (ii) before the Alutgama Church, 22 May 1889; (iii) before the Maggona Church, 25 May 1889; and (iv) before the Holy Cross Church at Kalutara, 29 May 1889.[46] This may also have been the case at Wattala on 25 February 1900, though there were additional allegations that the elephants in the procession had been used to uproot a cross.[47] Because the Catholics showed restraint on three of these occasions, no physical violence resulted. But at Maggona and Wattala affrays developed.[48]

On these occasions, therefore, these bodies of Buddhists were employing noise as a weapon, an invading force that was at once overwhelming, proprietorial and exclusive in its claims. That they should adopt this style of operation is a pointer to the transformative power of law as institutionalized practice (another example, arising from the modalities of non-statutory practice, being the degree to which Sri Lankans have adopted the Western practice of two minutes silence as a form of commemorative respect; even the Janata Vimukti Peramuna pursues this convention).

The adoption of such practices by some Buddhist activists, however, proved to be a two-edged sword. Administrators began

---

[46] Personal communication from Rogers with the citations being all from the *Ceylon Catholic Messenger*, 9 Nov. 1883; 2 Jul. 1889; and 28 May 1889. Also see Rogers (1987b), p. 590 for the Maggona disturbances involving Wahumpura villagers from Magalkande. The partisan nature of some sources is counterbalanced by what one can anticipate from the logic of retaliation.

[47] Cf. the official viewpoint in Dep (1970), p. 351 and the report in the *Ceylon Independent*, 27 Feb. 1900, with those in the *Ceylon Observer* and *Times of Ceylon*, 26 and 27 Feb. 1900. The report in the *Dinapata Pravurti*, 27 Feb. 1900, describes the attempt to uproot the cross as the spark. Also see Rogers (1987a), pp. 196–7. As Rogers observes, this conflict probably had its roots in a long-standing enmity between the Wahumpuras of Paliyagoda and the Salagamas of Wattala-Modara which dated back to the 1860s and 1870s. Though Goyigama and Karava Catholics appear to have been involved in the 1900 battle, all those charged in court were either Salagama Catholics or Wahumpura Buddhists.

[48] There were other localized clashes between Catholics and Buddhists which did not originate from objections to music but developed out of processions. E.g. at Galle Road, Colombo in 1889 when an exchange of words led to one such contretemps (*Admin. Repts. 1889*, G.A., W.P., 18 Apr. 1890, p. B12).

to regard processional music as a danger. A senior administrator in charge of the Western Province was even driven to the exasperated suggestion (in 1890) that 'all religious processions of whatever description should be strictly prohibited'.[49] Thus, Catholic and Muslim dignitaries were able to raise the spectre of a 'riot' and to activate the strict enforcement of the Ordinance.[50] By starting a riot themselves in front of Ambagamuwa mosque on 27 May 1907, the Moor Muslims set up the condition which led the government to apply the rules regulating processional music at Gampola.[51] This induced the Walahagoda Devala authorities to dig their heels in, to call off the *perahara* in 1912 and to challenge the legality of the regulations. The Gampola Perahara Case, as it was known, became a *cause celebre*.

A striking feature of the religious disturbances in the period 1865–1915 is the fact that there do not seem to have been any confrontations between Buddhists and Hindus, even though Hindu concentrations had developed in Colombo by the late nineteenth century.[52] Likewise, Christians and Muslims do not seem to have had any clashes *qua* Christians and *qua* Muslims.[53] These phenomena support the argument of this essay: that the imposition of British cultural premises about the importance of silence for

[49] Ibid. Also see the editorial in the *Ceylon Standard*, 27 Feb. 1900.

[50] E.g. Letter from J. Missillamany to I.G.P., 6 Mar. 1883 in *Riots Commission*, p. 8.

[51] *Admin. Repts. 1907*, G.A., Central Province, 29 Apr. 1908, p. B11, and P. B. Nugawela (1912).

[52] Dowbiggin's review of past disturbances in 1915 does not speak of disturbances between 'Sivites and Buddhists', while Rogers' research did not turn up evidence of clashes between Tamils and Sinhalese (1987a), p. 201. This tentative assessment is in disagreement with Kannangara (1984), p. 151 on this point, though I agree that economic factors were less important as the cause of the strike than made out by observers.

[53] In the disturbances at Chilaw in Dec. 1897 many of the Sinhalese involved were Karava fisherfolk who were Catholics, but it *would seem* that they hated as 'Sinhalese' rather than as 'Catholics', and, as such had support from non-Catholic Sinhalese within the locality (see DNA, Pending File 45 and *Times of Ceylon*, 29 Dec. 1897). This tentative assessment is in disagreement with Kannangara (1984), p. 151 on this point, though I agree that economic factors were less important as the cause of the strike than made out by observers.

religious worship worked to the advantage of the Christians and the Muslims, while disadvantaging Buddhists and Hindus.

In pressing this advantage to the hilt in obdurately demanding processional silence before their churches or mosques at all times, localized bodies of Catholic Christians and Muslims were imposing their worldview on the Buddhists in whose midst they lived. As such, their demands were political assertions and a delimitation of symbolic space. These demands were considered to be political impositions by the Buddhists. They were resented by them as the encroachments of minorities working within the shadow of the colonial power. In pressing their advantage, therefore, the Catholics and Muslims were not so much belling a cat as tweaking a lion. To the Sinhala Buddhist activists of this era, after all, the Moors and other Muslims were *paradessakara* or aliens, while the Sinhala Catholics were a particularly dangerous species, turncoats who were a cancer in the body politic of the Sinhalese.[54] It is towards a clarification of this background that I now turn.

Buddhist Revitalization and the Preservation of Sacred Realms: Towards the 1915 Pogrom

In British Ceylon during the nineteenth century one witnessed a relatively rapid extension of the market economy, with cash crop plantations as the spearhead of this process of commoditization. These developments promoted the emergence of an indigenous bourgeoisie as well as an overlapping but not synonymous status group which came to be described locally, in all its ambiguity, as the 'middle class'. A Western education was one of the boundary markers of the middle class and with the rapid expansion of print capitalism this middle class became the vehicle of liberal and

---

[54] E.g. a leaflet notice in Sinhala entitled 'Prasiddha Danvima' which was circulated in the Chilaw area in December 1897 (kindly supplied by John Rogers); Piyadasa Sirisena, *Maha Viyavula* (1984), pp. 7–13, 115–16 & Jayawardena (1970), p. 224; a summary of P. H. Abraham Silva's pamphlets by a British official: Roberts (1981), p. 125n and P. V. J. Jayasekera (1970), pp. 106–11, 318 & 325.

Ameer Ali, I suggest, errs in considering this antipathy a new development in response to the Pan-Islamic ideas of the Moors (1981), p. 14.

nationalist ideas. The middle class was at the centre of what one can describe as 'a cultural awakening' during the latter half of the nineteenth century.[55]

The Buddhist revitalization movement can be viewed as one facet of this cultural awakening. It is best known in the island historiography through the writings of the Anagarika Dharmapala (1864–1933), the son of a *nouveaux riche* Sinhala furniture manufacturer and a zealot who immersed himself in the liberation struggle of Buddhists and Sinhalese.[56] The zealotry of Dharmapala and others like him, one should note, was a reactive bigotry rising in opposition to the bigotry of Christian missionaries in the nineteenth century and the processes of Christian proselytization taking place around them. K.M. de Silva and Kitsiri Malalgoda have amply demonstrated how the British Protestant Evangelicals castigated the indigenous religions and their followers at the same time that they sought converts.[57] After a period of puzzled tolerance the Buddhist monks began to arm themselves with the same tools as the Christian bigots; the printing machine and the pamphlet, intolerance and polemic. The diffusion of printed publications enabled increasing numbers of Buddhist laymen to join the monks in this counterattack.[58]

One of the earliest Buddhist protagonists in this confrontation was Mohottivatte Gunananda *Thera* (1823–90). He was among the monks who engaged Sinhalese Protestant priests in a series of debates in the Sinhala language between 1865 and 1873. Before a massed audience at the Panadura Debate of 1873 he was popularly believed to have vanquished his opponent. By that point of time, he had established himself at a temple in Kotahena, in the northern suburbs of Colombo, and pursued his reformist goals in the midst of a population containing a Catholic majority.[59]

Though the famous mid-nineteenth century public debates

---

[55] See Roberts (1979c), for the background.

[56] On Dharmapala, see Amunugama (1985) and Obeyesekere (1976).

[57] K. M. de Silva (1965); especially pp. 68–86 and 119–22 and Malalgoda (1973).

[58] Malalgoda (1973) and Ames (1973).

[59] Malalgoda (1976), p. 220 and Amunugama (1985), pp. 704–5 and 728n. See Table 1 for population data.

engaged the Protestants, the Buddhist activists soon came to regard the Catholics as a greater danger and became embroiled with some of them in polemical tract warfare.[60] This is not surprising. Utilizing the foundations provided by the existence of a substantial body of Catholics from pre-British times and the freedom of the British institutional order, the Catholic missionary organizations had been growing in strength during the British era. The Catholics far outnumbered the Protestants in most parts of the island: in there were more Catholics as against Protestants, and by 1921 the figures were 368,499 Catholics, so that they made up 83 per cent of the Christian populace by that date.[61] Their biggest concentration has always been in the coastal belt immediately to the north of Colombo where they constitute a majority. This concentration extended into parts of Colombo, as Table 1 indicates. Indeed, Tables 1 and 2 are quite revelatory in displaying the relatively low proportion of Buddhists and Sinhalese in Colombo and some other towns. In the result, in such localities the Catholics were not slow to assert their claims or to defend their valued symbols.

The diffusion of Catholicism and Catholic assertiveness drew Buddhist fire. Some of these salvos were fired by a protege of Dharmapala, Piyadasa Sirisena (1873–1946). Sirisena is best known today as a Sinhala novelist, but he was also a journalist who edited the *Sinhala Jatiya* and the *Sinhala Bauddhaya* in the 1900s and 1910s and the revived *Sinhala Jatiya* in the 1930s. He was a leading spokesman during the temperance campaign in the years 1912–15, an active member of the Lanka Maha Jana in the 1920s, launched the Sinhala Pakshaya in 1931, and was a founder member of the Sinhala Maha Sabha in the 1930s.[62] As a journalist he was in a position to influence the thinking of his readership on an 'everyday' basis. Thus, the content of his novels gains in significance from this dual occupation. Given his subsequent political involvements, it is hardly a surprise to find that his novels are political documents. They are saturated with didactic moralisms. However, such moralistic themes were braided within a romantic melodrama and were conveyed through prose that was embellished by verse.

[60] Rogers (1987c), p. 176 and Malalgoda (1973).
[61] *Census of Ceylon 1901* and *Census of Ceylon 1921*.
[62] See Roberts (1970), pp. 27, 44, 47, and Amunugama (1979).

The popularity of Sirisena's novels during his own time seems to have rested upon this combination. His first novel, *Jayatissasaha Roslin, Hevat Vasanavanta Vivahaya*, which was serialized in 1904 and appeared in book form in 1906, is said to have sold 25,000 copies by the time of its fifth reprint in 1916, an unprecedented figure for that day.[63] This venture was followed by *Apata Vecca De* (What Happened to Us) in 1909 and a serialized story, *Maha Viyavula* (The Great Calamity) in the same year.[64]

As Sarath Amunugama has shown, *Jayatissa saha Roslin* is, in part, a diatribe against Catholicism: within it 'Catholicism, anti-national activity and criminality converge'.[65] In his first three novels (and subsequently too) this polemic is part of a broad attack on the process of imitative Westernization among the Sinhala people. Sirisena believed that these trends were destroying the traditional customs and virtues of the Sinhalese. His avowed goal was to arrest this disastrous decline by castigating those Sinhalese who adopted a Western lifestyle, became Christians, and indulged in mixed marriages with Burghers and other non-Sinhalese.[66]

As this summary will suggest, Sirisena was not merely defender of Buddhism, but was also a Sinhala nationalist. Indeed, his accent seems to have been on the latter aspect. Looking back on the motives which led him to launch the *Sinhala Jatiya* in 1903, in the year 1910 Sirisena observed that his intention was to diffuse 'modern knowledge' so that the Sinhalese could rid themselves of their 'unfounded fears and their sense of inferiority'—his point being that 'so long as such a sense of inferiority remained the Sinhalese nation would not be rich and powerful'.[67]

[63] Sarachchandra (1950), p. 95. In English translation, the title reads: 'Jayatissa and Roslind or A Happy Marriage'.

[64] *Maha Viyavula* was first published in the *Sinhala Jatiya* from March 1909 onwards (information kindly supplied by A. V. Suraweera) and then appeared in book form in 1916.

[65] Amunugama (1979), p. 325.

[66] For elaboration, see Roberts (1987). I have benefited from a conversation with B. K. A. Wickramasinghe of Colombo University. Wickramasinghe has one chapter on Sirisena in his 'Samskrtika Sangattana: Sinhala Navakatava Mukya Temava' (University of Kelaniya, Ph.D. dissertation, 1976).

[67] Quoted in Amunugama (1979), p. 320.

Such nationalist goals directed towards raising the self-respect of the Sinhalese people could easily be shared by Sinhala Catholics and Protestants. Indeed, they had been anticipated by James de Alwis in the mid nineteenth century and were echoed in the early twentieth century by such Christians as E. W. Perera, C. E. Corea, Lionel Mendis, Revd. John Simon de Silva and E. T. de Silva.[68] The Sinhala ideology of these Christian activists, however, appears to have been framed within a Ceylonese nationalism that was girded by Liberalism and was pluralistic in leaning. These constraints were either muted or non-existent in the thinking of such ideologues as Anagarika Dharmapala and Piyadasa Sirisena. Underlying the critiques presented by Dharmapala *et al* was a belief that the island was the land of the Sinhala people and was destined to preserve Buddhism in its pristine form. In brief, they adhered to the *Dhammadipa* and *Sihadipa* concepts propounded by the *Mahavamsa*. In these terms, 'Ceylon' and 'Sinhala' became synonyms and Dharmapala was able to shift, often unreflexively, from one to the other. This meant that the concept 'Ceylonese' became subsumed by the concept 'Sinhalese'.[69] The force of this ideology was all the stronger because the thinking of the Sinhala ideologues, as Kannangara has observed, was powered by 'a strong sense of nativistic grievance' which held that the Sinhalese majority, and especially the Buddhists, were 'under-privileged as against other ethnic and religious groups'.[70]

The ideological pursuits of Sinhala Buddhist revitalization had as their vehicles not only the pamphlet, journal, newspaper and public oratory, but also the association (*samagama* or *sabhava*). In most of these associations laymen rather than monks seem to have provided the leading edge. The most significant of these associations, perhaps, were the Buddhist Theosophical Society (with various branches) formed in 1880 and the Maha Bodhi Society initiated by Dharmapala in 1891. Not all the Sinhala-media associations were directed towards explicitly religio-political goals. Several

[68] See Roberts (1979c) and Kannangara (1984), p. 139.
[69] Dharmapala (1965), pp. 501–18 and Roberts (1978), pp. 363–5, 373–4.
[70] K. P. Kannangara (1984), p. 139. Also see Rogers (1987a), p. 189. For an illustration, see letter from H. S. Perera to Dadabhai Naoroji, 20 Feb. 1894, encl. with despatch no 84 in CO 54/614.

were inspired by the cultural awakening referred to earlier, a search for knowledge, which had spawned numerous English literary associations as well: so much so that, at one point in 1898–9, the *Ceylon Standard* was led to remark that 'almost every street in every town throughout the island has its association, while in the country districts they are numerous'.[71] For our purposes in this essay, however, what matters is that several religious associations directed towards the propagation of Buddhist doctrines were functioning along the south-western coast from the 1880s and that several of these bodies took up the cause of temperance in the 1900s and 1910s as one thrust in their opposition to Western influences.[72]

Thus charged and thus organized, the Sinhala Buddhist activists in the late nineteenth and early twentieth centuries were in a position to combat further encroachments into their valued domains. These acts of resistance sometimes occurred with a forethought, and at other times burst forth suddenly. They had the capacity to transform themselves into what we, from our point of view, may regard as acts of aggression—although the participants regarded them as legitimate punishments inflicted on transgressing others. In either form the legitimacy of action derived from the Sinhala activists' belief that they were defending their faith or defending the honour of the Sinhala people. For this reason I would describe such pursuits broadly as 'actions in preservation of sacred realms'. The term 'realm' is used here in a broad sense so as to encompass (i) attempts to protect the honour of one's women-folk, for instance, from alleged enticement into concubinage in Moor households;[73] (ii) the avenging of insults to one's religion; and (iii) the defence of sacred territories or sacred rights (inclusive of rites) in the face of alien intrusions.

---

[71] *Ceylon Standard*, 16 Sep. 1899 and 2 Dec. 1898. Also see E.A.A., 'The New Spirit' in *The Sinhalese*, Mar. 1913, vol. 1:1; Roberts 1970 and Roberts (1979c).

[72] On the temperance movement, see Fernando (1971); Jayasekera (1984–5) and Rogers (1987c).

[73] There were several complaints on this score. The ill-feeling which pro-moted the so-called 'rice riots' in Chilaw in December 1897 may have had more to do with a case of abduction by Moors than economic discontent

In the emerging worldview of Buddhist activists the temples, the Buddha statues, the bo-trees and the hallowed ground around the religious edifices at Anuradhapura were among these sacred territories. To this day Buddhists complain that the British authorities located St Paul's Church in immediate contiguity to the Dalada Maligawa (Temple of the Tooth) at Kandy, an action which is regarded as a deliberate intrusion into symbolic space during the early nineteenth century; and at the turn of the twentieth century Buddhists assembled in force on at least two occasions to defend such sacred space against government action.[74] Disturbances, injuries and court cases arose on both occasions.

That at Kalutara on 26 November 1896 originated in the belief that the local British district officer was about to uproot a bo-tree and shrine on Crown land. The Buddhist crowd of a thousand or so that assembled was not only from the town, but included 'villagers' from the coastal areas who arrived by train.[75] That at Anuradhapura in June 1903 was even less localized. A campaign had been mounted since the 1890s to protect the area that was deemed sacred, the proposed construction of an Anglican church within this area being among the targets of protest. Low-Country Sinhalese from further south, notably Walisinha Harischandra, were among the activists at the vanguard of this agitation. When an incident sparked off a riot during the pilgrim season in June 1903, imported Low-Country toughs and locally resident Low Countrymen appear to have been in the vanguard of the disturbances.[76]

(see Cumberland's letter, 3 May 1898 in DNA 59/45, and Rogers 1987a, pp. 168–71). Also see Ameer Ali (1981), pp. 11–12 and Kannangara (1984), p. 132. Note the Census Commissioner's comment: 'the number of Sinhalese women married to or living with Moors is fairly large': Denham (1912), p. 237. Cf. how the Moors in Colombo reacted when one of their women eloped with a Sinhala carpenter in 1879; an anti-government riot developed Rogers (1987a), pp. 169–70.

[74] Note Paul E. Pieris's caveat: Thalgodapitiya (1963), p. 60.

[75] Rogers (1987a), pp. 181–3. Also see the Dinakara Prakasa, Dec. 1896 which notes that Buddhists (Buddhagamkarayo) arrived 'from every district', presumably meaning every area in the surrounding environs. Note that they are also expecting reinforcements from Paliyagoda (thus Wana-wahala included), an expectation which did not eventuate: Rogers (1986), p. 32.

[76] Letter from S. N. W. Hulugalle to Sir West Ridgeway, 26 June 1903 in

In such a context, therefore, the construction of new temples, mosques or churches had a political import. They were iconic markers of the battle for minds which was taking place throughout the Low-Country districts of the south-west as well as the urban centres in the Kandyan districts. The late nineteenth and early twentieth centuries appear to have been characterized by the construction of many new religious edifices, holy work that was both the product, and the promoter, of religious revivalism among the Hindu, Buddhist, Christian and Muslim peoples. It is significant that newly-constructed or renovated places of worship were the site of struggle on at least four occasions: at Kotahena in 1883, at Ambagamuwa Road in Gampola from 1907 to 1916, at Castle Street, Kandy in 1915 and at Nakandapola in Gampaha in 1927.

Likewise, religious processions also had geo-political significance. They were symbolic proclamations on the march. For centuries past the Asala Perahara at Kandy has been a circumambulatory *pradaksina* which marks the conquest of the symbolic centre of Sinhala Buddhist society, the capital which stand at that moment for the whole kingdom of the Sinhala.[77] Religious processions, therefore, could be statements of territorial claims by the specific temples which organized them.

Processions provided the spark for two major skirmishes which exacerbated the existing hostility between Catholics and Buddhists on the western coast: that at Wattala-Paliyagoda in 1900 and that at Kotahena in 1883. It is difficult to work out how the fight between Catholics (mostly Sinhalese) and Buddhists originated at Wattala on 25 February 1900, though it is evident that a Buddhist procession from Paliyagoda passing a church provided the spark. Government officers were convinced that the Buddhists (many of them of the Wahumpura caste) started the fight without provocation, but some news reports stated that the Catholics had objected to the processions's music.[78]

The struggle between Buddhists and Catholics at Kotahena in March 1883 was the outcome of territorial competition and reli-

DNA, Pending File 1001 (i.e. lot 59/1001); and account of the disturbances in Rogers (1987b), pp. 184–7 and Nissan (1987), pp. 18–20.

[77] Seneviratne (1978), pp. 72, 85, 114. On the significance of processions, also see Kapferer (1983), pp. 26, 32.

[78] See the references in fn. 47.

gious tension that went back a decade or so. As indicated earlier, Kotahena was a predominantly Catholic area in which Mohotti-vatte Gunanada Therd had established himself at Dipaduttaramaya temple since 1843. Mohottivatte was a polemical activist and several Catholics believed that he trampled a Bible while preaching inside his temple. Worse still from the Catholic viewpoint, he made his presence felt in an iconic mode: he organized the construction of a new shrine within the premises which he occupied. This was completed by the beginning of the year 1883, thereby outpacing the completion of St Lucia's Cathedral 400 yards away, a work which had commenced in 1870. The culminating act in this renovation work was a netra pinkama, a ceremony to set the eyes on a Buddha statue. The Buddhists in and around Colombo organized a series of merit-partaking processions to bring offerings in procession to the temple from various localities between 8 February and 31 March. The latter part of March was the Easter period and a Catholic priest sought a ban on Buddhist processions during the three holy days. While this was partially affected, the Superintendent of Police, Colombo, permitted the Buddhists to conduct one procession on Easter Sunday afternoon after securing approval from the Roman Catholic Bishop.[79] This procession was attacked by a mass of Catholics. Many of these Catholics had crosses painted on their foreheads: it was their crusade. This aggressive assault generated a Buddhist backlash in and around Colombo which left a couple of Catholic chapels in embers. Such retribution notwithstanding, this series of events left the Buddhist activists in the Low-Country with a sense of grievance which was embodied in the Buddhist Defence Committee formed on 28 January 1884.[80] The Kotahena riots, therefore, were not localized in their import. They left smouldering memories which had the potential to fuel Buddhist-Catholic conflict in other parts of the country.

It would seem that the Catholic activists in the Kotahena locality saw the Buddhists and the Buddhist procession as intruding forces, as interlopers. But, as I have indicated, to the Sinhala Buddhist

[79] The I.G.P. to the Lord Bishop of Colombo, 22 Mar. 1883 in the *Riots Commission*, 1883, p. 12.

[80] This summary is based on the *Riots Commission* 1883 and Rogers (1987a), pp. 176–9.

revivalists of this era the Catholic population as a whole were interlopers within a Buddhist land, being composed of Sinhala heretics as well as 'foreigners' (i.e. Burghers, Tamils, 'Cochinese' and 'Paravas'). Such sentiments, of course, were particularly pronounced where a new Catholic church emerged in a predominantly Buddhist area. These underlying sentiments were at the root of the Buddhist opposition to the demands presented by Catholics and Muslims to the effect that Buddhist processions should cease music whenever they proceeded past a church or temple. Behind it all was the idea: 'this is our country, not theirs'.

The presentation above is my construct, a logical one built out of my awareness of the Sinhala Buddhist ideology as it was espoused at this point of time by Buddhist activists. The finer lineaments of the Buddhist response, in all its variety, both inchoate and refined, can only be constructed after extensive research. But two fragments have since supported my hypothesis. One is a passing reference in P. B. Nugawela's letter of 2 September 1912 to the effect that the Government Agent of the Central Province in the 1880s had rightly paid no head to an attempt by the Moors to interfere with *'the religion of the land'*.[81] For another, John Rogers has generously supplied an instance of a protest in the form of a letter to the editor of a Sinhala newspaper in 1889:[82]

When there is a Buddhist procession, Catholics take offence. So do other religions, but the Catholics are the worst. . . . It is astonishing that Sinhalese Catholics should want to attack *those of the Sinhalese national faith*. . . . [They] want all processions banned by the government. First they try violence, then they go to law to stop processions. Like the Irish, the Sinhalese Catholics are always fighting. It is not surprising when one considers the nature of their God (drowning people in a flood). . . .

There is no doubt, therefore, about the fact of Buddhist opposition to these Catholic and Muslim demands. It is also attested to Olcott's intervention in 1884, the work of the Buddhist Defence Committee in the 1880s and the legal challenge initiated in 1913 by the lay

---

[81] P. B. Nugawela (1912).
[82] From the *Sarasavi Sandarasa*, 4 June 1889. The translation is that provided by Rogers. Also see another reference which he supplied: a letter from a correspondent in Galle in the *Ceylon Independent*, 7 Mar. 1891.

manager of Walahagoda Devala at Gampola. Moreover, evocative proof of the long-standing and simmering Buddhist reminder of Buddhist resentment on this issue is provided in a summary of the situation by the Solicitor General in October 1927.

After summarizing the government's policy on the issue of tom-toming in front of places of worship, the Solicitor-General had this to say:[83]

These Buddhist processions, especially the tom-tomings, are an essential part of the Buddhist religion, and the activities of the Police in stopping tom-toming in the vicinity of the places of religious worship *have been always resented* by the Buddhist people. This was the direct cause of the riots in 1915. . . .

The Muslims argued that their mosques were open all day and night for individual worship and that therefore, as a worshipper would be disturbed, that the top-toming should ceasé at any time. I thought, and I still think, that this was an unreasonable request on the part of the Muslims. In any event after John Anderson's intervention in 1916 the Gampola mosque authorities agreed to a compromise, namely, that tom-toming should only cease when a service was held either on Fridays or on their festival days . . . (emphasis added).

The Solicitor-General then observed that 'unfortunately', this ruling only applied to the Gampola mosque. He went on to refer to two recent disputes of the same order, that at Nakandapola 'church' in the Gampaha District and at the Aranayaka mosque in Kegalle District. At Nakandapola the Attorney-General withdrew the prosecution cases against the Buddhists because he concluded that the Catholic position was an 'unreasonable one'—since the church in question was merely a building within school premises destined to become a church. In

. . . Aranayake the Buddhists had a procession and they insisted on tom-toming past the mosque there, in violation of the terms of their licence. On the application of the hon'ble Mr D. B. Jayatilleke [*sic*] the Attorney-General held a conference with the three Muslim members at which I was present. Unfortunately it was not possible to induce the Muslim members to adopt a conciliatory spirit in this matter, mainly because they were reluctant to bind themselves on behalf of their community.

[83] Akbar (1927).

The Attorney-General (L. H. Elphinstone) had therefore to proceed with the prosecutions. However,

It seems to the Attorney-General and me that the ruling in the Gampola Perahera case should be followed throughout the Island . . . to force such processions to go in silence past a place of worship of another religion which may be untenanted at the moment or even closed will only tend to rouse the resentment of Buddhists. I cannot, of course, understand why the Muslim members did not take this opportunity to adopt the reasonable compromise which was arrived at in 1918 [*sic*] in the Gampola Perahera case. . . . The Buddhist leaders including the Hon. Mr Jayatilleka are perfectly willing to abide by such a compromise and allow the same concession to processions of other religions when going past their temples. But they urge that to stop tom-toming whenever a procession went past a place of worship at all times would be seriously to restrict their religious rights, specially in large towns where there are mosques and churches at every street corner.

This review of the situation is particularly valuable because the Solicitor-General happened to be a Ceylonese, one with a Cambridge degree and experienced as a crown counsel since 1907. And not merely a Ceylonese, but also a Muslim, albeit of Malay stock: being none other than M. T. Akbar (1880–?). His letter not only confirms the fact of Buddhist resentment; it also discloses the intransigence of both Catholic and Moor (Muslim) dignitaries.

Akbar's appraisal, and his mediatory programme, were presented in the language of equity and reasonableness. However appealing as this might be to us today, it did not go to the root of the problem. The solution which he offered embodied the same principle of universality and uniformity of practice which was pursued within the Police Ordinance. It is the argument of this essay that the cultural premises embedded in that Ordinance were at variance with Hindu and Buddhist practices. In extending these premises democratically and equivalently to all the religions in Sri Lanka, the Ordinance was, in effect, disadvantaging the latter religious communities. In brief, the universal rationality of the Enlightenment and its equivalences can generate subordinations in settings in which there is no cultural homogeneity.

Such subordinations can then become inscribed within the

actions of those subordinated. It is clear that, in 1927, D. B. Jayati-
laka and other Buddhist notables were negotiating in terms of the
principle of reciprocal equivalence. They do not seem to have
taken up the cue provided by Paul E. Pieris and argued that the
'ritual of an Oriental religion was adamantine'. They did not press
their case in terms of tradition and precedence, nor contend that
music and drumming were conducive to religious worship. These
failures may conceivably have been the product of their Westernized education, a marker of their acceptance of the cultural
premises which informed British policy. It is my surmise, however,
that they did not press their case in these terms because they realized
it would not take them very far. The cultural premises which
conceived of noisy crescendos as disturbing to sleep and worship
were far too entrenched within the corridors of power for them to
be challenged head-on.

This was not only true in 1927. It was also true of the Sinhala
Buddhist opposition to the government regulations on processions in the years before 1915: there *does not appear to have been* a
persistent challenge articulated in the language of particularism;
instead, opposition was couched in a legalistic discourse which
was grounded upon Article 5 of the Kandyan Convention of 1815
(an argument that was fatally flawed and was easily overtuned:
see below). These 'failures' raise a significant question for our
historiography, albeit one that I cannot hope to answer here: a
question relating to the arguments that are placed on the agenda
for debate, or, in other words, the conditions which structure
knowledge and the forms of legitimation that can be deployed in
particular periods of history.

In pursuing a pragmatic course during the 1920s, the Buddhist
notables were much better placed than they were in the decades
before 1915. Several of them were elected members of the Legislative Council, a Council which contained a majority of unofficial
(i.e. Ceylonese) members. Both the Ceylonese and the Buddhists
had arrived. The British officials, moreover, had gone through
the cautionary experience of the 1915 pogrom against the Moors.
They were more willing to pursue a conciliatory line. This is
revealed in the manner in which they arranged mediatory confe-

rences whenever a religious dispute emerged.[84] In contrast, during the 1890s, 1900s and early 1910s, as I have shown, the British temper was intransigent. The tendency was to rule by fiat.

It follows that in the period 1890–1915 the Muslims and Catholics were able to more easily insist upon their pound of flesh: no music and drumming in front of places of worship *at all times*. They were able to do so in the language of universal equivalence, and its legitimating implication of fairness: 'we will pursue the same policy in relation to your places of worship'.

Thus disadvantaged, and thus subordinated, Sinhala Buddhist activists in the pre-1915 era appear to have adopted three modes of opposition. One was the flouting of the law (as illustrated earlier in this essay). Another was the localized riot against Muslims or Moors, usually in retaliation (as at Colombo in 1883 and Kurunegala in 1915). The third course was the legal challenge instituted by the Walahagoda Devala in 1913. The latter challenge argued its case, in major part, in terms of legal constitutional principles. Its documentary foundation was the Kandyan Convention of 2 March 1815, presented as an inviolable treaty which nullified the applicability within the Kandyan districts of such laws as the Police Ordinance of 1865. The legal proceedings nevertheless provide us with a glimmer of the worldview of Sinhala Buddhists and point to the chasm which separated their understandings from the cultural order which they were confronting. Both the *devala* tenants and Buddhist officials who gave evidence on behalf of the plaintiff claimed that unless the procession went along the traditional route and beat tom–toms continuously 'the god in whose honour the ceremony takes place will send great calamities upon the people and they could attribute to this cause the recent floods at Gampola and the sudden death of a certain Kapurala' (lay *devala* officiant).[85] The god in question was Skanda

[84] Ibid.; Memo by M. D. M. Gunasekera (A.S.P., W.P.), 28 Jan. 1927 and memo by A. Peiris (A.S.P., W.P.), 13 Jan. 1931, both in DNA 80/566. Also see Rogers' comment on similar lines (1987a), p. 192.

[85] De Sampayo summary of their views in 18 *NLR*: 203 and Paul E. Pieris in Thalgodapitiya (1963), p. 57. In the year 1913 the town of Gampola was in

or Kataragama, to whom a shrine was dedicated at Walahagoda Devala.[86] Kataragama was (and is) a powerful retributory god in the Sinhala tradition, known for the vengeance he wrecks upon those who cross his path. Woe be unto those Buddhists, therefore, who did (do) not defend his territory.

Such beliefs were entirely in accordance with the causal theories of the Sinhalese Buddhists and their understanding of the role of gods and kings (the state) in the maintenance of Order and Harmony.[87] Stretching the point somewhat, this implies that the claims of the Muslims were an imposition of Disorder, that elemental and frightening state which threatened the well-being of a Buddhist society.

Such arguments cut no ice with the two Supreme Court judges who heard the case in appeal. Neither T. E. de Sampayo (a Sinhala Catholic) nor Justice Shaw (British) were swayed. Nor were they convinced by Pieris's arguments: indeed, they decimated his reasoning, utilizing Article 8 of the Kandyan Convention to argue that its clauses were not immutable and introducing the political *raison d'etre* of 'higher considerations of State' to protect the sovereignty of the British government *vis-a-vis* the Convention-as-immutable-treaty.[88] Accordingly, they decided against the Basnayaka Nilame of Walahagoda Deval. Their decision was handed down on 2 February 1915.

---

fact subject to floods on four occasions (*Admin. Repts 1913*, G.A., Central Province, pp. B1, B7).

[86] Pieris in Thalgodapitiya (1963), pp. 48–53.

[87] Seneviratne (1978: 2), pp. 95–8 and *passim*.

[88] 18 *NLR*: 193–213. De Sampayo's judgement is marred by its class prejudice, as manifest in the manner in which he dismissed the oral testimony of 'illiterate' temple tenants. And his hegemonic incorporation into the Western worldview was such that his comments reveal a hostility to one of Pieris's most pertinent contentions, namely that the issue should 'be judged not according to the standards of a Christian or Agnostic of the Twentieth Century, but according to the ideas of a Sinhalese Buddhist before 1815': Thalgodapitiya (1963), p. 68.

Thomas de Sampayo (1854–1927) was the son of a Navandanna headman who was educated at St Benedict's and Royal and went to Cambridge on a University Scholarship.

Already, segments among the Muslim populace had revealed the same sort of aggressive assertiveness that had prompted their activities at Gampola from the 1900s: immediately after Pieris's judgement was announced, in March 1914, a body of Muslims had organized a riot in Balangoda against a Buddhist procession passing their mosque;[89] and on 27 January 1915, as the Supreme Court ruling was awaited, a body of Muslims at Kurunegala disrupted a Buddhist procession which had not ceased tom-toming and music-making near their mosque.[90] After the Supreme Court decision, one can surmise, Muslim boldness was accentuated. One expression was the demand from the Muslims of the new (or renovated?) mosque at Castle Street in Kandy that the Buddhist processions associated with the Wesak celebrations (May 1915) should be routed away from their place of worship or forced to pass silently.[91] This was a reiteration of the position adopted by the Ambargumuwa mosque at Gampola and, as with that claim, took place in the heartland of the Kandyan Sinhalese country. In 1915 they were also making the claim in the hundredth year after the Kandyan kingdom lost its independence, an anniversary occasion which many Sri Lankan nationalists had marked in various ways.[92]

Tension built up very quickly in May 1915 (though the govern-

[89] Thaine (1915), p. 251.

[90] *Ceylon Morning Leader*, 4 Feb. 1915 and extract from the weekly report of the A.S.P., North Western Province, for the week ending 30 Jan. 1915, encl. in DNA 80/1501. The incident took place in the morning. That evening some Sinhalese 'collected near a tavern on the Kandy road and assaulted and abused every moorman who passed'. Rumours were rife that Sinhalese from Colombo would turn up and support the attack on the Moors.

[91] Statements by E. L. Wijegoonawardane and Perumal Kangany in Appendix 3 of *The Sinhalese Memorial* in Co 54/786; evidence of F. T. Coore and C. L. Tranchell in *Sessional Paper XVI of 1916*; and Kannangara (1984: 134–5). It appears that a new mosque had been built at Castle Street around 1913, with E. N. Kader Saibo and Co. as the principal sponsors, but it is unclear whether a mosque had existed at the same site for some time. Cf. Kannangara (1984), p. 134 and 'A Dream Come To Reality' in *Souvenir of the Opening Ceremony of the Jamul Aalam Hanafi Mosque on 2nd Aug. 1985, Kandy*.

[92] Jayawardena (1972), pp. 226–7 and Blackton (1970), p. 236.

ment appears to have been unaware of it). Both parties in the town of Kandy girded their loins for confrontation, importing muscle for the purpose.[93] Unknown to the Muslims in Kandy (or so I surmise), however, there were Sinhala Buddhist activists elsewhere who were preparing to teach the Muslims a lesson.[94] In the many religious and temperance associations which existed and the network of temples and monastic fraternities they had the organizational vehicles for this work. The stage was set for the 1915 anti-Muslim pogrom.

The analysis of these communal riots is another story.[95] In revealing the subordinations and resentments promoted by British colonial rule as a consequence of its intellectual and cultural premises, this essay has been designed to set the stage for that story.

[93] Wahumpura men from the Paliyagoda-Wanawahala locality near Colombo were present in Kandy on 28 May 1915 [Kannangara (1984), p. 148 and Rogers (1987a), pp. 196–8] just as they were present at Anuradhapura on 9 June 1903. I have no proof of the Moors in Kandy bringing in muscular support, but the Moors of Chilaw did so in late December 1897 as tension built up in the town (*Times of Ceylon*, 29 Dec. 1897 and Cumberland to Col. Sec., no. 1263, 29 Dec. 1897 in DNA, Pending File 15) so it is a fair assumption that this occurred in Kandy. There are Moor clusters nearby at Akurana, Gampola and Mawanalla, while Colombo was perhaps four hours away by train. In brief, I suggest that it was standard practice for religious communities to draw support from their counterparts elsewhere whenever heightened tension developed in their locality. Certainly, a small gang of Moors from the Low-Country were on the way up to Kandy by night mail on the 29th May, but were intercepted and arrested at Kadugannawa (see Evidence of K. A. P. Singh in App. III of *The Sinhalese Memorial*, CO 54/786).

[94] E.g. at Attanagalla in the Western Province (Rept of the I.G.P., i.e. Dowbiggin, 20 May 1916 in *Admin. Repts 1915*: Part III B6); and at Rambukkana where the temperance society leader and trader, P. H. Abraham Silva, sent the whole of his property down to Galle about 29 May 1915 (Evidence of G. F. Forrest before the Police Inquiry Commission, *Sessional Paper XVI of 1916*, p. 118).

[95] This story has already been analysed in Fernando (1969); Jayawardena (1970); Jayasekera (1970), chaps 4, 5 and 6; Roberts (1981); Ameer Ali (1981); and Kannangara (1984). I intend writing up a review in the light of the new work, including Kannangara's and Rogers', a review which will emphasize the degree of dispersed and localized preparation for 'battle' which occurred in late May 1915.

Summary

This essay has revealed how the British raj introduced certain institutionalized practices through the Police Ordinance of 1865 which were alien to Sinhalese and Sinhala Buddhist ways. These clauses of the Police Ordinance were extended equally to all the religions. On the face of it, and in British eyes, these articles were in keeping with the Enlightenment: they embodied the concepts of religious tolerance, equality and uniformity of principle. It is my contention that this form of universalism created inequality because of the fundamentally different relation between drumming-cum-music and worship in Buddhist (and Hindu) culture on the one hand and Western Christian (and Islamic) civilization on the other.

The effects of these new practices were not immediately revolutionary because they were only extended to some urban areas; and even in these urban centres their application was piecemeal, partial and uneven. This article has shown that, to the extent that one can generalize, this Ordinance was applied haphazardly in the period 1865–1880s, that the policy became more imperative and rigid from around 1890 to 1915, and thereafter became more negotiatory and cautious. The Ordinance could nevertheless be activated by zealous localized communities of Catholics and Muslims.[96] It could be utilized as a weapon in the competition for symbolic space. From the 1880s or thereabouts, this occurred from time to time. Such assertions, at a time of developing Buddhist revivalism, drew the fury of those Buddhists who were at the butt end of these demands. The power of this anger was the power of righteous

---

[96] The Catholics in the south-western areas were mostly Sinhalese, but included Tamils, Burghers, Bhartha people and others. To the best of my knowledge the Protestants did not make as great a fuss about music in front of churches as the Catholics. The history of Moratuwa would be the best locality to pursue this issue. Note, however, that my argument in this essay implies that drumming-cum-music was generally tolerated by Sinhalese of all faiths till the British and the missionaries taught them to regard it as a 'disturbance' and a mark of disrespect. When precisely this transformation began to emerge I cannot say, though I suspect it was at some point of time in the nineteenth century. But what were the practices in Dutch times along the coast?

indignation against intrusions into traditional practice and impositions by privileged minorities upon the 'sons of the soil'.

At this interface, at the sites of confrontations with localized
bodies of Catholics or Muslims, the Buddhists began to use noise
in a manner that was founded upon the premise that they were
challenging: as an intruding weapon which annoyed worshippers,
i.e. Catholic and Muslim worshippers. They utilized noise in the
sense in which it was understood by the British rather than their
own traditional understanding, a tradition which perceived specific
forms of noise at religious rites as something that was celebratory, as
a modality that involved a non-exclusive extension of religious
fervour.

These conflicts invariably engaged the British as 'mediators'.
From the analytical point of view, there is a sense in which the
British officials were called upon to arbitrate these conflicts. But,
by itself, such a statement is incomplete. They were not arbiters
above the tumult. Their mediation occurred at a time of burgeoning
nationalist currents in the late nineteenth and early twentieth
centuries, a multifaceted tide which involved Buddhist revivalism,
Sinhala nationalism, Ceylonese nationalism and their combina-
tions. Thus, by the 1910s key British officials tended to regard the
temperance work of Buddhist activists as a form of seditious politic
under the cloak of religion.[97] Both Dowbiggin's statements in
1915 and Cookson's comment on the Catholic-Buddhist riot at
Wattala-Paliyagoda in 1900 suggest an antipathy to the Buddhists
which would have favoured the latter's opponents.[98] In any event,
an adherence to the letter of the Police Ordinance could only work
against the Buddhists. As I have shown, by the 1890s and 1900s, if
not earlier, religious processions were perceived as a source of
disturbance and the application of this Ordinance was regarded as
the appropriate solution. This could only fuel Buddhist resentment.

One can secure a more complete picture of the structured position
of the British raj if one also places oneself in the position of Sinhala
Buddhists (whether that of zealots or moderates). The essential
point is that during this same period these Sinhala Buddhists were
struggling against the inroads of Westernization and Christian

[97] V. K. Jayawardena (1970), p. 225 and Rogers (1987c), pp. 2 and 10.
[98] Citation 42 and quotation in Dep. (1970), pp. 351–2.

proselytization. A significant part of this struggle from the 1890s was the attempt to protect sacred Buddhist space from governmental claims. These attempts, as we saw, produced disturbances at Kalutara in 1896 and Anuradhapura in 1903. Both confrontations resulted in 'Buddhist Defence Committees' and the second of these confrontations was of national import insofar as it engaged notables and thugs from beyond the locality.

The significance of these contemporaneous battles with the British raj was that the British were placed in structural opposition to the interests of Sinhala Buddhism and Sinhala tradition at the same time as the Catholics and the Muslims who interfered with Buddhist processions.[99] In the nationalist thinking of the time, therefore, the Sinhala Buddhist way of life was under threat. The temperance agitation of the 1900s and 1910s added yet another 'Western import' to this array of threats.

These threats were regarded as emanating from outside, from the *paradesakkara* (a Sinhala word that goes back to medieval times and usually carried the meaning 'others, foreigners', with the additional connotation, at least more recently, of 'low and vile persons'). By definition, the British, the Burghers (virtually all of whom were Christians), the Moors, and the Malays were *para*. What is especially significant about the Buddhist–Christian confrontations of this period is that they rendered the Sinhala Christians into an anomalous, and thus particularly dangerous, species.[100] They too were potentially *para*. But this potentiality was constrained by their ability to participate in the awakening of 'Sinhaleseness' as it was embodied in history and language.

These conceptual linkages and the several struggles over symbolic space between 1880 and 1915 show how it was feasible for *some* Buddhist activists to make the analogic extensions which placed the British, Christians and Muslims in the same threatening domain.[101] The experiences and structures were in place for them to make another analogic equation: to attack the Muslim was to attack the British and to protest against the injustices of the British

---

[99] See Roberts (1987) for some details.
[100] On this issue, see Amunugama (1979) and Obeyesekere (1979).
[101] Regarding the nature of analogic extension, see Roberts (1987).

TABLE 1

Distribution of Religious Groups in the Wards of Colombo, 1901

	Fort	Pettah	St. Paul's	San Sebastian	Kotahena	New Bazaar	Maradana	Slave Island	Kollupitiya	Colombo
FIGURES										
Christians	355	1,619	6,512	1,582	18,683	3,858	7,288	3,158	6,297	49,352
Buddhists	493	2,218	2,830	2,545	8,519	5,513	13,474	5,047	7,773	48,412
Hindus	146	1,192	6,850	695	2,589	2,205	2,631	2,215	2,770	21,293
Mohammedans	282	2,498	4,067	4,518	3,539	5,880	6,968	6,328	1,328	35,412
Others	3	34	1	9	20	14	16	16	109	222
	1,279	7,561	20,260	9,349	33,350	17,470	30,377	16,764	18,281	154,691
PERCENTAGES										
Christians	27.7	21.4	32.1	16.9	56.0	22.1	24.0	18.8	34.4	31.9
Buddhists	38.5	29.3	14.0	27.2	25.5	31.5	44.3	30.1	42.5	31.3
Hindus	11.4	15.8	33.8	7.4	7.8	12.6	8.7	13.2	15.1	13.8
Mohammedans	22.0	33.0	20.1	48.4	10.6	33.6	22.9	37.7	7.3	22.9
Others	0.2	0.4	0.0	0.1	0.0	0.1	0.0	0.1	0.6	0.1

Source: *Census of Ceylon 1901*

Note: In the year 1901 the boundaries of Colombo city were not the same as they are today. Most of Wellawatte, for instance, was outside the city limits.

Abbreviations

A.G.A.	=	Assistant Government Agent
CO	=	Colonial Office series in the PRO
DNA	=	Department of National Archives, Sri Lanka
G.A.	=	Government Agent
I.G.P.	=	Inspector General of Police
NLR	=	New Law Reports (published by the Government of Ceylon)
PRO	=	Public Record Office, London
S.P.	=	Superintendent of Police
SCC	=	Supreme Court of Ceylon

raj. The historiography on the anti-Muslim pogrom of 1915 must be revised in these terms.

REFERENCES

Akbar, M. T., 1927: Letter from Akbar to the Colonial Secretary, Confidential, 6–8 Oct 1927 in DNA 80/566. Also available in DNA 80/338.

Ameer Ali, A. C., 1981: 'The 1915 Racial Riots in Ceylon (Sri Lanka): A Reappraisal of its Causes', *South Asia*, 4, pp. 1–20.

Ames, Michael M., 1973: 'Westernization or Modernization: The Case of the Sinhalese Buddhism', *Social Compass*, xx, pp. 139–70.

Amunugama, Sarath, 1979: 'Ideology and Class Interest in One of Piyadasa Sirisena's Novels: The New Image of the "Sinhala-Buddhist" Nationalist', in M. Roberts (ed.), *Collective Identities, Nationalism and Protest in Modern Sri Lanka*. Colombo: Manga, pp. 314–36.

———, 1985: 'Anagarika Dharmapala (1864–1933) and the Transformation of Sinhala Buddhist Organization in a Colonial Setting', *Social Science Information*, 24, pp. 697–730.

Bayly, C. A., 1985: 'The Pre-history of "Communalism"? Religious Conflict in India, 1700–1860', *Modern Asian Studies*, 19, pp. 177–203.

Blackton, Charles S., 1970: 'The Action Phase of the 1915 Riots', *Journal of Asian Studies*, xxix, pp. 235–54.

Denham, E. B., 1912: *Ceylon at the Census of 1911*. Colombo: Govt. Printer.

Dep, A. C., 1970: *A History of the Ceylon Police*, vol. ii, 1866–1913. Colombo: Times of Ceylon Press.

de Silva, K. M., 1965: *Social Policy and Missionary Organizations in Ceylon 1840–1855*. London: Longman, Green & Co.

———, 1981: *A History of Ceylon*. London: C. Hurst & Co.

Dharmapala, Anagarika, 1965: *Return to Righteousness*, ed. by A. Guruge. Colombo: Ministry of Education & Cultural Affairs.

Dowbiggin, H., 1915: Letter from Dowbiggin (I.G.P.) to the Attorney General, no. 526, 3–4 Feb. 1915 in DNA 80/1501.

Fernando, P. T. M., 1969: 'The British Raj and the 1915 Communal Riots in Ceylon', *Modern Asian Studies*, 3.

———, 1970: 'The 1915 Riots and Martial Law in Ceylon: A Study of the Campaign for Justice,' *A Symposium on the 1915 Communal Riots.* Peradeniya: Ceylon Studies Seminar. An abbreviated version of this essay appeared in the *Journal of Asian Studies*, xxix, 1969.

———, 1971: 'Arrack, Toddy and Ceylonese Nationalism: Some

Observations on the Temperance Movement, 1912–1921', *Modern Ceylon Studies*, 2, pp. 123–30.

Jayasekera, P. V. J., 1970: 'Social and Political Change in Ceylon, 1900–1919'. London University, Ph.D. dissertation in History.

———, 1984/5: 'Temperance and Nationalism in Sri Lanka', *Kalyani*, 3 & 4, pp. 283–312.

Jayawardena, V. Kumari, 1970: 'Economic and Political Factors in the 1915 Riots', *Journal of Asian Studies*, 29, pp. 223–33.

———, 1972: *The Rise of the Labor Movement in Ceylon*. Durham, N.C.: Duke University Press.

Kannangara, A. P., 1984: 'The Riots of 1915 in Sri Lanka: A Study in the Roots of Communal Violence', *Past & Present*, 102, pp. 130–65.

Kapferer, Bruce, 1983: *A Celebration of Demons*. Bloomington, Illinois: University of Indiana Press.

Malalgoda, Kitsiri, 1973: 'The Buddhist-Christian Confrontation in Ceylon, 1800–1880', *Social Compass*, 20, pp. 171–200.

———, 1976: *Buddhism in Sinhalese Society 1750–1900*. Berkeley: University of California Press.

Nandy, Ashis, 1987: 'Reflections on Ethnic Conflict—Some Conceptual Issues, the Politics of Secularism and the Rediscovery of Ethnic Tolerance', Conference on Ethnic Violence in South Asia, organized by the International Centre of Ethnic Studies, Kathmandu, February 1987.

Nissan, Elizabeth, 1987: 'The Making of a Sacred History: Anuradhapura', paper presented at a Conference on Sri Lankan Studies, University of Sussex, September 1987.

Nugawela, P. B., 1912: Letter from Nugawela (President, District Committee, Buddhist Temporalities) to the G. A.; Central Province, 2 Sep. 1912, in Appendix II of *The Sinhalese Memorial*, encl. in CO 54/786, Public Record Office, London.

Obeyesekere, Gananath, 1976: 'Personal Identity and Cultural Crisis: The Case of Anagarika Dharmapala', in Frank E. Reynolds and Donald Capps (eds.), *The Biographical Process: Studies in the History and Psychology of Religion*. The Hague: Mouton, pp. 221–52.

———, 1979: 'The Vicissitudes of the Sinhala Identity through Time and Change', in M. Roberts (ed.), *Collective Identities, Nationalisms and Protest in Modern Sri Lanka*. Colombo: Marga Institute, pp. 279–81.

———, 1984: *The Cult of the Goddess Pattini*. Chicago: University of Chicago Press.

Ranasinghe, D. D., 1976: *The Lion of Kotte, His Life and Times*. Colombo.

Riots Commission, 1883: 'The Kotahena Riots. The Report of a Commission appointed by the Governor to inquire into the Cause of the

Recent Riots in Colombo', *Sessional Paper IV of 1883*.

Roberts, Michael, 1970: 'The Political Antecedents of the Revivalist Elite in the MEP coalition of 1956', Ceylon Studies Seminar, 1969/70 series, no. 1, August 1970.

———, 1978: 'Ethnic Conflict in Sri Lanka: Barriers to Accommodation', *Modern Asian Studies*, 12, pp. 353–76.

———, 1979a: 'Meanderings in the Pathways of Collective Identity and Nationalism', in M. Roberts (ed.), *Collective Identities, Nationalisms and Protest in Modern Sri Lanka*. Colombo: Marga Institute, pp. 1–90.

———, 1979b: 'Elite Formation and Elites, 1832–1931', in ibid., pp. 153–213.

———, 1979c: 'Stimulants and Ingredients in the Awakening of Latter-Day Nationalisms', in ibid., pp. 213–42.

———, 1981: 'Hobgoblins, Low-Country Sinhalese Plotters or Local Elite Chauvinists? Directions and Patterns in the 1915 Communal Riots', *Sri Lanka Journal of the Social Sciences*, 4, pp. 83–126.

———, 1987: 'Pejorative Phrases: The Anti-Colonial Response and Sinhala Perceptions of the Self through Images of the Burghers in Sri Lanka', paper presented at the Conference on Ethnic Violence in South Asia, Kathmandu, February 1987. A revised version will appear as chap. 1 in M. Roberts *et al.*, *People In Between*, forthcoming.

Rogers, John D., 1986: 'The Assertion of Sacred Space and the Imperial Response: The Kalutara Bo-Tree Agitation in Sri Lanka, 1891–97', *South Asian Research*, 6, pp. 27–37.

———, 1987a, *Crime, Justice and Society in Colonial Sri Lanka*. London: Curzon Press.

———, 1987b: 'Social Mobility, Popular Ideology, and Collective Violence in Modern Sri Lanka', *Journal of Asian Studies*, 46, pp. 583–602.

———, 1987c: 'The 1904 Temperance Movement in Sri Lanka', paper presented at the Conference on Sri Lankan Studies, University of Sussex, September 1987.

Samaraweera, Vijaya, 1979: 'The Muslim Revivalist Movement, 1880–1915' in M. Roberts (ed.), *Collective Identities, Nationalisms and Protest in Modern Sri Lanka*. Colombo: Marga Institute, pp. 243–76.

Sarachchandra, E. R., 1950: *The Sinhalese Novel*. Colombo: Gunasena & Co.

Seneviratne, H. L., 1978: *Rituals of the Kandyan State*. Cambridge University Press.

Thaine, R. N., 1915: 'Report on the Riots in the Ratnapura District', by R. N. Thaine, G. A., Sabaragamuwa, 8 Sep. 1915, in *Eastern 128*, CO 882/10/128, pp. 250–57.

Thalgodapitiya, W., 1963: *Studies of Some Famous Cases of Ceylon.* Colombo.

Wickremeratne, L. A., 1969: 'Religion, Nationalism and Social Change in Ceylon, 1866–1885', *Journal of the Royal Asiatic Society, GB & Ireland,* LVI, pp. 123–50.

Woolf, Leonard, 1965–66: *Leonard Woolf's Diaries in Ceylon 1908–11,* printed as *Ceylon Historical Journal,* XI.

Chapter Eleven

Political Economy of Ethnic Violence in Sri Lanka: The July 1983 Riots

SUNIL BASTIAN

Introduction

This paper attempts to look at the relation between the ethnic riot that shook Sri Lanka in July 1983 and the politics of the development process. Various kinds of violence are usually lumped together under the single term 'ethnic riots'. In much of the scholarly and popular writings on such violence in Sri Lanka and India, it is common to use the expression 'communal riots'. This is understood to mean a conflict between two or more groups of people with different ethnic identities who have an equal or near-equal chance of inflicting violence on each other. In other words, it is a 'free for all', where all parties make use of the chance to attack the other group or groups. However, not all violence related to the ethnic issue can be categorized under this. A cursory observation shows the different types of violence that are categorized under the term 'communal riot'. Therefore, there is a need to arrive at some form of a typology that will help us understand this diversity.

Gunasinghe (1987) has recently identified the following types of ethnic violence in the context of Sri Lanka:

(a) Violent ethnic conflict
(b) Ethnic riot
(c) Pogrom
(d) State violence against an ethnic group
(e) Guerilla violence against an ethnic group
(f) War between state forces and guerillas

According to this classification, only the first type approximates to what has traditionally been termed a 'communal riot'. The ethnic riot of the second type differs from the first in that it is violence inflicted by *one group* (usually the majority) on the other. There is not even exchange in this type. Most of the ethnic violence in South Asia seems to be of this type. Pogrom differs from all these because of the organized nature of the violence. It is not a spontaneous outburst of irrational passion but an organized form of violence by one group against the other. The other three forms of violence are self-explanatory.

When using this typology it is necessary to remember that the actual event is in many instances a mixture of these types. In fact, the larger the scale of the event the more likely this is to be so. Even in these instances, however, it might be possible to identify the dominant characteristic of the event. Such characterization is important for discerning the relationship between the event and the other processes in society.

In Sri Lankan society today we encounter all these types of violence. Here I shall focus upon one particular event, which is more easily characterized as a pogrom rather than as a riot. The evidence later presented is taken from governmental and non-governmental sources. Although there were many spontaneous and unorganized aspects of the violence in July 1983, two facts stand out. The first is the organized nature of the riots and the second the distribution of victims—they belonged primarily to Tamil minority groups and were not equally distributed among both contending groups. On the basis of these two features I would suggest that the July 1983 events in Sri Lanka are closer in character to an anti-Tamil pogrom rather than to a riot.

Ethnic Riot as 'Event' or 'Process'

The initial reaction of articulate public opinion to ethnic riots is one of revulsion. Very often, this reaction comes from political parties, religious organizations and other mass organizations. Although the strength and character of the reaction can differ in different places and circumstances, most organizations and individuals active in the public domain react to ethnic riots with outright condemnation. Very often, the liberal intellectual community is in the forefront of this reaction.

Along with this initial reaction is the belief that ethnic riots represent an 'event' which is not 'normal' in civilized society. The violence perpetrated at the time of an ethnic riot can be horrendous. It can include hacking people to death, or burning them alive. 'Retaliation' and 'punishment' meted out to members of other communities may include violence against children, old people and women. Thus, violence during a riot is indiscriminate and creates a moral problem for observers. It is often considered an aberration within civilized living. There is a feeling of disbelief and horror, especially at the manner of the violence; the evil seems central, yet liberal opinion tries to hold on to the idea of goodness of human nature.

It is in this context that we need to understand how a strongly moralistic approach to the understanding of communal riots may distort our analysis of such events. If human nature is bestowed with an innate goodness, then the tendency is to regard communal riots as an aberration and to search for 'culprits' who can be held responsible for perpetrating the horrendous violence one encounters during communal riots. This is not to deny the importance of fact-finding commissions and of recording such events. Such records are important for political activities concerned with the protection of human rights, but we do need to recognize their limits.

In Sri Lanka, as in other parts of South Asia; the recurrence of communal riots is seen as a manifestation of communalism. Riots are considered to reflect the 'irrational' passions of backward sections of society. Thus the liberal, modernist tradition uses the opposition of reason and passion to distinguish between the progressive course of history within which the processes of nation-building and development take place, and the occasional regressions reflected in isolated outbursts of the passions of what are considered 'communal-minded' and 'backward' people. In this kind of analysis such aberrations are to be condemned and the culprits punished so that the 'normal' processes of nation-building and development can proceed. The point is that, within this approach, ethnic riots are isolated events, discontinuous in time, and reflective of an outdated, false consciousness.

Opposed to the view of ethnic riots as isolated incidents is the suggestion that we look at them in relation to the changes in society in which they occur. The main issue is whether ethnic riots are a manifestation, in an acute form, of the very structures that characterize normal society. In other words, by refusing to treat these riots as aberrations, we may be able to understand the structure of a society at the precise moment of such violence. We may even ask if ethnic riots can be seen more as an aspect of certain stages of a society which is following a particular path of development, rather than isolated occurrences.

This paper looks at the anti-Tamil ethnic pogrom that took place in Sri Lanka in July 1983 as a *process*, the attempt being to link it to the contradictions generated by the development process that Sri Lanka is undergoing. I shall also here develop the framework for this linkage by looking at the relationship between the development experience of Sri Lanka, and ethnicity. This will be followed by an attempt to show the link between processes thrown up by present development strategies and the anti-Tamil pogrom of July 1983.

Development Policies and the Ethnic Issue

Before we come to the relationship between present tendencies in the economy and the ethnic issue, it is necessary to understand this link as it was constituted before 1977. We look at the policies before and after 1977 as two phases within a capitalist framework. In contrast to what is happening now, the previous phase can be characterized as a period when state-regulated inward-looking policies dominated. The policy prescriptions in this period looked towards the state as the main engine of economic growth. Protected markets, price controls, restrictions in foreign-exchange movements, and quotas in production were the hallmarks of this period. All these amounted to a greater dependence on state regulation on the one hand, and state involvement for economic development and greater protection of the economy from external factors on the other. What is also important to note about this moment is the fact that state intervention was also legitimized with a social-justice argument. Intervention of the state in various spheres of economy and society was apparently made to redress injustice; and some even characterized this transfer into state ownership within a capitalist framework as 'socialism'. It is my contention that this interventionist role played by the state had an ethnic dimension.

The fundamental political problem in the ethnic issue is related to the fact that it is the majority Sinhala community that enjoys state power in Sri Lanka. Thus, the state that emerged in post-independent Sri Lanka was heavily biased in favour of Sinhala interests. The intervention of the state in the economy and other spheres of society carries with it the interests of the majority community. This is a dimension largely ignored in the discussions of policies that came to dominate in Sri Lanka after 1956.

In the Sri Lankan context the expanded role of the state in the economy introduced three main mechanisms that could go against the interests of minority ethnic groups:

(a) The state's expansion of the economy could mean taking over areas of economic activity by the state in which the minorities had been involved. If the state sector creates monopolies in such areas, it could mean a continuous shutting-off of the minorities from such sectors.

(b) Expansion of state regulations in the economy also mean the introduction of systems of quotas, permits and licenses even in economic activity in the private sectors. Normally, political patronage and the influence of the state bureaucracy play a significant role in granting these licenses and permits. The ethnic factor could play an important role in this process.

(c) With the expansion of the state in the economy, the state becomes the major avenue of employment. Here too political patronage becomes critical. Loyalty to political parties that come into power becomes extremely important. Since the major parties that have been sharing political power in Sri Lanka are largely backed by the Sinhalese, it is they who stand to benefit from political patronage. Therefore, if an economic policy emphasizes the state as the prime agent of economic activity in a context where a system of political patronage operates, the minorities are affected.

Some writers, such as Shastri (1983) have used Kalecki's model of 'intermediate regimes' to explain the political economy of state-dominated populist policies that emerged in the Sri Lankan context. Intermediate regimes have a state with a multi-class character. In this class coalition, middle-level landowning class and petty-bourgeois sections play a key role. The petty-bourgeois will include many others, like sections of the trading class, those employed in minor positions within government, and the vernacular intelligentsia. Their role is crucial in intermediate regimes and, in a way, they are in the best position to benefit from these policies.

While Kalecki's theory of intermediate regimes throws light upon the class force behind state-dominated populist development policies, it has to be supplemented with their ethnic characteristics. This aspect is seen more clearly in the area of state power.

Emergence of the Sinhala State and
the Ethnic Issue

Sri Lanka is a multi-ethnic society. Sinhalese (74.6 per cent), Sri Lankan Tamils (12.6 per cent), Indian Tamils (5.5 per cent), Muslims (7.4 per cent), Moors (7.1 per cent), Malays (0.3 per cent) form the major ethnic groups. As Sri Lanka moved towards independence, this multi-ethnicity became a central issue in defining state structures. Although in the late twenties some of the political leaders and representatives of certain ethnic groups put forward the idea of a federal constitution for Sri Lanka, what was introduced into the constitution of Sri Lanka at the time of independence was the mechanism of trying to safeguard the rights of minorities through checks at the centre. Some of the measures adopted were the distribution of seats in parliament so that minority voices could be heard, multi-member constituencies where there were pockets of minorities, a second chamber into which minority representatives could be appointed, and clauses in the constitution to safeguard minority rights. The political history of post-independent Sri Lanka shows the ineffectiveness of these safeguards at the centre.

The ineffectiveness of these safeguards appeared in face of the emergence of Sinhala Buddhist nationalism as a dominant political force. The electoral process helped to bring these pressures on the state. The elections in 1956, by which a government with a hegemonic Sinhala Buddhist ideology came to power, was a turning point in this process. Although the influence of this ideology was

seen immediately after independence, when a section of a minority was disfranchised, it was after 1956 that Sinhala Buddhist
nationalism became the dominant ideology of the ruling class. It
is from this point onwards that a class block similar to the class
block of Kelecki's intermediate regime came to dominate state
power. As already mentioned, one result of this was the institution of state-dominated populist development policies within a
capitalist framework. The other development was the hegemony
of Sinhala Buddhist ideology and the systematic dismantling of
the safeguards for minorities that had been introduced at the time
of independence.

This process shows the contradictions of a bourgeois-democratic
system in a multi-ethnic society. Due to the importance of numerical strength within the bourgeois-democratic framework, the
Sinhalese Buddhists came to occupy a dominant position. Further,
the minorities began to feel that they did not have the numerical
strength to exercise power within the system. Thus, ethnic issues
began to dominate the electoral process and came to occupy an
important position in mass consciousness. Even the bourgeoisie,
whose objective interests within an internationally operative
capitalist system is to overcome narrow ethnic nationalism,
begins to play politics with it in order to stay in power. Thus, in
Sri Lanka all the major parties identify themselves with a Sinhala
Buddhist ideology. This does not mean that ethnicity in politics is
only a result of the manipulation of the ruling classes, for ethnic
consciousness has a real basis within popular consciousness. This
is true of all ethnic groups. Both the rulers and the ruled form part
of a society where ethnic consciousness has come to dominate.

The response of the minorities to the process of emergence of
Sinhala Buddhist ideology into dominance came from the Sri Lanka
Tamils who form the numerically biggest minority. Tamil political
leadership agreed to the safeguards at the centre at the time of
independence, although the demands of some of them were more
than what was agreed upon. These demands soon changed to one
based on concepts of regional autonomy. In the mid-fifties the
major Tamil party put forward the demand for a federal system
of government and by the early seventies this had escalated to the
demand for a separate state. The escalation of these demands also
saw the emergence of a new political leadership within Tamils and a

change in the form of the political struggle. The social background of the leadership was more of a petty-bourgeois character. They were less westernized than the earlier leadership, and had a regional base in the northern province, where there is a concentration of Tamil population. Armed struggle became the dominant form of struggle of the political movements led by this group. In some ways they are a mirror image of the Sinhala petty bourgeoisie which spearheaded the ethnic nationalism of the south.

The enactment of the First Republican Constitution in 1972 saw the beginning of the emergence of armed groups within the Tamil social formation. This constitution removed the earlier safeguards for the minorities in the previous constitution, gave pre-eminence to Buddhism in the constitution in addition to the Sinhala language, and concentrated all power in the Sinhala-dominated legislature. The early seventies also saw the aggravation of ethnic issues on account of the introduction of new admission schemes for entrance into the university. These schemes had discriminatory elements against Tamil students. All this led to the emergence of a separate state demand from the Tamil minority. Therefore, by the time the United National Party (UNP) was getting ready for elections in 1977, the ethnic contradiction was aggravated. This resulted in the Tamil United Liberation Front (TULF)—the organization that spearheaded the demand for a separate state—not only winning the elections in the north and to a lesser extent in the east with a separate state demand, but also becoming the major opposition party. For the first time in Sri Lankan history, parliament reflected the ethnic polarization in the country. While the United National Party (UNP) with a five-sixths majority obtained largely from a Sinhalese majority, was on the government side, the TULF was leading the opposition after winning the Tamil vote on a separate state demand.

The Post-1977 Development Experience of Sri Lanka

In the present context of capitalist growth, Sri Lanka's development policies are internationally determined. This determination emerges not only because of the greater intervention of bodies like the IMF and the World Bank, but also because international capitalism as an objective historical force determines these policies. What we are observing now is the greater influence of this international system in the economies and societies of not only Third World countries, but also in the Second World. More specifically in the case of Sri Lanka, international bodies began to advise on the economic affairs of Sri Lanka in 1952. Then, in 1965, this took a new turn by the establishment of the 'Aid Ceylon Club' under the auspices of the IMF, and since then its influence has grown. At the moment, IMF/WB influence in policy formation in Sri Lanka is significant (Lakshman 1987). This is parallelled by greater penetration of the international capitalist system as a fact into all forms of production in Sri Lankan society. Today, even the cultivation process of a small farmer in a remote village area of Sri Lanka is touched by forces that can be traced to an international system.

The post-1977 economic policies of Sri Lanka are influenced by recommendations of the IMF and the WB. These in turn are influenced by what has come to be known as 'monetarist' theories of economic development, and some authors have referred to 'Monetarist/IMF/World Bank (MIW)' policies.[1] Briefly, MIW-type recommendations may be summarized as being in favour of economic liberalization, export-led growth and fiscal balance: 'Great faith is placed on the market mechanism as a panacea for economic ailments, and government intervention in the economy is opposed in almost any form'.[2] These policies have two aspects, namely structural change and stabilization. The structural policies recommended are liberalization of trade and financial dealings with the world, the development of financial institutions and money markets, and the reduction of the state. As regards stabilization, balanced budgeting and maintaining a stable growth in money supply are emphasized. As can be seen, these recommendations are based on well-known tenets of free-market theories that emphasize market forces, comparative advantages, reliance on private capital (local and foreign), balanced budgets (cutting down government expenditure and welfare) and control of money supply as the principal means of economic growth.

These more liberalized economic policies, implemented now

---

[1] Howard (1987).
[2] Ibid.

for ten years, have to be understood in the context of the socio-political forces within which these policies are implemented.

Imperatives of the Liberalised Economy
in Ethnic Relations

The outward-looking economic policies adopted by the UNP government after 1977 had implications for ethnic relations in Sri Lanka, of which the two following aspects are most important:

(a) Outward policies make political stability an important pre-requisite. The ethnic issue was the main candidate as a destabilizer when these policies were initiated. Therefore, it was necessary to manage it.

(b) The policy framework, with relatively little importance being attached to the state sector, had the potential of reducing the importance of ethnically-biased structures that the earlier state interventionist policies had brought into prominence. However, in class terms this meant overcoming the influence of petty-bourgeois sections.

Certainly a government that had in mind a strategy of development based on a greater integration with international capitalism could not afford to ignore the contradictions arising out of ethnic relations. The policy depended heavily on foreign sources of finance. Attracting foreign investment is a cornerstone of these policies, and for foreign investors, political stability is a *sina qua non*. Thus, liberalized economic policies have built-in pressures for political stability.

The strategy of the UNP leaders in facing this issue was to try and arrange an accommodation with the representatives of the Tamil bourgeoisie and the traditional Tamil leadership. This was not a new thing for the UNP, whose previous period in power was a coalition with the leading Tamil political party—the Federal Party. The UNP itself had Tamil members as well as Tamil-speaking Muslim members from the eastern province—a province dominated by the minorities. The UNP was also able to get the participation of the leader of the Ceylon Workers Congress (CWC) in its new cabinet. The CWC is virtually the sole representative body of the Indian Tamil community. As revealed by the leader

Recent Riots in Colombo', *Sessional Paper IV of 1883*.

Roberts, Michael, 1970: 'The Political Antecedents of the Revivalist Elite in the MEP coalition of 1956', Ceylon Studies Seminar, 1969/70 series, no. 1, August 1970.

———, 1978: 'Ethnic Conflict in Sri Lanka: Barriers to Accommodation', *Modern Asian Studies*, 12, pp. 353–76.

———, 1979a: 'Meanderings in the Pathways of Collective Identity and Nationalism', in M. Roberts (ed.), *Collective Identities, Nationalisms and Protest in Modern Sri Lanka*. Colombo: Marga Institute, pp. 1–90.

———, 1979b: 'Elite Formation and Elites, 1832–1931', in ibid., pp. 153–213.

———, 1979c: 'Stimulants and Ingredients in the Awakening of Latter-Day Nationalisms', in ibid., pp. 213–42.

———, 1981: 'Hobgoblins, Low-Country Sinhalese Plotters or Local Elite Chauvinists? Directions and Patterns in the 1915 Communal Riots', *Sri Lanka Journal of the Social Sciences*, 4, pp. 83–126.

———, 1987: 'Pejorative Phrases: The Anti-Colonial Response and Sinhala Perceptions of the Self through Images of the Burghers in Sri Lanka', paper presented at the Conference on Ethnic Violence in South Asia, Kathmandu, February 1987. A revised version will appear as chap. 1 in M. Roberts *et al.*, *People In Between*, forthcoming.

Rogers, John D., 1986: 'The Assertion of Sacred Space and the Imperial Response: The Kalutara Bo-Tree Agitation in Sri Lanka, 1891–97', *South Asian Research*, 6, pp. 27–37.

———, 1987a, *Crime, Justice and Society in Colonial Sri Lanka*. London: Curzon Press.

———, 1987b: 'Social Mobility, Popular Ideology, and Collective Violence in Modern Sri Lanka', *Journal of Asian Studies*, 46, pp. 583–602.

———, 1987c: 'The 1904 Temperance Movement in Sri Lanka', paper presented at the Conference on Sri Lankan Studies, University of Sussex, September 1987.

Samaraweera, Vijaya, 1979: 'The Muslim Revivalist Movement, 1880–1915' in M. Roberts (ed.), *Collective Identities, Nationalisms and Protest in Modern Sri Lanka*. Colombo: Marga Institute, pp. 243–76.

Sarachchandra, E. R., 1950: *The Sinhalese Novel*. Colombo: Gunasena & Co.

Seneviratne, H. L., 1978: *Rituals of the Kandyan State*. Cambridge University Press.

Thaine, R. N., 1915: 'Report on the Riots in the Ratnapura District', by R. N. Thaine, G. A., Sabaragamuwa, 8 Sep. 1915, in *Eastern 128*, CO 882/10/128, pp. 250–57.

Thalgodapitiya, W., 1963: *Studies of Some Famous Cases of Ceylon.* Colombo.

Wickremeratne, L. A., 1969: 'Religion, Nationalism and Social Change in Ceylon, 1866–1885', *Journal of the Royal Asiatic Society, GB & Ireland,* LVI, pp. 123–50.

Woolf, Leonard, 1965–66: *Leonard Woolf's Diaries in Ceylon 1908–11,* printed as *Ceylon Historical Journal,* XI.

process of dialogue and discussion was sought to be given a concrete shape.

The Anti-Tamil Pogrom of July 1983

Sri Lanka has seen several incidents of large-scale ethnic violence in its post-independent history; 1958 saw the first incident, followed by ethnic violence in August 1977, August 1981, and July 1983. In order to understand these events it is necessary to place them in the context of large-scale socio-political processes. Therefore, the anti-Tamil pogrom of July 1983 has to be analyzed while keeping in mind the processes generated by development policies in the post-1977 period.

Most of the large-scale events of ethnic violence since 1977 have occurred against a backdrop of various kinds of political moves which were attempts to begin a process of dialogue and discussion. What preceded the August 1977 riots were the pre-election discussions and dialogue between the UNP, representatives of the Tamil bourgeoisie, and the traditional leadership. The post-election incidents of violence in July 1977, during which members of the opposition were attacked, continued into anti-Tamil riots. The August 1981 attack on Tamils occurred within a context of the first District Development Council elections, which was a measure agreed upon as an interim solution by the moderate Tamil leadership. However, the brunt of the attack in these riots was borne by the Indian Tamil community. The July 1983 riots also coincided with an attempt at calling an all-party conference to settle the issue. This was first called only to discuss the so-called 'terrorist' problem, but later its scope was expanded to include the entire issue of ethnic conflict in Sri Lanka. The expanded scope of this consultation even had such issues as the removal of the draconian Prevention of Terrorism Act and the limiting of the role of armed forces in the northern and eastern provinces. This consultation was to be held on 27 July. The July 1983 event started on 23/24 July. Therefore, all instances of anti-Tamil violence since 1977 coincided with various attempts by the system to come to terms with the contradictions. This is necessary for the system for its own self-interest. However, it generates a reaction from Sinhala chauvinist elements.

These elements could be found both within the government and outside, although it seems that those who are in positions of power within the government have a greater chance of perpetrating violence and yet escaping the consequences of their actions. The large-scale ethnic pogroms were the organized reaction of Sinhala chauvinism whenever the government tried to accommodate the moderate Tamil leadership. Such events became more frequent after 1977 because the imperatives of development increased the necessity for accommodation.

The Event

The incident that provoked the July 1983 violence was the killing of soldiers by Tamil militants who had been waging a guerilla war with the objective of setting up an independent state, Tamil Eelam. Militants had lured out the army with false information, and they were ambushed around 11.30 p.m. In this incident thirteen soldiers were killed. On the same day, the army had begun certain operations to remove some of the state Tamil population that had been settled in the predominantly Tamil districts of Manner, Vavuniya and Trincomalee. These were refugees of the August 1977 and August 1981 riots who were later settled in these lands. The settlement of these people, who were victims of ethnic riots, had been strongly opposed by Sinhala chauvinist elements. A former cabinet minister of the regime in power led this opposition. According to a statement issued by the Ceylon Workers Congress, around 600 people were removed from this area in the early hours of the morning of 23 July and brought to Nuwara Eliya district, where there is a preponderant Indian Tamil population. As we shall see later, the role of the army is an important factor in the anti–Tamil pogroms of Sri Lanka. In the case of the July 1983 outbreak, this seems to have begun from these actions by the army against the Indian Tamil population.

Just after the soldiers were ambushed in Jaffna, the army retaliated against Tamil civilians. During this retaliation, which took place in Tirunaely and Kantharamadu area, a number of people died. The figure is 20 according to official sources, 51 according to TULF sources, and over 70 according to others. Similar incidents seem

TABLE 1

Distribution of Religious Groups in the Wards of Colombo, 1901

	Fort	Pettah	St. Paul's	San Sebastian	Kotahena	New Bazaar	Maradana	Slave Island	Kollupitiya	Colombo
FIGURES										
Christians	355	1,619	6,512	1,582	18,683	3,858	7,288	3,158	6,297	49,352
Buddhists	493	2,218	2,830	2,545	8,519	5,513	13,474	5,047	7,773	48,412
Hindus	146	1,192	6,850	695	2,589	2,205	2,631	2,215	2,770	21,293
Mohammedans	282	2,498	4,067	4,518	3,539	5,880	6,968	6,328	1,328	35,412
Others	3	34	1	9	20	14	16	16	109	222
	1,279	7,561	20,260	9,349	33,350	17,470	30,377	16,764	18,281	154,691
PERCENTAGES										
Christians	27.7	21.4	32.1	16.9	56.0	22.1	24.0	18.8	34.4	31.9
Buddhists	38.5	29.3	14.0	27.2	25.5	31.5	44.3	30.1	42.5	31.3
Hindus	11.4	15.8	33.8	7.4	7.8	12.6	8.7	13.2	15.1	13.8
Mohammedans	22.0	33.0	20.1	48.4	10.6	33.6	22.9	37.7	7.3	22.9
Others	0.2	0.4	0.0	0.1	0.0	0.1	0.0	0.1	0.6	0.1

Source: *Census of Ceylon 1901*

Note: In the year 1901 the boundaries of Colombo city were not the same as they are today. Most of Wellawatte, for instance, was outside the city limits.

Abbreviations

A.G.A.	=	Assistant Government Agent
CO	=	Colonial Office series in the PRO
DNA	=	Department of National Archives, Sri Lanka
G.A.	=	Government Agent
I.G.P.	=	Inspector General of Police
NLR	=	New Law Reports (published by the Government of Ceylon)
PRO	=	Public Record Office, London
S.P.	=	Superintendent of Police
SCC	=	Supreme Court of Ceylon

Friday, 29 July

Rumour spread in Colombo that the Liberation Tigers were invading the city to exact revenge. Mobs beat to death Tamils who strayed from the security of the refugee camps or their homes. About 100 persons were reported killed. On this day the security forces took serious measures against looters, shooting or arresting some. This was the last wave of violence in Colombo. It was also the day on which Indian Foreign Minister, Narasimha Rao, arrived in Colombo with a message from Mrs Gandhi.

The toll of the riots was immense. According to official sources the number of dead was around 400. But there were other estimates. These varied—more than 500; around 1000; more than 2000; and even a figure as high as 4000. According to official sources, around 100,000 were rendered homeless. But according to others, this was the figure only for Colombo. Outside Colombo there were 175,500 refugees. An estimate of the damage to trade and business establishments was done by a government task force. It covered 116 industrial establishments that had been damaged within a 30-mile radius of Colombo. In addition it estimated that 492 trading establishments had been damaged at Pettah, which is a wholesale and retail trade area in Colombo.

The political response of the government to the riots began to emerge during the course of the events. It was contradictory and showed the confused position of the government on the issues. On the one hand the government said and did a lot to appease the sentiment of the Sinhala Buddhist majority. This began with the head of state saying that the riot was a legitimate expression of anger by the Sinhala Buddhist majority. The ministers who followed gave assurances that the government would do all it could to safeguard the rights of the majority. This culminated in legislation which made espousing the cause of separatism illegal; it resulted in the removal from parliament of legitimate representatives of the Tamil people.

The second response of the government was an attempt to find scapegoats from the Left as elements behind the riots. Several theories of conspiracy were floated. One talked of an attempt to promote conflicts between different ethnic groups of the country, starting from Sinahala and Tamil. This was expected to lead to general destabilization. This same speculation extended to a coup theory in which sections of the army were also supposed to be involved. Therefore, for the government, on the one hand the riot was a legitimate expression of Sinhalese anger, and on the other it was an attempt to overthrow the government: a classic contradictory situation reflecting a crisis.

Although the July 1983 event ended a week after it began, a similar pattern of events continued within the context of intensifying ethnic conflict in Sri Lanka. Such a pattern of events was characterized by a backlash on the Tamil civilian population provoked by the actions of militants. Significantly, the army was involved in several such incidents after July 1983, showing how institutions of the state themselves became the perpetrators of violence and lawlessness.

It was hoped that the Indo-Sri Lanka agreement signed on 27 July 1987 would be able to break the cycle of violence. However, immediately after signing the accord, there were violent protests all over southern Sri Lanka. The government responded with massive police operations against the JVP, the major militant group opposed to the accord and against concessions to Tamil demands for self-government.

The Indian peace-keeping force (IPKF), which was charged with keeping peace in the northern and eastern provinces, launched military operation against the LTTE to disarm them. In the offensive several charges of human-rights violation were made against the IPKF. The victims were mainly Tamils in Jaffna and the Sinhalese in Trincomalee. Many of the charges were supported by signed affidavits, eyewitness reports and reports by respected journalists.

A report by the Asia Watch Group summarized the problems arising from the LTTE and IPKF operations. The LTTE was charged with having used civilians as shields or with having executed Indian soldiers who had been taken prisoner.

The report stated, however, that this would not fully explain the casualties sustained by the civilian population during the IPKF offensive:

Civilian casualties were indeed heavy, heavier than the Indian government would prefer to admit. It appears that the Indian forces did observe some

seen immediately after independence, when a section of a minority was disfranchised, it was after 1956 that Sinhala Buddhist nationalism became the dominant ideology of the ruling class. It is from this point onwards that a class block similar to the class block of Kelecki's intermediate regime came to dominate state power. As already mentioned, one result of this was the institution of state-dominated populist development policies within a capitalist framework. The other development was the hegemony of Sinhala Buddhist ideology and the systematic dismantling of the safeguards for minorities that had been introduced at the time of independence.

This process shows the contradictions of a bourgeois–democratic system in a multi-ethnic society. Due to the importance of numerical strength within the bourgeois–democratic framework, the Sinhalese Buddhists came to occupy a dominant position. Further, the minorities began to feel that they did not have the numerical strength to exercise power within the system. Thus, ethnic issues began to dominate the electoral process and came to occupy an important position in mass consciousness. Even the bourgeoisie, whose objective interests within an internationally operative capitalist system is to overcome narrow ethnic nationalism, begins to play politics with it in order to stay in power. Thus, in Sri Lanka all the major parties identify themselves with a Sinhala Buddhist ideology. This does not mean that ethnicity in politics is only a result of the manipulation of the ruling classes, for ethnic consciousness has a real basis within popular consciousness. This is true of all ethnic groups. Both the rulers and the ruled form part of a society where ethnic consciousness has come to dominate.

The response of the minorities to the process of emergence of Sinhala Buddhist ideology into dominance came from the Sri Lanka Tamils who form the numerically biggest minority. Tamil political leadership agreed to the safeguards at the centre at the time of independence, although the demands of some of them were more than what was agreed upon. These demands soon changed to one based on concepts of regional autonomy. In the mid-fifties the major Tamil party put forward the demand for a federal system of government and by the early seventies this had escalated to the demand for a separate state. The escalation of these demands also saw the emergence of a new political leadership within Tamils and a change in the form of the political struggle. The social background of the leadership was more of a petty-bourgeois character. They were less westernized than the earlier leadership, and had a regional base in the northern province, where there is a concentration of Tamil population. Armed struggle became the dominant form of struggle of the political movements led by this group. In some ways they are a mirror image of the Sinhala petty bourgeoisie which spearheaded the ethnic nationalism of the south.

The enactment of the First Republican Constitution in 1972 saw the beginning of the emergence of armed groups within the Tamil social formation. This constitution removed the earlier safeguards for the minorities in the previous constitution, gave pre-eminence to Buddhism in the constitution in addition to the Sinhala language, and concentrated all power in the Sinhala-dominated legislature. The early seventies also saw the aggravation of ethnic issues on account of the introduction of new admission schemes for entrance into the university. These schemes had discriminatory elements against Tamil students. All this led to the emergence of a separate state demand from the Tamil minority. Therefore, by the time the United National Party (UNP) was getting ready for elections in 1977, the ethnic contradiction was aggravated. This resulted in the Tamil United Liberation Front (TULF)—the organization that spearheaded the demand for a separate state—not only winning the elections in the north and to a lesser extent in the east with a separate state demand, but also becoming the major opposition party. For the first time in Sri Lankan history, parliament reflected the ethnic polarization in the country. While the United National Party (UNP) with a five-sixths majority obtained largely from a Sinhalese majority, was on the government side, the TULF was leading the opposition after winning the Tamil vote on a separate state demand.

The Post-1977 Development Experience of Sri Lanka

In the present context of capitalist growth, Sri Lanka's development policies are internationally determined. This determination emerges not only because of the greater intervention of bodies like the IMF and the World Bank, but also because international capitalism as an objective historical force determines these policies. What we

too categorically separates the violence which is rational and characterizes the modern state, from both traditional domination based on the force of custom, and from habit and charismatic leadership which call forth the essentially irrational force of personal devotion based on fath.[3]

Clearly, this concern with distinguishing different kinds of violence and assigning 'value' to them shows that the epistemic space of violence itself has become prey to the the tyranny of the norm. Thus, for instance, in an underdeveloped country where a premium is put on modernization and progress, atomic or industrial accidents are treated as regrettable 'costs' of development, whereas communal riots are seen as pathological expressions of an irrational past which impede development; at any rate they are not treated as 'costs' of progress. But what we have to consider here is whether, by unthinkingly following this general trend in the understanding and 'treatment' of violence—supposedly typical of our societies— we do not lose out on its inherent transformatory and experimental potential. With this I think I have jumped straight into the heart of my methodological purpose in this essay: to raise doubts about the typological, behaviourist approaches to violence through an examination of the hermeneutic 'alternative'. The category of the survivor, its epistemological emergence and heuristic potential will be treated as critical to this evaluative exercise.

The fascination with the survivor—the one who is touched by violence but manages to 'get away' and lives to testify to the brute facts of violence—is surely very new to the study of violence. Yet it is linked to the historical and cultural category of 'witness' and the spiritual significance accorded to the 'historical' being of man within the Christian tradition. In religious terms the one who suffered and died or at least was prepared to die—the martyr, confessor and penitent—was honoured as interpreting and confirming the truth about an entire textual and historical tradition.[4] The survivor as a heuristic construct is inextricably, not fortuitously, bound to the study of violence, within a philosophy of history which builds intelligible reconstructions of the past as a series of 'interruptions' or 'ruptures' of the normal social order. When the

[3] Weber (1947), pp. 87–123.
[4] Ricouer (1978).

principal criteria for establishing historical causation makes an appeal both to the 'abnormality' and 'unexpectedness' of an event and to the allied power of human volition,[5] then violence is woven into the very stuff of historical praxis. It was not without thought that Gandhi declared history to be a record of 'every interruption of the even working of the force of love or the soul . . . an interruption in the course of nature'.[6]

It was in the production of a new kind of evidence, whose documentation would compensate for the unexplained 'residues' of rational history-writing, that the survivor proved crucial. As an ordinary member of society speaking from private memory and experience, the survivor furthermore provided a corrective to the understanding of history as an exclusively specialist activity. Since, by very definition, his testimony did *not* take the normal for granted as something known and in need of no explanation, the survivor represented a historical source which facilitated the movement of history away from events to structures. The earlier preoccupation with the unique could now give way to an interest in the ordinary responses and actions of men in society. Given the lack of recorded historical data on average people in everyday situations, the survivor's privileged epistemic position as one mediating life and death, chaos and order, speech and silence proved very valuable in permitting the historian to smuggle the social structure into his studies, through the back door as it were. Ultimately, it was acknowledged that the mechanisms of remembering and forgetting, describing and classifying, recounting and recreating, explaining and expressing, reflected in the survivor's testimony, all led back to the social fabric itself and the secrets of the collective life of which he served as a receptacle. The outbursts of mass hysteria, aggression, totalitarianism and confrontation to which the survivor was witness, certainly dwelt on the irrational forces of history; but at the same time they pointed to the hidden and intangible forces that shaped society. The apparent tendency of the historian, therefore, to concentrate, via the survivor, on shattering experiences and periods of disturbance and stress, was only to highlight the tension between rational structures and instinctual reactions common to social life

[5] Ricouer (1978), p. 126.
[6] Gandhi (1984), pp. 78–9.

condemnation. Very often, the liberal intellectual community is in the forefront of this reaction.

Along with this initial reaction is the belief that ethnic riots represent an 'event' which is not 'normal' in civilized society. The violence perpetrated at the time of an ethnic riot can be horrendous. It can include hacking people to death, or burning them alive. 'Retaliation' and 'punishment' meted out to members of other communities may include violence against children, old people and women. Thus, violence during a riot is indiscriminate and creates a moral problem for observers. It is often considered an aberration within civilized living. There is a feeling of disbelief and horror, especially at the manner of the violence; the evil seems central, yet liberal opinion tries to hold on to the idea of goodness of human nature.

It is in this context that we need to understand how a strongly moralistic approach to the understanding of communal riots may distort our analysis of such events. If human nature is bestowed with an innate goodness, then the tendency is to regard communal riots as an aberration and to search for 'culprits' who can be held responsible for perpetrating the horrendous violence one encounters during communal riots. This is not to deny the importance of fact-finding commissions and of recording such events. Such records are important for political activities concerned with the protection of human rights, but we do need to recognize their limits.

In Sri Lanka, as in other parts of South Asia; the recurrence of communal riots is seen as a manifestation of communalism. Riots are considered to reflect the 'irrational' passions of backward sections of society. Thus the liberal, modernist tradition uses the opposition of reason and passion to distinguish between the progressive course of history within which the processes of nation-building and development take place, and the occasional regressions reflected in isolated outbursts of the passions of what are considered 'communal-minded' and 'backward' people. In this kind of analysis such aberrations are to be condemned and the culprits punished so that the 'normal' processes of nation-building and development can proceed. The point is that, within this approach, ethnic riots are isolated events, discontinuous in time, and reflective of an outdated, false consciousness.

Opposed to the view of ethnic riots as isolated incidents is the suggestion that we look at them in relation to the changes in society in which they occur. The main issue is whether ethnic riots are a manifestation, in an acute form, of the very structures that characterize normal society. In other words, by refusing to treat these riots as aberrations, we may be able to understand the structure of a society at the precise moment of such violence. We may even ask if ethnic riots can be seen more as an aspect of certain stages of a society which is following a particular path of development, rather than isolated occurrences.

This paper looks at the anti-Tamil ethnic pogrom that took place in Sri Lanka in July 1983 as a *process*, the attempt being to link it to the contradictions generated by the development process that Sri Lanka is undergoing. I shall also here develop the framework for this linkage by looking at the relationship between the development experience of Sri Lanka, and ethnicity. This will be followed by an attempt to show the link between processes thrown up by present development strategies and the anti-Tamil pogrom of July 1983.

Development Policies and the Ethnic Issue

Before we come to the relationship between present tendencies in the economy and the ethnic issue, it is necessary to understand this link as it was constituted before 1977. We look at the policies before and after 1977 as two phases within a capitalist framework. In contrast to what is happening now, the previous phase can be characterized as a period when state-regulated inward-looking policies dominated. The policy prescriptions in this period looked towards the state as the main engine of economic growth. Protected markets, price controls, restrictions in foreign-exchange movements, and quotas in production were the hallmarks of this period. All these amounted to a greater dependence on state regulation on the one hand, and state involvement for economic development and greater protection of the economy from external factors on the other. What is also important to note about this moment is the fact that state intervention was also legitimized with a social-justice argument. Intervention of the state in various spheres of economy and society was apparently made to redress injustice; and some even

in any depth and preferred to keep lay perceptions and understandings of the collective crisis free of exogenous theory. But this did not reduce the material's inherent explanatory potential. Even a perfunctory analysis reveals the significance of these narratives for unearthing the social context of individual memory and consciousness. Some of the schemes, both moral and cognitive, to emerge from the speech of the Delhi survivors will now be examined for the methodological light they throw on the study of violence.

The Survivor's Past as Distinctive Time and Space

The most significant break after November 1984 may be found in the crystallization of the Sikh's new psycho-social identity as a 'minority' within the secular Indian nation. This was inextricably linked to their understanding of the past as experienced both temporally and spatially, individually and collectively. This is best demonstrated in the way in which the carnage against the Sikhs was interpreted within a sequence of earlier events.

A few key events and spaces provided the necessary conjunctures for the retelling of history as the gradual development of a sense of community alienation and political separateness. Invoked again and again in the survivors' speech as milestones to private memory were the facts of Indira Gandhi's death and the retaliatory violence and counter-violence; Operation Bluestar and the rise of Bhindranwale; the dissection of Punjab on a linguistic basis; the Punjabi Suba agitation and the partition of 1947. Having once taken place, the November riots were permitting connections to be made between previously unconnected events of national significance. In an exceptional, even substantial, sense, the reconstruction process found it possible now to merge individual time with social time given the simple but very real fact that those who experienced 1984 in Delhi were the same as those who experienced or inherited the collective memory/amnesia of Pakistan in 1947: 7.5 per cent of Delhi's total population, it must be kept in mind, is made up of Sikhs, most of whom settled there *after* Partition. Before this they only constituted 1.2 per cent of the population of Delhi. It was the distinctive time-space axis of the Delhi Sikh identity that made it possible for partition to appear as a precursor of the November events. But if partition was perceived as an unfortunate but inevitable happening of the collective past—the price one had to pay for independence—it had at least taken place in a *gair mulk* (alien country). The November 1984 atrocities, on the other hand, brought the horror back 'home' once again. For many of the survivors, November 1984 was a reminder of their received birth-defect as a nation. The memory of conflict and divisiveness which had hitherto been projected onto an alien country was now turned inward upon the self.

The violation of the home, whether religiously or domestically defined, formed a common thread in the Sikhs' own perception of Operation Bluestar (a military action) as an outrage of essentially the same order as the November killings (a populist action). Both together served to crystallize their new historical identity and stereotype: 'Beginning with Operation Bluestar and culminating with the November carnage, the Sikhs began to feel like a marked community.'[9] Whether it was tanks invading the Golden Temple or mobs hunting and killing men in front of their women and children, both amounted to an attack on sacred space. The fact that the agressors were those to whom one ordinarily looks for protection only served to increase the sense of alienation and persecution amongst the Sikhs. If the role of the army was condemned in connection with Operation Bluestar, it was the role of the police, local leaders (*netas*) and neighbours, particularly in the congested JJ (*jhughi jhopdi*) colonies of outer Delhi, which came in for condemnation in the context of the November carnage. Crucially, it was felt that the military atrocities of June 1984 had trespassed the moral boundary separating 'citizens' from the 'enemies' of the state, just as the atrocities of November 1984 had trespassed the moral boundary separating the innocent from the criminal and the guilty. Significantly, the injustice of these historic events was expressed in spatial metaphors. For instance:

When the Indian army has the power to challenge and defeat a different nation (*quam*), why did they have to use the army and tanks against Bhindranwale, who was after all an Indian?

It (the operation on the Golden Temple) was like someone coming into your house, forcing their way into your house... it was a violation which was wrong and most of all, cruel. . . . It was like having a war right next

<hr>

[9] Chakravarty and Haksar (1987), p. 22.

door . . . the way to effectively mount an operation against this kind of a place is to send in commandos, not from the front, not have a frontal assault with a whole battery of arms. But even by their [the government's] account they first sent in the army. It was exactly as if they were launching a war. I mean they were behaving in a totally war-like situation—20 tanks and a complete frontal assault.

The police took away quite a few people (after the *danga*). But all of them have been released. Now we see them roaming the streets and we feel terrified. Sometimes the children come and go, and we feel scared that they might be attacked. . . . It has become impossible for us to live here now. All of them are now our enemies. . . . And all the killers are from here. It's all lies that they were outsiders. No one was from outside. They were all from here. . . . Now of course they are all saying that they helped a lot. The same people were killing and the same people were doing everything else.

What happened at the time of Partition happened in a different country (*gair mulk*) but all that has happened now has happened in one's own country, the country which one thought was home, one's nation. For sometime now one has begun to feel that there is nothing for us here. Four or five years ago the freedom one felt in a place or the joy one experienced even in a jungle or a deserted place, is gone. Even in the home there is no peace of mind anymore.[10]

The survivor's need for sanctuary after the events of November 1984 found political expression for some Sikhs in a spatial metaphor, of Khalistan as a place where one could go and be safe permanently. This emotional reaction appeared at least in part as a direct response to the ambiguous role played by the state and society, by the police and neighbours in the Delhi carnage. The neighbours had, after all, actively participated in the killings or directed the mobs in their murderous tasks in the resettlement colonies. They had stood directly accused. In these colonies, the survivors saw no possibility of returning and setting up house once again. Many survivors, mostly widows and young children, positively refused to go back and rebuild their homes and start life afresh from where they had left off. They preferred instead to move to camps *en route* to being resettled in a new locality. But even where neighbours had actively helped save lives without thought of their

[10] All these and the following quotations are from Chakravarty and Haksar (1987), unless otherwise stated.

own safety, it was significant that Sikhs *had* to leave their homes in order to take refuge. Khalistan represented in this context an almost utopian dream of a new country where Sikhs could live in security without fear and humiliation:

We'll go to the Punjab, we'll go to Khalistan. . . . If this had not happened to us could we have ever left our *watan* (country)?. . . . Sardars are now in a position of weakness. [In Khalistan] they will make some place for themselves. . . . When they make it [Khalistan] we will go. It isn't made as yet. When it's made, only then we'll go.

The Survivor as Historical Stereotype

It is obvious that the survivor of the Delhi violence was not a unified subject and his experience remained influenced by differences of sex, age, social class, neighbourhood and the stage of the family's development cycle. But in an even more important sense, his self-identity as a 'marked' person flowed not merely from the Sikh perception of a shared, distinctive past, but also from the status that had been ascribed to him as 'victim' and 'survivor' by the Other. After November 1984, the mould into which the Sikhs were fitted by unspoken agreement remained itself a product of the rather ambiguous and uneven history with which their community had come to be associated over time. There can be no denying that, in the recent past, temporally more proximate memories of the Sikhs as a problem had tended to drive out more distant ones, which conveyed an image of the Sikhs as brave and faithful soldiers who had put up a fight for the Indian homeland against invaders, both Muslim and British. If the growing fortification of the Golden Temple had raised apprehensions about Sikh terrorism, separativeness and religious fundamentalism, and then the assassination of Indira Gandhi at the hands of two security guards from their community, conclusively branded them as people who had betrayed the trust of the nation and violated its sanctity and who therefore deserved to be 'taught a lesson'. By killing a leader who was readily assimilated to the category of 'mother', the Sikhs had shown their power and mad ambition, which posed a threat to everyone. Significantly, sections of the Hindus who had by and large approved of Operation Bluestar could nonetheless immediately connect Indira Gandhi's murder by a Sikh assassin as 'inevitably' flowing from that one action of the political past. It was the 'natural' link between the Sikhs and their fanatical, vengeful and violent behaviour, which was thereby sought to be highlighted.[11] For many Hindus a violent reprisal was what a Sikh not only richly deserved but all he could expect, given that he had flouted the norms of brotherhood and decency. The emerging stereotype of the Sikh as one to be feared *and* hated is given voice by the Other:

We won't spare any Sardars, when they could kill Indira Gandhi, they can kill us.

. . . *khoon ka badla khoon, tumne hamari ma ko mara* [blood in vengeance of blood: you killed our mother] *ham sardaron ko marange, sardaron ko jala denge* [we'll kill the Sardars, we'll burn them].

These Sikhs have killed her . . . these *sala* Sikhs should be taught a real lesson. . . . They've really gone too far in the last four or five years. . . . *Unko to ye mar padni hi chahiye* [they deserve this bashing].

Viewed in this light, Operation Bluestar and, later, November 1984, appeared to many Sikhs retrospectively to have been motivated by a desire to set right the balance of history against the community. Going by their personal testimony, state and society came to a tacit agreement on this matter. If the army's show of force in June 1984 had widespread public legitimacy and was seen overall as a 'good' thing which needed to be done to curb the Sikhs, the public's show of force in November had the covert and not-so-covert approval of the state. Whatever the truth of this general assessment, what is significant for our purpose here is that the Sikh survivors of the Delhi violence *believed* it to be true. As they saw it, their new ignominious historical role and condition as 'victims' and 'survivors' was not fortuitously linked to the violence but was itself part of the larger vengeance that had been plotted against them to check their growing social, political and economic pre-eminence. It is another matter that the category of survivor as it came to be applied to the Sikhs remained a fundamentally unstable and ambivalent group representation. In a remarkable irony the Sikhs came to be suspected and accused even during the November violence of essentially the same crimes as were being committed

[11] Chakravarty and Haksar (1987), pp. 510–13.

against them. The widespread credence given to the rumours circulated after Indira Gandhi's assassination, to the effect that Sikhs were celebrating, dancing the *bhangra* and distributing sweets, that trainloads of dead Hindus were coming in from the Punjab, that the Sikhs had poisoned the water in Delhi, had cut off young girls' hands and were raping and killing the very people who sheltered them, and that groups of them were roaming the streets with sten-guns in their hands and 'nothing in their heads'—all makes sense only in the context of their historically complex stereotype.

In the days since the November events the emergence of the Sikhs as challengers in the deadly game of ping-pong going on between terrorism and the state has only confirmed and hardened the contradictions inherent within the image others have of them. For the public at large, Sikhs combine in themselves, to an unacceptable degree, the qualities both of the aggressor and the aggrieved, the feared and the fearful, the winner and the loser, the martyr (*shaheed*) and the survivor. These historical ambiguities found clearest expression in November 1984 when all those who 'participated' in the violence, whether as victims, victors or voyeurs saw themselves in some sense as its 'survivors'. This was only to be expected given the unprecedented terror unleashed by the public, nature of the killings, arson and the manner of death.

Well-intentioned neighbours were made to feel that it was a sign of 'weakness', to shelter or save Sikhs. They were either taunted: 'Have you worn bangles?', or they were beaten up and warned that their own houses and lives would be in danger if they so much as showed any sympathy to the Sikhs. Where police cases did get registered it was remarkable that the killings were justified in the reports as a form of self-defence: 'A small group was gathered at a point when they were faced by a large number of Sikhs with *kirpans*. Feeling threatened they began attacking Sikhs.'[12]

Elsewhere, the police reassured those who had participated in mob activity by playing on similar sentiments: 'We gave you 36 hours. Had we given the Sikhs that amount of time they would have killed every Hindu.'[13]

---

[12] *Report of the Citizen's Commission*, 1985, p. 27.
[13] *PUDR and PUCL Report*, 1984, p. 5.

The mental exchange of places with the Sikh survivor became possible through a peculiar combination of anxieties that had come to oppress the ordinary person during all the chaos: the fear on the one hand of reprisal by the Sikhs and on the other of attack by the Hindus for sheltering Sikhs. A Delhi housewife thus found it possible along with others in her train compartment to climb on to the top berth in order to protect herself from the Sikhs, even after she had witnessed members of the Sikh community being dragged off from the train and being burnt alive on the platform before her very eyes.[14] Then again, a professor of Delhi University was looked upon with disfavour by his neighbours not only because he had helped a member of the 'marked' community but, more particularly, because he had thereby brought on the threat of an 'attack' on their particular street.[15] In such a context the 'loss of self-respect' given voice to by many Sikhs after November 1984 was a reflection of what they had seen in the Other's eyes and heard reported in his speech:

I knew that something was going to go wrong. It was already there on the faces of the people who didn't do anything during the riots. It had been there in their faces after Bluestar. And I was less shocked frankly by the riots than I was by Bluestar. Simply because for the first time in my life I saw very strange expressions in people's eyes. . . . In November I felt that I saw the same look in the eyes of the people which I had seen earlier. I didn't see any of the rioters. I'm not saying that. But I felt that I saw the same look in people's eyes.

No one has said anything to me. But the manner in which the propaganda through the media is being carried out . . . their role is clear from it. . . . Their [friends'] minds are being affected by what they see in the newspapers, what they see on the T.V. . . . They've made such allegations that I cannot bring myself to state them. . . . Its not that I cannot say them for fear or through hesitation. . . . They were such base allegations, such cheap words, that my tongue cannot repeat them.

In the final analysis the specificity of the survivor's experience and 'mentality' dissolve in the confusion of Self–Other images, as a Sikh and a young Hindu boy give voice separately and from opposite sides as it were, to an altered social consciousness:

[14] Chakravarty and Haksar (1987), p. 451.
[15] Ibid., p. 550.

I do not trust people anymore. I will not give them a lift.

One day a friend of mine who takes lifts regularly had a punctured tyre. Suddenly an elderly Sikh just offfered to take him in and put his cycle in the dicky. I was quite astonished, and in fact I even thought of going to him and saying 'Don't go'. . . . Because usually people don't go around offering help. . . . Very few people come and ask, 'Want to have a lift?' It seemed quite strange, and on top of it he was a Sikh.

The Survivor and Political Time

The survivor's record of the November hostilities—the unreason of fear, the dullness of prejudice, the minutiae of killing, the pragmatics of survival, the violence of need, the confession of despair— is an atrocious, even pornographic, one. But the question to be asked now is whether the 'obscenity' of this history is not merely the symptom and the sign of the more general inversion of order which prevails to mark the passing away of a great leader?[16] For many survivors, Sikh victims had not died a 'political' death in the November violence; thus, even though they saw analogies between the latter and partition, they clearly distinguished between the two on the basis of the mode of death prevalent. In November 1984 the 'political' death, according to the Sikhs, had been that of Indira Gandhi, who was assassinated for her 'responsibility', as leader of the nation, in the Operation Bluestar atrocities. Despite its public nature, the act, they said, was nonetheless clearly the action of two Sikh *individuals*, who out of a sense of anguish and anger had utilized their opportunity as Indira Gandhi's security guards, and killed her in order to take revenge.[17] The November 1984 carnage, on the other hand, insofar as it gave collective expression to essentially private, local quarrels ('*ghar-ki-larai*', '*khundak baji*'), jealousies ('*chidh*') and resentments against Sikh neighbours for whatever reasons—economic or social—was a perversion of the

[16] It has been noted by some historians that the death of an important political or religious leader is often accompanied by frenzied violence in the society. Carlo Ginzburg compares this to a rite of passage as order is restored only with the instalment of a new leader.

[17] At the same time, many of them acknowledged the widespread adulation the two assassins had since received among the militant sections of the community.

political order, which reflected itself on the temporal plane as a purposively organized period of anarchic liberty (*chhuta*). In the three days between 1 and 3 November 1984, the Hindus were allowed by the authorities to settle old scores of whatever nature against the Sikhs, and this was supposed to 'redeem' the Hindu community.[18] It was also important that the powerful organizers of the riots used, as their instruments, those people who could be terrorized or were already indebted to them for their very '*roti, kapda*, and *makan*' (food, clothing, and shelter). These were the lower castes and the displaced persons who made up the majority of the people in resettlement colonies. The reversal of positions was expressed by an old man whose two sons were burnt to death, '*jisne kabhi billi nahin mari ho wo aadmi marr rahe they*' [people who had never attacked even a cat were now killing men].

In the ghastly rites-of-passage that were performed unofficially before Indira Gandhi's last *samskara*, the weak killed, the *khanjars* purified, the 'criminals' judged, the 'martial' race observed purdah, and men (not women) were burnt in their homes. The very act of witnessing and later recording all this was a function of the temporary breakdown of structure which permitted a certain kind of gaze to be directed towards that which would normally have remained hidden from view. For many observers, what was significant about the violence of those three days—and lent credence in fact, to the belief in its 'motivated' and 'theatrical' nature—was that it appeared to have its 'own' time. The raucous glee and exultation on the faces of the looting and killing mobs made it appear more 'festival' than mourning time.[19] The violence, furthermore, only picked up on the day after the assassination, achieving its crescendo by the second day and dying its own death by the time of the cremation on the evening of the third day. Mobs moved in wave-like surges, sometimes returning two or three times to the scenes of their crimes with an increasing intensity of violent intent. Looters and arsonists robbed and burnt at leisure in an entirely relaxed manner and, significantly, without mutual disputation. It is in such periods of reversal that one may ask: does the state protect only its territorial or also its temporal integrity by a monopoly on the use of force? This

---

[18] Chakravarty and Haksar (1987), pp. 421–34, 533.
[19] Vishwanathan (1985).

would appear to be the case when we consider that events like the political death of a great leader tend to get reflected in society as a temporary condition of generalized and diffused disorder, violence, and feeling of timeless being.

The resettlement colonies, it could be said, became, in the three days after Indira Gandhi's death, self-sufficient microcosms of violent space and time reflections of the violent cosmology of the macrocosmic state. As pre-eminent representatives of the anonymous, uprooted, migrant and mixed or 'hotchpotch' culture of the state, they appeared to demonstrate at the time of crisis a fundamental social fact that 'artificial' disorder can only be a function of 'artificial' order.[20] In such a situation the restoration of 'order' can only proceed by way of disorder and violence and the enlarging of a political calamity to the inevitable natural plane. Does political death then serve as the thin line that separates the acts of violence, legitimate to the institution of the modern state, from the more general 'state of violence' prevalent in modern society? In any case violent *events* like assassinations and the like appear to be a necessary function of violence as a continuing *condition* of life in the contemporary political order. If November 1984 was predicated on Indira Gandhi's death, the Partition, it could be said, predicted Mahatma Gandhi's. History, by operating itself within the violent cosmology which gave rise to the modern state, has hardly found it possible to provide us with proper answers. It is from the epistemological space that the survivor occupies that we can perhaps interrogate the exact nature of the relation between society and state.

REFERENCES

Barraclough, G., 1978: 'History', *Main Trends of Research in the Social and Human Sciences*. Part 3, vol. I, pp. 227–487. Paris: Mouton/Unesco.
Chakravarty, U. and N. Haksar, 1987: *The Delhi Riots. Three Days in the Life of a Nation*. New Delhi: Lancer International.

[20] See Indermohan (1985) for an examination not only of the uprooted and unstable character of the JJ Colonies, but also of their violent history as organized targets for various state programmes such as enforced sterilization, resettlement, etc.

Das, V. and A. Nandy, 1986: 'Violence, Victimhood and the Language of Silence', In *World and the World: Fantasy, Symbol and Record*, ed. Veena Das. Delhi: Sage.

Durkheim, E., 1966: *Suicide*. Glencoe, Illinois: The Free Press.

Foucault, M., 1984: *The History of Sexuality, vol. I: An Introduction*. (tr. from French by Robert Hurley). Harmondsworth: Penguin.

Gandhi, M. K., 1984: *Hind Swaraj* (First Gujarati edition, 1908). Ahmedabad: Navjivan.

Hastings, J. (ed.), 1912: *Encyclopaedia of Religion and Ethics*, vol. 5. Edinburgh: T. and T. Clark.

Kishwar, M., 1985: 'Gangster Rule: The Massacre of the Sikhs', *Manushi*, vol. 25, 1984, New Delhi.

Marx, K. and F. Engels, 1975: 'The Holy Family or Critique of Critical Criticism', Karl Marx and F. Engels, *Collected Works*, vol. IV (Marx and Engels 1844–45). Moscow: Progress Publishers.

Mcgrath, A., 1987: *The Intellectual Origins of the European Reformation*. Oxford: Basil Blackwell.

Mohan, Inder, 1985: 'Re-Settlement: The Other Delhi', in *Voices from a Scarred City*, ed. S. Kothari and H. Sethi. Delhi: Lokayan.

Ricouer, P., 1978: 'Philosophy', in *Main Trends of Research in the Social and Human Sciences*. Part 2, vol. 2. Paris: Mouton/Unesco.

Smitu Kothari, S. and H. Sethi (ed.), 1985: *Voices from a Scarred City: The Delhi Carnage in Perspective*. Delhi: Lokayan.

Vishwanathan, S. 1985: 'The Spectator as Witness', in *Voices from a Scarred City*, ed. S. Kothari and H. Sethi. Delhi: Lokayan.

REPORTS

1984: *Who Are the Guilty? Report of a Joint Inquiry into the Causes and Impact of the Riots in Delhi from 31 October to 10 November*. Delhi: PUDR and PUCL.

1985: *Report of the Citizen's Commission*. Delhi, 31 October–4 November 1984.

1984: *Manushi*, vol. 25, New Delhi.

1985: *Manushi*, vol. 26, New Delhi.

Chapter Thirteen

July 1983: The Survivor's Experience

VALLI KANAPATHIPILLAI

Introduction

Sri Lanka has seen ethnic strife between the Tamils and the Sinhalese in 1958, 1977 and 1981, but the riots in 1983 were unprecedented in their scale of violence and brutality. Although they were aimed primarily against Tamils living in South Sri Lanka, the riots left the entire Tamil population of the country insecure and uncertain of their future. The middle classes in the South saw mob violence and frenzy unleashed upon them: it brought home to them the painful fact that regardless of their political ideology they were identified as Tamils and not as Sri Lankans. The polarization of the Sinhala and Tamil communities, which was gradually widening, increased dramatically after the violence of 1983.

For this study I have mainly interviewed victims of the July violence from the predominantly Catholic areas of Hendala and Wattala in Colombo. The victims were primarily Tamils belonging to different social classes and a few Colombo Chettis. The violence subsequently spread to the South and Central highlands, including both urban areas and plantations, but due to limitations of time I have had to confine my interviews to the Colombo area. Given the sensitive nature of the subject and the political situation in the country, it was possible to interview only those with whom great trust had been established. Out of the thirty in–depth interviews that I conducted, I now present four case-studies. For the conclud-ing section, however, I have drawn on all thirty interviews. The emphasis in my descriptions is not on validation and verification but on seeing the symbols through which narratives about survival and re-definition of everyday life were organized.

Case 1

Name	Saroja Solomon
Area of Residence	Dehiwela
Occupation	Teacher
Age	Late 40

Saroja Solomon is a Hindu Tamil married to a Catholic. Her husband is a retired foreman. They have two adolescent children, a son of eighteen and a daughter of sixteen. The house that they presently occupy is rented from a Sinhala landlord. They have lived here for seventeen years. At the time of the interview, I found that their house (not unlike other Tamil houses which were attacked) was sparsely furnished since the occupants had lost most of their things during the riots. Dominating the two rooms was a figure of Christ mounted on the wall, with an oil-lamp beside it. In her narrative, Saroja often mentioned that this figure had provided constant solace during the troubled period. Two other Tamil families had lived in this area but, following the riots, they moved out, leaving Saroja's family as the only Tamil family in the neighbourhood.

The events of July 1983 were recalled by Saroja primarily in terms of the changing relationships with her neighbours and the constant effort entailed in the interpretation of historical events as they impinged more and more on their personal lives.

On the morning of 25 July, according to Saroja, her children and husband had set off, respectively, for school and work, as usual. On hearing from various sources that there was likely to be 'trouble', she first went to the school where she taught and, having warned others of the impending trouble, she set off to fetch her son and daughter. When they returned home they were warned by a neighbour to close their windows and doors and stay indoors as Tamil shops were being broken at Galle Road. 'So I closed the windows and doors and sat with a pocket radio in hand, waiting anxiously, hoping to hear that a curfew had been announced.' After a while, the landlady advised them to open the windows and doors and go elsewhere: Tamil houses that were closed were being attacked.

The next few hours were shot with nightmarish uncertainty for Saroja. Having sent her daughter to a neighbour's house for safety, she waited with her husband and son under a tree. Except for one neighbour who invited them to come into their house, they were completely ignored. At one point they saw about a hundred thugs coming in their direction, and they fled in panic. While fleeing from the crowd, running directionless, they met unexpected kindness from the owner of a bicycle-repair shop who urged them to take cover in his shop. He locked them into a small room for safety. They could hear the sounds of destruction as their belongings were vandalized and broken. As she said:

'We waited for some time until the noise stopped; then as time passed we began to wonder where the shop owner had gone. My son said that the man did not have a good reputation, and for all we knew he could be an accomplice of the crowd and could burn us in the room. We tried to open the door, but could not. In panic we pushed and banged; nothing happened. Then my son noticed that the door had only been latched. With great relief we unlatched the door and came outside.'

The crowds seemed to have dispersed. However, they faced fresh trouble as their landlady tried to prevent them from entering their house. Fortunately a Muslim neighbour intervened on their behalf. They saw that their house had been vandalized, the furniture lay in ruins. Too scared to stay now, they went out and were roaming around aimlessly when a Muslim neighbour offered to take both the Tamil families of the neighbourhood to a camp. They gratefully accepted this offer and were taken to the Ratmalane camp.

Life in the Camp

Saroja and her family stayed in the Ratmalane camp from 26 July to 24 December 1983, the longest period in camp spent by any of those who were interviewed. They had entered the refugee camp with just the clothes on their backs. Their houses were no safe havens, but, rather, scenes of destruction. They did not know who to trust among friends and neighbours and the future appeared bleak and uncertain.

Like many other Tamils who were similarly displaced, camp life appeared extremely hard in the beginning. In the first few days there were 10,000 people in the camp and they had to stand in queues to use the toilets or to get drinking water. However, a community life began to emerge in the camp soon after and Saroja found there her brother, teachers from her school, and other Tamils (even people who were married to Muslims or Sinhalese). In the camp they were not fearful for they felt protected by the crowds. The richer people soon left the camps going off to Jaffna or India or to relatives elsewhere. Towards the end only those remained who could not afford to leave.

In September the schools started functioning again and Saroja and her children began to go to school from the camp itself. Her husband also resumed work. One day, on her way back from school, she met an old classmate, a Sinhalese girl who was shocked to learn of their plight. She offered the facilities of her house. For the rest of their stay in camp, Saroja and her family bathed and took all their meals in their friend's house, returning to camp only to sleep.

Saroja found that although camp life was terrible in the beginning, things began to improve as they made friends with others, including the officials. Some of these friendships continued beyond the life of the camp.

The Changes in Local Relations

While violence of the kind that Saroja encountered can be seen to constitute an extremely important historical moment in the life of a nation, it was also simultaneously a momentous event in the personal lives of people that shook the nature of their everyday life. Relations in everyday life that were marked by a certain ambivalence, such as landlord–tenant relations, now became much more defined. Thus it is not surprising that one of the dominant motif in the narrative of Saroja came to be her changing relations to her Sinhala landlord, and the harassment which her family had to suffer at his hands. Prior to 1983, there were many irritants which are part of such relations everywhere, but after 1983 these irritants were transformed into open hostility.

Saroja resented the fact that the landlord had not offered them shelter when they were attacked by thugs. The landlord, on his part, was probably scared of having a Tamil family live in his house and by the fact that REPIA (Rehabilitation of Property and Industries Authority), which had been set up by the government to help victims of the riots, had become involved in the dispute over the house. While in camp Saroja and her husband had appealed to REPIA for financial help to repair the house. The landlord, who found Tamil tenants an encumbrance, tried to create obstacles. In order to help Saroja and her husband, REPIA issued them a letter of authority, authorizing them to repair the house and move in; they were also instructed to pay Rs 200 per month to the landlord, which was their normal rent. The landlord sent a letter to the chairman of REPIA stating that the area was not safe for the habitation of Tamils and that he took responsibility for possible future trouble.

Encouraged by the REPIA chairman, Saroja's family had minimal repairs done and moved into their house with police protection, despite the hostile attitude of the landlord. Thus, relations between Saroja's family and the landlord continued to deteriorate. The landlord subjected them to continuous harassment. The worst incident in the pattern of intimidation occurred on the night of widespread disturbances in the city after the Peace Accord had been signed between Sri Lanka and India (28 July 1987). Taking advantage of the fact that political discontent was being widely expressed, the landlord tried to harass them by the use of local headlines. As Saroja recalled:

On the 28th July, [1987], there were disturbances in the Mount Lavinia junction. That evening the power supply went off, so did the telephones. At 11.00–11.30 p.m. my children, husband and cousin were sitting in the living room casually chatting with each other when we heard a knock on the door. I opened it on the assumption that perhaps it was a neighbour. A thug walked right into the house and asked us to switch on the lights. We replied that there were no lights. Then he took the torch from my husband and flashed it into the room, asking if we were the only inmates of the house. Then he went round the house, came back and said: 'We have surrounded the house. In about ten to fifteen minutes we shall set fire to it. Do not shout for help, just wait here.' We were stunned.

After a while I stepped out to go to the toilet and my son and cousin followed me. The man asked, 'Where are you going'? In a flash I saw the figure of another man standing by the entrance to my landlord's house. Later my cousin said he had seen another man on the other side. We knew we were surrounded. The man told me to get into the house. Then I remembered that in 1983 some Tamils managed to escape by pleading with the thugs. So I started to talk for whatever it was worth. I said, 'Don't you feel sorry to do a thing like this'? He went off without replying. Again he came back and said 'I spoke to the others but they refuse to go. They are quite drunk and I do not know what they may do.'

I was wondering whether to send my son through the side entrance to get help, but my husband thought that could be dangerous. The only thing was to pray, so we all gathered and prayed for our safety. The man came back again and said that his friends refused to go. He remarked, 'Any way in 1983 also you escaped'. His remark made it clear that someone must have given him information about us. He challenged us to call the police, but he knew that the phones were not working. Then he said, 'Why can't you go and stay elsewhere even for 15 minutes'? We refused, for we could now understand that they wanted to loot the house. He went away, then returned again, and said his friends might throw stones at us. Then after a while he told my children to go and sleep but they refused. He went out again. By now it was between 2.30–3.00 a.m. He returned, sat on a chair, asked for a drink of water; then said, 'You do not look like Tamils. So why don't you go somewhere else and live like Sinhalese'? I was convinced this incident had been set up by the landlord. It was part of a continuing series to intimidate and harass us—so that we may leave and he may rent out the house to someone else at a higher price.

That night the man who had intimidated them thus, left without harming them. The family prayed together after he left. The next afternoon, when Saroja was out in the garden, the same man passed by on a bicycle and shouted, 'Remember me? I was the one who saved you last night'.

It is important to note that this particular incident did not happen at the height of ethnic violence but almost four years later, and it shows how patterns of violence get embedded into local contexts and continue even after mob violence has subsided. It is part of this pattern that every change in the Sinhala-Tamil relationship at the national level leads to a new uncertainty in the lives of the Tamils. For example, most Tamils feared violence on 18 August 1987, when Parliament was to meet over the Peace Accord. For Saroja it was not simply a generalized fear that there could be violence against Tamils by anonymous crowds, but also the fear that the landlord could use that occasion to intimidate and harass her. Her fears were confirmed when, on the 18th evening, the landlord's son and a few others came and started shouting filthy abuses at them: '*Ado Varang*', '*Para Demala*', '*Chakhili Damale*' (low-caste Tamil). Saroja and her family did not join or respond. They had to simply bear up with the insults.

An unexpected consequence of these incidents was that Saroja, who at one point was considering reconciliation with the landlord, now became firm in her resolve that she would not allow herself to be intimidated by him: 'Even if I am killed I shall stay here. I do not want to take the house forcibly but I shall not come to a settlement after what they have done to us'.

In Saroja's account it seems that the deteriorating relationship with the landlord crystallized the meaning of national events in her everyday life. Thus, local-level events—such as fights in the neighbourhood and landlord-tenant disputes—are grafted on to national events by reasons of contiguity. What dramatizes the impact of ethnic violence at the national level in the everyday life of the people is the transformation they see in local-level relations. There is, ofcourse, a sharpening of conflicts, but there is also the creation of new intimacies which come about due to the need to offer and accept help and succour.

What appeared remarkable in Saroja's account was her ability to unravel and understand clearly the nature of the conflict in which she was involved. She said that she would continue to live in the house despite all the difficulties, for she realized that whatever happened to them was due to the landlord's interest in having the house vacated, for which the ethnic strife simply provided the pretext.

It is obvious that the violence of July 1983 and the protracted period of harassment has required a new understanding of the self and the world on the part of its victims. Such violence often seduces the victims to totalize the categories of their world.[1] It would have been easy enough for Saroja to translate the conflict with her landlord into the idiom of ethnic strife. As stated earlier, every event at the national level is also an event at the local level. This grafting of the two levels on each other allows victims as well as perpetrators

---

[1] The concept of totalization in the context of violence has been developed by Perkin (1986).

of violence to constitute an event in terms of a variety of categories. Saroja showed courage and clarity in defining the conflict with her landlord as one over local issues rather than national ones. For such an interpretation to become a guiding force to action, as in the case of Saroja, her mental resistance to totalization of categories seems to have played an important part. Thus, in Saroja's account, we found not only reference to her intimidation by the landlord but also the help she received from her Sinhala friends.

Another important point here is the family's construction of reality. Saroja, though herself a Tamil, is married to a Catholic and her children practice the Catholic faith. Her construction of events, therefore, is part of the whole family's construction of reality. This comes out best in her reflections on her Tamil identity and what this has meant for her family.

We turn now to these reflections and their narrative framing. One may summarize Saroja's reactions to her Tamil identity by her poignant statement that 'to be Tamil is to live in fear'. She remembered with nostalgia the times when she used to dress up in typical Tamil fashion. Now she avoids wearing *puttu* (an auspicious mark over the forehead which would identify her as a Tamil). The children, she said, resented her Tamil identity. Whenever she wore an Indian saree and a *pottu* they remarked, 'She is dressing to go out and get hit again'. The fear of being identified as a Tamil pervaded relations within the family, for although Saroja and her husband spoke in Tamil the children spoke Sinhalese, even at home. Saroja encouraged the children to identify themselves more and more with the Sinhala community and to hide all marks of a Tamil identity. 'I have told them', she said, 'to marry persons from any ethnic community but the Tamil'. Ensuring a better future for the children, she felt, was to ensure that they moved away from being identified as Tamils. It is in these reactions of Saroja that we see the deep scars of violence.

The events of July 1983 and the subsequent intimidation that Saroja faced has meant that the family has had to make many adjustments within their own internal structure. It is noticeable that it is not the male head of the household who seems to have taken the difficult decisions since the violence erupted, but Saroja. In fact it seems that, in times of violence, women come to play a far more active role in decision-making, taking risks and dealing with the hostile external world. In her turn, Saroja has moved much more towards the religion of her husband to provide relief and succour. She explained that she had a figure of Christ mounted on their living-room wall in July 1983 so that the family could pray daily.

She firmly believed that in periods of crisis prayers have saved them. Her positive feeling towards Catholicism has been strengthened by the fact that Catholic church organizations have provided relief and help during times of need.

Case 2

Name	Sylvia David
Age	42
Occupation	Primary schoolteacher in a leading Catholic school in Colombo.

Sylvia is a Catholic woman of Jaffna, of Tamil origin. She comes from a large family, with six sisters and four brothers. Her father died in 1974. At the time of the riots the family was living in a suburb of Colombo, in a rented house, where they had lived since 1967. Sylvia remembers the initial few days of the riot as days of utter confusion and chaos. Pictures of shops burning, cars running amok, crowds smashing and hitting at old people and children— these dominate her memory. It was, she said,·'a world gone mad'

On the fateful day of 25 July 1983, Sylvia had gone to school as usual but discovered that there had been a ethnic riot in Colombo. She was sent home in a van where she found that some members of her family had been taken to a Sinhala neighbour's house: others, including her brother, she was told, had taken shelter in a friend's house. She joined the family in the neighbour's house. What appears vividly in her accounts is the role played by neighbours as well as the Catholic church in saving the family. Sylvia and her family were themselves in such a dazed condition that they simply could not interpret the events and had to put themselves completely in the hands of the neighbours. Thus it was one Mrs Pereira who had dragged her mother and sister out in the morning and taken them to her own house, insisting that 'their lives were at stake'. The parish priest moved around giving messages and bringing news from the outside. He had tried to save their house, unsuccessfully as it turned out, which had been set alight by hoodlums.

Sylvia remained in Ms Pereira's house till the evening. At six o'clock another neighbour came rushing to the house where they were hiding and insisted that they jump over a side wall and hide there to avoid the crowds that were attacking Sinhala houses suspected of harbouring Tamils. 'Today if someone asked me to jump a wall', said Sylvia 'I would not be able to do so, but that day I do not know how I got the strength'. Across the wall they found themselves in the premises of a nearby convent and were given shelter there for two days. Sylvia emphasized that the convent sisters had taken considerable risks in giving them shelter, for the hoodlums suspected the parish priest and the sisters of hiding Tamils within the premises of the church and the convent. At seven o'clock the next evening, a van was organized to take them to a police station under cover of darkness, with an assurance by the sisters that their prayers would 'accompany them'.

The experience of the crowded police station stood up in Sylvia's mind as offering a complete contrast to her experience in the convent. 'The smell of blood was overpowering.' A pregnant women asked for water but the policeman refused and joked saying, '*get it from Elam* [the Tamil militant organization]'. The next day more people with injuries were brought to the police station. One of the fearsome incidents that Sylvia recalled was being told by a young Tamil boy to try and lose herself in the crowd because he had heard a policeman say that they would rape the two women (meaning her and her sister) and throw them into the river. After they had been herded in the police station in this manner till the next evening, the Tamils were told that their safety could not be guaranteed at the police station and, therefore, they should go to a camp. However, the police refused to provide them with any escort which would help them reach camp in relative safety. Finally, the Tamils collected money among themselves for petrol and a young Tamil boy who looked like a Sinhala agreed to drive them in a private van. It was during curfew hours and the roads were deserted but, as Sylvia said, crowds seemed to materialize from nowhere. Fortunately, there were two Navy personnel with them who fired in the air and the crowds vanished. 'As I talk to you', said Sulvia, 'I can see the crowds before my eyes'. When they arrived at the Mahanama camp at 6.00 p.m., having been on the road for four hours, the army personnel guarding the camp pointed guns at them and, ironically, made *them* walk with their hands in the air.

Fortunately for Sylvia, the other members of the family were safe and joined them in the camp. She stayed there along with her family till September. Her youngest brother fell ill and was diagnosed as having a 'nervous illness'. He had to be hospitalized. The doctors said he would suffer all his life. 'At this stage', said Sylvia, 'I lost whatever hope I had'.

In reformulating their lives, Sylvia, like the other Tamils who were interviewed, has had to come to terms with a totally new way of looking at the world. A most profound change in the life of her family was entailed by the necessity to live separately after the riots. Sylvia rented a room in Bambalapitya while her brother boarded in a room elsewhere. Her mother and younger sister have had to accept the hospitality of her married sister. Thus, from a close and strongly-knit family, they became spatially dispersed. Not only was this financially burdensome, it was psychologically crippling. Sylvia missed, above all else, the comfort and closeness of her family, crystallized in her memories of the protected and sheltered life she had lived earlier. Especially difficult for her was the recognition that her mother and younger sister had become dependent relatives, with all the humiliation that such dependence implies.

The events of 1983 were in some ways a repeat of the earlier events of 1958, when their house had been attacked and when they had been robbed of all their possessions. Subsequently, their father had sold their house in Jaffna. Saroja felt that these riots of 1958 had so affected her father that he had been unable to recover from the shock. He had been a strong and active man earlier but had become totally dejected later, dying in 1974. The money they had made from selling the house was all lost in the riots of 1977. And then again there was a repetition of this experience in 1983. All this had left the family without a will to start anew to create a home. It was not only the large issues but the little things that gave pain. For instance, Sylvia grieved for the loss of all the knick-knacks that had made up the memories of their lives together. Yet in 1987 Sylvia and her family had recovered enough to begin to make plans for the future and to try and find a house to rent so that the family could be together again.

We saw in the earlier case of Saroja that the individual's relationship to the group is inevitably renegotiated in the case of ethnic violence. There is a strong tendency on the part of victims of violence to totalize the characteristics of a group. However, the notion that groups have characteristics comes in conflict with one's experiences of the particular individuals of a community, which is varied and rooted in concrete events.

Sylvia had to reformulate her relation with the Sinhalese as a group. As we saw, her experience of her immediate Sinhala neighbours, who had helped her family during the crisis, was a positive one. Yet feelings of anger and hatred were projected by her to groups of Sinhalese who were outside her immediate experience. For example, she had come to dislike intensely the armed forces. She referred approvingly to the terrorist attack at Chavakachery in which several soldiers were killed, as she felt avenged by this distant violence. Yet when she happened to meet the widow of a solider killed in that attack she felt very sorry for the woman. It is significant that she always referred to those who attacked them as 'thugs'. For most middle-class people who were attacked during the riots, the source of violence was not the immediate neighbours but, inevitably, lower-class hoodlums. Thus they brought a split focus to bear in their attitudes to the Sinhalese as a group, for they identified them as the perpetrators of violence when they thought of them in the abstract. At the same time, the experience that they had (with exceptions) of concrete individuals, such as neighbours and friends, was of having received help and succour even when this endangered the lives and property of the people who offered such help.

Whereas Sylvia's attitude to the Sinhalese as a group was one of ambivalence, there was no such ambivalence towards the state; towards the state she had a feeling of complete betrayal. This feeling was compounded by the fact that Sylvia's family had been UNP supporters. During the 1977 elections her brother had campaigned for the MP of the area. Yet during 1983 when he called the MP and told him that their house had been burnt, the MP promised to look into the incident but did not follow it up with either help or sympathy. Sylvia had also heard rumours that the MP had personally told the Sinhalese in the area that they should not give shelter to Tamils. In addition to local factors, the first speech which President Jayavardena gave came as a great disappointment for not a word of sympathy was offered to Tamil victims in this speech. In Sylvia's words, 'It was as if our suffering was nothing'.

The recognized institutions of the state, such as the police and the armed forces whose duty it was to help the victims and to control the violence, were seen as manifestly failing to do their duty, while, in contrast, the Church had offered kindness and help. For the victims it was the informal network of friends and neighbours, and the church organizations, which had provided the means for reformulating their lives. It is not surprising, then, that they should have felt most betrayed by the state.

Case 3

Name	Kamala
Area of Residence	Wellawatte
Occupation	Teacher
Age	41

At the time of my interview with Kamala, she and her family were preparing to migrate to New Zealand. In her case one could see the dilemmas faced by middle-class Tamils who had lived most of their lives in Colombo and who did not have many roots in Jaffna. Kamala had always seen herself as totally integrated with other ethnic groups in the country; yet she found herself a target of vicious violence during the riots. She found it difficult to come to terms with the ethnic polarization that she saw around her. She refused to identify with the emerging Tamil nationalism, which she considered chauvinistic, but neither could she cope with the Sinhala chauvinism that was beginning to emerge. She was equally opposed to the violent methods adopted by Tamil militants and considered that a non-violent struggle following the Gandhian methods would have been more humane and effective.

Kamala saw no future for herself and her family in Sri Lanka. More than anything else, she was very disturbed by the impact that the violence had on her children. She felt that the decision to migrate had become necessary to ensure that the children had a secure future; this did not seem possible for them in Sri Lanka.

I shall first give an account of the direct violence that Kamala and her family had to face in July 1983 and then describe how she had tried to reformulate her life.

This is how Kamala described the riots:

On Monday, 25th July, several Sinhala friends called in the morning and warned us that there was likely to be trouble in Colombo and it would be advisable not to send the children to school. The whole neighbourhood became tense as information and warnings began to pour in. My sister and her family who live in our neighbourhood joined us by 10 a.m. We decided that the best course to follow, under the circumstances, was to go to the Ramakrishna Mission, which was situated close by. As we set out, I saw CTB buses full of young men stopping at Galle Road. They got off and ran towards Ramakrishna Mission. This was followed by the sound of breaking and smashing. I was in a panic, when a Sinhala lady shouted at us to get inside our house. At that moment I had to make a quick decision. I could not stand outside exposed to the violence. So I took my family and ran into the house. I suppose at that moment instinct makes us run to the security of our home, but I regreted my decision. Anyway, my brother, my two children of 6 and 3 years, my 12-year-old niece, and I ran upstairs to a room on top of the garage and locked ourselves in. My mother, sister and aunt had got separated from us, as they were stopped by three men, holding large knives, who shouted at them in Sinhala, 'What are you doing here? Run inside.' In terror, they ran into my sisters' house.

In a while, we could hear shouts followed by sounds of glass breaking. We knew the mobs were inside the house. I was terrified. The children were crying. The sound of breaking and smashing seemed to go on for ages. We cowered and waited as quietly as possible. Then I heard a voice, from the vicinity of the garage, saying in Sinhala, 'There's a beautiful car here, let's burn it'. I heard another voice say, '*Aney pow*—do not burn the car' to which the first voice threateningly responded, 'If you do not, we will hit you and put you inside the car'. Then they probably set fire to the car for the smell of something burning wafted to our room. I felt trapped. Soon we heard footsteps coming up. There was the sound of banging and pushing on the door. The thugs were trying to get inside. My nephew and I pushed with all our might against the door to prevent it from opening. We were terrified in case they broke open the door. Then with relief, I heard one of them saying, 'There is no one here, let's go away'. While holding on to the door all I could do was to pray. I told the children not to make a sound, and told them to silently pray with me. One of them asked me, 'Amma are we going to die'? How could I answer that? Meanwhile smoke from the car started coming into the room. Once we were sure the thugs had gone away, I opened the door cautiously and looked out, the staircase was on fire. I had to find a way to escape. I decided to get on to the roof. I told my children to follow and in a flash my daughter, niece, and nephew ran up to the top of the roof. My son was clinging to me, frightened, but finally I persuaded him to do the same. From the roof I could see that my neighbour's house was untouched. Their name is Joshua, so probably the thugs did not realize they were Tamils. Meanwhile from the roof we could hear the thugs talking in a garden. It was imperative that we were not seen. The only course open to us was to jump from the balcony on to the neighbour's wall and into their garden. The other children quickly slid from the roof and got on to the balcony, but my daughter got scared. I told her that a broken foot is better than a burnt foot and cajoled her to jump. She finally jumped onto the balcony. Then I discovered that my niece was missing. I called for her and saw her still sitting on the flat part of the roof. I pleaded with her to get off. She was twelve years old and I was frightened to even imagine what the men would do if they saw her. I pleaded with her and finally scolded her. Then she slid down a pipe and landed on broken glass. As she went sliding down I saw two men approach her. I was terrified. She was frightened herself, but had the presence of mind to say, 'I don't live here, I come from the front house', pointing to the Peiris' house. She is a fair child and so is Mrs Peiris, who was watching all this. Mrs Pieris promptly called to the men imploring them not to harm her as she was her daughter, and took her into the house. Stealthily we all joined Mrs Pieris. When my niece saw me she cried in relief, for she was very afraid that her own mother had been killed by the thugs.

It was quick thinking on the part of several neighbours that saved many Tamils that day. My brother, at one point, stepped out of the house to look for my mother when the thugs caught him and hit him. Seeing this, an 18-year-old Sinhala neighbour shouted that this boy (my brother) was a Muslim and not a Tamil. He took in my brother who was badly bruised.

After a while, a second crowd formed and started systematic destruction of Tamil houses. I heard a man on a motorbike shouting out the house numbers of the Tamils and warning the crowds not to touch Sinhala houses. The second mob even came into the Pieris house and enquired if any Tamils were hiding there. At grave risk to themselves Mrs Pieris replied in the negative and chased off the hoodlums.

One of the most difficult situations that Kamala had to face that day was arranging the return of her father, who had been admitted to hospital earlier for a routine check-up. At about 9 o'clock one of their Sinhala friends drove by to see if they were well and on hearing about the father, agreed to drive him back from the hospital. On the way the car of the Sinhala friend was stopped several times by crowds and they were asked if they were Tamils. Somehow the friend managed to bring the old man home, but on finding their houses burning, he left his father in front of the Pieris house. Kamala saw her father and came out to take him in. He was pale and bathed in sweat. Right then, some men came running with big poles. They were shouting: 'If you are Tamils, we will kill you'. Kamala barely managed to drag her father into the house. 'By 3:30 in the afternoon', said Kamala, 'the noises of the crowd had died down. There was an eerie silence. The only sounds were those of the beams of the houses that were breaking and falling at regular intervals. There was no other sound, not even an echo of human voices.'

Kamla's experience in the Ramakrishna Mission and subsequently in the camp was similar to the experiences of the others, described earlier. In this case Kamala and her family did not have to stay more than two days in the camp. As soon as their Sinhala friends heard of their plight, they came and fetched them to their own house, where they stayed for one month.

Subsequently, Kamala's sister decided to migrate to New Zealand as a refugee and at the time of the interview Kamala and her family had also decided to migrate.

It seemed in my discussions with Kamala that there were two major factors which led to her decision to migrate. The first was the constant fear with which the children had to live after the 1983 violence. The second was a construction of their own identity as minorities who would have to live in constant awareness of this fact, wherever they chose to live.

The children bore psychological scars from the violence and continued to have nightmares when asleep. Kamala related the following instances: 'One night my eight-year-old daughter came running to me, crying that some people were coming to kill her. Another day, early in the morning I was in the kitchen making coffee when my daughter came in crying hysterically and said that she had seen thugs come in and cut off *amma's* legs.' She was hugging Kamala and crying, and it took a while before she could be made to see that Kamala's legs were still intact, and that it was only a dream. Her children went for a holiday to visit her sister in New Zealand in 1986. As soon as her eleven-year-old daughter reached her sister's place from the airport, she announced, 'Now I do not have to worry if the army is killing the terrorists, or if the terrorists are killing the army, and if the Sinhalese are going to burn our house'.

As in the case of Saroja, Kamala's children also identified their Tamil identity as the cause of much pain and suffering. 'After 1983 the children were pestering us to change our names to a less Tamil sounding one. And also to get rid of the name board on our front gate.'

Fear of revealing their Tamil identity would surface on all kinds of occasions. Once when they were in a shop in New Zealand, Kamala's daughter called her *amma* but was promptly scolded by her brother, 'I told you not to call her *amma* outside the house but to call her *ammi*'. Thus he wished to adopt the Sinhala term for 'mother', along with other Sinhala ways, so that they could be protected from the ruthless consequences of being Tamil.

The only positive transformation in the lives of the children, Kamala felt, was the deepening of faith in God. According to her, their belief in God had been like a convenient vehicle before they had experienced the violence. For instance, just before the school sports-day, Kamala's son had been known to declare that if he said 'Muruga' thrice he would win the race.[2] In July 1983 the children discovered a different meaning of prayer when they stood behind the door which the thugs were trying to push open. They were convinced that the door did not open because God heard their prayers and they could save themselves despite the fact that the whole staircase was on fire.

Apart from the experiences of the children, which were very important for Kamala in making her decision to migrate, there was also a deep sense of betrayal by the state. The tragedy was compounded by the fact that the events of 1983 culminated in the death of her own father.

---

[2] Muruga is the name of a Tamil deity, who presides over games of competition.

It may be recalled that her father had been discharged from hospital on 25 July and had reached home when the violence in the city was at a peak. Kamala had just about managed to save his life by dragging him into the Pieris house, as the thugs came running to assault him. A month after this riot he died of a heart attack, and it is likely that the coronary attack was provoked by the trauma of the violence. All his life, Kamala's father had been a nationalist. He was a doctor and had done considerable work among the Sinhala peasantry. Now, after the violence, he was a broken man. He told Kamala to leave the country and 'not to stay with these animals'.

For Kamala and her father the violence of 1983, in which they were identified as Tamils and attacked, constituted a threat to their entire existence. The violence brought home the fact that despite their ideological commitment to Sri Lanka as a nation and their antagonism towards Tamil militants, they were objectified as Tamils. In the previous riots of 1958 or 1977, middle-class residential areas had been protected, because the residents had been able to use their influence to get police or army protection. In 1983 they were made homeless overnight. The violence happened so quickly that there was no time to call for help, and even when they did call for help it never came, or came too late.

Unable to identify herself with the Tamil militants and equally unable to find a place and an acceptance among the dominant Sinhalese, Kamala felt that the future of Sri Lanka now had no place for them. 'If we have to live as minorities', she said, 'we might as well live in a place that promises security to the children'. In taking the decision to migrate, Kamala had killed all those nationalist aspirations on which her father had brought her up. But in the final analysis it was not the daughter who was abandoning the father, but the father who had betrayed the daughter. Commenting upon the fact that the victims of violence received no support or protection from government officials, she made the poignant statement: 'It is as though your own father has let you down, so all you can do is to leave'.

Thus, the loss of her own father in death is conjoined with the loss of a legitimate place in the future and the betrayal by a government that she had come to regard as her own. The personal and the political meet in this instance is the decision to leave Sri Lanka as well as to relinquish the past on which Kamala and her father had based their political identity.

Case 4

Name	Chellappa
Age	50s
Occupation	Business executive
Area of Residence	Kollupitiye

Chellappa is a Hindu of Jaffna, of Tamil origin, with a wife and two children of 26 and 23 years, respectively. At the time of the violence Chellappa was living in his own house in the affluent area of Hugegoda where some of his other relatives had also bought property.

The violence of 25 June was preceded by a couple of strange incidents. On 21 July strangers came to Chellappa's house to raise a donation. Although he refused to give any money in donation, they invited him to inaugurate a new community centre at Kirillapone on Saturday, 23 July.

Chellappa had a premonition that all was not well. So he sent his driver ahead to check on the address to which he had been asked. The driver found the house in complete darkness. Chellappa assumed that he had been invited by 'con-men'. Only later did he learn that rich Tamils had been thus ambushed, and sometimes killed.

On 24 July Chellappa had gone to Havelock Town for community prayers when he heard rumours of the trouble that was brewing following the killing of thirteen soldiers by Tamil militants. Thus, unlike the other survivors whom I interviewed, Chellappa was a little better prepared in anticipating the violence of 25 July. That morning he telephoned a high-ranking police officer to ask if it was safe to send his son to the university. The police officer warned him of the impending dangers and advised him to stay at home. However, Chellappa took all important documents, including passports, from the house and asked a Sinhala friend to drive him to the office.

As tension mounted in the area, the family moved out to the

houses of various Sinhala friends. His daughter and a cousin moved to a different locality (Nawala) where he joined them later. His wife, his son, and his brother's family moved to the house of a neighbour. According to his wife, she was told by a Sinhala neighbour that a crowd of 400–500 hoodlums had gathered during curfew hours, set their house on fire and looted all they could carry.

Chellappa and his family decided to leave for Malaysia, along with a niece. Other close relatives could not join them, either because they did not have passports or because they could not make their way to the airport. Later, on 31 July, when they reached Malaysia, they received a phone-call from Colombo and were given the tragic news of the death of a nephew, a cousin, and a friend. All three men had gone to Nawala to take a bath in a friend's house. While returning, their jeep was diverted by the army to another route on which it was ambushed by a gang of hoodlums. The three unfortunate men were hacked to death and burnt.

Although Chellappa returned after two weeks from Malaysia, he could not feel secure. So he sent his son to England to pursue his studies there and later arranged for his daughter too to study in England.

In his account Chellappa dwelt upon the losses to his property and the economic reorganization of his life. Only when questioned did he talk about the three close relatives who died in the violence. For months after they heard of these deaths, Chellappa and his family blamed themselves for the death of their relatives. In the interview he said, somewhat defensively, 'It was a case of each man for himself. I could only think of my family's safety. Anyway in those days of chaos, there was no means of tracing missing persons. I try to understand my losses in terms of Hindu karmic theory. Our experiences in life depend upon our past deeds. May be it was that boy's destiny to die. May be it was God's will.'

Chellappa felt his son was the one who had to bear the brunt of the violence. He had been compelled to leave home abruptly for England and then go to the USA, but he never visited Sri Lanka again. If ever asked about his plans to return, the son retorted: 'Why should I come back? To get humiliated?'

Concluding Comments

The four cases presented here represent different ways in which families exposed to sudden violence reformulated their lives. These cases represent the kind of muted violence that seeps into the everyday life of ordinary people. The ethnic violence of 1983 was unique in the experience of so many Tamils precisely because the middle and upper classes that were normally protected from such violence suddenly came to realize what it meant to become homeless over a single night.

The kinds of resources used by members of the upper classes to reorganize their lives were not available to members of the middle and lower classes. For instance, richer people such as Chellappa left for Malaysia and did not have to experience camp life at all. On the other hand, despite his wealth and social position, Chellappa lost some close relatives in a brutal fashion, for in the anonymity of the streets they were identified by only one mark—their Tamil identity.

It is particularly useful to think of the concept of totalization in such situations, for violence homogenizes people and renders them indistinct. Kamala found that, regardless of her political ideology, she was identified as a Tamil. Conversely, the violence was seen to be perpetrated on behalf of the whole Sinhala community, even though the crowds consisted only of 'thugs' and 'hoodlums', and even though many Sinhala neighbours and friends risked their lives to provide help.

Moments of political crisis such as the one witnessed in July 1983 become a crisis in the everyday life of the community. One notices the heterogeneity of everyday life reflected also in periods of crisis. Thus, some risked their lives to save their Tamil neighbours. Others used the opportunity to trick them out of jewelry or expensive belongings. It is, therefore, important to understand that time took on an extraordinary character, in which various events came together. On the one hand we saw the implicit renegotiation of power that took place, with hoodlums and thugs controlling the streets, whereas people who normally wielded power in society searched for protection and help. On the other hand in the crowded camps, Tamils of the middle classes lived in intimate contact with lower-class Tamils and, in some instances, felt themselves protected by the large crowds in which they could merge.

The impact of violence went much further than the two or three days of violence. We have seen, in all these cases, that a virtual reformulation of life took place at the level of the family. The threat to the family was most visible in the case of Sylvia, for members of her family had to disperse spatially in order to survive. In the other cases, children started to demand that parents should take on a different social identity so that they did not have to face the humiliation of living with a Tamil identity. In some cases, the entire relationship to the past was altered as one or the other family decided to migrate 'for the sake of the children'.

We saw in these cases that the personal meaning of violence was organized around different kinds of narrative themes. In the case of Saroja the entire meaning of the ethnic violence came to centre around the conflict with her landlord—thus, what was ethnic conflict seen from the perspective of the nation became landlord-tenant conflict from the perspective of the neighbourhood. Saroja, as the organizer of this narrative, resisted seeing such conflict as Sinhala-Tamil conflict and instead constructed it as located in local events.

For Sylvia the violence meant the dispersal of her family, whereas for Kamala it was the betrayal by the state that provided the narrative leitmotif. It was Kamala who felt most betrayed as a citizen: the death of her father and the betrayal by the state became interpenetrating themes in her personal experience of ethnic violence. Her sense of loss at the death of her father, who was traumatized by the violence, was projected on to the state, which had behaved like a father who did not protect his children and thus compelled them to migrate.

One of the striking features in the narrative of these women is the decisive role that they played in giving direction to the re-organization of the family. The qualities that they brought to this task of reorganization were those which were hidden in their normal life. Sylvia recalled her sheltered life and how she used to be accompanied by a brother if she ever had to go out alone after dark. Yet, after the riots, she was able to board alone and pay for her sister's education. It was she who encouraged her mother to consider renting a house once again, so that the family could reunite and experience the closeness which had become threatened by their dispersal to different parts of the country. It seems that there was an aspect of the self which was like an outsider to the family; this the women were able to bring out, to the task of family reformulation.

The role of the outsider seemed very important in periods of crisis for the survival of the family. In each case we saw fleeing families helped by neighbours or even remote acquaintances. In the case of Sylvia, the entire rescue operation was carried out by neighbours. This opening of the boundaries of the family was sometimes experienced as threatening. Consider the case of Saroja, who felt she had to be extremely cautious in dealing with the demands of her neighbours over the use of various facilities of her house, for she needed their support to deal with her landlord. But clearly, the opening of these boundaries was one way in which the family came to cope with continued stress.

The survivor's experience was strongly influenced by social class, kinship network and past history. Whereas the classic studies of survivor experience, such as those of Lifton (1968), have emphasized the processes by which the self is reformulated, in my own interviews I found that the primary concern of the victims of violence was reorganization of the family. Decisions regarding the future of children, the need to find safe areas to live, to reorganize economic life, and to constantly interpret political events as significant signs, figured prominently in this reorganization. The violence did not just 'erupt' and then disappear. Perhaps the difference between threats from natural disasters, and violence coming from human agencies, is that the latter is experienced as *continuous* violence. It is not contained in time; like waves created by throwing a stone in the river, it has repercussions which far exceed the moment of its occurrence.

REFERENCES

Lifton, Robert Jay, 1968: *Death in Life: Survivors of Hiroshima*. New York: Random House.

Perkin, David, 1986: 'Violence and Will', in *the Anthropology of Violence*, ed. David Riches. Oxford: Basil Blackwell.

Reiss, David, 1981: *The Family's Construction of Reality*. Cambridge: Harvard University Press.

Chapter Fourteen

Our Work to Cry:
Your Work to Listen

VEENA DAS

This paper describes the survivors of the riots which followed the assassination of Indira Gandhi in Delhi in 1984.[1] These accounts came from my encounters with the survivors in the overall context of providing for their relief and rehabilitation. The context was not that of a researcher and his or her subjects, and I was by no stretch of the imagination in 'control' of 'the field'. The methodo-logical implications of this have been recounted elsewhere.[2] Here I only try to open a window to the world of the survivor.

The survivors described here were from one of the refugee colonies, called Sultanpuri. The victims belonged to the Siglikar (ironsmiths) community of Sindh. They had migrated from Sindh to Alwar in Rajasthan in 1947 and were now residents of Delhi.

[1] The kindness and help of so many people went into the making of this paper that it is simply not possible to acknowledge all of them. During my work among the survivors, I was part of a team of Delhi University teachers and students. My two colleagues, Mita Bose and Sanjib Dattachowdhary, gave unstinting help and I cannot now distinguish between their voices and mine. The Indian Express Relief Committee provided material and moral support for the rehabilitation of the victims. I want to especially mention B. G. Verghese for the trust he reposed in us. The Delhi University Relief Committee provided help towards transport. Many friends have given criticisms of earlier drafts which are gratefully acknowledged. I want to especially thank Amitav Ghosh, Dorothy Austin, Dennis Hudson and David Wills for their perceptive comments. I owe a special debt to Paola Bacchet a for making me aware of my own silences. Most of all, it was the courage of the victims that showed us how one can live at the limits of human endurance.

[2] See Das (1984) and (1987a).

Most of the victims lived in two blocks (A/4, C/3) and the *jhuggis* of Block P. Other blocks in Sultanpuri were not so seriously affected. Here I shall describe the survivors of A/4 but I have included one case study of a woman who lived in Block P as it offers a contrast to the women of Block A/4.

Death may be considered at one level as essentially marked by its non-narratability, by its rupture of language.[3] I have described elsewhere how ordinary language becomes transformed in the process of making death narratable by focusing upon the laments of women mourners.[4] This transformation, however, occurs at the level of cultural paradigms for the expression of grief. The relation between these paradigms and the individual experience of grief remains problematic. Especially when death has occurred in violation of all cultural ideas about a good death, the bereaved cannot easily take recourse to customary forms of mourning. Yet there was a great need on the part of the survivors to tell their story over and over again. As they said to a professor of the Indian Institute of Technology, 'It is our work to cry and your work to listen'. This paper is arranged so that the reader may 'listen' to the 'speech' of different women and children as they narrated the stories of these deaths to us. The subject who articulates this speech is sometimes an individual woman or child. But even when they have a definite identity, their voices are interwoven in a polyphony of other voices. These are the voices of women as they sat huddled in camps or parks, mourning the loss of loved ones, of homes, of things they had built together, of people who were convinced that the whole world had become a cremation ground.

Let me begin with Shanti, who lost her husband and three sons in the riots and who later committed suicide, leaving behind two orphaned daughters.

Shanti Devi: The Maternal Lamentation

Shanti's house was at the edge of the colony. Unlike the women of Block A/4, who lived in a kin-neighbourhood, Shanti did not live surrounded by close kinsmen. Her natal family was from

---

[3] On the non-narratability of death, see Freud (1973), Poulet (1977), Todorov (1967), Stewart (1984).

[4] See Das (1986b).

Alwar, where the Siglikar Sikhs had migrated after the Partition of 1947. Her brothers were quite prosperous and owned land in Alwar. Her conjugal family, though Siglikars by caste, were considered a cut above the others.

Let me first give an account of how Shanti described the riots and then come to the organizing images through which she tried to communicate the destruction of her soul. I have retained the fractured quality of her narrative as essential to this description.[5]

My husband had expected that the riots would remain confined to the A/4 Block because of the previous fights between the Siglikars and the Jat/ Bania faction of the Congress Party there—we thought some *goondas* may loot our houses. But what did we have to do with the assassination of Indira Gandhi? Why should we have thought that anything would happen to us?

Then, how did her husband and children die?

Some people, the neighbours, one of my relatives, said it would be better if we hid in an abandoned house nearby. So my husband took our three sons and hid there. We locked the house from outside, but there was treachery in people's hearts. Someone must have told the crowd. They baited him to come out. Then they poured kerosene on that house. They burnt them alive. When I went there that night, the bodies of my sons were on the loft—huddled together.

It was my own *mama* (mother's brother) who had advised my husband to hide. He revealed the hiding places of the Siglikar Sikhs to the leaders of the mob. He bartered their lives for his own protection. Go and see his house. Not even a broken spoon has been looted.

They hurled challenges upon my husband to come out. If he was brave he would have come out and then my little children would have been spared. But he remained mute. The mob burnt the house.

In the initial formulation of this narrative, we see that Shanti saw the violence as stemming equally from her own kinsmen as from the 'mob' (*bhida*). The general and vague characterization, 'some people, the neighbours, one of my relatives', comes to be particularized at a later time to her mother's brother. That the betrayal should have come from her mother's side is poignant for, in contrast to her mother's brother, her own mother, as we shall see, made

---

[5] It must be noted that these fragmented organizing images were articulated at different times in the course of our communications over six months.

every effort to save her from the devastating consequences of this violence, and from the pathological mourning which claimed her life.[6]

Shanti's ambivalence to her husband—'if he were brave'—also resonates in the rest of the text. This is the first formulation of the relations that recurred in her narrative. Its elements are: the violence of a crowd over a political issue with which Shanti or her husband were never involved, either at the national or the local level; the betrayal by her mother's brother; the 'lack' in her husband in Shanti's eyes as he was unable to sacrifice himself for his sons. The traumatic violence of the crowd suddenly revealed to her the fragility of her kinship universe.

One particular incident, recalled by Shanti's daughter, a ten-year-old girl, held special importance for Shanti, although it never occurred in her own narrative. The girl told us that when she (the daughter) saw the crowd in front of that house, she broke loose from the terrace in which she was hiding, and, recognizing some of the people in the crowd, begged them to spare her baby brother. 'Uncle Ji, Uncle Ji', she shouted, 'my little brother is hiding inside'. For a while, no one in the crowd heard her. When one of the men did, he was furious. 'Why did you not say so earlier?' he roared, 'Do you think we have come here to kill *children*?' At this stage the girl felt that the fury of the crowd would turn upon her and she fled. She did not remember anything after this incident.

Shanti remained hidden on the terrace till nightfall. When darkness fell, she stole into the charred house, where she found the bodies of her husband and her three sons. The younger two were sitting huddled together on the loft in the room where, perhaps, her husband and older son had hidden them while they steeled themselves to come out and face the mob. This they had been unable to do. Shanti could not have cremated them. Uncertain, she came back to her terrace. By the next morning the bodies had disappeared.

Even the most articulate among us face difficulties when we try to put ambiguous and jumbled thoughts and images into words. This is even more true of someone who has suffered a traumatic

---

[6] On the distinction between normal and pathological mourning, see Freud (1973).

loss. Let me now try to present some of the organizing images through which Shanti tried to describe what had happened to her.

I want sukha *(peace)—Won't you give me* sukha?

I remember these as almost the first words that Shanti uttered to me when I met her in her house. She was sitting on a bed in a rather dark room within her house. Covered with quilts, she seemed to shrink into the smallest space her body could occupy. On one side of the bed sat her mother, who had come from Alwar to look after her. Her younger sister, who had also come to help, was sitting on the floor beside her. An old neighbour, a woman from Bihar known as the old amma, was standing by the door. 'What do you mean?' I asked her, unsure of how to react. Shanti looked expectantly at the others. It was my introduction to her mode of speech. She would make very condensed statements and assume the truth of it was known and understood by everyone. She would leave it to the others assembled around her to explain the statement. 'She is asking to be given a medicine so that she can die', explained her mother. 'I tell her again and again—daughter do not talk so. But does she listen? Does she care?' Almost on cue, Shanti responded: 'What is there to listen and why should I care? If my baby at least had been spared I would have hugged him to my bosom and somehow I would have gone on living'.

This was the point at which the neighbour, who was standing by the door, interjected. 'She carries on as if she were the only one to suffer a loss. Look at the world around us. Everyone was affected. A storm came upon us and it destroyed everything in its way. Can we save anyone from such a storm?'

In this first encounter we can see a community of women as healers, forming around Shanti, into which my colleague Mita and I were immediately drawn. Shanti's obsessive courting of death had, as its counterpoint, the community of women who were trying to exorcize her terrible feelings of guilt. Thus the old woman blamed the 'storm' that had come upon them—it was not the fault of women that they were unable to save their men and their children. The maternal and sisterly care by which they attempted to heal the daughter, the sister, was in stark contrast to Shanti's inability to bestow maternal care upon her daughters, whose need for Shanti was no less urgent than Shanti's need for the healing community of women.

For as long as I thought everyone had been affected I remained in control of myself. But when I went to the camp and found that other women had been able to save their children, my heart burnt out. My mother took me to Alwar where I got worse. I could see all around me. There were children— laughing and playing. My nephews—I felt terrible.... Why were they alive and my children dead?

One of the repeated themes in Shanti's memories was the allusion to the fact that her children had died, whereas other children lived. In these memories, she would not acknowledge her own daughters as her children. She took a stoic attitude to the death of her husband. 'Well the Sardars did it to Indira Gandhi. So the fruits of those evil actions (*karma*) would have to be borne, wouldn't they?' But what she could not understand was that the other women had managed to save their children while she had failed to do so herself. It was her failure as mother, but primarily as mother of sons, which she found most difficult to bear. She alternately held her husband, her eldest son, her eldest daughter, the community, and herself responsible for the death of her youngest child. 'I had sent my daughter to my husband, where he was hiding, begging him to give the baby to me. But he just said, your mother is feeble-minded, she will not be able to protect my son. Had he shown more trust in me, the baby would have lived.'

At other times she would begin to beat her daughter, saying she should have persuaded her father to give her the baby, or she should have shouted more loudly when the crowd was burning the house, and then the child might have been spared. Here, the daughter was being treated as a mere extension of the self of the mother—Shanti's own ideal self (mother of sons). Her own conflicts were being directly transferred to the daughter, who she expected should bear the guilt of their joint failure to save the son. At one time she put the blame on her husband and older son. 'Why did they not open the room and come out and give themselves up to the crowd? The crowd was not out to kill young children. My little baby would have been saved if they had shown the courage to give themselves up.'

'How were they to know?' I asked, to which she immediately

said that one of the neighbours had done exactly *that* when the crowd went to his house, and his son had lived—the crowd having become honour-bound to let the child go free. Again, she would say, it was the community which was to blame for her plight. 'If the women knew that the crowd was not killing the children why did they not tell me? They only told me that women were not being touched.'

Although Shanti did talk about the responsibility of others in the death of her child, it was around herself that she gathered the final blame and guilt. 'It is true, what my husband said. I am feeble-minded. I am half-witted. I am mad. That is why I could not under-stand what the crowd wanted. They wanted vengeance from adult men. They did not want the blood of children.'

How did Shanti gather and crystallize all the floating guilt around her and attach it upon her own self? It is my contention that the community around her collaborated in reinforcing her own feelings of guilt. I shall try to describe how this was done. Shanti's mother, who was with her, had allowed her circumstances to retreat into a kind of childhood. The mother washed her, fed her, followed her around everywhere to see that she did no harm to herself. All Sikhs, she said, had suffered and then she tried to tell Shanti she was not alone in her sorrow. However, after some time Shanti's husband's father came to live with her, which is when relations within the family became very tense. On the surface, this eighty-year-old man had come to provide support and succour to his widowed daughter-in-law and orphaned grandchildren. There was no question that the death of his son and grandsons had affected him deeply. *Hum to ghar se beghar ho gaye.* (From being people with homes, we have been made homeless.) He would describe his plight in these simple words. For a time I was blind to the power-struggle which was taking place in the house. On reflection, it seems to me that the man spoke with two voices. Sometimes he would implore Shanti to try and recover from her state of para-lysing sorrow, to throw away all thoughts of suicide. Once he even bent down and touched her feet, begging her to think about her two daughters. These dramatic gestures were, however, accompanied with another message, which was that a wife as devoted as Shanti could not possibly recover from such a trauma. The message would be delivered to the ever-present audience of neighbours. He would sigh and say: 'We try our best—but how can she possibly recover? It is the dead who call her.' 'Poor woman—she has gone mad. Ostensibly, she was feeble-minded. That is why Tehal [the son] could not trust her with the baby.' To aid her recovery and to bring peace to his dead son and grandsons, he arranged for an elaborate prayer ceremony but, as we shall see later, it was also to deprive Shanti of whatever sources of strength remained in her.

Shanti had received Rs 10,000 for each of the dead kin as compensation from the government. As the days passed, a struggle for control over the money began to take place. Shanti had not been able to refuse money for the elaborate ritual which the old man had demanded from her, for that would have been impious, but she was unhappy to be required to spend extravagantly on religious ceremonies regardless of the uncertain future of her daughters. I find here the essence of tragedy, because even a fleeting concern for her daughters—barely given voice to by Shanti—could be construed by her husband's father as a betrayal of the male line. There were other indications of struggle. The old man insisted that he would manage the household expenditure. He insisted that Shanti was feeble-minded and incapable of handling the money she had received. He also hinted that as the oldest surviving male of the family, it was he who should have received the compensatory sum from the government. Shanti was mute in the face of such allusions, woven into the web of everyday interactions. Outwardly deferential, she seemed to be struggling with her anger and yet imbibing his judgement of her as the bringer of this unprecedented misfortune.

The struggle over money between a widow and the dead man's natal kin was not unique to Shanti's case, as we shall see later. But unlike other women, Shanti was not able to express her rage, partly because she prided herself on her refined manners. In Block A/4, the struggle for money was expressed in bitter quarrels. Abuses and obscenities were hurled at each other by different members of the family, where each saw the others as depriving him or her of a proper share of inheritance. Shanti could only give an indication of her inner turmoil when, sometimes, she would whisper: 'He sits around with the old men of the whole community in my house. Who is providing the money for so much tea?' At another time she made my friend and colleague Mita, who was her dearest confidante, promise that she would take care of her daughters 'if anything happens to me', expressing distrust in her father-in-law's ability to provide care to them.

The struggle between Shanti and her husband's father appears at one level as the attempt by the latter to gain control over Shanti. At another level, however, it is possible to see it as a struggle to create female genealogies in opposition to male ones. The money that Shanti had received was in compensation for the death of her male kinsmen. Her husband's father tried to establish the legitimacy of his own claims over this money on the basis of his membership within the male line. Shanti's resistance, however muted, was an attempt to secure the survival of the female line. Hence, while the old man wanted to spend the money on rituals for the propitiation of his son and grandsons, Shanti wished to conserve the money for securing the future of her daughters. It was a struggle over her own annihilation. Similarly, her appeals to other women, including her mother and Mita, to take care of her daughters, was an effort to activate the potential that was inherent in the female connections but was subverted by superior male controls.

This struggle between the female connectedness and the exercise of authority to break those connections and appropriate each woman *individually* into the male line soon manifested itself in Shanti's mother's decision to leave her daughter's house. The kinship norms in north India only allow fleeting interactions with a maried daughter in her conjugal house. The insinuations that she was staying on with the daughter in order to gain control over her money became impossible for the mother to bear, and she departed for Alwar.

The departure of her mother created a vacuum for Shanti. Although Shanti's younger sister was staying with her to look after her, the accusations against Shanti increased. Once I encountered a woman who said to Shanti, 'If you were really so grief-stricken why did you not kill yourself the day your sons died?'

Thus, Shanti's life had become a statement against the dominant norms that would allow a woman life and daughters only if she succumbed to the male world. This is not merely a question of the exercise of power, for a woman may herself exercise power, at least during certain *moments* of her relationships, whether erotic or maternal; nor is it a question of female autonomy *versus* male dominance; the point really is that a life built around female connections is not seen as a life worth living. It is when they themselves occupied that discourse and took that voice as their own (as in this woman's question to Shanti—'why did you not kill yourself the day your sons died?') that healing turned into poison. Finally, just as Shanti was most wounded by such women, so she herself, in her refusal to acknowledge herself as the mother of daughters, failed to provide any emotional healing to her shattered daughters.

How can I live? You tell me to look to my daughters—to be comforted by them. But they are not my children. They are counterfeit (*nakli*) children. I cannot bear them around me. If my little son had lived I would have somehow clasped him to my bosom and lived. But I was cheated.

One important difference between Shanti and the women we came to know in Block A/4 was that Shanti rarely showed any interest in the variety of objects given out as charity by various individuals and organizations. Whereas other women clamoured for the things brought by members of relief organizations for distribution, Shanti hardly ever left her bed or followed them around. This lack of interest in the outside world was also reflected in her inability to relate to her daughters any more. Towards her older daughter she was positively hostile. Neighbours would report that she would slap the daughter whenever she tried to touch her. She was sometimes quite explicit in blaming this child for the loss of her youngest one.

She showed compassion towards the younger daughter but was unable to show her any love. If the girl came near her mother and tried to touch her or hug her, she would be pushed away. Sometimes the old lady, who was their neighbour, would push the younger girl towards Shanti, exhorting her to hug her mother in the hope that the physical contact would awaken the dormant and now suppressed motherhood in Shanti. But Shanti would not allow herself to be touched. 'Take her away', she would say, 'this is not my child—she is counterfeit, a fraud—my child died.' 'Look at her', the neighbours would say, 'was this not a girl born of your own womb like the others? Why is she not your child?' 'Oh she is a girl. Just send her away—take her away, I cannot look after her.'

Shanti's daughters understood the rejection but still tried to comfort her, till the last day. One day Shanti told me that the younger daughter had tried to persuade her that she could be like a son. 'I will not marry. I will become a doctor and look after you.' Shanti was touched by this and even told me how the little girl had been a great favourite of her father. 'When her father used to ask her who she wanted to marry, she would say—the same kind of man that my mother married.' For a fleeting moment, mother and daughter had smiled together, almost as if the negation of the daughter's female identity could restore the relation to the mother. Soon she relapsed into the theme of daughters being counterfeit children because they could not continue the line—their father would be without ancestral oblations.[7] In effect she was saying that even if the daughters could provide for her in the secular world, they could not replace sons in the cosmic scale of time. In that sense the greatest gift a woman could give to her husband's line—that of descendants who could rescue their ancestors from hell by giving them ancestral oblations—had been lost by the death of her sons. In a cosmic scale she and her family had been erased and obliterated.

We can see here the difference in a mother's construction of her self in relation to her sons and daughters. The birth of a son is a gift that a woman makes towards the continuity of the male line. A commonly heard statement in this community was: 'A man has to lean on a woman in order to be reborn as a son'. Who is then renewed through the birth of the daughter? Not the woman. For just as she hands over the son for the continuity of the male line, so she hands over the daughter to be circulated further as a gift given by men to other men. Whatever the possibilities for the father–daughter relation in this formulation, the mother–daughter relationship cannot be seen as a mirror of the father–son relationship.

Was the body of my sons and husband only there for pigs and dogs to eat upon?

The survivors were haunted by the absence of dead bodies.

[7] I refer here to the Hindu and Sikh belief that it is the ancestral oblations offered by sons that release a dead man from a particular kind of hell.

Shanti would often get up in the middle of the night and go to the park opposite their house, where she would gather sticks and make little piles which she would proceed to burn. She was unable to explain what she was doing, but some neighbours believed that she was trying to cremate the bodies of the dead. They said, 'They burnt them alive but the dead bodies were not cremated. They must wander around as ghosts and spirits. What peace will they get?'[8] What peace shall we get? This was always asked, although the ceremony of *antim ardas* for the placation of the dead was held and the *prasad* for peace was partaken of by a pious congregation. Shanti felt that they were deceiving themselves with these rituals. As long as the dead bodies had not been properly cremated, the souls of the dead could not be appeased.

According to some neighbours, Shanti had gone to the park when she found some pigs burrowing in a hole and retrieving human bones. Shanti was convinced that these were the bones of her husband. She was unable to look at this decayed body as the body of her husband. Although there are many Indian legends about mutilated bodies of warriors lying on battlegrounds among which women wander in search of their dead husbands and sons, in these legends the mutilated bodies are symbolic of the heroism of men. The deaths in the riots were not seen as 'heroic'. In certain kinds of public discourse, for example in the preaching of some *gurudwaras*—the dead men were treated as heroes who had died for a noble cause. But for the victims, as well as for the survivors, there was no heroism in these deaths. The cause of Sikh separatism had never been their own. As Shanti repeatedly said, 'All we wanted to do was to lead a quiet and peaceful life. We did not want to die for other people's ideas'.[9] Hence the bones she took to be the

[8] Fire is a polyvalent symbol and appears here in both its malevolent and benevolent aspects. In its malevolent aspect it was used by mobs to burn people alive, but its benevolent aspects of purification and release, as represented by the sacrificial fires of the cremation ground, were denied to the dead. See Das (1976).

[9] In similar terms, Bettleheim reacted sharply to the tendency to glorify the victims of the Nazis by calling them martyrs. He believed that we glorify the fate of the victims because, 'in doing so we cope with our distorted image of what happened, not with the events the way they did happen'. Bettleheim (1982), p. 92.

mutilated body of her husband could not signify any heroism to her. It was symbolic of an utterly futile and meaningless death.

Unable to bear this reminder of how their lives had ended, Shanti soon found an opportunity 'to do her work', as her daughter said. Her father-in-law had gone to the ration office. Her sister had gone to the 'fields' and her daughters were away at school. Her sister came back to find the door closed but not locked. When she opened the door, Shanti's body was hanging from the ceiling. The police were called and the case registered. After the formalities were completed, she was taken to the cremation ground and given the funeral that she had so craved for her husband. Shanti's suicide raised very important moral questions to which I am not sure we had the answers. Since she had so often indicated her desire to find peace in death, we repeatedly asked ourselves how we could have prevented her death. We did try to persuade her to go to a hospital but were unsure about conditions in state hospitals for mental patients. Further, Shanti was also receiving advice and some medication from a doctor who used to visit her. Any aggressive action on our part to insist that she be hospitalized could have jeopardized our position in the community, especially if she had died in the hospital. These dilemmas were faced anew when we tried to arrange for the adoption of her two daughters. Both girls pleaded that they wanted to live with Mita and me. They were permitted by their grandfather to come and stay with us for a few weeks. However, the grandfather felt that he would lose an important source of income if he left the girls with foster parents. Many Sikh families offered to adopt them but did not want to cope with threats from the grandfather and other relatives. The only person who supported our plans for their adoption was Shanti's mother. In the end, we could not persuade their paternal relatives to allow us either to adopt them, or to have them adopted by a Sikh family, or even to arrange for their education in a boarding school. The community itself became hostile at the thought that the two girls might receive more care than other people. We could not press our claims or take recourse to a court as both these actions would have made us stand in hostile relation to the community and obstruct any long-term measures that we wanted to plan out for work among the children.

A few salient points about this case need to be made before we describe the bereavement patterns of other women. The most important aspect of this case was the persistent refusal of Shanti to find in her daughters any form of symbolic immortality for herself and for her dead husband. [10] At one level one may consider the patriarchal structure of society responsible for her inability to accept her daughters as legitimate heirs. Yet this would be inadequate, for the reason that Indian society, like many other patriarchal societies, provides for mechanisms by which families may find continuity in daughters in the absence of sons. It is true that patriarchal structures provide different valuations of sons and daughters, but the complete psychological incorporation of this valuation by Shanti can only be understood in the context of what Lifton (1967) calls 'counterfeit nurturance'. I shall have occasion to comment on this concept later. Here it is only intended to point to the fact that Shanti felt that the nurture she was receiving from her daughters was not authentic in terms of the kinship norms of her society. She repeatedly stressed the fact that if one of her sons, especially the youngest, had lived, she would have been able to give him nurturance and receive nurturance from him. I suspect that there was some element of guilt in her reaction to the daughters, for, much as she had loved the elder daughter, she probably wished her dead in place of her son.

As Lifton (1967) has pointed out, the psychological process of 'numbing' is adaptive for survivors of disasters, in as much as it protects the inner self against assaults it cannot bear by a psychological closing off. By ridding themselves of all capacity to feel any emotion, survivors create a protective wall around themselves. However, although numbing begins as a defence against exposure to death, it can become a way of life and inundate the organism with the imagery of death. Survivors who have numbed themselves in this manner may be especially threatened by the caring of others. Shanti's constant denial of any succour offered by her daughters seems to have been located in a similar psychic economy. To have

---

[10] The concept of symbolic immortality is used in anthropology to convey continuing relations between the living and the dead. For its use in psychology, see Lifton (1983), who argues that collective disasters raise doubts and lead to loss of faith in the traditional methods of establishing connections between death and life.

accepted her daughter's need for her would have been to acknowledge the possibility of affection within herself. This was realized
clearly in the wisdom of the old lady who was Shanti's neighbour,
who kept reiterating the view that her numbed feelings had to be
reawakened, which meant awakening the dormant motherhood
in her.

The second significant point to be made in Shanti's case, is the
manner in which she framed time.[11] The entire dialogical relation
between Shanti and myself was concentrated on the day of the riots.
Her entire present was now nothing more than a slow unfolding
and mental replaying of the decisions and events of the riots. Unlike
Freud's analogy of the recall of the past as the 'looking' at a passing
landscape from a running train, Shanti had no means by which
she could distance herself enough from the past so that the present
could be made 'present' in her consciousness. The traveller in the
train, looking at his past as a passing landscape, can describe it
from a vantage point of distance.[12] Shanti, on the other hand, could
not move from that particular day. Her laments were all about
her, or about other people's failure, to read correctly the signs by
which her son could have been saved. Paradoxical as it may seem,
I hope to show that it was Shanti's inability to find any structure
within which her symbolic immortality could be expressed that
made it impossible for her to frame her immediate future. This
was in complete contrast to other women, who I will describe
shortly, whose attention could be focused upon the near future

[11] Humphreys (1983) has indicated the importance of studying the 'management' of time in the study of death. As she says, 'restricting of relationships
within the family and with outsiders, the psychological adjustment of the
bereaved, the preparation of the material equipment and the summoning of
the personnel needed for funeral rites, the process of decay undergone by the
corpse and the experiences ascribed to the spirit of the dead, do not necessarily
all harmonize easily on a temporal scale' (p.279). All the examples of time
management indicated above, however, point to the model of normal death.

[12] In his classic statement on free association, Freud (1976) compared the
patient in psychoanalysis with a passenger on a train. The patient's job is to
look at the passing scene and describe all its features to his companion, who
cannot see outside the window. Despite the powerful imagery that such a
model of 'remembering' conjures in the mind, it is not very appropriate for
remembering recent and traumatic events. For a critique of Freud's model
within the psychoanalytic frame, see Spence (1982).

and who could be thereby taught to live. Lifton (1967), following Freud, has identified this concern with the traumatic event as the classic syndrome of obsessional review and shown how survivors go over the traumatic events over and over again, building different scenarios in their mind by which the outcome of the trauma could have been altered. Shanti's attempts to make piles of wood and set them on fire, which also had an obsessional quality, was seen by her neighbours as an attempt to cremate the dead.

One of Shanti's laments was that she alone had been unable to save her child. As we have seen, this fact weighed more heavily upon her than anything else she had experienced. It seems that victims try to universalize their suffering. If their suffering can be universalized, it can be related to an overarching frame, whether this be the operation of a malignant fate, an incomprehensible god, or past *karmas*—these are all means by which the malignancy and contingency of evil can be comprehended and made simultaneously universal and impersonal. It is as if the universality of the suffering provides a guarantee that it was not the *particular* failing of the victim but an impersonal force, such as a storm or lightning, that had brought about the disaster. Such a neutral force is seen as indifferent to who it hits and who it spares. The fact that other women had been able to save their children while Shanti had failed became a symbol, for Shanti, of her particular failure as a mother to save her sons.

Then there was the final question: what was her responsibility towards the dead?

Every death raises the issue of the obligations of the living towards the dead. These obligations can be expressed at the level of ritual, in a well-articulated manner, while at the psychological level the work of mourning allows the living to be sufficiently disengaged from the dead, enabling them to resume the business of life. All the themes of mourning—the loss of a loved object, the desire to regain it, the guilt and the fear—are encountered in the case of violent death in a very stark manner. The question of the obligation of the living towards the dead takes on a new meaning in the context of violent deaths. Due to the complex nature of the events that occurred in this particular case, Shanti could only frame her obligations to the dead in terms of her responding to their call. The heterogeneity of the dead—the difference between the death of the husband and the son—was transformed into a homogeneous community of the dead. She was the only survivor who committed suicide in the colony. Her willingness, even compulsion, to take her own life was the only proof she could offer herself that her guilt could be assuaged by joining her husband and dead sons in their destiny. She was not able to take the risks of a re-engagement in the world, including the possibility that she might in time be able to 'forget' what had happened to her dead. The forgetting would have included a forgetting of the dominant definition of a woman, as integrated individually into the lines of men and a reformulation of life in terms of female connections. Death and masculinity finally broke the hold of life and femininity.

Shanti lamented that she alone had been unable to save her child (although she persistently interpreted child to mean son), whereas other women, she felt, had not failed as mothers of sons. We have an example here of Devereux's (1973) distinction between the disorders that are collectively structured, and idiosyncratic disorders. It seems that when disorders are given a cultural meaning which is collectively shared, the individual victim does not have to experience himself or herself as personally responsible. Whether it be the operation of a malignant fate, an incomprehensible god or past *karmas*, an impersonal force is held responsible for the disaster. Shanti could not experience herself as part of a collective in the loss of her sons, which explains the nature of her maternal lament.

Underlying the lament of a mother for her son, however, is another lament—that of a mother for her daughter. All around Shanti a community of women healers was forming, but in order for this community to be effective it would have been necessary for the male society around to accept its legitimacy, and also for it to allow Shanti to accept her place within the female genealogies. For example, she accepted an infantile status in relation to her mother, allowing the latter to provide succour. This relation was broken by her husband's father. Her concerns for her daughters, however muted, were made to appear as betrayals of her obligations to the male line. Similarly, in her attempts to secure a future for her daughters, she turned to her mother and to the two women from the outside world (Mita and me). In this case, also, the paternal line and the community of men reclaimed the daughters, thus negating the female community even after Shanti's death.

The Collective Mourning of Women

I will describe now the manner in which women in Block A/4 recounted and coped with the violence and deaths that had come suddenly into their lives. Although many women appear in sharp relief in this account, none of them could be described as standing alone as characters. This was partly because they were able to deal with these deaths in a more collective manner than Shanti, and partly because the nature of our relief work in this block did not allow for individual relations to develop. There were eighty deaths among the 150 households in this and the adjoining block. The majority of the dead were adult men, though one woman was burnt with her husband because she refused to leave him. Another woman had severe burns on her hands and face, which she got when she tried to extinguish the fire. All the men killed were burnt alive in the presence of their wives. Many men had managed to escape, either by donning the clothes of women or by hiding in neighbouring houses. The patterns of mourning and bereavement showed a temporal structure which I shall now try to describe.

We went into this block for the first time after four days of riots. We had met some of the women of this block in the crowded conditions of the relief camp, where we learnt that many of the women were still within the colony. On our first visit we were taken around, primarily by a self-styled social worker who was assigned by the rioters to keep them informed of events in the colony. We had been able to shake this man off on some pretext or other, and had then been shown around by Vakil Singh, who had lost two sons in the carnage. We saw blood splattered on the walls, bullet holes, heaps of ashes in which one could still find bits of hair or skull and bone. But what we encountered in the women was mainly fear. Their men had been killed before their eyes. Their children had been spared but been threatened with dire consequences if they spoke about the murderers. A sullen resistance was beginning to take shape. They felt surrounded by the murderers, who had established a 'camp' in the colony and were ostensibly doing 'relief work' to impress the press and social organizations that had come to discover the carnage. Under these conditions, the women wanted to find some way by which the truth of their suffering could be made known to the world, and by this they could resist the silence imposed upon them.

They have asked us to clean up our houses and to go in and settle down. How can we settle down here? Do you see the heaps of ashes? Do you see the blood? Here, put your hand inside this heap and you will see the melted skulls. They would not even let us have the dead bodies. We begged them; you have killed our men. Let us have their bodies at least—let us mourn them properly. The whole night we hear the voices of our dead. I hear my husband asking for water. The killers would not even let us give water to our dying. My son cried, mother—mother—as he used to when he was small but I could not go to him. This street is now a cremation ground for us. The living have become silent shades, while the cries of the dead float up to the sky and fall on us like weights.

The first act of autonomy that the women performed was in their insistence that their state of mourning be not hidden but be publicly proclaimed. As the local politicians began to put pressure upon them to clean up their houses, to wash themselves and appear decent for the sake of the many important functionaries that were beginning to visit the colony, the women defiantly hung on to their filth and their pollution. They would not go into the houses, they would not light the cooking hearths and they would not change their clothes. Although many relief agencies saw them as dirty and slovenly, we felt a great sympathy for them and could not bring ourselves to ask them to return to normalcy: the heaps of ashes, the abandoned houses, the blood-splattered walls—these were not abstract; they were concrete and indexical symbols of what had happened to their men and to them.[13] It was part of their obligation to the dead to display these, but also it was part of their obligation as *women* to bring to the collective consciousness the grievous wrongs that had been done to them. The prolonged period in which symbols of dirt and pollution dominated the area—

[13] Index was defined by Peirce as the process of signification to which the signifier and the signified are existentially related. See Buchler (1955).

for women did not move into their houses till these had been completely repaired and cleaned by relief workers (a task which took three months to complete)—was one in which no visitor to the area could ignore the plight of these families.

Although the women took on the symbols of mourning and pollution and gave it a political meaning, they were not able to mourn the dead in the traditional manner. This was not because of any cultural uprootedness, for such mourning songs are sung normally after a death in the community, even in Delhi. I was struck by the fact that the only time when traditional laments for the dead were spoken or sung was when relatives from Alwar visited a family and were able to treat the deaths as 'normal'. One of the most moving sights that I saw on the first day of our visit to the colony is perhaps best recalled as I wrote it in my diary:

As I talked to the women, three or four very old women were wandering round the street in a kind of convoy, each holding the edge of the other's *dupatta*. Like spirits they stood in front of each house—mute—but seeing things that were invisible to us. The laments for the dead would not come to their lips. There they stood, before broken doors and scorched walls—unseeing eyes calling softly the names of those who had died just two days ago.

As the days passed the question of the obligations that the women had towards their dead took on new meanings and structures. But before I can describe these, I need to say a few words about the framing of the future that began to take place in this period. Most of the survivors in these families had lost one or two members, but there were young children in all the families who needed to be cared and provided for. It was the surviving children who became symbols of the future, and with reference to whom the future could be framed. It seems to me that the women accepted these children as representing their symbolic immortality, and therefore could be taught to reintegrate these terrible events into structures of significance. Since all the women I worked with—who had been married long enough to have children—had one or more surviving sons, it is difficult to compare their formulations with those of Shanti.

On our first encounter with the women, and even as they were mourning and displaying the mourning through their bodies, we did not find them hesitant to point out that they had not had any food for almost twenty hours. 'It is all right for us but how do we quieten these wailing babies?' In fact, food was being brought in by a local organization and one of the industrialists of the area had been working day and night to raise money for food, but its arrival tended to be sporadic and unpredictable. This was understandable because the meagre resources of relief agencies were going to the management of many such colonies and relief camps. Further, information about the needs of the different sections of the population was difficult to get and supplies of food were cordoned off by those who had not been severely affected since they were in a much better position to guide people who brought in relief.

My purpose in drawing attention to all this is simply to point out that the need to provide food framed the immediate future, both for the women and for us. There were immediate needs which could not be postponed, while other things could wait for later. Once we were able to supply rations to the women on a fortnightly basis, so that they did not have to wait every day for charity to appear, we could think of the next step. The next need was housing. This would require further effort to structure the future, and to make a commitment for two or three months. The beginning of the activities—to have houses mended—signalled our involvement for longer periods and provided the women a further means by which the future could be structured. As an indication of the involvement of the women, I should point out that some engineers, who were working on the repair of the houses as volunteers, found the women very obstructive because they, the engineers, were constantly plied with requests to do things differently. Everyone wanted more doors, better windows, new floors, and any suggestion that one family was getting more than another or better doors or windows could provoke major quarrels.

Once the immediate needs of the women were guaranteed, they developed a further interest in finding out more about the different kinds of relief goods that were available, and to which they would be entitled. They learnt things about the bureaucracy when we filled compensation forms for them, and in due course the widows received compensation for deaths. They also learnt that sewing machines or rations or bicycles were distributed by various philanthropists and *gurudwaras*. They became experts in finding out where these were distributed and went about in groups, claiming whatever goods came their way.

The behaviour of the women— especially their tendency to grab every opportunity to get whatever they could from the various relief agencies—did not match middle-class ideas of dignified behaviour, and since most of the people offering relief were members of the middle classes, the women came to be known as covetous and greedy, in addition to being constantly engaged in quarrels with each other. It was impossible for those who did not know them well to distribute goods in an orderly way in the colony. But what was disorderly and undignified behaviour for many was for us the sign that the women were recovering and re-engaging in life. This is perhaps because we had become conscious of the fact that the people who were most difficult to deal with were those who could not be made to take any interest in the objects that were being made available. The need to corner as many relief goods as they could get gave some structure to women's activities and helped them to think of the future, to symbolize it in the new commodities that relief was bringing in their lives. It was also symbolic of the engagement of the external world into their lives.

It was mentioned earlier that prolonged mourning and an adoption of the symbols of dirtiness and pollution became important political symbols for the women and were an effective rejoinder to those who would have silenced them completely. As time passed, the question of the obligations to the dead took on a new significance for the women. However, I would like to make a distinction here between the young widows (normally below the age of twenty-five) and the older widows, for the nature of the commitment to the dead was different in these cases.

The Siglikar Sikhs have traditionally practised levirate and leviratic marriage. In addition, the divorce rate appears to have been high in this community. Whereas it was not possible to collect statistical data to compare the incidence of marriages terminated by death to those by divorce, we did find that of the 65 women above the age of 30 who appeared in our survey, 50 had been married to another man, often a brother or cousin of the present husband. Under the circumstances, it seems to have been the expectation of all members of the community that the young widows would be soon married again. The particular mode of death of the men, however, created new and complex conditions. First, many families lost more than one male member. Thus, other men were simply not immediately available for leviratic marriages to take place. This meant that the widow would have to be married to a man outside the conjugal family. Second, since in the modern judicial and administrative structures in India the widow is considered for many purposes the legal heir, compensation money was awarded to her. Most members of the community thought this very unfair, for they assumed that the widow would remarry and considered the rights of parents of the dead to have been severely compromised. This led to many fights between the natal family and the conjugal family of the widow, each accusing the other of being money-grabbers who wanted to profit by an untimely and unnatural death. Some young widows accused their conjugal kin of beating them up so that they would be coerced into giving up their legitimate inheritance. Finally, the caste *panchayat* met and a compromise was reached. It was decided that a widow would be given permission to remarry only if she agreed to equally share the money with the father of her dead husband. In every case where a widow was under the age of twenty-five or so, I found that this agreement was adhered to. *Talaknamah*, or documents of divorce, were drawn up on court paper in which the father of the widow and the father of the dead man signed an agreement to the effect that the widow would give fifty per cent of the money she had received in compensation for her husband's death to her husband's father, and the latter would agree that all relations with the widow were severed after this.[14]

The anthropological literature on the psychological consequences of leviratic marriage on the widow is sparse. With the exception of Kolenda (1983)—who has described levirate in the context of

---

[14] The normal assumption that divorce occurs between spouses is not valid in this case, for upon marriage a woman is seen as the 'property' of the conjugal family. Therefore, the conjugal family had to terminate its claims over the women by the granting of divorce. Similarly, the court paper on which agreements were signed may not have had any legal validity, but these were nonetheless symbols of a formal contract in the community.

the personal history of a woman in the village she studied—and a sensitive fictional account of this by Bedi (1962), we do not have many accounts of how this institution affects the processes of grief and bereavement.[15]

It seems that when a system places a strong obligation on a widow to remarry within the overall context of patriarchal values, it places a heavy burden on young women. Unable to retain their psychological ties with their dead husbands, such women became completely inarticulate about the death of their husbands, although we found that others could speak on their behalf. For example, a woman, whose son had been married just a few weeks before he died in the carnage, took the hand of her son's widow and, showing the auspicious signs of henna which still decorated her hands, she said, 'Look at my grief. Even the henna of her hands is not dried and my son is dead.' The remark incorporated the grief of the widow into the grief of the mother.[16] The general assumption, shared by almost all members of the community, was that young widows could not be expected to mourn for their husbands for long, as they must already be imagining a new marriage for themselves. A young girl said rather bitterly to me, 'You do not know how it is with this community. Just as a donkey is tied to a new owner the moment his old owner dies, so a girl is married to a new husband the moment her husband dies. Here a cremation is taking place and there the preparations for a ceremonial.'

The obligation to become sexually active, it seems to me, could be as coercive on the individual woman as the restrictions upon

---

[15] In their cross-cultural study of grief and mourning Rosenblatt *et al.* (1976) say that customs for breaking ties with the dead spouse would be encountered more frequently in societies with levirate and sorrorate than in societies without these. Without going into the usefulness of establishing such statistical correlations, I would only like to draw attention to the fact that their concern seems to be more with finding what inhibitions would come in the way of establishing new marital ties with a dead spouse's siblings rather than the manner in which this may affect the process of bereavement.

[16] This incorporation, on the one hand, pointed to the lack of ego boundaries between women; but, on the other hand, it was a negation of the subjectivity of young widows. It was only if we came across a young widow alone that she was able to speak of her experience in her own terms.

remarriage which are typical for higher-caste widows in India. In this case it did not allow young widows to express sorrow or grief in terms of a personal time. Rather, the social definition of a widow's supposed readiness to remarry provided a socially constructed boundary to signal the end of grief. In turn, this meant that the social order did not define any further obligation within the widow to her dead husband. It was as if this part of her past life would have to be erased or renounced by the widow in order to enter the new marital relationship. In fact, we found that parents of young widows were very concerned about finding grooms for their daughters. The death of so many young men resulted in the anomaly that conjugal families could not find new husbands for the widows of their sons from within the family, creating new sources of tension.

One example may illustrate how the ideal of the young widow was formulated in the community. According to many people, one of the young widows had gone to her father-in-law and placed the cheque she had received in compensation for her husband's death in his hands with the following words: 'Father, this money rightly belongs to you and you may do with it what you will.' On being shown such honour from her dead son's wife, the old man had apparently said, 'From today you are to me a daughter and not a daughter-in-law. I will use this money to find a worthy bridegroom for you.' This, everyone agreed, was an honourable solution to a wretched problem which the community had never faced before. They said that both the girl and the old man had behaved in an honourable manner, not only towards each other but also to the memory of the dead man. I should add that in every other case the resolution of the problem was fraught with bitterness, violence and abuse.

It is clear from this discussion that the deaths of their husbands, and the aggression that young women had to face from their conjugal kin, placed a heavy burden upon them. They were expected to behave as if the husband–wife tie had been erased. Thus the ideal ego construction was one in which the young widow placed herself completely under the authority of her conjugal kin, while erasing the particularity of her relation with her husband by her readiness to be immediately married to one of his kin. This must have required a radical reordering of the past and the framing of a future in a manner which ensured that the reality of death was denied. The social structure thus gives directions to the way in which grief and bereavement are to be handled. This, however, may place impossible burdens upon certain categories of people. The remark of the young widow who complained that the community did not permit women to mourn their husbands was a formulation of this very burden.

In contrast to the young widows, women who had been married for a longer time, or who had four to five children, were seen as more integrated into their marriages. Even if they did decide to remarry later, there was no expectation that this would happen soon. These women were able to articulate their grief and were able to speak for themselves. The two women who had refused to leave their husbands alone in the hands of the killers, despite dire threats, as mentioned earlier, were older women with adult children. For these women the question of obligation to the dead took on a different meaning, which I shall now describe.

At one level, the riots were understood in the language of feud. In the colony, many people assumed that since the Sikh guards of Indira Gandhi had killed her, the killing of Sikhs was an act of vengeance. The slogans shouted at various times—*khun ka badla khun* (blood in return for blood)—had stressed this theme. At the more immediate level, however, the vengeance had a more personal meaning. The killers were known to the people. The major organizers of the riots in this colony had been locked in factional struggle with the Sikh leaders of this locality, and fights on a smaller scale had happened earlier. The majority of the people who died, however, had not been involved in these disputes, but it was assumed by many that they had been made to pay the price for the political ambitions of their leaders.

Whatever the pre-history of the riots, the deaths had created a new awareness among the survivors of their vulnerability, heightened by the fact that killers and victims continued to live in close proximity. For instance, when a young boy pointed to a man and said, 'I saw him kill my father', the killing had necessarily to become a personal truth. It was not an anonymous crowd that had done the killing, but people who were known and who continued to live in the colony. The question that haunted men and women was: what is our obligation to the dead now?

At this stage the entry of civil-rights organizations, social workers and legal-aid groups changed the definition of the situation. Within the traditional system it would have been the responsibility of the men to avenge the deaths of their kinsmen. Yet whenever this topic was broached, 'outsiders' like us, who had entered the community and in whom considerable trust had been reposed, constantly reiterated the undesirability of such an approach within modern state structures.[17] Direct vengeance, we repeatedly told them, would be considered a criminal act and would lead to arrests and punishment in court. The women realized that new kinds of structures were available to them by which the guilty could, perhaps, be brought to book—if they had the courage to give evidence against them. In these new structures, wherein justice replaced the notion of vengeance, the women found that they had an important role to play. Hence, taking great personal risks, they submitted affidavits in the Supreme Court. Many of them appeared before the Police Enquiry Commission and gave evidence against the police. All of this was conceptualized as the fulfilment of their obligations to the dead. Sometimes a woman would show fear—fright that 'they' would learn she had given evidence against 'them' and then 'they' would come after her— but such a woman was always reprimanded by others: 'You have eaten the money of the dead. Now do what you can for them'.

One particular incident, which happened four months after the riots, will show how the traditional relations between men and women had been completely reversed in relation to the external world. As the plight of these women came to be better known and publicized, the arrogant belief of the perpetrators of violence that they would not be touched by the police because of their political connections was somewhat shaken. Due to changes in the police set-up, some of the alleged killers had been arrested and had not been released on bail. Further, after the elections, two

---

[17] The illegality of modern law was writ large in these discussions, for the women always pointed out that no punishment had been meted out to the offenders who had murdered their men.

prominent leaders had been arrested, contrary to all expectations. What I would like to recount here is the event that took place on the day that these two prominent leaders were released on bail. A meeting had been held in the street on which the *chamars* lived. Tempers were running high, for it was the *chamars* who had played a major role in the killings. We could feel the tension in the streets ourselves. There was gloom in the streets where the Sikhs lived. They were persuaded that the other faction was going to wreak vengeance on them for having given evidence against the killers. As I was going from one house to another, I was taken aside by a group of women while the others were asked to go around normally so that no one would know a plot was being hatched. They told me that they needed to send a petition to the 'highest official of Delhi' because they knew that their lives were in danger. I said I would try to contact whoever I could so that their fears were communicated to the authorities who were responsible for their protection. But they urged me to take action immediately, for there was no time for delay. I was told, 'You write out in English what we say and then fix up something for us so that we can meet the highest official immediately'. All my pleas—that I was a rather inconsequential teacher in a university and that I would be turned out unceremoniously if I tried to reach the 'highest official'— were dismissed. I wrote out the petition on a dirty piece of paper that was torn out of an exercise-book, and they put their thumb impressions upon it. They would meet me the next day on a specified spot and would take care that no one in the colony learnt they were going to present a petition.

Following their advice, I rang up the Chief Secretary of Delhi. My earlier experience with the Deputy Chief Secretary had been most unfortunate and I had been politely but firmly accompanied out of his office by a policeman. This time I was received with great courtesy. The change in attitude was rather mysterious. The Chief Secretary agreed to see the women and consider their petition. The next morning I found that eight women had come as representatives of the colony. We held a meeting on the lawns of the Chief Secretary's office. I pleaded with them to put forward their case in a cogent way, to speak one at a time, and to avoid getting into quarrels regarding the distribution of relief and mutual accusations about the failure to save someone or the other. They, in turn, wanted to know the polite expression for such words as 'defecation' and 'widow' which they needed to use without shocking the sensibility of the Chief Secretary by their rude speech.[18] The Chief Secretary received them with courtesy. The women made two points. First, with the release of the leaders of the rioters, their lives were not safe. Even if there was a police picket in their street, the police could not be expected to go everywhere with them. For example, when they went to the toilets which were out on the streets, they could be accosted by the murderers and raped or killed. Hence it was imperative that they be provided housing in other areas. Second, the government had plans for rehabilitating them by teaching them such skills as knitting and sewing, but they were ironsmiths and knew how to forge most things if they could only establish *bhattis* (anvils) outside their houses. Therefore, they did not want apartments in multi-storeyed buildings, where they knew that widows from other areas were being accommodated; they wanted open plots of land where they could live in shanties and begin to produce goods for sale. Third, any policy that separated the widows from the rest of the community would not only create problems of security but also jeopardize their economic life, for they were dependent upon the men to go and sell the products they made. Their petition was accepted and the Chief Secretary promised to do whatever he could to alleviate their suffering. On the way out one of the women suddenly started to cry in the traditional manner and to beat her forehead repeatedly, saying, the *sarkar* is said to be our mother and father—so why did you all

---

[18] As in most other languages, Hindi also uses circumlocutions for such bodily functions as defecation and urination. The women wanted to know what these circumlocutions were. One of the points to which they wished to draw attention in their petition was the dangers they faced when they went to perform these functions, either in the fields or in public toilets, where many of the men had been murdered. The polite term for 'widow' in Hindi is vidhava, and in Punjabi beva, but in the community the word most frequently used was randi, which can refer to both a widow and a prostitute. This term is never used in polite forms of speech among upper castes. The speech of lower castes, such as the Siglikars, is often marked by the use of such tabooed words. Clearly, I appeared to them as someone who could mediate between their world and the outside, defined by class, gender, and culture.

fail to protect us? She was gently pushed outside by the other women. Although their demands were not eventually met, the women had established their capacity to reorient themselves to their reality in terms of the external world, a world of which they had been totally ignorant just a few months back; they also showed an understanding of the social structure which was superior to that of the officials.

In summing up this discussion, let me point to some of the salient differences in the case of Shanti and the other women. First, the women of Block A/4 reacted to the tragedy in a collective manner. The availability of outsiders led to a different cognitive understanding of these events for the women, and they learnt to restructure their responsibilities in the context of a democratic state. Nevertheless, the women spoke in two voices. First, the traditional meaning of mourning, and the public display of pollution and dirt, were given a political meaning. The bodies of the women and the state of their houses proclaimed to the world their fate and the malign intentions of their tormentors. It was an ambiguous symbol, for it could also be interpreted as a reproach to their own men for their inability to save their kinsmen; I shall take up the meaning of this for the man later. However, there was also a restructuring of roles and relationships when women took it upon themselves to repay the debt to the dead by using every available means in the modern political structure for the procurement of justice. They worked simultaneously to try and have the guilty punished as well as to find the ways and means to build a secure life for their children. In contrast to Shanti, who could not reorder the past and orient herself to the future, these women learnt to frame the future so that they could redefine their responsibilities to the dead. It is my contention that it was the acceptance of the symbolic immortality of the dead, in the form of the future of their descendants, which allowed the immediate future to take shape. In this, their encompassment in a collectivity—however quarrelsome and difficult this collectivity may have been—proved to be a major help. Through this collectivity their suffering could be universalized and the survivor guilt could be given a shape. It should not, however, be forgotten that the social definition of affinity gave this freedom and scope of redefinition only to the older widows. The younger widows were securely tied within their roles and had to move into remarriage without the exploration of any of the possibilities that had opened up to their older counterparts.

The Legacy of the Child

In a recent survey of psychiatric literature on death, loss and grief, Harvey (1985) compares the findings of studies that have been conducted on the reactions of children to the loss of a parent by death. One of the important conclusions of this comparison is that there is considerable doubt about the accuracy of parents' perceptions and interpretations about their children's behaviour following bereavement.

We encountered the children and their grief in two different contexts and it may be useful to compare these contexts. Whenever we visited the community, we were always followed around by scores of adults and children. In these contexts we encountered the children's grief primarily through the voices of the adults. A mother or an aunt or a grandfather might emphasize the reactions of the children in order to make a point in their own narrations. For example, when people were describing the gruesome nature of the death, they would point to the children and say that they (the children) had been so frightened that they could no longer sleep at night. The imagery used was that of a screen on which the gruesome scenes of those nights were being forever repeated. In all these discussions what was emphasized was *fear* and not *sorrow*. The children who listened to these stories rarely showed the appropriate affect. For instance, a child would sometimes be listening to the most horrific details about how his father was killed, but with a beatific smile on his face. Once I heard a number of children having a heated argument about whether the murderers had come to one person's house first or another's—almost as if they were engaged in a kind of competitive sport. I wrote in my diary that the children's narratives seemed to have a very 'third person quality'.

We were fortunate, however, in that we were given an opportunity to conduct a one-month summer camp for the children of riot hit families, a consequence of the generous support of a local newspaper. In the camp we had not only regular volunteers who had known the children, but also teachers from a nursery school, and children from some of the local schools in Delhi. None of us had any expertise in providing therapeutic support to children suffering from post-stress trauma, but since we had not been able to find experts who could have worked in such conditions, we felt we could at least try to provide a reasonably stress-free environment for the children.[19] On their part, the children showed great enthusiasm, and the implicit trust of their mothers made it easy for them to come to a local college where they were given food, an opportunity to paint, play and act.

The children were brought to the summer camp in two vans. I would go in one of these to fetch them in the morning. I soon realized that the journey from home to camp, which took about an hour, was an occasion when many of the children began to talk about the riots. Often the memory was provoked by either the sudden recognition of a space where a parent had been killed, or by watching someone perform an activity in which a member of the family had once been engaged. The children who had seemed most unable to articulate their memories suddenly found language pouring out of their mouths. It is possible that groups of children had discussed these events amongst themselves but had been discouraged by adults from discussing them; or perhaps they found an assurance from my presence, so that these memories could, indeed, be narrated. Let me give an account of the manner in which their memories were framed.

One of the children in our group was Avatar, an eleven-year-old who had a severely damaged eardrum and was described as deaf mute. His mother would say, 'He cannot speak, but he understands everything and his actions can say more than words'.

One day the van took a slightly different route and passed through a street we had not been in before. Suddenly Avatar became very excited and pointed to a tree. His shoulders were heaving and he gave the impression of jumping up and down on the seat, although he was, in fact, not moving at all. As he forced

---

[19] I would like to pay tribute to the teachers of Shiv Niketan and all the school and college students who generously gave time and love while running the camp.

my attention towards the tree, pointing to it repeatedly, I asked him what that tree was. Then Avatar did a bit of a mime: his hands first gripped an imaginary object and began to drag it, his face showing the resistance and the struggle of a person being dragged against his will to a terrible fate. He then stretched his hands as if over an imaginary rope, and made it into a lasso. The lasso was sprung to catch a branch of the tree and, on the other side of the hanging rope, a noose was made which slipped round a neck. His face now became the face of a person around whose neck a noose is tightened, and then his head slumped forward, the face becoming that of a dead man. One of the children, who had perhaps watched the performance earlier, told us that it was the tree from which his father had been hung. 'Were you watching?' I asked, and an emphatic nodding of the head affirmed his presence during this gory act. In the mime, it seemed to me that the hands had become those of the murderer's, and the face that of the victim. His body had become a repository of the knowledge which he had not revealed to us earlier.

The children psychologically stood with each other in these remembrances. The more articulate ones often lent their voices to those who were numbed and could not speak. When remembering something, each would contribute to the story so that memory became a collective event. For example, a little girl, who was perhaps five years old, would not speak at all. But whenever we passed a particular spot the children would say, that is where Ballo's father was burnt. The crowd left him to burn and she ran to him holding his hand while he died. Ballo would nod shyly to affirm that the children were telling the truth, but could not be brought to put any of this into her own words.

Most children found a way of talking about their dead fathers or other relatives by creating figures of ghosts. Shanti's daughters would affirm that their mother came to them as a ghost. The youngest one was given to weeping much more than the older one. Her father's sister would threaten her, saying that if she did not stop crying her mother's ghost would come and take possession of her body. The girl would be terrified of her mother's ghost and was unable to say anything at all. Once, when she was standing in a completely inert position, I asked her: 'Are you thinking of your mother? Do her memories come to you?'. She nodded and said,

'Yes, but *Bua* [father's sister] says if you cry she will come and haunt you'.

The adults, then, did not feel that they had to provide any explanations to the children about what had happened, or even discuss with them anything of how they had experienced the loss of a parent. Many children showed signs of distress—for example fear of going to dark places and fear of ghosts—and hallucinated about voices which they heard in the night. But children had to construct their own knowledge about the riots and what the future was likely to hold for them. This may explain why we had so many discussions about the nature of the world, as will become apparent a little later.

It seemed to me that, in the period when I was involved with the children, I was constantly engaged in discussions that had a fairly abstract character. The issues they raised did not seem to arise from day-to-day concerns. For example, one day as we were driving along in the van, Avatar excitedly pointed to the symbol of the hand painted on a wall. He then looked at me with expectation. 'That is a hand', I said, and he nodded encouragingly. 'It is a symbol of the Congress Party', I declared, for the slogan accompanying the hand asked you to vote for the Congress (I). His head moved from side to side in vehement denial. 'It is not a symbol of the Congress Party?' I asked. He then showed me the palm of his hand and pointed to the wall which had already disappeared from our view. 'You are going to tell me what that hand meant?' 'Yes', he gestured. Then he proceeded to mime with his hands an episode from the life of Guru Nanak, the founder of Sikhism. One hand brought a boulder towards his head. Next, he mimed the coming of a ray of light from the raised hand of Guru Nanak and the light stopped the hand that presumably held the boulder. Then his right hand was raised in the traditional gesture of protection, in which benevolent deities are iconically represented. For a moment he was the iconic representation of Guru Nanak. Then he raised his hand again and pointed to the wall where he had first spotted the hand. Now he was going to tell me the story of the Congress hand. A vicious, murderous look came on his face. Both hands became a flurry of movement—killing, dousing people with petrol and burning them alive. The hands and face were again a dialogue of gestures in which the hands portrayed the acts of killing whereas the face represented the expressions and the pain of the dying. At the end of this performance Avatar showed us the auspicious hand of Guru Nanak and gestured protectively; he then switched to the hand of the Congress Party and mimed the brutalities to which that hand had subjected them.

The attempt to find symbols on the part of the children, by means of which the brutalities to which they had been subjected could be expressed, may seem to have a rather abstract character. Perhaps in order to express affect they needed non-verbal means to express the impact of the events to which they had been subjected, whereas what I have described is the verbal discussions. Some of the pictures that the children drew point to distorted body images, but the difficulties of interpreting these pictures cannot be underestimated. I would argue, however, that the cognitive needs of the children cannot be ignored. They tried to understand the events in a manner by which their world could be made meaningful again. In this context it is especially notable that the time-frame they used was invariably a mythic rather than a narrative one. In other words, when they wanted to discuss what had happened in their colony they tended to evoke mythic images and events either as analogy or polarity. The symbol of the hand could provide a contrast between the protective hand of the Sikh guru and the destructive hand of the local leaders of the Congress Party. Similarly, the burning of the gurudwaras in the locality was immediately assimilated to the destruction of the Darbar Sahib, the holy temple of the Sikhs in Amritsar, in various historical and imagined episodes. It is possible that the latter mode of representing the events was sometimes used in sermons in the gurudwaras. It was clear that since the parents had not explained the events to the children, they had borrowed the construction of these events from different contexts, including the stories and sermons they had heard in the gurudwaras. That, however, was not the whole story, as evident from the manner in which Avatar tried to portray his personal tragedy: he did so in terms of the mythic imagination and the narrative traditions of the whole culture.

I also found that children developed a great curiosity about the external world. Hukam, another eleven-year-old, told me in great agitation one day, that soon all the children of the Sikhs were going to be killed because Rajiv Gandhi, the Prime Minister, was going to Russia where his mother had once gone. He would order the killing of all Sikhs—every child among them—so that his mother's soul could be avenged. I found myself vehemently assuring him that the Prime Minister had made no such statement before his departure, and that if he had heard this from someone, he should disregard it as rumour. It seems to me that part of this anxiety on the part of the children to interpret every sign in the external political system for its relevance to their future mirrored the anxiety of the adults. The latter were constantly interpreting the signs according to which decisions about the future had to be made, and the children had simply picked up their anxiety. But it also seems that the distress of the children arose from the fact that their world had been irretrievably altered by events which they did not understand, and for which they were not prepared. The destruction of the world was traumatic for them, and they required of us an attempt to explain it. Hence, political discussions, which would have had an abstract character if the political system had not been seen to have been responsible for the destruction of their world, acquired a concreteness in this context. It was of immediate relevance to them.

One fact which surprised us was the readiness with which the children came to the summer camp and even tried to negotiate with us ways and means of spending a longer time in the camp. We wondered whether this partial separation from the family would add to their already awesome burden. Yet it became clear that they did not experience their families as particularly protective. If the family was presented as protective, it was only so in relation to the external world, which was even more hostile and dangerous. Children were quite frequently subjected to violence within the family. Older men regularly got drunk and beat up their children. Sometimes a child would bare parts of his body and display the scars he had incurred during such beatings. The body, it seemed, was a picture of the abuses the child had been subjected to by a parent, an older relative or an employer. Those children who went to school were no better, for corporal punishment was part of the reality, if not the ideology, of the schools in this area. The difference between the kind of violence that they had been used to and the new kind of violence that they had witnessed was that the first kind could be incorporated within their worlds, whereas the second kind of violence had brought them face to face with the reality of a world for which they did not have any categories. Hence their fantasies had transformed parental deaths into the known categories of ghosts and witches. However, the world which had been suddenly transformed by grotesque violence could not be so comprehended.

The children were on intimate terms with violence. This was not simply because of the use of physical punishment by parents and other caretakers to discipline the children, but because they were steeped in a climate of poverty and crime. They had witnessed gang fights on the streets, knew that some people made their living by hiring out hoodlums whom they controlled, and had sometimes themselves been used for petty criminal activities. So much was violence a part of their lives that they assumed all problems ultimately led to violence, and that the solution of problems could only be found by external authorities.[20] Once, when two groups among them had fought for almost half an hour, one of the young adults who was assisting in running the camp suggested that the children find some means of settling their differences. Unanimously they said, you *find a solution—a solution has to come from outside.* One of the most difficult problems for us was to devise any form of activity in which objects, such as dolls or soldiers, could be made available for play. The children assumed that an adult had to be in command even during play, for otherwise the stronger children might beat up the weaker and younger ones. Older siblings were extremely solicitous about the younger ones, but would not hesitate to use force to make them comply with their wishes.

The teachers and other young adolescents who were engaged in the running of the camp had to devise activities that would engage all the children simultaneously. It seemed that unbearable anxiety was created if a child had to wait for his or her turn to come. For example, if the children were to engage in clay modelling, then

---

[20] There is a growing literature on violence against children. See, for instance, Gil (1970), Herman (1981). Unfortunately, we do not have reliable documentation of violence against children in India, although reports on child labour point to institutionalized violence against children.

clay would have to be placed at each child's seat so that they could all begin together. Or, if a theatrical improvization was to be attempted, then ways would have to be found to have all the children present on stage. It is possible that the idea of a co-operative morality, which Piaget (1960) proposed as an index of the moral development of a child, was completely absent in this context. This might either be because the game as a paradigm for the development of co-operative morality does not have much place among lower-class children—as it does among middle-class children—but could easily be due to the legitimacy that violence has acquired in the minds of children.[21]

As I said earlier, the adults seem to have generally ignored the grief of the children, though they were solicitous about their future. There was one important instance, however, in which I found that people had very different ideas about the manner in which grief affects children. The event happened in the following manner: A widow who had three children was pregnant. She had no means of supporting herself and the rations distributed by relief agencies were cornered by her husband's mother, so that both she and her children were finding it very difficult to get enough food. Her parents stayed in a different block of the same colony and had given her temporary refuge. But she did not want to burden her parents any further. The Delhi branch of the Sisters of Charity, who had been providing excellent medical aid, were willing to give her and the children temporary shelter in an orphanage run by them. After a great deal of hesitation, she was persuaded by her natal family to accept the offer of the Sisters, and one day she asked me if I could take her to their place. She was reassured that my house was not far from the orphanage, and that I would come to meet her every day. I took her along with her three children to the Sisters, who gave them a warm welcome. But the next day, when I went to see her, I was informed that she had borrowed some money from the door-keeper and left in the morning. Somewhat

---

[21] There is some evidence that children with prolonged exposure to war may accept the legitimacy of violence, and kill as a consequence of their direct experiences in war. See Nasr *et al.* (1978), Nassar (1985), Yacoub (1978). Much more research is needed on the impact of collective violence on children.

panic-striken as to whether she had reached safely, I rushed to the colony to find her safe and sound.

When asked why she had rushed back in such a panic, the woman told me this story. Apparently the orphanage had a rule that children were not allowed to sleep with adults. They had to sleep with other children. These children, however, were terrified of sleeping without their mother because they were afraid that their mother would disappear in the same way as their father. So, in panic, they screamed and shouted the whole night, banging at the windows and trying to break open the doors in order to reach their mother. The mother had tried to tell the Sisters that the children were given to fits of panic if they did not see their mother, and that 'their livers would burst with the sorrow and fear', but the Sisters, for their part, were persuaded that the children needed to be dealt with firmly. 'They told me that the liver cannot burst like this. The whole night I heard my children cry and fear gripped my heart in case I lost them too. So in the morning I came back to my community. Here I may not have enough to eat but at least my children are in no danger. First I lost my husband; I do not want the children to slip out of my hands too.'

The Sisters had assumed the primacy of normal rules as still operative, though they had been working with riot victims of the area. Further, they understood 'bursting of the liver' to be a symbolic statement, whereas the mother had meant it literally. It was evident that though parents had not discussed the grief of their children with us, they were sensitive to the manner in which the children had been affected. There was a whole language about the 'symptomatology of grief', that was available and shared by the community, which allowed them to offer some recognition to the grief and fear of the children. Adults, for example, would often bemoan the fact that their bodies had not withered by the experience of such tragedy, as if the body had a will of its own. In the case of the children, this woman was saying, the capacity of the body to be transformed, broken and withered by grief was much greater than that of adults, and hence protection took the form of protecting the inner organs of the body rather than by an encouragement to verbalize grief and fear. I shall say more about the 'embodiment' of such emotions as grief later in this paper.

One of the consequences of this way of understanding the needs of children was that though their world was altered suddenly and traumatically, no attempts were made to explain these changes to them. As we have seen, the children were intensely interested in the nature of the world and how it was likely to affect their future. Their cognitive need to 'make sense of the world' could not be separated from their affective needs. The children had to piece together this world from various bits and pieces that they could gather from sermons they had heard in gurudwaras, from rumours, from television, and from their discussions with us in the camp. Whereas the women in Block A/4 had also learnt how to piece together a world, their orientation was framed in terms of their obligations to the dead. For the children, the question was of finding what components of their identities were relevant in reordering the world. In one particularly poignant case that I remember, rumours were rife that a fresh round of violence would begin because Sikh terrorists had planted bombs in public-transport buses in Delhi. One little boy of ten ran to his mother and said, 'hurry up and dress me as a girl so that I can escape'. The children were engaged in interpreting and reinterpreting every event that came their way as indexical of the possibilities that the future held for them.

We found that the children were engaged in discussions about ghosts and witches more than were the adults. Whereas the adults would refer to the dead as restless spirits who would not let the living return to life in peace, the children had particularized the identity of the ghosts; Shanti's younger daughter was scared that if she cried her mother's ghost might possess her. Her sister often dreamt that her mother's ghost appeared to her in a dream and scolded her. Another boy dreamt of fighting with witches. He claimed he had overcome his fear of witches and ghosts by fighting and defeating them with a rifle.

Survivor Guilt and Shame: The Case of the Men

By contrast with the emotional lives of women and children, the inner lives of men remained largely inaccesible to me. This was not only because of my being a woman but also because neither my male colleagues nor I could take part in activities within which the men really allowed themselves to talk. Usually this happened at night, under the influence of alcohol or drugs, both of which were used regularly in the colony.

In retrospect it seems to me that my relations with the men were structured around the effort to get them economically rehabilitated. Most of our discussions centred around the kinds of tools that were required for them to resume their work. The men felt their economic loss very deeply, and getting back to the tools of their trade seems to have become symbolic of a return to their previous identities. Often I would accompany a man into a house which was small and now broken down, and his eyes would fill the empty spaces and he would say, *look at the house now, and yet at one time what did I not have in it?*

The men were convinced that they had been attacked because they had made good and had become the targets of envy. They were anxious to get back to their livelihood. Yet one question haunted them. If they stayed on in the same colony, then, one day, they might feel impelled to take revenge. This thought of the impulse towards revenge was always something which emanated outside the person. As many of them said:

Seeing the murderers go around freely, hearing them taunt us, may one day suddenly make our blood boil. Something may impel us to take up arms and do to them what they did to us. We are not cowards. But we have to look after our children who have lost everything. Please get us houses elsewhere so that we never have to see the faces of our murderers again.

After I had heard many statements like this, it appeared to me that the men who had survived felt both guilty that they had managed to survive and ashamed that they had failed in their obligations to the dead. Lifton (1967) has paid special attention to the death guilt within the survivor's struggle with guilt. To quote him:

Since survival, by definition, involves a sequence in which one person dies sooner than another, this struggle in turn concerns issues of *comparative deaths timing*. Relevant here is what we have spoken of as guilt over survival priority, along with the survivor's unconscious sense of an organic social balance which makes him feel that his survival was purchased at the cost of another's (p. 489).

In this particular case, the feeling of guilt was compounded by the fact that the men felt they had been able to survive only by betraying the dead or by emasculating themselves. As I mentioned in the case of Shanti, there was a suspicion among the widows that some men who survived had done so by revealing the presence of others, and by bargaining for their lives with the lives of others. Although people did try to explain why some had survived and others had failed by evoking the notion of fate, suspicions surrounding the survivors could not be erased. Second, some men had forgotten close kinsmen in the attempt to save themselves. For example, one man had run away, leaving behind his adolescent son, who had been discovered and killed. Third, many men had escaped in the garb of women and this caused them great shame. Fourth, all the survivors had been gathered together in the police station where the local Station House Officer had engaged a barber to cut off their hair and shave off their beards—both important signs of Sikh identity. Although the Station House Officer had explained his actions by saying that he had been trying to save the Sikhs from the anonymous crowd which killed all Sikhs indiscriminately, this explanation is hardly credible. This officer was alleged to have been responsible for the planning and execution of many of the acts that helped rioters. People generally understood this act, of having their hair forcibly cut, as a public humiliation and emasculation of Sikh men. A jeering crowd had watched this performance, and the men were now ashamed to be seen out in the streets.

The overall impact of these events on the lives of the men was translated into a great desire to flee. They wished to move away from the colony, and whenever they apprehended danger their first reaction was to take flight. For example, just before the national elections, the whole colony became deserted as the men fled to Alwar, where they felt they would be safe. This, as we have seen, was different from the reactions of the women, who felt that they would have to articulate their demands for safer living conditions within Delhi. So, although the women also fled with the men just before the elections, they were the ones who proved more responsive to suggestions that they might be able to use wider political structures to secure a safer life. This difference in the attitudes of men and women was also due to the fact that there was much sympathy for the women among the bureaucrats, while the men were viewed with suspicion as possible terrorists, or as people who might be recruited in future to help terrorism. For example, one administrative officer told me that all help to the bereaved should be given in the form of goods and not money, 'as the money may go for financing guns'. Although there were many who did not share this view, it certainly affected the perception of Sikh men about the political climate of the country.

The men constantly talked about their loss of face. They were reluctant to talk about their departed kinsmen. Usually, any enquiries about how a particular person had managed to escape was met with a perfunctory answer. In some cases a man would be willing to explain why he had left his wife or son behind. One example of this is found in the statement of one of the men that, as he and his wife were trying to run away, the crowd started raining lathi blows upon them. 'My wife tried to come between them and me, when one of them said to her courteously, "sister, please move away". When I realized they were calling her sister, I knew that no harm would come to her. So I left her and ran. They intended no harm to women. Since then I have sent my wife to get rations or to gather news.'

All our discussions with the men led to topics relating to loss of face, of their reduced financial circumstances, and the failure which the men experienced in being unable to take revenge. Sometimes this need for revenge was expressed in the hope that the men who perpetrated violence would automatically meet the same fate. For example, one man asked me if it was true that one of the hospitals in Delhi had admitted a number of patients who suffered from strange complaints, the most frequent of which was that the patients thought their bodies were 'on fire'. At another time one man said that those who had burnt men alive would never sleep in peace again. It was, however, equally true that this idea of retribution was considered somewhat abstract. The generalized feeling that haunted the colony was that the terrible violence which had been given a form in the riots was somehow incomplete. The Sikhs were constantly anticipating a further round of violence, either initiated by the Sikhs themselves in order to avenge their honour, or by the rioters as further punishment. The others in the colony were also apprehensive of the desire for vengeance, and sporadic incidents of violence continued for almost three months.

When rumours spread in the colony in the month of April that two Sikhs had killed a neighbour who had participated in the riots, there was a feeling that this was inevitable and completed a logical circle. Girard (1977) contends that violence at the height of crisis becomes 'subject, object, instrument, and purpose of action'; this would have been well understood by the men in the colony. The events of the riots not only provoked reflections which one may define as coming from *within* one's membership of the society, but also as coming from without. In other words, the men reflected *about* the nature of their society as much as they expressed concerns as members within it. One of these reflections was provoked by my own involvement. One of the men was wondering aloud about past karmas which led me to be among them, hungry and thirsty, the whole day. I said jokingly that I was probably paying past debts, when he said, 'You are wasting your time. Nothing is to be gained by this involvement. After all, our deaths do not mean anything. Alive, we are useful to the Government for we can be hostages against the lives of the Hindus in Punjab. Dead, we are useful to the terrorists for we can become statistics in the Sikh grievances.' Earlier, the victims had wondered how Hindus could have killed other Hindus, for they had always assumed Sikhism to be related to Hinduism, as had many Hindus. The riots had forced them into a separate identity of Sikhs, for they had been compelled to die as Sikhs. Now many wondered if anyone was interested in them as persons or if they were to be forever pawns in the games of others. None of us had answers to these questions.

Concluding Comments

What is a good death? What is a bad death? The survivor of a collective disaster makes us pose this stark question. As Lifton (1967) has remarked, all of us may become survivors in the modern world when unlimited technological violence and absurd death demand that we use our imagination in the service of a continuity of life. The people in Sultanpuri repeatedly charged us to write their story. Enmeshed as their lives were in cycles of crime, poverty and absurd death, this level of violence made them, for a time, concerned with using their experience to expand *our* consciousness.

Many of the psychic processes that Lifton and others have identified for disaster victims could be identified in this study.[22] Yet various studies show that there are important differences in the manner in which the world and the self are reformulated in different kinds of disasters. In the case of Hiroshima, the violence was sudden and total and it also permanently tainted the survivors due to recurring fears of 'A Bomb disease'. In contrast, the victims of concentration camps were subjected to prolonged assaults on the body and the psyche, and the generalized nature of this violence led to diffuse and severe psychic impairment (Lifton, 1976; 1982; Bettleheim, 1980; Luchterhand and Sydishe, 1971). In the case of Sultanpuri, there was both sudden and total death, and prolonged periods of assault on the body and minds of the victims. In all these cases, death was absurd and indecent; and yet there were subtle distinctions in the form of what Lifton, in his various studies, calls the death imprint.

People in Sultanpuri had been subjected to violence not by a distant and somewhat abstract enemy, but by their own, albeit hostile, neighbours. Violence had been inflicted upon, and by, people with known identities and histories. In this whole process, some had been saved and others subjected to a terrible death. There had also been a kind of implicit 'contract' by which adult men had been the targets of violence, whereas women and young children had been spared. Unlike disaster from natural causes, over which human beings may not be able to exercise control, the violence wreaked by other human beings is constantly subjected to interpretive reading by the victims, who are haunted by the possibilities of their own roles in it. In Sultanpuri, being able to read the signs properly made the difference between life and a grotesque death. Under these conditions, it seems to me that the survivor cannot be constituted as a unified subject. His position in the social structure intervenes and gives direction to his grief as well as to restructuring the world. I have therefore tried to indicate how the differences in notions of masculine responsibility and feminine obligation structured the death imprint, gave shape to

---

[22] A large body of literature on post traumatic stress has grown in recent years. See, for instance, Bettleheim (1980), Lifton (1967, 1973, 1983), Matussek (1975), Krystal (1969).

survivor guilt, and influenced the reformulation of the world.

Before recapitulating the differences between the categories of the survivors and the manner in which they reformulated their` world, let me remark on the similarities. As Bowlby (1980) and Lifton (1967) have shown, death, loss and separation are psychically interchangeable, and survivors are subject to a reactivation of death imagery when confronted by any of these. In normal people the experience of a total annihilation of the self and the world is usually associated with psychotic delusion. In the case of the survivor, this contact with total annihilation is *actually* experienced in the body and the mind. In Lifton's own words, 'The "world destruction" fantasies of the psychotic reflect his radically impaired relationship to the world and his projection upon it of his own inner sense of "psychic death". But the survivor of mass death reverses the process so that an overwhelming external experience of near absolute annihilation makes contact with related tendencies of the inner life.'[23] In other words, it is the external reality which is annihilated and which has to be mapped on to the inner reality. We have seen how images of separation, annihilation, helplessness and inability to move dominated the process of making this external reality 'real' to the psyche. The obsessive review of the events of those days, the constant questioning of whether events could have been reversed, the search for bodies which could not be found, and the concern that one's own body would not be able to withstand such an onslaught—all were attempts to make inner sense of the reality of what had happened. The people mourned not only for the dead, but for the loss of face, the destruction of a known way of life, and even for inanimate objects such as one's tools of trade.

It is the contention of this paper that the social structure intervenes decisively in directing the manner in which such emotions as guilt or sorrow are formed, and the way in which the world can be reformulated. Within the overall patriarchal values of the community, it was considered the responsibility of men to have protected women, and to have avenged their honour. Since the circumstances of the riots did not allow men to provide this protection, it led to a tremendous loss of face. The ideology of the

[23] Lifton (1967), p. 486.

heroic death demands that men do not desert their brethren in danger. Yet many men had to do precisely that in order to save themselves. Second, a person saw himself as having stolen life from the dead, not only in a symbolic sense, as in the case of Hiroshima, but in the literal sense of having abandoned a son or a relative to the killers or, even worse, of having been compelled to reveal their place of hiding to the killers.

Women, in contrast to men, felt their responsibility to their children intensely but were not customarily required to take responsibility for the protection of the men. I saw only one case where the woman felt herself to have been responsible for the death of her husband. She had fought with him that day and had refused to light the *chulah* (cooking hearth). He had left her to go to his mother's house, in a different block of the colony, where he had been confronted by rioters and killed. There was a constant note of regret in the laments of this woman—*if only I had not fought with him he would have lived; as it is he died hungry.* It is significant that the woman felt her failure lay in the feminine function of providing nurture through food. This guilt was compounded by the fact that a cold hearth is a symbol of a family which has lost a member through death; and thus she felt that she had symbolically brought about her husband's death. Women grieved for their dead husbands or sons, were torn by remorse that they had been unable to provide their dying men with water. However, the nature of their remorse was different from that of the men, who were assaulted by the feeling that they had lost face.

The survivor is not only confronted with the task of creating patterns of mourning for a whole lost world, but also with recreating the world. Lifton (1967) calls this process formulation, and defines it as the process by which a survivor establishes those inner forms which can serve as a bridge between the self and the world. The psychological work of formulation includes, for him, the important psychological work of creating a sense of connection, a sense of symbolic integrity, and a sense of movement. The survivor is in a state that is marked by isolation, meaninglessness and stasis, and the establishment of these three processes is part of the psychological work of reformulating the world. It is comparable to the work of mourning in normal death.

The survivors in Sultanpuri were, indeed, engaged in this

work of reformulation. I have tried to show that movement was essential to the task of reconstructing the self and the world, and I have emphasized their framing of the future. Their sense of connection and integrity could be established in the context of how the future was to be framed. In the case of Shanti, I have tried to show that movement became impossible because her sense of symbolic immortality was defined completely by her husband's genealogical continuation and was seriously impaired. Unable to establish connections with the living, Shanti could not sever her bonds with the dead. Her suicide was a desperate repaying of the debt which she felt she had incurred by her inability to save her son. Lifton (1967) remarks that parents who had survived the death of children in Hiroshima felt the most guilt, and he traces this to the imagery of an unfulfilled life. Shanti's case shows the power of kinship norms in defining the nature of the parent–child relation: Shanti would have been willing to, or even wished to, buy the life of her son at the cost of her daughter.

In the case of other women, their encompassment in the community and the possibility of new kinds of movement helped to frame the future. Some felt they had a mission as survivors, and this was to secure justice for the dead. To others the availability of relief goods gave a direction to their movements, and the securing of these goods became symbolic of continuity and movement. Here also we should remember that young widows were not permitted to retain their connection with the dead; hence they had to frame their future in a manner whereby the death of the husband could be erased from the reconstruction of their lives.

The formulations of children while framing time were, indeed, special. The intrusion of the mythic into the narrative in their understanding of the violence showed how present events were understood as part of a mythic or imagined past. Within this the personal history of the children merged into the mythic history of the community to which they now felt they surely belonged. The adults in the community, on the other hand, could not see these events as emblematic of a repetitive pattern of Sikh history, despite the attempts in some gurudwaras to place the violence in that context. The children, it appeared, needed to understand such violence within the mythic framework. This emphasis upon the mythic was also found in the case of those who had not directly experienced the pain of the victims. For example, there were attempts by some visitors to transform the deaths of the victims into deaths that were heroic. 'They were martyrs', I heard a middle-class Sikh say once, 'their bodies may be eaten by crows and vultures but heaven will not be denied to them'. This kind of framing of death simply did not make sense to the survivors in the midst of their grief, although it is possible that, in a retrospective framing of the meaning of death, they may, one day, come to accept this formulation as a resolution to the problem of meaning.

In their immediate struggle to establish meaning and build the bridges between the self and the world, the survivors were surely helped by various gurudwaras, relief agencies and citizens who came to their aid. This kind of help, however, also raises the problem of what Lifton (1967) has called the suspicion of 'counterfeit nurturance'. The existence of intense conflict and jealousy has been noted for all communities of survivors. Lifton feels that this is because of the competitive aspect in the quest for nurturance in which all survivors engage. This competition is expressed in the fear that, (a) they will not receive the nurturance they need; (b) they will receive help, but it will be counterfeit; and (c) others less deserving will receive more help than they. While we found all three fears in the community, they cannot be classified under the same phenomenon of 'suspicion of counterfeit nurturance'.

As far as the first and third aspects of the phenomenon identified as 'counterfeit nurturance' are concerned, the need for help and the assessment that one is deserving of help get woven into the social definitions of the person. For example, there was much sympathy among relief workers, and even government officials, for the needs of widows. Hence, the rehabilitation of widows became an important programme in the ministry of social welfare, and the community was quite aware of the official recognition of the category of 'widowhood'. Yet old parents who had survived the death of their adult children felt that their needs for nurturance were not sufficiently met. The suspicion of the claims of young widows in the community—and also of the agreement that widows would share the money they received in compensation for the husband's death in exchange for the right to remarry—stemmed from the social definition of affinity rather than from any personal decisions. The claims of the young widows to relief, as well as any obvious symptoms of grief on their part, were viewed with suspicion because the tie of marriage was not considered strong enough for young women to endure beyond death. Counterfeit nurturance, in this context, would imply that the recipient of the nurture was unworthy.

In contrast to this were events when the *giver* of nurturance was considered fraudulent. The most obvious example of this was the 'camp' put up by functionaries of the local branch of the Congress (I), where relief was supposedly provided to widows. This camp had been hurriedly put up to convince various reporters, and others visiting the area, that the victims were being cared for by the local community. Naturally, the victims were terrified of this relief, for they were too scared to reject it and too pained to accept such nurturance. Another form of succour was provided by various rich people who were willing to provide material goods, as long as they did not come into direct contact with their beneficiaries. The typical *modus operandi* of such people was that they would go to a local gurudwara and distribute clothes, food, medicines, quilts, sewing machines, etc. to the victims. There was no systematic method for identifying the needs of the victims, or to distinguish between genuine and fake claims. Such help was very useful for the relief agencies, which soon learnt to channel these resources in a manner that ensured they would reach the needy. Yet, from the point of view of the victims, there was a counterfeit element in all this, in that they sensed the need of the rich to maintain a distance from them. They were aware of how uncomfortable the distributors of such charity felt in making any real contact with the victims. This, the victims felt, gave them a license to devise the means to cornering as many resources as they could, regardless of their need. Such behaviour on the part of both providers and receivers of nurture made for caustic comments: 'There are people who have filled up their houses with clothes to last ten winters', one of the persons in the colony told me. 'We say they have lined up enough clothes for ten shrouds.' Or, at another time, when someone was trying to trick me into giving her some extra money, the woman was reprimanded thus: 'Do you think our sister [i.e. me] is one of those rich people who live in bungalows and earn merit by giving out handouts? Be ashamed of yourself— hungry and thirsty she wanders among us all day.' Strangely, it was the fact that I had to struggle to find help for them that established my authenticity for some, if not for all.

I would suggest, then, that intense hostility results from the fact that there are undeserving recipients of help as well as undeserving providers of nurturance. The existence of the former results in hostility and jealousy within the community. The existence of the latter may lead to a cynical manipulation of people providing relief, but may also become sinister when, for example, the help is a continuation of patterns of victimization. Related to, but different from, the patterns described here is the case of Shanti, who could not accept nurturance from her own daughter. This was not only because the daughter could not provide the kind of nurturance and assurance Shanti needed, but also because Shanti wished to barter the daughter's life for that of the son that she had thus begun to experience herself as *unworthy* of such nurture.

In the final analysis, the differentiation in patterns of the 'survivor syndrome' that I have underlined in this paper can be related to the nature of the violence to which the community was subjected. Their feeling of near annihilation was caused not by indiscriminate 'nature', but by the discriminate oppression of men. The killings were accompanied by humiliating episodes, and the burning alive of people could not be assimilated into the imagery of normal death. The people who were alive were burnt like corpses, while the corpses were not properly cremated. All this left people with a diminished sense of their own being. This is why they eagerly accepted the opportunity to simply talk to us, to construct the events as they remembered they had happened, and to help in the writing of these events. All this signified the fact that their lives held a meaning, and that their suffering would not go untold.

The continued involvement of the community with the sources of this violence also altered its meaning for them. They had to make decisions about where they would live, and what their political and religious identity would be, the violence having been perpetrated in the context of a political and religious ideology.

Recent research has shown the psychic impairment of individuals of mass disasters such as war, concentration camps and natural calamities. The case of death in man-made disasters points not only to the psychological but also to the traumatic social costs of such disasters. The legacy of the riots in Delhi was a wounding of persons and society that will probably take several generations to heal.

REFERENCES

Bachelard, G., 1949: *La Psychanalyse du feu*. Gallimard.

Bedi, B. S., 1962: *Ek Chadar Maili Si*. Delhi: Rajkamal Publications.

Bettleheim, B., 1980: *Surviving and Other Essays*. New York: Vintage Books.

Bowlby, J., 1980: *Loss, Sadness and Depression. Vol. III: Attachment and Loss*. New York: Basic Books.

Buchler, J., 1955: *Philosophical Writings of Peirce*. New York: Dover Publications.

Das, V., 1977: *Structure and Cognition: Aspects of Hindu Caste and Ritual*. Delhi: Oxford University Press.

———— 1984: 'Collective Violence and Anthropological Knowledge'. *Anthropology Today*. London.

———— 1986a: 'Violence, Victimhood, and the Language of Silence'. *The Word and the World: Fantasy, Symbol and Record*, ed. Veena Das. Delhi: Sage Publications.

———— 1986b: 'The Work of Mourning: Death in a Punjabi Family'. *The Cultural Transition: Human Experience and Social Transformation in the Third World and Japan*. Ed. M. I. White and S. Pollak, pp. 179–210.

———— 1987a: 'The Anthropology of Violence and the Speech of Victims'. *Anthropology Today*. London.

———— 1987b: 'The Legacy of Despair'. *Illustrated Weekly of India*. Bombay. February.

Devereux, G., 1973: *Essais d'ethnopsychatrie générale*. Paris: Gallimard.

Freud, S., 1976: 'Recommendations to Physicians Practicising Psycho-analysis'. *The Complete Psychological Works*. Standard Edition, vol. 12. ed. and trans. James Strachey. New York: Norton. (First published 1912.)

———— 1987b: 'Mourning and Melancholia'. *The Collected Works of Sigmund Freud*. Standard Edition. London: Hogarth Press (first published in 1915.)

Gil, B., 1970: *Violence Against Children*. Cambridge: Harvard University Press.

Girard, R., 1977: *Violence and the Sacred*. Baltimore: Johns Hopkins University. (Original French edition, 1972.)

Harvey, M., 1985: 'Death, Loss and Grief: Assessing the Mental Health Needs of the Bereaved' (typescript).

Herman, J. L., 1981: *Father-Daughter Incest*. Cambridge: Harvard University Press (with Lisa Hirschman).

Humphreys, S., 1981: 'Death and Time'. *Mortality and Immortality*, ed. S. C. Humphreys and H. King. London: Academic Press.

Kolenda, P., 1983: 'Widowhood among "Untouchable" Churas'. *Concepts of Person: Kinship, Caste and Marriage in India*, ed. Akos Ostor, Lina Fruzzetti and Steve Barnett. Delhi: OUP.

Krishna, Gopal, 1985: 'Communal Violence in India: A Study of Communal Disturbance in Delhi. *EPW*, vol. 20, no. 3.

Krystal, H., 1969: *Massive Psychic Trauma*. New York: International University Press.

Lifton, R. J., 1967: *Death in Life: Survivors of Hiroshima*. New York: Random House.

———— 1973: *Home from the War: Vietnam Veterans, Neither Victims nor Executioners*. New York: Simon and Schuster.

———— 1983: *The Broken Connection: On Death and the Continuity of Life*. New York: Basic Books.

Lynch, Owen M., 1981: 'Rioting as Rational Action: An Interpretation of the April 1978 Riots in Agra'. *Economic and Political Weekly*, 1981, vol. 16, no. 48.

Lindemann, E., 1941. 'Symptomatology and Management of Acute Grief'. *Archives of General Psychiatry*, 101:141–8.

Luchterhand, E. and Sydiaha, D., 1966: *Choice in Human Affairs: An Application to Aging-Accident-Illness Problems*. New York: New College University Press.

Matussek P., 1975: *Internment in Concentration Camps and its Consequences*. Berlin and New York: Springer Verlag.

Nasr, A. *et al.*, 1978: *Moral Judgement of Lebanese Children after the Lebanese War*. Institute for Women's Studies, Beirut University College.

Nassar, C., 1985: 'Psychological Effects of the War on Lebanese Children of various Social Groups'. Doctoral thesis. Sorbonne University, Paris.

Piaget, J., 1932: *The Moral Judgement of the Child*. London: Routledge and Kegan Paul. Reprinted 1960.

Poulet, G., 1977: *Proustian Space* (trans. Coleman, Elliott). Baltimore: Johns Hopkins University Press.

Rosenblatt, P., *et al.*, 1976: *Grief and Mourning in Cross-Cultural Perspectives* (Comparative Studies Series). Human Relations Area File: New Haven, Yale University Press.

———— 1983: *Bitter Bitter Tears: Nineteenth Century Diarists and Twentieth Century Grief Theories*. Minneapolis: University of Minnesota Press.

Spence, D., 1982: *Narrative Truth and Historical Truth*. Cambridge: Harvard University Press.

Stewart, G., 1984: *Death Sentences: Styles of Dying in British Fiction*. Cambridge: Harvard University Press.

Todorov, T., 1967: *Litterature et signification*. Paris, Larousse.

Yacoub, G., 1978: *Psychological Disturbances in Lebanese Children During and After the War*. Educational Council for Research and Development.

Subject Index

Author Index